Political Parties and Elections in American States

Fourth Edition

MALCOLM E. JEWELL
University of Kentucky

SARAH M. MOREHOUSE
University of Connecticut

CQ PRESS

A Division of Congressional Quarterly Inc.
Washington, D.C.

For our children and grandchildren

CQ Press
A Division of Congressional Quarterly Inc.
1414 22nd Street, N.W.
Washington, D.C. 20037

(202) 822-1475; (800) 638-1710

www.cqpress.com

Printed and bound in the United States of America

05 04 03 02 01   5 4 3 2 1

Designed and typeset by Nighthawk Design, Grand Rapids, Michigan

Cover Design by Gary Gore

Library of Congress Cataloging-in-Publication Data

Jewell, Malcolm Edwin, 1928–
Political parties and elections in American states / Malcolm E. Jewell, Sarah M.
Morehouse.—4th ed.
p.   cm.
Includes bibliographical references and index.
ISBN 1-56802-481-9 (pbk.)
1. Political parties—United States—States.   2. Elections—United States—States.   I.
Morehouse, Sarah McCally.   II. Title.
JK2261 .J48 2000
324'.0973—dc21   00-059912

Contents

Tables and Figures   vii

Preface   ix

Introduction   1

State Political Parties Have Been Changing   1
Political Parties in the Fifty States Differ in Many Ways   3
Money Plays a Major Role in State Politics   5
The Linkages Between State and National Parties Are
    Growing and Changing   5

1   State Political Systems in a National Setting   7

Distinctive Characteristics of State Political Systems   7
National Factors That Influence State Politics   14

2   The Growth in Two-Party Competition   21

Historical Patterns of National Party Competition   22
The Impact of National Trends on State Party Competition   25
Trends in Two-Party Competition   28
Prospects for Greater Two-Party Competition   37

3   State Party Organization   47

Theories of Party Organization   47
The Functions of State Party Organizations   49
Campaign Finance   61
The Structure of State Party Organizations   70
Party Workers   83
Measuring Party Strength   92
Party Organization Matters   98

4   The Nominating Process   100

Requirements for Voting in Primaries   102
Candidate Nominations and Party Endorsements   106

Levels of Competition in Primaries 118
Voter Participation in Primaries 121
Factors Explaining Primary Election Outcomes 128
The Impact of Primaries on General Elections 136

5 General Elections: Candidates, Campaigns, and Issues 141

Candidates 142
Campaigning for Office 147
Issues in the Campaign 158
The Role of Money in Gubernatorial Elections 163
Governors: Strong But Not Invincible 175

6 Voting Behavior in Gubernatorial Elections 176

Are State Elections Autonomous from National Elections? 177
Party Loyalties of Voters 180
The Impact of Gubernatorial Incumbency 182
The Impact of Ideology and Issues 185
Variations in Voting Turnout for State Elections 195
The Voters Choose 200

7 State Legislative Elections 201

Nominating Legislative Candidates 201
Electoral Competition and Incumbency 202
Campaigning for the Legislature 208
Financing Legislative Races 211
National Trends and Legislative Elections 218
Partisan Implications of Legislative Districting 219
Growing Two-Party Competition for Control
   and Divided Government 221
Conflicting Trends in Legislative Elections 225

8 Political Parties in State Legislatures 227

Patterns of Legislative Organization 227
Party Leadership 229
The Governor as Party Leader 238
Partisan Decision Making in the Legislature 243
The Future Role of Political Parties in Legislatures 251

9 State Parties and National Politics 253

State Parties and the Presidential Nominating Process 253
Electing Members of Congress 256

State Parties: Captives or Partners? 258
A Partnership of Strength 271

10 Conclusions 272
Evaluating the Parties 273
Differences among the State Parties 277
Money and Politics 280
The Evolving Partnership of State and National Parties 282
State Parties: New Responsibilities and Capabilities 283

References 285

Index 297

Tables and Figures

Tables

2-1 Indexes of State Party Balance   30

2-2 Republican Growth in Southern States   34

2-3 Party Identification in the States   40

2-4 Party Registration in the States   44

3-1 Contribution Limits to State Parties and from State Parties   66

3-2 Comparing the Views of Party Convention Delegates and Voters Identified with a Party on Ideology and Issues   90

3-3 Gubernatorial Nominations and Party System Strength   97

4-1 State Requirements for Voting in Primary Elections   103

4-2 Success of Endorsed Candidates in Primaries, by Time Period, Legal and Party Rule Endorsements, and Party, 1960–1998   109

4-3 Viewpoints of Delegates to 1994 and 1998 Conventions on Endorsements   116

4-4 Contested Gubernatorial Primaries, 1968–1998   119

4-5 Average Gubernatorial Party Primary Vote as Percentage of Party Vote in General Election, 1968–1998   123

4-6 Comparison between Proportion of Votes That Incumbent Governors Received and Proportion of Campaign Funds That They Spent in Contested Primary Elections, 1988–1998   132

4-7 Comparison between Proportion of Votes That Winning Gubernatorial Candidates Received and Proportion of Campaign Funds That They Spent in Contested Primary Elections without Incumbents Running, 1988–1998   133

5-1 Comparison between Proportion of Votes That Incumbent Governors Received and Proportion of Campaign Funds That They Spent in General Elections, 1978–1998   167

5-2 Comparison between Proportion of Votes That Winning Gubernatorial Candidates Received and Proportion of Campaign Funds That They Spent in General Elections without Incumbents Running, 1978–1998   168

6-1 Electoral Record of Incumbent Governors and Their Impact on Party Turnover   184

6-2 Factors Affecting the Outcome of Incumbent's Defeat in Gubernatorial Elections   187

6-3 Turnout of Voters in Gubernatorial Elections as a Percentage of Voting-Age Population in Presidential and Nonpresidential Election Years, 1990–1996   196

7-1 Percentage of Two-Party Contests and of Competitive Two-Party Races in Legislative Houses, 1984–1994   205

7-2 Unified and Divided Government by Two-Year Time Periods, 1965–2000   222

7-3 Unified and Divided Government by State, 1965–2000   224

8-1 Differences between Democratic and Republican Legislators in Levels of Support for Governors' Bills in 1983   249

8-2 Index of Party Differences on a Sample of Roll Calls on Bills   251

9-1 State Party Percentage of Various Categories of Funds, 1995–1996   266

9-2 National Party Committees' Transfer of Funds to State Parties   270

Figures

3-1 Sources and Flows of Money in State Election Campaigns   63

3-2 Diagram of Typical Formal State Party Organization   71

7-1 Democratic and Republican Gains and Losses in Legislative Chambers, 1972–1998   218

Preface

This book's origins go back to the late 1970s, when Malcolm Jewell and David Olson decided that there was a need for a textbook on political parties and elections in American states to fill a gap for students with an interest in state politics. This collaboration led to the publication of three editions of that book—in 1978, 1982, and 1988. When Malcolm Jewell and Sarah Morehouse decided that it was time for a new edition of the book, David Olson, whose research focus has shifted into other fields, encouraged us to pursue this project. Although the book has been completely rewritten, the scope and structure of this fourth edition closely follow those of the earlier editions. We are indebted to David Olson for his encouragement and for his many contributions to the earlier editions.

The purpose of this book is to compare the political party and election systems in the fifty states. We want to enable readers who are familiar with politics in one state to place that knowledge in perspective and so to understand it better. Compared with other states, how competitive are the parties, how strong and effective are the party organizations, how broadly based is political competition in the state? We seek to identify the most important dimensions of the political systems on which the states differ, to classify the states along these dimensions, and then to explain why these differences have arisen and to identify significant trends in political systems among the states. Because it has been a dozen years since the third edition was written, we are particularly conscious of the need to show how and why state parties and political systems have been changing and to what extent these trends have been similar or have differed among the states.

Over a number of years—working together or separately—we have carried out research on a number of topics on state politics, and we have made use of that research in this book. We are indebted to many persons who answered questionnaires or submitted to interviews. Over three election years (1982, 1994, and 1998) several thousand delegates to state party conventions responded to our questionnaires on the endorsement process, and a number of party leaders were interviewed on the same topic. Gubernatorial candidates and campaign managers were interviewed about nominating campaigns. Political party leaders in fifteen states answered questionnaires and sat for interviews on the relationships between state and national parties in raising and spending campaign funds. Several were particularly helpful: Christine Dudley, R-Ill., George Gallo, R-Conn., Jorge Ramirez, D-Texas, Joe King, R-Ga., Hank Hollowell, R-Pa., and Kathy Czar, D-Minn. Several hundred state legislative leaders participated in interviews or answered questionnaires on leadership styles and techniques; recruiting and supporting legislative candidates; and financing legislative races. Legislators in nine states were interviewed on the representative process.

We learned a great deal from the answers given us by these practitioners, who have a first-hand view of the party and electoral systems. We are deeply grateful for the willingness of these political leaders to take time from busy schedules to talk to us, and we appreciate the interest they showed in our work. We also appreciate the cooperation of the many people who filled out questionnaires for us, often taking time to describe their experiences and viewpoints in considerable detail.

Anyone writing about comparative state politics must rely on political science colleagues across the country who know their own state better than others; they have answered countless questions through the years about how the political system really works in their respective states. We are particularly indebted to a number of colleagues who let us use their data or who found data for us. John Aldrich generously gave us an advanced look at data from a new study of state party organizations included in his Southern Political Science Association presidential address, to be published in the *Journal of Politics*. Bruce Anderson and Keith Hamm gave us state-by-state data on contested and competitive legislative races over many years. Gerald Wright made available to us recent data on party identification in the states. Thad Beyle gave us access to his large collection of data on campaign spending in gubernatorial races. Randall W. Partin gave us data on party voting in governors' races. John Bibby helped us to verify the most recent state laws on requirements for voting in primary elections. Some of our information and examples on legislative recruiting and campaigns are the result of collaboration with Gary Moncrief and Peverill Squire. Obviously none of these political scientists are responsible for our analysis of their data.

We also want to acknowledge the major role Marcia L. Whicker played in interviewing legislative leaders and analyzing data from that study of leadership. Her untimely death in 1999 was a shock to all who knew her.

We are very much indebted to the careful reading of this manuscript and the excellent suggestions of the three reviewers: Wayne Francis, L. Sandy Maisel, and Ronald Weber, whose contributions have made this a better book.

The National Science Foundation provided funding for Jewell's studies of gubernatorial nominations and the party endorsing process in 1982, and we jointly received grants from the National Science Foundation in 1994 and 1998 for further research on this topic. The University of Connecticut and the Russell Sage Foundation provided funding for Morehouse's research and analysis of gubernatorial candidates in 1982 and 1983, and the project was augmented and completed because of a National Science Foundation Visiting Professorship for Women Award in 1991. The State Legislative Leadership Foundation provided funding for Jewell's study of state legislative leaders in 1991. None of these organizations is in any way responsible for the analysis and conclusions of these studies.

Introduction

This book on state political parties and elections includes four major themes, and we will return to each of them in many of the chapters. The first theme emphasizes that state political party systems are alive and well, but they are different in important respects from the state parties of the 1950s and even the 1980s.

The second theme highlights the major variations among the state parties. Despite national trends and the influence of national parties on state parties, both traditional factors and current political realities create important differences.

The third theme is the importance of money for political parties and candidates. To provide candidates with services and financial aid, and to perform other functions, state parties must raise large sums of money.

The fourth theme shows the increasingly important relationships between state and national parties. This theme is closely related to the issue of campaign finance because the laws specify the means by which soft money and hard money are handled by the state and national parties.

STATE POLITICAL PARTIES HAVE BEEN CHANGING

State political parties have larger and more professional offices at party headquarters than in the past. They have become more complex organizations because there are linkages between the formal party headquarters and other organizations. To a large extent, the state parties have become service organizations for their candidates, providing them with funding and other kinds of assistance. The parties must raise much more money than in the past to maintain well-staffed, up-to-date headquarters and to provide candidates with funding and services.

The local party machines that used to mobilize voters efficiently and distribute patronage to reward party workers and maintain discipline gradually faded away after the first third of the twentieth century. In the 1940s and 1950s many state party organizations appeared to be almost empty shells, particularly in those states that were dominated by one party and lacked the electoral competition that encouraged organizational growth.

Since that time, the state parties have been transformed into much more active, complex organizations, with greatly increased resources. As the Democratic and Republican Parties have grown more competitive in most states, it has become both possible and necessary for both parties to be much better organized. Most parties today operate modern, well-equipped state headquarters that are staffed with several, full-time professional employees and that use computers for a variety of purposes. Their budgets are much larger than they were in the 1970s.

We will describe modern political party organizations in some detail in Chapter 3; we will analyze the impact they have on nominations and general elections in Chapters 4 and 5; and we will examine the relationships between state and national parties in Chapter 9. The formal structure of state parties has not changed much since the 1940s. It includes a state central committee, headed by a party chair. An elected convention usually chooses members of the central committee. Local party committees generally are in place at the county, city, or town levels, as are committees for electoral units, such as the congressional districts.

But, in reality, the state party includes several other components. Most state legislatures have Democratic and Republican campaign committees, run by the party's legislative leaders, that recruit candidates for the legislatures and provide them with campaign funding and assistance. The party's officeholders, particularly at the statewide and congressional levels, inevitably are important members of the party. Persons who raise money for the party and its candidates as well as activists who work for its candidates are important "cogs in the party machine," whether or not they serve on any party committee. In recent years important linkages have developed between state parties and the interest groups that are closely aligned with them; for example, labor unions are aligned with the Democratic Party, right-to-life and Christian right groups with the Republican Party.

Those who write about modern elections often describe what they call candidate-centered campaigns, suggesting that most candidates raise their own funds, hire campaign managers and media experts, plan their own campaign strategy, and decide what issues to emphasize. Increasingly, however, state party organizations have been trying to play a role in these campaigns. If it can raise enough campaign funds, a state party can provide its candidates with experienced campaign managers and workers and offer them a wide variety of services, including help with fund raising, lists of voters, polling data, and advice on handling the media. Legislative candidates, who usually lack the political skills and resources of candidates for governor or Congress, have the greatest need for such help, which may be provided by the state party, the legislative party, or both. State parties make an effort to register voters, mobilize them, and get them to the polls— an effort that relies heavily on phone banks; this service is important for all of the party's candidates. State parties may even run television and radio commercials in support of, but independent of, their candidates, thus giving them an opportunity to shape the issues in the campaign. We describe these party functions in more detail in Chapter 3.

If a state party is going to operate a modern, well-staffed headquarters and also provide funding and services for its candidates, it obviously has to raise a lot of money. In recent years, money has become increasingly important in every aspect of state and national politics. Consequently it is not surprising to discover that the state party must devote a great deal of its time, effort, and resources to raising money. Unless it has substantial resources, a state party cannot play any real role in the political game.

POLITICAL PARTIES IN THE FIFTY STATES DIFFER IN MANY WAYS

In each of the states, the two major parties are the Democrats and the Republicans. Governors and other statewide officials run on a partisan ticket, as do legislators in every state except Nebraska. Almost all state officials and nearly every member in each legislature is either a Democrat or a Republican. On paper, at least, the parties in the various states are organized in similar fashion.

But we must recognize that, in reality, there are many differences among the state parties. Students who know something about politics and parties in their state may believe that what applies in their state is typical of what one would find in every other state, but that is not the case. Parties and politics are very different in California, Iowa, and Vermont, simply because of differences in size and population. Events in the distant past explain differences at the start of the twenty-first century. There are still differences between southern and northern states because the South lost the Civil War and southern states remained solidly Democratic until the 1950s. Political parties are different in the states that received large waves of immigrants in the late nineteenth and early twentieth centuries; and they are different in states that now have large numbers of racial and ethnic minorities. Politics is different today in the midwestern and western states where the Progressive movement was strong in the early twentieth century. Many of the variations in state political systems are described in Chapter 1.

In a broad sense, we can divide state parties into those that are strong, those that are weak, and those that are emerging. Party strength is closely related to party competition. As we will explain in Chapter 2, competition at the state level is usually stronger when there is a relatively close balance between the two national parties in the state. From the end of the Civil War and Reconstruction until the beginning of the New Deal in the 1930s, one national party, and therefore one state party, won most of these elections in many states. Parties usually were weak in states where this situation prevailed because the dominant party did not need a large, well-financed organization to win elections, and the minority party—with little chance of winning statewide elections—lacked both adequate resources and enough committed workers to become competitive.

The strong parties, found predominantly in the Northeast and Midwest, have a tradition of strong organizations that is meaningful today even though the old-style urban machines have largely disappeared. In a majority of these states, including most of those that are heavily urbanized, the state party makes some effort to influence the choice of its nominees (described in Chapter 4). It is in these states that we are most likely to find strong legislative parties, each of which is likely to be cohesive on many of the important issues arising in the legislature (described in Chapter 8). Most of these are states where there has been relatively strong two-party competition in elections at least since the 1940s, and in some cases much earlier.

Weak parties are found primarily in western states, particularly the more rural ones. In a number of these, and in a few midwestern states (like Wisconsin, Minnesota, and the Dakotas), the Populist movement was strong in the early twentieth century. The Populist Party was critical of party organizations and particularly of political bosses. It promoted direct primary elections, which developed first in these states and later spread to all the states. Open primary laws, which permit voters to shift back and forth between the party primaries, have the effect of weakening the party's control over the nomination; but some states with open primaries are, in other respects, relatively strong.

When the parties in a state are weak, the legislative parties are also likely to be weak. The two parties are not likely to be very cohesive on issues, and voting in the legislature does not often follow party lines (Chapter 8). Some of these states do not have strong two-party competition, though in others competition has been developing more of late.

Until recently, southern states were dominated by the Democratic Party; in the Deep South, the Republican Party was so weak that politics was almost nonpartisan. However, in the 1950s and early 1960s Republican presidential candidates began to make serious and increasingly successful efforts to win southern states, so very gradually Republican Parties in southern states began to develop into more than empty shells.

Southern parties can now be described as emerging parties. The Republican Parties were slow to take advantage of the popularity of their presidential candidates, but they have begun to elect an increasing numbers of governors, senators, members of the U.S. House and, more recently, substantial numbers of state legislators. Republican Parties in the Deep South have been slower to win victories because they were so far behind. The Democratic Parties can also be described as developing because they have reacted to Republican gains by raising the level of organizational and campaign activities. (We pay particular attention in Chapter

2 to the emergence of a competitive Republican Party in the South.) In southern legislatures, however, there are often few differences on issues between Republicans and those Democrats who are quite conservative, and therefore issues often are not decided along party lines.

MONEY PLAYS A MAJOR ROLE IN STATE POLITICS

It is impossible to discuss any aspect of state political parties and elections without talking about money, and thus inevitably campaign funding will be a pervasive theme in this book. We have already said that the state party cannot even join the political game unless it raises large amounts of money. If campaign contributors give all their funds directly to candidates, and none of it to political parties, then the parties have nothing to offer their candidates—no direct funds, no services, no tangible support. Consequently the raising of money and decisions about how to allocate it become important to our discussion of party organizations in Chapter 3.

One of the criticisms of direct primary elections is that money may play a larger role in their outcome than it does in general elections. In Chapter 4 on the nominating process, we will try to measure the effect of campaign funding on nominations, and we will also raise questions about whether a party organization's preprimary endorsement of a candidate can be very effective unless the party provides tangible help—funding and services—to the endorsee.

In our discussion of gubernatorial general elections in Chapter 5, we will examine how gubernatorial candidates raise money, how much help they get from their party, and the conditions under which funding is critical to the outcome of the election. We will also look at the states that provide public funding directly to gubernatorial candidates or to the political parties.

Similarly, when we examine the role of political parties in the legislature, we will look at what it costs to get elected to the legislature and how legislative candidates raise campaign funds. We will also describe the role that legislative leaders and campaign committees play in allocating funds to legislative candidates—both incumbents and nonincumbents.

THE LINKAGES BETWEEN STATE AND NATIONAL PARTIES ARE GROWING AND CHANGING

The state parties have not become pawns of national parties, but their relationships have become closer and more complex. These trends are discussed in some detail in Chapter 9. The national parties exercise considerable control over how and when state parties select delegates to the national convention and even how delegates' votes are cast at the convention—although state parties have some flexibility in these areas.

Major changes in the relationships between state and national parties involve campaign finance and its regulation. The state and national parties are both involved in campaigns for presidential and congressional office. The Federal Election Commission (FEC) in Washington regulates the funding of these campaigns, and its rules limit how state and national parties allocate funds for these races. Funds raised and spent in accord with federal regulations are often called "hard money." Unlimited funds contributed to national and state parties for limited purposes, such as party overhead expenses, are called "soft money." The state and national parties raise both hard and soft money and spend these funds for direct aid to candidates and for so-called party-building activities. The FEC rules specify how hard and soft money can be raised and how these funds can be spent. Hard and soft campaign dollars move back and forth between the national and state parties in bewildering fashion, and in practice the ways in which these funds are used varies considerably from one election year to the next. The national party campaign committees also give some funds directly to state candidates, including legislative candidates, without going through the state parties. In Chapter 9 we will try to make these complex procedures and practices a little less bewildering and a little more understandable.

1 State Political Systems in a National Setting

Each of the fifty states has a unique, distinctive political system. At the same time, state political systems are affected by national political forces and by many of the characteristics of the U.S. political system. Our job in this chapter is to untangle the state and national political systems, to show in what respects the states are different, and to show how they are influenced by national traditions and trends.

DISTINCTIVE CHARACTERISTICS OF STATE POLITICAL SYSTEMS

States differ in a wide variety of ways. The political system is directly affected by a number of constitutional and legal provisions, ranging from the structure of the legislature to the organization of political parties and the operation of primaries and general elections. Elections are also shaped by the patterns of two-party competition, which are not only very different among the states but are changing rapidly, particularly in the South. State politics is also affected by factors that are not obviously political, such as the geography and the social structure of the state. Furthermore, states have different political cultures, shaped by their history and by widely held attitudes toward political matters.

Constitutional and Legal Factors

Anyone who undertook the arduous task of reading the fifty state constitutions would find many similarities but also some important differences. Some of the constitutions are relatively brief, and others are so detailed that large numbers of amendments must be adopted every couple of years. Some were originally drafted in the early nineteenth century, many were drafted or thoroughly revised in the late nineteenth century, and a few have been completely rewritten in recent years.

Although all of the constitutions establish three branches of government in very similar forms, some significant differences do exist. Almost all governors now serve four-year rather than two-year terms and may serve two consecutive terms, but some place restrictions on additional terms. Only Virginia prohibits a governor from serving a second consecutive term. The amount of authority granted to the governor over the executive branch varies significantly.

Legislatures vary in size, the senate from 20 to 67 members and the house from 40 to 400, with the numbers usually reflecting state population. Three of the smallest states—Delaware, Alaska, and Nevada—have the smallest senates and houses. Most of the largest states have large legislatures; for example, there are 203 House members in Pennsylvania, 180 in Georgia, and 150 in Texas and in New York. But the largest state, California, has only 40 senators and 80 Assembly members and consequently its Senate districts are larger than its congressional districts. Most of the relatively small states of New England have large legislatures; and New Hampshire, entitled to only two members of the U.S. House, has 400 members in the state house.

Some constitutions restrict the length of legislative sessions or their frequency (every year or every two years), while an increasing number allow the legislature to meet whenever it wants. Roughly half of the states limit the scope of legislative power by providing that voters can adopt laws or constitutional amendments by initiative or can pass judgment on laws by referendum. Constitutional provisions such as these establish the framework for the distribution of power in the state, particularly between the governor and the legislature, and help to explain some of the differences in the operation of the political system.

Statutory law has a less enduring effect on the political system because it can be more easily changed, but its impact can be just as great. Of course such laws, even more than the constitution, reflect the preferences of the dominant political forces in the state. For example, if state law makes it difficult for third-party or independent candidates to get on the ballot, we may assume that this law results from the two-party dominance of state politics and it thus helps to perpetuate that dominance.

Some states impose rather detailed legal control over the structure and activities of party organizations; other states (including many in the South) have a minimum of regulatory legislation. The fewer the legal restrictions, the more freedom the parties have to organize and operate as they wish. A number of states specify, sometimes in great detail, how parties shall be organized and governed, but recent court decisions (see *Eu, Secretary of State of California v. San Francisco County Democratic Central Committee*, 1989) have given state parties greater freedom to organize as they wish. States regularly specify the conditions a party must meet to have access to the ballot and define what is considered a major political party.

The fact that the direct primary is now conducted in all of the states means that detailed legal provisions cover the nomination of candidates. Some states establish procedures for political party endorsement of candidates in primary elections; others used to prohibit such endorsements until the courts overruled such limitations. State laws determine whether registered voters may vote in the primary of any political party or whether they must register in advance with a particular party to vote in its primary. We discuss these differences and their consequences in Chapter 4 on nominations.

Almost all states regulate how parties and candidates may raise and spend funds in political campaigns. In recent years these regulations have become stricter and more detailed, but they vary considerably from state to state. A number of the states also have been experimenting with various forms of public financing for political parties or the campaigns of candidates. We will explore the complexities of campaign financing in several chapters.

The timing of elections, of course, is a matter of law. It makes a difference whether the governor is elected in a presidential election year, a congressional election year, or some other year and whether local officials are elected when statewide candidates are. The use of nonpartisan elections in many local governments weakens the local power base of the parties. In the past, before the Supreme Court began intervening to protect voting rights in the 1940s and Congress passed the Voting Rights Act in 1965, the political system in many southern states was shaped in large part by laws that made it difficult for racial minorities to register and vote. Even today, differences in registration requirements such as the lead time required between registration and election day can affect the size and makeup of the electorate.

Constitutional and statutory law on legislative apportionment and districting determine how popular votes are translated into seats and may significantly affect the balance of power between the parties in the legislature. Although the Supreme Court's decisions on apportionment have severely limited the states' freedom of choice in this field, the majority party in the legislature can still draw district lines that favor its legislative candidates, as long as the population of the districts is approximately equal.

This list is not exhaustive, but it is long enough to show that states determine who can vote, when they can vote, whether primaries are open or closed, how long officials can serve, how many statewide officials are elected, the size and shape of districts, and what kinds of issues are submitted to the voters for a decision. Although many of these political ground rules are statutes rather than constitutional provisions, they are not frequently changed. Although the federal government (usually through the courts) has imposed certain standards—generally to broaden voter participation and prevent discrimination in voting—there are many areas in which the states are free to make their own choices. The constitutional and statutory ground rules perpetuate a certain kind of political system in each state. Although these rules result from political traditions and practices, they have a continuing impact on the political system and the political culture within which that system operates.

Patterns of Political Competition

One of the fundamental differences among the states concerns the character and intensity of two-party competition. Some states have had close competition between the Republican and Democratic Parties with hardly any interruption since the Civil War. In other states, such competition has been interrupted for long periods of time or has only recently developed. Most southern states did not develop real two-party competition at the state and legislative levels until the 1980s and particularly the 1990s. The level of competition can be measured by several criteria: turnover in partisan control of the governorship, other state offices, and the legislature; closeness of elections for major office; the proportion of offices contested by each party; the number of voters registering with each of the parties in closed primary states; and the proportion of voters who tell pollsters that they identify with each of the parties.

The factors that explain the differences in two-party competition are described in Chapter 2. The pattern of party competition is rooted in each state's political history, and traditional partisan loyalties and voting habits are not easily changed. Changes in the level of state party competition often result from national trends but the effect of such trends on state competition is often delayed because of these traditional party loyalties.

Geographic, Economic, Social, and Historical Factors

At the risk of appearing to state the obvious, we should emphasize the enormous variety that exists among American states. They differ in natural resources, urbanization, the extent and types of agriculture, size and density of population, immigration patterns (past and present), racial and ethnic diversity, and many other important respects. Each of these distinctions has some effect on the political system that has evolved within each state. The types of interests that are organized and influential, the form of partisan alignment, and the major issues that have arisen in a state are all shaped by these factors.

The political history of each state is different and some states have a much longer political history than others. Massachusetts and Alaska illustrate this difference. Massachusetts was one of the original thirteen states, while Alaska was the forty-ninth state, joining the Union in 1959. Whether a state belonged to the Union or the Confederacy during the Civil War, or had not yet been settled, still has an impact on state politics some six generations later. Conflicts between different regions of a state or the urban and rural areas may have historical roots that go back a couple of hundred years. In some of the border states the deep divisions that arose over the issue of slavery and the question of secession in 1861 are reflected in partisan divisions that exist today.

Differences in the Political Culture of States

Anyone who studies or observes various states carefully is likely to reach the conclusion that there are differences in the styles and customs of politics that cannot simply be explained by such tangible characteristics as laws, elections, or economic realities. Sometimes we are tempted to explain some aspects of politics in a state by saying, "That's just the way they do it." As political scientists, we resist an explanation that appears unscientific and unsystematic and we grasp for something better.

The best answer may be to borrow a term—*political culture*—that has been used frequently by scholars who are interested in cross-national comparisons of political systems. Sydney Verba has defined political culture as "the system of empirical beliefs, expressive symbols, and values which defines the situation in which political action takes place" (Verba 1965, 513). We might clarify the concept further if we specified that these beliefs, symbols, and values are widely shared in a society and have an enduring quality that is based on history and tradition. Daniel Elazar has described political culture as "the historical sources of such differences in habits, concerns, and attitudes that exist to influence political life in the various states" (Elazar 1972, 85).

If it is possible to define and identify national political culture, does that necessarily mean that there is a distinct political culture in each of the fifty states? We recognize that there are cultural differences between North and South, but are there, for example, significant differences among the southern states? Is it not likely that cultural differences within a state, among its various racial and ethnic groups or between its urban and rural residents, would be more important than cultural characteristics that distinguish a state from its neighbors?

In suggesting that state political culture is a meaningful concept, we are not arguing that the most significant existing differences in political culture are necessarily those that follow state lines or that the beliefs and attitudes of Texans or of Hawaiians are homogeneous. We are suggesting that the political system of any state is affected by what the citizens of that state think and believe. The viewpoints on some questions that are widely shared by the people of one state may be quite different from those that predominate in another state. Moreover, each state has a history and traditions that are unique and that will help to shape the dominant beliefs and attitudes in that state. In that sense, it is useful to discuss and to study political culture (see Patterson 1968).

The first step in understanding a state's political culture is to identify the kinds of people who inhabit that state. We can identify patterns of immigration from one state to another and can identify the most important racial, ethnic, and religious elements in a state's population, and we can analyze how they affect state political culture. The attitudes of whites and blacks differ on some issues and the importance of these differences depends on the distribution of the two groups in a state. The religious views held by large groups in a state affect its decision making. Members of southern churches are likely to be more conservative in their views on both religious and political questions, particularly those related to social issues. No one would attempt to analyze Massachusetts politics without understanding the role that Irish Catholics have played in its history; nor would one ignore the role of Jewish influences on New York politics. The politics of both California and Texas are changing because Latinos are beginning to vote in larger numbers and to plan more active political roles than before.

Economic and social developments in a state also affect its political culture. Those who live in large metropolitan areas often have viewpoints about the range and variety of services that government should provide that are different from those in rural areas. States like Arizona and New Mexico, which are growing rapidly in population and becoming heavily urbanized, are developing a different political culture as a result. Historians have emphasized the effects of the frontier on American culture; therefore it is not surprising to find different attitudes about law and order and greater hostility toward the role of the federal government in the lives of those who inhabit some of the more sparsely populated western states.

The ethnic, economic, and social forces that we have been discussing help to explain differences in the political histories of the states, which in turn affect their political culture. The Populist movement had a lasting effect on the political culture of western states, extending beyond anything that can be explained by the quality of the soil or the number of silver mines in the state. The influence of the Progressive movement in the early twentieth century in such states as Wisconsin, Minnesota, and the Dakotas resulted not only from the ethnic background of their citizens but also from the political strength that the movement developed and the issues it emphasized. The political culture of southern states has been shaped not only by the cotton economy that existed in the 1950s and the high proportion of African Americans in these states but also by the fact that these states seceded, lost the Civil War, and were occupied by federal troops during the Reconstruction years. The current southern political culture is changing, at least in urban areas, because of the influx of people into such cities as Atlanta, Memphis, Houston, and Dallas.

Thus the political culture of a state today is a product of its entire history. National political developments, such as the Civil War and Reconstruction, Populism, the Progressive movement, the New Deal, and the civil rights movement have left different imprints on each state, depending on its geography, economy, and population characteristics. Moreover, particularly important political leaders, controversies, and crises within individual states have left their marks on the political culture as well. For example it would be impossible to understand the political culture in Louisiana today without some knowledge of the political dynasty of Huey and Earl Long. Martin Luther King Jr. had a lasting impact in many southern states, particularly Georgia and Alabama. To understand Michigan politics today, it helps to recall the labor union movement that developed in the auto industry during the 1930s and 1940s.

Elazar (1972, 1984) has made the most extensive attempt to identify and describe political culture in the American states. He has identified three major types of political culture—individualistic, moralistic, and traditionalistic—and has identified the states, and the sections of states, in which one or more of these cultures is dominant. It is an ambitious effort, but because the designation of state and substate cultures is more impressionistic than systematic, it is open to criticism. Actually, anyone who is fully acquainted with several states can play the game of describing their dominant political cultures.

We can identify some linkages between political culture and public policy in the states. Much of the economic and social regulatory legislation developed first in states where the Populist and Progressive movements were strong. The eastern and midwestern states established systems of public education before southern states did, although differences in education policy have grown smaller in recent years. A study by Jack Walker (1969) showed that New York, Massachusetts, New Jersey, Michigan, Connecticut, Pennsylvania, and California were often the first to adopt legislative innovations that eventually spread to most of the other states. The states that lagged behind were often in the South, along with some in the Southwest and West. But in the most recent period, innovations designed to put limits on the growth of taxes and spending—often adopted by voter initiatives—were more likely to develop in those western states where the distrust of government is more prevalent.

In recent years it has become more difficult to recognize differences in state attitudes toward the role of government because the federal government encouraged and almost forced states to introduce a wide variety of programs by providing matching funds. This remained true into the 1990s, even as the federal government was allowing states somewhat more flexibility in how they spent federal funds.

Some states have a much higher rate of participation in general and primary elections than other states, because state laws make it particularly easy to register and vote and because citizens seem more likely to take advantage of those opportunities. In some other states many citizens do not seem to believe it is either possible or desirable for them to have much impact on the decisions made by government. Even at a time when polls suggest that public cynicism about the political process is both widespread and growing, variation in the rate of participation still exists among states. The differences in such laws and practices are the consequences of different norms and attitudes regarding the breadth of participation in the political process; these differences are very important in understanding state political culture.

There appear to be differences among the states in attitudes toward political parties and party organizations. Party loyalties seem stronger in the East and Midwest than in the West and South. In some states voters appear to vote consistently (in one election and over time) for a party and are more willing to follow the advice of the party organization on nominations. Voting patterns in New York and Indiana are examples of this trend. States in which the Progressive movement was strongest appear to harbor the greatest distrust of party organizational leadership. Despite these apparent differences, we lack recent public opinion survey data that would confirm interstate differences in attitudes toward party.

Some states seem more willing than others to elect governors who either are independent or belong to third parties. For example between the 1970 and 1998 elections, Maine elected independents three times (in 1974, 1994, and 1998). Alaska and Connecticut elected an independent and a third-party candidate, respectively, in 1990, although both had previously held statewide office as Republicans; and in 1998 Minnesota elected Reform Party candidate Jessie Ventura, who attracted far more attention than the others.

Political styles differ from state to state in ways that are difficult to measure or explain. Certain norms exist, based on habit and tradition, about how politics is conducted. In some states a variety of distinctions—racial, ethnic, and religious—still permeate politics and affect how parties are split into factions and how candidate coalitions are constructed. Race is a more pervasive factor in the politics of most southern states than it is elsewhere. Ethnic factors have some importance in the most urbanized northeastern and midwestern states. Differences among various religious groups over moral issues seem to be growing in importance in a number of states. Political conflict appears to have a much stronger ideological base in some states than in others. In some states, including those in which party machines used to be strong, corruption seems to be a way of life, a norm that is accepted by the politicians and tolerated by the voters. On the other hand, the standards seem to be much higher in states like Minnesota and Wisconsin.

NATIONAL FACTORS THAT INFLUENCE STATE POLITICS

There are national factors that affect all of the states. Some of these result from provisions of the U.S. Constitution, the policies adopted by Congress and the executive branch, and judicial decisions—particularly those made by the Supreme

Court. Trends in two-party competition at the state level are profoundly affected by national partisan trends, particularly party realignments. There are also a wide variety of changes in the national political culture that threaten to make the states less distinctive. Political perceptions and opinions of everyone from Maine to California are shaped by the same national events as reported by the same media.

Constitutional, Statutory, and Judicial Factors

The similarities among state constitutional structures are more obvious than their differences. The structures of the executive and legislative branches in most states are similar, with officeholders elected for fixed terms of two or four years, on partisan ballots, and with bicameral legislatures. (Nebraska is the exception, with its unicameral, nonpartisan legislature.) The states are similar partly because as new states joined the Union they adopted constitutions that were modeled on those of the existing states and to some extent on the national government.

Moreover, throughout our history, major changes in state constitutional structure have spread quickly from state to state. For example, from the Revolution to Andrew Jackson's administration (which ended in 1837) the franchise rapidly expanded to include all adult males in almost all states. In the early twentieth century the direct primary election spread rapidly throughout most of the states. Other changes, such as the reorganization of state government and the development of the executive budget, were adopted in many states after having been pioneered by a few. Other changes resulted from amendments to the U.S. Constitution, such as women's suffrage, the vote for eighteen-year-olds, and the popular election of U.S. senators.

Since the start of the New Deal, the actions of the federal government have had a profound effect on state governments. Congress has passed many laws designed to encourage the states to adopt particular programs by providing federal funds on a matching basis. As a result, the policy outputs of the states have become increasingly similar in areas ranging from highway construction, environmental protection, and education to welfare policy—although in the 1990s the states were given somewhat more freedom in this last area. Federal tax policy has shaped state taxes as well. Almost all of the states have come to rely heavily on the general sales tax because it is the only major source of tax revenue left untouched by Washington (other than local property taxes). In some states the Democratic Party might be expected to oppose the sales tax because it typically is regressive. However, Democrats often support the tax, knowing that it is essential to cover at least some of the costs of state government programs they favor.

Some federal legislation has had a direct effect on the structure of state government. It has banned the use of political patronage in agencies receiving federal funds. Federal programs that provide direct assistance to urban governments have affected the relationship between state and local governments, sometimes increasing the political power of mayors in large cities. By encouraging growth in a variety of state programs, federal activities have resulted in stronger governors with larger staffs in the gubernatorial offices.

The extensive influence of the federal government and its policies on the states does not mean that the states are declining in importance; in fact, just the opposite is true. One reason is that during the 1980s and 1990s many federal government programs grew more slowly than they once did or even were cut back, leaving the state governments to fill the void and assume greater responsibilities than they had in the past. State government has revitalized in other ways as well.

State legislatures are becoming modernized and gaining in capacity. Legislators are becoming more professional and serving longer terms, except in states where term limits have taken effect. Governors are growing in importance, and the governorship is taken more seriously as a stepping stone to the White House or at least to the presidential nomination, as evidenced by the fact that Jimmy Carter, Ronald Reagan, and Bill Clinton were elected and Michael Dukakis was nominated. There is a declining belief among citizens that the federal government can solve all problems and a growing conviction that the states should be given more opportunity to make crucial decisions and set priorities.

U.S. Supreme Court decisions have also had a major impact on all the states, for the most part resulting in smaller differences among them. The most obvious example is the series of Supreme Court and lower court decisions on school desegregation and busing, which have forced the states to make major changes in their school systems but which have not eliminated considerable segregation in practice. The Supreme Court's decisions on the rights of defendants in trials have reduced the variations in state judicial systems. The policies adopted by the Supreme Court, along with congressional legislation, have eliminated the obstacles to voting by African Americans, thereby ending one of the most important differences in state electoral practices. Judicial and congressional actions have also forced states to eliminate long residence requirements as a prerequisite to voting.

The judicial decisions with the most direct impact on state politics and parties have been those dealing with state legislative apportionment. Before 1962 the constitutional and/or statutory base of apportionment in many states grossly discriminated against urban residents; in states where the party alignment had an urban-rural base, this often had the effect of guaranteeing one-party (usually Republican) control of the legislature, whatever the electoral trends in the state. A series of judicial decisions in the mid-1960s, starting with *Baker v. Carr* (1962) declaring that state constitutional and legislative provisions violated the U.S. Constitution, required substantial population equality for legislative districts, or "one person, one vote." As a consequence, urban areas are no longer seriously underrepresented in any state, and no party is barred from a legislative majority by the apportionment system.

The courts have not, however, prohibited partisan gerrymandering—the practice of drawing district lines to handicap the other political party—as long as the principle of population equality is followed. The majority party in some legislative bodies has been skillful in creating district boundaries that give it an advantage in translating votes into seats.

The courts, and the U.S. Justice Department, have been much more concerned about preventing racial gerrymandering for state legislative or congressional districts, which reduces the chances that candidates who belong to racial minorities can get elected. In some states black voters are not concentrated geographically but are widely scattered in some areas; legislatures have had to create districts that are strangely shaped and far from compact in order to get districts with a majority of black voters.

The Supreme Court in the 1990s sometimes rejected districts that appeared to be a form of reverse racial gerrymandering (*Shaw v. Reno,* 1993). The Supreme Court has held that whenever a state uses race "as the dominant and controlling rationale in drawing its district lines," it has engaged in racial gerrymandering that may not be permissible (*Miller v. Johnson,* 1995). A majority of the justices seem to be committed to race-neutral criteria for districting. The Supreme Court has recognized, however, that what appears to be racial gerrymandering may be a consequence of partisan gerrymandering, which it considers legitimate (*Hunt v. Cromartie,* 1999).

The courts remain heavily involved in determining how racial majorities are represented in state legislatures as well as in Congress. This issue also has implications for the party balance in state legislatures because black voters are most likely to vote Democratic. One result of concentrating black voters in districts is to make surrounding districts more heavily white and thus reduce the number of districts that the Democrats have a good chance of carrying (Lublin and Voss 1999).

The Justice Department and the courts (see *McMillan v. Escambia County of Florida,* 1981) have also been critical of multimember districts in state legislatures if these have the effect of reducing the electoral power of racial minorities. In fact, the use of multimember, rather than single-member, districts may make it more difficult for any minority—racial, ethnic, or partisan—to translate into seats the votes their candidates receive.

In most multimember districts voters may cast as many votes as there are members to be elected. If a county elects three members to the legislature, for example, and two-thirds of its voters are white and one-third are black, and if voting often follows racial lines, the election of any black candidates may depend on the districting system used. If the county is divided into three single-member districts, one of which has at least a majority of black voters, one black candidate is likely to be elected. If the county consists of one three-member district, all three candidates elected are likely to be white (Jewell 1982; Grofman, Migalski, and Noviello 1986).

The use of single-member or multimember districts has a similar effect on the proportion of Democrats and Republicans elected. Voters are probably less likely in a multimember district to vote a straight party ticket than to vote for all whites or all blacks.

Because the Justice Department and the courts have been persuaded that multimember districts tend to dilute the vote of racial minorities, particularly in the South, they have been able to eliminate most multimember legislative districts, particularly in the southern states. One of the byproducts of this shift to single-member districts has been to help the party that is in the minority in a particular area, and in southern states recently this has often been the Republican Party.

During the 1990s North Carolina continued to make some use in both the House and Senate of districts electing two or three members, particularly in urban areas. The House had seventeen three-member and two-member districts. In the three elections from 1992 through 1996 twelve districts always elected all members from the same party in any given year, and five had a split in one or more elections. These districts were drawn up by a Democratic majority in the legislature, and in 1992 twelve of them elected all Democrats. However, Republican gains in 1994 and 1996 reduced the all-Democratic districts to seven and gave the Republicans almost as many.

Partisan Trends

State political party systems do not exist in isolation from national political trends. National party alignments determine the approximate proportion of Democrats and Republicans in a state and establish the bases for (or make unlikely) two-party competition in a state. The actual development of vigorous two-party competition at the state level, however, depends on a number of state variables as well as on national alignments and trends. Much of Chapter 2 is devoted to an explanation of how national and state factors combine to determine the level of state party competition. Major national party realignments, such as occurred in 1896 and in the early 1930s, and in the South beginning in the 1950s and 1960s, have had a profound effect on state party systems. The Democratic gains in national politics during the early 1930s gradually led to Democratic gains in state politics, and thus to closer two-party competition, ten to twenty years later in many northern states. The national Republican gains in the South in the 1950s and 1960s led very slowly to a revitalization of party competition at the state level in the 1980s and 1990s.

In addition to these national realignments, in every national election there are political trends favoring one party or the other, and these have some effect on state elections. Every two years some or all legislators in most states are elected; only about one-fifth of governors are chosen in presidential election years; three-fourths are picked in congressional years or, in a few cases, in odd-numbered years. But major political trends can occur in presidential election years, such as 1964 and 1980, or in congressional election years, such as 1974 and 1994. Lyndon Johnson's landslide election in 1964 helped produce Democratic gains in Congress, and Ronald Reagan's election in 1980 launched twelve years of Republican control of the White House. There were large Democratic gains in congressional races in 1974 (the post-Watergate election), and the Republicans captured control of both branches of Congress in 1994 after a very long dry spell. Incumbent governors and state legislators are politically stronger than they used to be and thus are less likely to be swept out of office in a national partisan landslide. But there are data showing that the electoral success of both governors and state legislators is somewhat affected by national trends.

National Political Culture

Changes are occurring all the time in the national political culture, in the attitudes and beliefs of Americans generally, that have an effect on state political culture. Just as no state is isolated from national partisan trends, none is isolated from the national media and from events that are national in scope. If the public is growing more cynical about politics and politicians, these attitudes presumably apply at the state as well as the national level, though possibly to different degrees.

More important, there appear to be some nationalizing trends in the country that may be reducing the importance of differences in regional and state political cultures. The growing population mobility, particularly in states such as Florida, Nevada, Arizona, and California that have had large influxes of residents, may erode state political culture. If a person has grown up in New York or Massachusetts, where parties are relatively strong, and moves to California or Washington, where they are much weaker, does that person get a different perception of how political parties work or should work? The Progressive movement, which flourished in the first quarter of the twentieth century, may have shaped political culture in Minnesota and Wisconsin, but why should this influence the thinking of someone who moves to one of these states from Texas or Pennsylvania?

We live in an age when we all see and hear about the same events on national television at the same time. But the Internet gives those who have some interest in politics a chance to explore an enormous variety of specialized materials, ranging from debates over issues to newspaper coverage of elections or political developments in other states. Sometimes it seems as if state political culture has some effect on the style and content of television ads in state campaigns, but we know that the same political advertising firms sometimes use similar tactics and even similar ads in a variety of states over a period of a few years. The changing rules and practices at the national level regarding the use of soft money have an impact on the state as well as national campaigns.

National trends have effects on political culture that are so obvious and powerful that they are likely to overshadow the more subtle, underlying, traditional forces that continue to distinguish state political cultures. The differences among state political cultures presumably are becoming smaller, but they have not disappeared.

Some of these long-standing differences among the states in attitudes toward politics have become institutionalized; that is, the laws, procedures, and practices of state politics may remain in effect long after the public attitudes and political events that led to their establishment have disappeared. For a long time many states imposed rigid constitutional limits on the frequency and length of legislative sessions, restrictions that had been adopted in a number of states in the late nineteenth century as a way of trying to curb serious problems of legislative corruption. As the problem of corruption grew less serious and the workload of legislatures increased in the last third of the twentieth century, amending the constitution to let the legislature meet for longer periods was often a slow and difficult process.

In the early part of the twentieth century, a number of states amended their constitutions to create an initiative process that would permit voters to adopt new legislation rather than waiting for the legislature to take such action. The initiative has been adopted in about half of the states, primarily those in which the Progressive movement was strong. In the 1990s a strong national movement led about one-third of the states to place restrictions on the number of terms that state legislators could serve. Such a change was not very popular in the legislature; therefore, in almost every state where legislative term limits were adopted, it was accomplished through the initiative process. This is an example of how a national trend, reflecting a widely held public belief in such limits, was largely limited to those states where the Progressive movement helped to shape the political culture many years ago.

2 The Growth in Two-Party Competition

We have said that state political systems must be understood within the context of the U.S. political system and national political trends. This is well illustrated by the relationship between two-party competition at the national and state levels. There is greater two-party competition in some states than in others because of differences in political characteristics of the states and also because of national political developments. Changes in the amount of competition at the state level are driven in large part by national political trends. A major theme of this chapter is the trend toward increased competition in two-party politics in almost all states, a trend that began at the national level and has filtered down to the state level.

During the first third of the twentieth century, a large proportion of voters had strong loyalties to one major party or the other and usually voted for the candidates of that party. In many of the states a large majority of the voters were loyal to one party. Consequently, in such states or in large parts of such states, one party was well organized and the other was weak, and the same traditional voting patterns occurred in both national and state elections.

The trend toward two-party competition began at the level of national politics, as a result of major political realignments that undermined the traditional political loyalties of many voters and led them to vote more independently in national elections. This change occurred in northern states during the 1930s and 1940s and began in the southern states during the 1950s and 1960s. The results of these trends were first evident in the outcome of presidential elections and in some congressional races. It took a number of years, particularly in southern states, for these trends to affect the patterns of voting for state candidates, such as those running for governor, state legislature, and local office. By the 1990s it could be said that Democratic control had been broken, to varying degrees, in all of the southern states.

HISTORICAL PATTERNS OF NATIONAL PARTY COMPETITION

The Civil War and Reconstruction had a massive and enduring effect on national and state politics, establishing Democratic domination in southern states and Republican domination in most northern states. From the end of Reconstruction until the start of the New Deal in 1933, most political developments had the effect of strengthening and reinforcing this one-party dominance in most, though not all, of the states. One-party control of county and city governments was established even in states where there was stronger party competition at the state level.

V. O. Key, Jr. (1964, 232) has defined sectional politics as "a sharing of interests and attitudes by people of all sorts in a major geographical region against a similar clustering of interests and attitudes of the people of another region." The sectional division grew out of the loyalties and antagonisms generated by the Civil War and persisted largely because of regional economic differences. As long as it persisted, new partisan alignments based on class or urban-rural differences failed to develop. Moreover, each of the national parties was dominated by the political leadership located in the section of the country where that party held a dominant position.

We will be quoting and citing Key frequently in this book. From the late 1930s until his death in 1963 he was the most important political scientist writing about American politics, parties, and elections. His textbook *Politics, Parties, and Pressure Groups* was the standard in the field for five editions. His book *Southern Politics,* published in 1949, was a masterpiece and is still consulted by anyone studying southern politics. His book *American State Politics: An Introduction* (1956) was a pioneering work that effectively began the comparative study of state politics and first raised many of the issues that we continue to explore today. It was also, in fact, the inspiration for this book.

Sectional Politics

Because the pattern of politics in individual American states today has been shaped so much by history, it is important to trace briefly the main outlines of American political history since the Civil War. In Key's words (1964, 232), "The Civil War made the Democratic party the party of the South and the Republican party the party of the North." One-party control was strongest in the eleven states of the old confederacy—the Solid South. Between 1880 (following the end of Reconstruction) and 1944, Democratic presidential candidates carried every one of these states in every election, except in 1928 when Democrat Al Smith failed to carry five of them and in 1920 when Tennessee voted Republican. From 1916 (when they were first elected) to 1944 every U.S. senator from the South was a Democrat; and from 1880 to 1944 every southern governor was a Democrat (or, rarely, an independent), with a few exceptions in North Carolina and Tennessee.

The only centers of Republican strength in this period were in the Appalachian Mountain areas (western North Carolina, eastern Tennessee, and southwestern Virginia). Cotton could not be grown in these mountainous areas, so there was very little slavery and much opposition to secession. Consequently these areas became Republican and have remained somewhat Republican to the present time.

The North was never as solidly Republican as the South was Democratic, and Republican control gradually eroded between the end of the Civil War and the 1896 election, for a variety of reasons. Waves of immigrants from Europe settled in major urban and industrial centers in the Northeast and Midwest, and, as they became citizens and voters, usually became Democrats. The Republican Party was largely Protestant, middle class, and nativist in its orientation, and Republican organizations made few efforts to recruit the new immigrants. The Democratic Party in the northern urban centers was more Catholic and working class in composition. The Democratic organizations recruited the new immigrant voters, providing a variety of services for them and, in return, getting their votes, which were mobilized with considerable efficiency. Although the Republicans remained the majority party in most northeastern and midwestern states, the urban base of the Democratic Party became strong enough to challenge the Republicans for control in a number of states in the late nineteenth century.

In some western states the ethnic and religious loyalties to parties that the new immigrants had developed in eastern states persisted as they moved farther west. A majority of the western states had been populated primarily by northerners. They contained Protestant, rural majorities and tended to be Republican, though partisan loyalties seemed weaker than in the eastern states. Beginning in the 1870s, however, the citizens of many western states, and particularly the farmers, became disillusioned with the two major parties. They had been hurt by a series of economic setbacks, and they began to demand economic and political reforms, including cheap money and greater regulation of businesses, particularly the railroads. When the two major parties largely ignored these demands, westerners began to give their attention, and some of their votes, to a series of minor parties in both state and national elections. This political movement reached its peak in the 1892 presidential election when the Populist Party polled over one million votes (more than 8 percent), won a plurality in five western states, relegated the Democratic Party to third place in several states, and won the governorship in three western states.

The success of the Populist Party and the depression of 1893 led the Democratic Party to repudiate the economic principles of its president, Grover Cleveland, nominate William Jennings Bryan as its presidential candidate, and adopt the Populist economic program, particularly the inflationary free silver plank. As the Democratic candidate, Bryan carried some, but not all, of the western and plains states, but these gains were short-lived and Bryan was defeated by Republican William McKinley in 1896.

The long-run consequence of the 1896 election was the strengthening of Republican dominance in the more northern states. The Republican Party succeeded in winning the votes of many urban, middle-class, and working-class voters, who were dismayed by the inflationary policies advocated by the Democratic Party. A large proportion of the voters continued to elect Republican candidates in subsequent elections, and the Democratic base of support was limited largely to Catholics and recent immigrants. These national trends were reflected in state elections. Most of the northeastern and midwestern states elected Republican governors in a large majority of elections from 1896 through 1930.

The New Deal Realignment and the Post-War Period

The New Deal realignment in the 1930s destroyed the sectional base of American politics as well as Republican control over most northern states. Under Franklin Roosevelt's leadership, a new Democratic coalition was built in northern states that included not only Catholic and ethnic group voters but also a large proportion of the lower- and middle-income voters in urban and metropolitan areas. The working-class voters were mobilized by labor unions, which established a firm alliance with the Democratic Party. Because the metropolitan areas had been growing rapidly in population, large Democratic majorities in these centers usually resulted in Democratic majorities in the state (see Sundquist 1973, chap. 10).

In the years since the New Deal, the metropolitan base of the Democratic coalition in northern states has been changed but has not disappeared. One change has been the increasing role of black voters, who have identified overwhelmingly with the Democratic Party. A second change has been the growth of population living in suburban sections of metropolitan areas, where the Democratic Party has been weaker than in the central cities. A third trend has been the declining allegiances of Catholic and ethnic voters to the Democratic Party.

The Democratic coalition that elected Franklin Roosevelt four times from 1932 through 1944 also included the Solid South—the one remaining vestige of sectional politics. Roosevelt consistently won every southern state plus the border states, in most cases by large margins. The 1944 presidential election was also the last time that the Democratic Party carried every southern state. The most important changes in the New Deal coalition since 1944 have occurred in the South. We will discuss realignment in the South and its impact on southern state politics later in this chapter.

THE IMPACT OF NATIONAL TRENDS
ON STATE PARTY COMPETITION

The relationship between political trends at the national and state levels is complex and must be understood if we are going to understand the changes that have been occurring in state-level party competition. Clearly it is major political trends at the national level that have produced major changes in party competition at the state level. It is also obvious that there is usually a time lag, sometimes a long one, between national trends and changes in the individual states. There are a variety of factors that may delay or distort the impact of national political trends on state politics. If we understand these factors, we can see why some states react more quickly than others to these trends.

Key (1956, 229) has provided a useful definition of the two criteria that are required for two reasonably strong parties to exist in a state: "First, within the electorate itself two major groups must exist with each possessed of the capacity to maintain a corps of political leaders. . . . Second, a substantial similarity should prevail between the divisions created among the people of a state by the issues of both national and state politics." If a state is relatively homogeneous (entirely rural, for example) it is unlikely that two strong and closely balanced parties will develop. If there are several major interests in a state but they all share a loyalty to one of the national parties, there is also no reason to expect strong two-party competition in a state.

James Gimpel has defined those state party systems where the state or local party coalitions are "consistently different from the national party coalitions" as "autonomous," and he calls such elections "incongruent" (1996, 3–4). Such electoral incongruence usually leads to parties that are relatively weak and poorly organized, even though they may be quite competitive. (We will discuss Gimpel's perspective on state parties in more detail in Chapter 6 on voting patterns in gubernatorial races.)

How does two-party competition develop in a state that has been dominated by one party for a long time? The minority party that is seeking majority status starts out with a bloc of voters who have been traditionally loyal to that party. Northern Democratic Parties in the 1930s could count on the support of ethnic and Catholic minorities, particularly in the urban centers. In the 1950s some of the southern Republican Parties, such as those in North Carolina and Tennessee, could count on strong support in the mountain areas. In the Deep South, however, the number of traditional Republican voters was very small; this helps to explain why it took so long to build strong state Republican Parties, even though Republican presidential candidates were often winning in many of these states from 1952 onward. A minority party that starts out with the dependable traditional support of 35 or 40 percent of the electorate is much better off than one that begins with only 10 or 15 percent of the voters.

The other source of support for the minority party at the state level is that group of voters who have become supporters of the party's presidential candidates as a result of national party realignments. These voters are potential supporters of the party's candidates for U.S. senator and representative, governor, state legislator, and other state and local offices. The larger this group of voters, the greater the minority party's opportunity. The potential impact of the New Deal realignment in the 1930s was greater in those northern states that were heavily urbanized and industrialized than it was in the traditionally agricultural states. As presidential candidates, in the 1950s and 1960s, Dwight Eisenhower and Richard Nixon made their greatest southern gains among the middle- and upper-income voters in metropolitan areas. Consequently the potential gains for state Republican Parties were greater during that period in the more urbanized southern states, such as Florida, Texas, and Virginia.

We have said that those who have been voting for presidential candidates of one party are potential supporters for that party's state candidates. But several steps must be taken by the minority party in a state for this to occur. First, the minority party must recruit workers who are committed to the party, who will help to build state and local party organizations, and who are willing to work in both national and state and local campaigns. Often these are persons who were first motivated to become active in politics by national candidates such as John and Robert Kennedy, Eugene McCarthy, Barry Goldwater, and Ronald Reagan, and who then became involved in state politics.

To elect candidates it is of course necessary for the minority party to run candidates—for statewide, congressional, legislative, and local offices. Then the minority party must help its candidates to raise money and learn how to become effective campaigners; and it must work to get out the vote for these candidates—and not just for presidential candidates. The minority party is likely to run candidates for governor, U.S. senator, and some U.S. House districts before it runs many candidates for the state legislature. It is much easier for a southern state Republican Party to find one relatively skillful and experienced candidate for governor (perhaps a former Democratic officeholder) than to find fifty to one hundred state legislative candidates, some of whom would be running in districts where the party is not well organized and lacks supporters. It usually takes years for a badly outnumbered minority party to become seriously competitive at all or on most levels.

The Democratic Party won five consecutive presidential elections from 1932 through 1948 (the Truman election), but it was not until the 1950s and 1960s that state Democratic Parties in northern states became closely competitive with state Republican Parties. This occurred first in large urban-industrial states like New York, New Jersey, and Ohio, which had been quite competitive for many years. It occurred more slowly in such states as Maine, Vermont, Indiana, Wisconsin, and Iowa, which were less urbanized and thus had a smaller proportion of persons voting Democratic in presidential elections.

Democratic organizations in northern states were somewhat slow to capitalize on the New Deal realignment. The state Democratic Party was often run largely by organizations based in the urban centers that relied heavily on the traditional Catholic and ethnic voters, made little effort to recruit new members, and were reluctant to share political power with new political leaders. In the northeastern and midwestern states, Democratic strength began to grow as both labor unions and black political organizations started playing major roles in state Democratic politics. Individual political leaders like Edmund Muskie in Maine, Hubert Humphrey in Minnesota, and G. Mennen Williams in Michigan succeeded both as party builders and as gubernatorial and senatorial candidates.

In the southern states the Republican Party was even slower to take advantage of the success that Republican presidential candidates were enjoying in the South. Dwight Eisenhower, in 1952, was the first Republican presidential candidate to make a serious effort to win electoral votes in southern states. That year he carried four of the eleven southern states, and Republican presidential candidates won between three and five southern states in the next four elections (1956–1968); in 1972 Richard Nixon carried all of the southern states. But the Republicans did not elect a southern governor until 1966, and it was not until the 1980 election that they held the governorship in more than two or three southern states at the same time. During the period from 1952 to 1978 the Republicans did not have a majority in any southern legislative chamber, and in most of these legislatures they were heavily outnumbered by Democrats.

Why did it take so long for the southern Republican Parties to make significant headway in state elections? First, they started out with almost no political power in most southern states. In 1952 they had no governorships, only one U.S. senator (a converted Democratic senator), and only a few representatives in states with pockets of Republican strength. In some state legislatures, particularly in the Deep South, they had only a handful of members. In some southern states Republicans did not consistently run candidates even for governor and senator, and they let many congressional and legislative seats go uncontested.

In the 1950s and early 1960s most voters in southern states considered themselves to be Democrats, often lifelong Democrats. Southern Democrats tended to be more conservative than northern Democrats. Many of them refused to vote for Democratic presidential candidates whom they considered too liberal, such as John Kennedy, Hubert Humphrey, George McGovern, Walter Mondale, and Michael Dukakis. But a large majority of the Democratic officeholders and candidates at the state level were conservative, sometimes very conservative, and this made it very difficult for Republican candidates to find issues on which to run. Republicans had limited success in some upper-income metropolitan districts when they emphasized the kinds of economic issues that Republicans stressed at the national level. In rural areas they sometimes emphasized racial issues and criticized proposals for stronger civil rights legislation, but this sometimes put southern Republicans at odds with national Republican candidates who had to campaign in the North as well as the South.

TRENDS IN TWO-PARTY COMPETITION

The starting point for our study of two-party competition is to explain exactly how we are measuring partisanship and two-party competition in the states and to analyze changes over two time periods. We then turn to a much more detailed analysis of the Republican growth in southern states that has radically changed the levels of two-party competition in that region.

Measuring Partisanship and Two-Party Competition

We now examine the growth of party competition at the state level in the more recent period, particularly since 1980. To understand these trends, we need to know which states are becoming more or less competitive and also which states are becoming more strongly Democratic or Republican. Determining the level of two-party competition and changing competitive trends for elective offices is an empirical inquiry. Measures of two-party competition differ depending on the offices that are included, the time period chosen, and the method of aggregating the statistics that is used.

No single measure of two-party competition is the "best"; the question is what aspects of competition you want to emphasize. We could include votes in each state for president and for members of Congress, but we want to focus on state politics and minimize the effect of national trends. Therefore we will concentrate on the partisan vote for governor and partisan strength in the state legislature. The governorship, of course, is the most important state office, and partisan strength in the legislature is an excellent indicator of the breadth and depth of party strength.

If we look at partisanship and party competition for just the last few elections, we will get only a snapshot of the current pattern. If we examine forty or fifty years of election data, we may see the long-term pattern but miss the more recent changes. To understand recent trends in partisanship and two-party competition, we will concentrate on the elections from 1980 through 1998; for historical perspective, we will also look at election patterns from 1964–1978.

In Table 2-1 party competition is measured using the index developed by Austin Ranney (1976), that is designed to show each party's electoral strength in the governorship and the legislature and the proportion of time that each controlled these two institutions. Specifically it is an average of four measures of competition over the time period:

1. The percentage of vote for the governor's office.
2. The proportion of Senate seats won.
3. The proportion of House seats won.
4. The proportion of years the party controlled the governorship, the Senate, and the House, with these averaged together.

Table 2-1 is divided into two sections—one covers the 1964–1978 period and the other covers the 1980–1998 period. (Nebraska is omitted because it has a nonpartisan legislature.) The Ranney index can be calculated in two ways—to show how much control each of the two parties had over government and also how closely competitive the two parties were.

In the column of Table 2-1 labeled "party control" the states with the highest scores are the most Democratic, and those with the lowest are more Republican. The scale can run from 1.0 to 0; a score of 1.000 would mean that the Democrats won every governorship unanimously, always won every legislative seat and controlled the governorship and legislature all of the time. A score of 0 would mean that Republicans had accomplished this. In reality, for the more recent period the figures run from only .810 to .240.

In the column labeled "party competition" the scores can range from 1.000 for the most competitive to .500 for the least competitive. The states that are heavily Democratic and heavily Republican, at the top and bottom of the list, are the least competitive and those in the middle are the most competitive. The actual range of party competition scores in the most recent period are from .995 for the most competitive, to .690 for the least competitive Democratic state and .740 for the least competitive Republican state.

We will define states scoring above .750 in party control as heavily Democratic and those from .601 to .750 as predominantly Democratic; .250 or less would be heavily Republican and those from .251 through .400 are predominantly Republican. States between .401 and .600 are considered competitive; they score .901 or above on the party competition index.

Clearly in the period from 1980 to 1998 there are more Democratic states than Republican ones: twenty-one Democratic states scored over .600, and only eight Republican states scored under .400. This Democratic advantage is slightly smaller than it used to be (in 1964–1978); there are now no Democratic states with a score over .810, and there are more Republican states with scores less than .350. There has been a modest increase in the number of competitive states:

Table 2-1 Indexes of State Party Balance

State	Party Control[a]	Party Competition[b]
1964–1978		
Louisiana	.936	.564
Alabama	.928	.572
Mississippi	.903	.597
Arkansas	.875	.625
Georgia	.851	.649
Texas	.848	.652
South Carolina	.826	.674
North Carolina	.796	.704
Maryland	.795	.705
Rhode Island	.754	.746
Oklahoma	.741	.759
Hawaii	.740	.760
Florida	.726	.774
Kentucky	.718	.782
West Virginia	.714	.786
Missouri	.708	.792
New Mexico	.708	.792
Virginia	.698	.802
Massachusetts	.696	.804
Tennessee	.676	.824
Minnesota	.670	.830
Nevada	.652	.848
Connecticut	.638	.862
California	.609	.891
Montana	.590	.910
Oregon	.554	.946
Washington	.552	.948
New Jersey	.542	.958
Pennsylvania	.534	.966
Alaska	.532	.968
Michigan	.524	.976
Wisconsin	.523	.977
Delaware	.512	.988
Utah	.511	.989
Illinois	.481	.981
Ohio	.464	.964
Maine	.460	.960
Arizona	.458	.958
Iowa	.457	.957
New York	.455	.955
Indiana	.425	.925

Table 2-1 (*continued*)

State	Party Control[a]	Party Competition[b]
Colorado	.398	.989
North Dakota	.388	.888
Idaho	.386	.886
New Hampshire	.377	.877
Kansas	.375	.875
Wyoming	.369	.869
South Dakota	.361	.861
Vermont	.346	.846
1980–1998		
Maryland	.810	.690
Arkansas	.803	.697
Hawaii	.791	.709
Georgia	.786	.714
Louisiana	.772	.728
Mississippi	.762	.738
West Virginia	.753	.747
Rhode Island	.750	.750
Kentucky	.742	.758
Massachusetts	.740	.760
Alabama	.727	.773
North Carolina	.674	.826
Oklahoma	.674	.826
Virginia	.648	.852
South Carolina	.639	.861
Missouri	.624	.876
New Mexico	.624	.876
Texas	.623	.877
Tennessee	.621	.879
Florida	.603	.987
Minnesota	.601	.899
Nevada	.593	.907
Washington	.591	.909
California	.591	.909
Connecticut	.577	.923
Maine	.568	.932
Oregon	.544	.956
Vermont	.540	.960
New York	.530	.970
Wisconsin	.526	.974
Delaware	.508	.992
Michigan	.495	.995
Illinois	.488	.988
Alaska	.477	.977

Table 2-1 (*continued*)

State	Party Control[a]	Party Competition[b]
Iowa	.475	.975
New Jersey	.470	.970
Montana	.463	.963
Ohio	.455	.955
Pennsylvania	.436	.936
Indiana	.432	.932
Colorado	.412	.912
North Dakota	.391	.891
Wyoming	.358	.858
Arizona	.350	.850
Kansas	.334	.834
New Hampshire	.327	.827
Idaho	.321	.821
South Dakota	.275	.775
Utah	.240	.740

Source: Index developed by Austin Ranney, "Parties in State Politics," in *Politics in the American States: A Comparative Analysis,* 3d ed., edited by Herbert Jacob and Kenneth Vines (Boston: Little Brown, 1976).

[a]The scores can range from 1.0 for the most Democratic to 0 for the most Republican.

[b]The scores can range from 1.000 for the most competitive to .500 for the least competitive.

twenty of them in the 1980–1998 period compared with seventeen in the 1964–1978 period.

There are some clear and important geographical patterns to state partisanship. The twenty states found in the competitive groups in the 1980s and 1990s include sixteen states in the Northeast, Midwest, and Midwest; nearly all of the major urban-industrial states are found in the competitive category. A few of the larger competitive states grew more Republican in the 1980s and 1990s, including Pennsylvania, New Jersey, Michigan, and California, but New York grew more Democratic.

Seven of the eight Republican states (under .400) are located in the western plains and mountain areas (all except New Hampshire). Two other western states—Colorado and Montana—were barely competitive enough to avoid the Republican category. These nine states almost form a solid bloc in the West (but not on the West Coast): North and South Dakota, Kansas, Montana, Wyoming, Idaho, Colorado, Utah, and Arizona. (Nebraska could be considered part of this bloc, but it has nonpartisan legislative elections.) In the most recent period this bloc of nine states has grown even more Republican. In the 1994, 1996, and 1998 elections, eight of the nine consistently elected Republican governors and legislative majorities; Colorado had Republican legislatures and in 1998 shifted from a Democratic to a Republican governor.

Most of the twenty-one states that were Democratic in the 1980s and 1990s are either southern (11) or border (4) states. But all of the southern states had lower scores (and thus were less heavily Democratic) in the 1980s and 1990s than in the earlier period. In the 1964–1978 period the eight most heavily Democratic states were in the South, some with scores over .900. In the 1980–1998 period only four of the ten most heavily Democratic states were in the South and only one was barely over .800.

The change in the South is even more dramatic if we look at only the last three elections covered in the table—1994, 1996, and 1998. In this most recent period only six of these states were Democratic (above .600), five were competitive, ranging from Tennessee, which leaned Democratic (.550), to four states leaning Republican: South Carolina (.490), Virginia (.488), Texas (.475), and Florida (.425).

Republican Growth in the South

In the 1980s and 1990s the most important changes in party alignments and competition were in southern states. We noted earlier that the national political realignment, centered on presidential politics, laid the groundwork for Republican gains in southern states. The ability of Dwight Eisenhower and Richard Nixon to carry a number of southern states in 1952, 1956, 1968, and 1972 made possible the rebuilding of the Republican Party and the election of a growing number of Republicans to congressional, statewide, and sometimes legislative office. The Republicans started with an advantage in the southern states that were carried several times by Eisenhower or Nixon because those who voted Republican in presidential races were potential Republican voters in state races. Eisenhower or Nixon carried Virginia, Tennessee, and Florida four times and Texas twice between 1952 and 1968; Nixon carried every southern state in 1972. Although Barry Goldwater carried none of these states in 1964, he carried five states in the Deep South: Georgia, South Carolina, Alabama, Louisiana, and Mississippi. His victories provided a belated boost to Republican Parties in those states. But it took years to develop really competitive party systems in southern states, below the presidential level. Republican parties had to get organized, enlist workers, raise money, and recruit viable candidates. There were also great differences among the southern states in the pace of Republican growth. In comparing these states, we will concentrate on gubernatorial and state legislative races. The governorship, the most important state office, must be a major priority for an emerging party. Winning legislative seats is a major test of a party's progress because it requires the party to organize, recruit candidates, and mobilize voters throughout all, or at least most, of the state.

Table 2-2 traces the progress made by Republican Parties in the eleven southern states from the 1960s through the 1990s. The left-hand section of the table shows, for each state in each decade, the number of years that the state had a Republican governor. The right-hand section shows, for each state in each decade, the average percentage of legislative seats held by Republicans. The average percentage of seats is calculated separately for the Senate and House and these two are averaged. In the first column, for example, these data cover the ten years after the 1960 election, or, for states elected in odd-numbered years, the ten years after the 1961 election.

The states ranked near the top of the table are those in which Republican gains came earlier and in those nearer the bottom Republican gains came later. This is a rough ranking because Republican Parties making early progress in electing governors were not always the first to elect substantial numbers of Republican legislators. By the 1990s Republicans held one-third of the Georgia legislature but had yet to elect a Republican governor. In the 1960s the Arkansas governor was a Republican for four of the ten years, but only 1 percent of the legislature was Republican. In most states it is clear that the Republicans had significant success in electing governors before they had won more than a modest minority of legislative seats. It is easier to find one strong candidate for governor than to recruit and elect dozens of legislative candidates.

Republicans had a head start in Tennessee, Florida, Virginia, and to some

Table 2-2 Republican Growth in Southern States

States	Number of Years with Republican Governors				Average Percentage of Legislative Seats Held by Republicans (%)			
	1960–1969	1970–1979	1980–1989	1990–1999	1960–1969	1970–1979	1980–1989	1990–1999
Tennessee	0	6	6	6	28	37	35	42
Florida	4	0	4	2	18	29	33	50
Virginia	2	10	0	8	12	23	29	48
North Carolina	0	4	6	2	19	14	23	39
South Carolina	0	4	4	8	3	9	21	41
Texas	0	2	6	6	2	10	26	43
Georgia	0	0	0	0	8	12	15	33
Alabama	0	0	4	6	1	1	11	28
Arkansas	4	0	2	4	1	3	9	15
Mississippi	0	0	0	8	1	4	9	30
Louisiana	0	0	4	4	1	3	10	22

Source: Data tabulated from authors' research.

extent in North Carolina because of presidential campaigns and in both Tennessee and North Carolina because there had been pockets of traditional Republican strength in the mountain areas. These four states all elected Republican governors in the 1960s or 1970s, and all began to elect Republicans to about one-fourth of the legislative seats (slightly fewer in Virginia) by the mid-1960s and 1970s.

Republican Parties were slow starters in the next three states: South Carolina, Texas, and Georgia. In the 1960s they had virtually no strength in the legislature and elected no governors (with Georgia and South Carolina Republicans not even running a gubernatorial candidate in 1962). But in the 1980s and 1990s Republicans held the governorship more than half the time in both South Carolina and Texas. In the 1990s Republicans averaged over 40 percent of the legislature in these two states, and following the 1996 and 1998 elections they held a narrow majority in one of the legislative chambers in each state. By the 1990s Republicans in Georgia had won one-third of the legislature. We have noted that Georgia remained the only state that had consistently kept a Democratic governor, though the gubernatorial election had been very close a couple of times.

In the remaining four deep southern states—Alabama, Arkansas, Mississippi, and Louisiana—the Republican Party has lagged behind. Except for Louisiana, neither Eisenhower nor Nixon carried these states until 1972. They are less urban than most of the other southern states. In all four states until the 1960s the Republicans generally ran either no gubernatorial candidates or very weak ones.

The first Republican governor in Arkansas was Winthrop Rockefeller, elected in 1966 and 1968; his victory resulted from his political skills and ample campaign funds. The Arkansas Republican Party failed to press this advantage and did not capture the governorship again until 1982, when Frank White interrupted Bill Clinton's tenure for a single two-year term. In Louisiana the Republicans did not elect a governor until 1979.

The first Republican governor in Alabama was not elected until 1986 (and again in 1990). A major obstacle was that conservative, states' rights Democrat George Wallace (or in one case his wife) won five of six elections from 1962 through 1982, twice without a Republican opponent. It was not until 1991 (and again in 1995) that the Mississippi Republicans elected a governor.

Republicans in these four states were even less successful in electing members to the legislature. In 1958 there was not a single Republican in any of these four legislatures; in the 1960s Republicans in these states averaged 1 percent of the legislature. Even during the 1970s there was only a minuscule number of Republican legislators in these states. In the 1980s and 1990s Republicans in these four states averaged control of the governorship 40 percent of the time, but all of these governors faced legislatures where the Democrats held at least two-thirds of the seats and often much more.

The pace of Republican progress in southern states accelerated in the 1990s, even in states where progress had been particularly slow. The most significant Republican breakthrough occurred in the 1994 election. At the national level the Republican Party recaptured the Senate after eight years of Democratic control and won a majority in the House after forty years of Democratic control. Republicans also gained eleven governorships to give them a 30–19 majority. They won control of a majority of state legislative chambers for the first time since a 1968 tie and gained more than 500 state legislative seats.

In the South the 1994 election marked the first time since Reconstruction that a majority of U.S. senators and representatives and governors from the eleven southern states were Republicans. Republicans began the slow process of capturing control of southern legislative chambers by winning a narrow majority in the Florida House. In the 1994 election the Republicans gained 133 new seats in southern legislatures, about one-fourth of all seats they gained in the country. In southern legislatures in 1994 the proportion of seats held by Republicans increased from 30 percent to 37 percent.

During the six-year period beginning with the 1994 election, Republicans controlled the governorship some of the time in every state except North Carolina and Georgia (the latter has never had a Republican governor). They controlled the governorship all of the time or a majority of the time in eight of the southern states.

Even more dramatic Republican progress was made in the legislature. Republicans controlled the House or Senate or both for some time during this six-year period in Florida, South Carolina, North Carolina, Texas, and Virginia. After the 1998 election the Republicans held 42 percent of seats in southern legislatures. They controlled both chambers in Florida by over 60 percent; controlled the South Carolina House for the third consecutive time; controlled the Texas Senate for the second time in a row and were close to winning the House; held the Virginia Senate and in the 1999 election captured the House. On the other hand, the Republicans were still heavily outnumbered in the legislatures of Arkansas (over 3–1), Mississippi (2–1), and Louisiana (over 2–1), even though all three states had Republican governors following the 1998 election (the Democrats recaptured the Mississippi governorship in 1999).

After years of making slow progress in winning legislative states, why were the Republicans able to win so many additional seats in southern legislatures in 1994 and expand these gains during the remainder of the 1990s? One answer is that, beginning in 1990, the Republicans began to run more candidates for southern legislative seats and target more realistically the seats they had some chance of winning. By 1994 they were contesting almost one-third of the seats and for the first time winning two-thirds of those they contested.

Another important factor is that incumbents have a big advantage over other candidates in legislative elections (discussed in some detail in Chapter 7). Going into the 1994 election the Republicans held 30 percent of the seats; about four-fifths of these incumbents ran again and almost all of them won. More than 60 percent of these winning incumbents had no Democratic opponent.

New Republican candidates succeeded in winning almost all of the remaining seats that had been held by Republicans. Presumably in those districts the Republican Party was well enough organized to recruit good candidates and support them effectively. The result was that the Republicans held onto almost all of the seats that they had going into the election. They also contested about 40 percent of the Democratic seats, won almost one-third of these races, and increased their share of total legislative seats from 30 percent to 37 percent.

During the 1990s it became clear that both political parties in the southern states were following a strategy of running candidates in most districts where the other party did not have an incumbent running, but they were being much more cautious about challenging an incumbent. This means that in most southern states the proportion of seats contested by both parties has been dropping; by 1998 it was less than 40 percent. These contested seats are most likely to be open seats, with no incumbents running. Southern Democratic Parties, which once ran candidates in almost all districts, have been failing to contest many of the seats won by Republicans, particularly if they are in heavily white districts. Southern Republican Parties have been increasingly skillful about targeting the districts they will try to capture, avoiding those that have a substantial proportion of black voters, particularly if a Democratic incumbent is running (Martorano, Anderson, and Hamm 1999; Aistrup and Gaddie 1999).

After the 1990 census the Republicans also benefited from judicial decisions designed to increase the proportion of legislative seats with a concentration of black voters. As we pointed out in Chapter 1, this resulted in the surrounding districts being heavily white, reducing the number of districts where Democratic candidates had a reasonable chance of winning (Lublin and Voss 1999).

In the years ahead an increasing number of southern legislatures are likely to have close two-party competition for control. By the end of the 1990s in most southern states the Republican Party held at least one-third of the seats. And in another one-third of the seats the party was well enough organized, had learned how to recruit candidates, and had enough support from voters to be competitive for control of the legislature.

PROSPECTS FOR GREATER TWO-PARTY COMPETITION

Earlier we measured the strength of each party and of two-party competition in each state by calculating partisan control of the governorship and the legislature, particularly during the 1980s and 1990s (illustrated in Table 2-1). Now, to measure the potential of each party for growth and the prospects for more or less two-party competition in each state, we will examine the partisan loyalties of the voters using two quite different measures: party identification and, where possible, party registration.

Party Identification

Since the development of modern political polling in the 1950s, pollsters have been asking voters whether they considered themselves to be Democrats, Republicans, or independents (or rarely some minor party). It is possible to track changes in party identification over time and among the states, as well as among various kinds of people. After voters are asked the first question about identification, partisans are often asked if they are strongly or weakly identified with a party and independents are asked if they lean toward one party or the other. If both questions are asked, a seven-way classification of party identification is produced instead of a three-way one.

National surveys have shown that from the mid-1960s to the mid-1970s the proportion of people identifying with a party declined and the proportion calling themselves independents increased. But from the mid-1970s to the mid-1990s this trend was sharply reversed. Between 1976 and 1996, for example, the proportion of those saying that they "strongly identify" with a party rose from 24 percent to 31 percent, while the proportion who are "pure independents" (not leaning toward either party) dropped from 16 percent to 9 percent. In other words strong partisans in 1976 outnumbered pure independents three to two, but by 1996 the ratio was more than three to one. Voters are much more likely than nonvoters to identify with a party, not surprisingly, but the gaps between voters and nonvoters has grown much larger, from about 10 to about 20 percentage points (Bartels 2000, 36–37).

Research on voting behavior has consistently shown that those who identify with a particular party are much more likely to vote for candidates of that party than for other candidates. It is important to realize that the impact of party identification on voting for president has increased steadily from a low point in 1972 to a high point in 1996 and that it has even exceeded the previous high point (based on survey research) in the early 1950s. Party voting has also increased in congressional elections, somewhat less sharply, from the late 1970s to 1996 (Bartels 2000; see also Miller and Shanks 1996, 146–149). Although comparable longitudinal data are lacking from gubernatorial and other state elections, it seems likely that there has also been an increasing impact of partisanship on voting for state races.

Because we are comparing partisanship in the fifty states, we need to use voter surveys conducted at the state level. Wright, Erikson, and McIver (1985) aggregated CBS News–*New York Times* polls conducted in each state over a period of several years (1976–1982) to provide a large enough sample of voters in each state, as one way of measuring the strength of the two parties in that state. They later extended the series through 1988 (Erikson, Wright, and McIver 1993). We are using an updated version of this data set covering surveys for the 1989–1996 period (Wright 1998) and comparing it with the 1976–1982 data on party identification.

Table 2-3 shows, for each of these two time periods, the percentage of voters who identify as Democrats, independents, and Republicans in these surveys. (Data are not available for the earlier period in Alaska and Hawaii.) The columns labeled "party margin" show the difference between the percentage of Democrats and of Republicans and which party had the larger percentage of identifiers; the states are ranked from the most Democratic to the most Republican in the 1989–1996 period. The simplest way to examine changes in partisanship between the 1976–1982 and 1989–1996 periods is to look at changes in these party margins.

A careful examination of Table 2-3 shows that most of the states became more Republican from the first period to the second. Twenty-six states had more Democratic than Republican identifiers in both time periods (the first twenty-six on the list, except for Alaska and Hawaii). Only six states had Republican pluralities in both periods. Twelve other states shifted from a Democratic plurality in the first time period to a Republican plurality in the more recent period. Four other states had an even number of Democratic and Republican partisans in one or another period.

The clearest evidence of Republican growth is not the number of states becoming Republican but the shift in the proportion of voters identifying as Republicans, compared with Democrats. In forty-four of the forty-eight states where we can make comparisons, there was an increase in the proportion of party identifiers who were Republicans, and many of these shifts were large. The Republicans lost ground in only four states, and these losses were very small: West Virginia, Delaware, Vermont, and Iowa.

The Republican gains were greatest in the South. Two states, Virginia and South Carolina, shifted from Democratic to small Republican margins, and Florida shifted to a tie between partisans. In the remaining southern states the size of the Democratic margin, over Republicans, dropped by an average of 21 points. The southern states with the greatest shifts were, not surprisingly, those that had been most strongly Democratic. For example the Democratic margin over Republicans dropped from 33 to 3 percentage points in Alabama, from 45 to 19 percent in Louisiana, and from 38 to 9 percent in Georgia. The Republicans also made substantial gains in party identifiers in the Southwest and mountain states

Table 2-3 Party Identification in the States (percentages)

| | 1976–1982 | | | | 1989–1996 | | | |
State	Democratic	Inde-pendent	Republican	Party Margin	Democratic	Inde-pendent	Republican	Party Margin
Arkansas	50	33	17	33 D	44	35	21	23 D
West Virginia	47	26	27	20 D	50	22	28	22 D
Hawaii					43	33	23	20 D
Louisiana	60	25	15	45 D	48	23	29	19 D
Maryland	48	32	20	28 D	47	24	29	18 D
Oklahoma	50	24	26	24 D	49	18	33	16 D
Kentucky	49	28	23	26 D	47	22	31	16 D
Massachusetts	34	50	16	18 D	31	52	17	14 D
Minnesota	39	37	24	15 D	37	36	27	10 D
Georgia	54	30	16	38 D	39	31	30	9 D
Delaware	32	44	24	8 D	37	35	28	9 D
Rhode Island	27	60	13	14 D	27	55	18	9 D
New York	36	35	29	7 D	38	31	31	7 D
North Carolina	46	30	24	22 D	40	26	34	6 D
Alaska					29	48	23	6 D
Mississippi	48	32	20	28 D	40	25	35	5 D
Pennsylvania	38	29	33	5 D	40	24	36	4 D
Tennessee	39	36	25	14 D	36	32	32	4 D
Missouri	35	41	24	11 D	33	38	29	4 D
Washington	31	48	21	10 D	31	41	28	3 D
Alabama	50	33	17	33 D	35	33	32	3 D
Illinois	33	39	28	5 D	34	35	31	3 D
Ohio	34	37	29	5 D	35	32	33	2 D
Wisconsin	34	40	26	8 D	32	38	30	2 D
Connecticut	31	44	25	6 D	30	42	28	2 D
California	40	29	31	9 D	38	25	37	1 D
Oregon	38	33	29	9 D	36	29	35	1 D
Texas	44	35	21	23 D	34	32	33	1 D
Florida	41	30	29	12 D	36	28	36	0
Michigan	32	41	27	5 D	32	37	32	0
Vermont	22	53	25	3 R	26	47	26	0
Montana	31	43	26	5 D	31	37	32	1 R
New Jersey	33	43	24	9 D	31	37	32	1 R
Iowa	29	39	32	3 R	30	39	31	1 R
Maine	30	41	29	1 D	28	43	30	2 R
New Mexico	42	36	22	20 D	35	28	37	2 R
Virginia	35	40	25	10 D	31	35	34	3 R
South Carolina	39	37	24	15 D	33	31	36	3 R
Colorado	30	41	29	1 D	28	39	33	5 R
Indiana	32	38	30	2 D	31	33	36	5 R
North Dakota	31	38	31	0	25	44	31	6 R
Arizona	37	33	30	7 D	31	29	39	8 R

Table 2-3 (*continued*)

	1976–1982				1989–1996			
State	Democratic	Inde-pendent	Republican	Party Margin	Democratic	Inde-pendent	Republican	Party Margin
New Hampshire	23	47	30	7 R	20	50	30	10 R
Kansas	30	34	36	6 R	29	32	39	10 R
South Dakota	43	22	35	8 D	34	21	45	11 R
Nevada	40	31	29	11 D	30	27	43	13 R
Nebraska	29	29	42	13 R	30	24	45	15 R
Wyoming	36	39	25	11 D	23	33	44	21 R
Idaho	21	43	36	15 R	21	36	43	22 R
Utah	25	35	40	15 R	21	30	49	28 R

Sources: Data taken from Gerald C. Wright, unpublished data set, 1998; and Gerald C. Wright, Robert S. Erikson, and John P. McIver, "Measuring State Partisanship and Ideology with Survey Data," *Journal of Politics* 47 (1985): 469–489.

such as New Mexico, Arizona, Nevada, Idaho, Utah, and Wyoming; this last state shifted from a Democratic margin of 11 percent to a Republican margin of 21 percent.

Were there any states where the Democrats were holding their own? There were some, mostly in the Northeast. The Democrats gained slightly in West Virginia and Vermont, held steady in New York, lost slightly in Pennsylvania, Massachusetts, Connecticut, and Maine. There was also little change in several midwestern states: Illinois, Ohio, and Iowa, along with modest Democratic losses in Minnesota, Wisconsin, and Michigan.

Why is it important to examine trends among the states in party identification? The basic reason of course is that party identification is an important predictor of voting behavior. If the trend toward a higher proportion of Republican identifiers continues over several more years, a larger number of states will have a plurality of voters identifying with the Republican Party who are therefore more likely to vote Republican.

Changes in party identification are particularly important for understanding what has been happening in the South. The Republican Party began to make inroads into the South in the 1950s, 1960s, and 1970s, particularly in presidential races and some contests for statewide and congressional offices. But for a long time there were no substantial increases in the proportion of southern voters identifying as Republicans; although the proportion of Democrats was gradually decreasing, it was the proportion of independents that was increasing.

One reason was that African Americans were registering and voting in increasing numbers, and most of them identified as Democrats. Another reason was that the older generation of southern voters had been lifelong Democrats and were reluctant to change. A third reason was that southern voters often had little reason to vote Republican in statewide, legislative, and local offices. Often the Democratic candidates were as conservative as the Republican ones, and in many other contests there was not even a Republican candidate running. Moreover, voters were more likely to vote in Democratic primaries because they were much more likely to have serious competition than were Republican ones.

Because southern voters had little reason or opportunity to vote a straight Republican ticket or to vote in a Republican primary, they were more likely to begin thinking of themselves as independents than as Republicans. Most voters do not change their party identification lightly or quickly. In the 1980s and 1990s the Republican Party began to run more viable candidates and win more races in southern states; more and more frequently they began to have competitive primaries. Over a period of years, as conservative voters began to vote more consistently for Republican candidates and sometimes participate in Republican primaries, they began to think of themselves as Republicans. This change in identification made them even more likely to vote consistently for Republican candidates. One other factor is at work: A new generation of voters, without any lifelong ties to either party, is more likely to begin identifying with Republicans if they vote that way.

The evidence of this change in party identification is clear in Table 2-3. In southern states, between the periods 1976–1982 and 1989–1996, the percentage distribution of Democrats, independents, and Republicans shifted from a 46–33–21 ratio to a 38–30–32 ratio. The Republican percentage has grown, while the proportion of independents and particularly Democrats has fallen. By 1989–1996 five southern states had substantially more Republicans than independents, five had about the same proportions, and only Arkansas had substantially more independents. South Carolina and Virginia had more Republicans than Democrats. Florida and Texas had about the same numbers of each party.

This shift in party allegiance helps to explain why the Republicans made dramatic gains in congressional, statewide, and legislative races in 1994 and continued to make some further gains in southern states in the remaining elections in the 1990s. It is no coincidence that South Carolina, Virginia, Florida, and Texas— the four states where there were more Republican identifiers than Democrats or about the same number—were the four where Republicans controlled, or almost controlled, legislative chambers in 1998.

We cannot assume that the party allegiance of voters will grow increasingly Republican indefinitely in all or most of the southern states, partly because most of these states have a substantial minority of African American voters whose loyalties are heavily Democratic. But it is likely that most southern states will become and continue to be highly competitive and some of them will be more Republican than Democratic.

There is a surprising amount of variation among the states in the proportion of persons who identify as independents, rather than identifying with a party. In the 1989–1996 period the six New England states had the highest average proportion of persons identifying as independents: 48 percent. This is surprising because three of them, Connecticut, Rhode Island, and Massachusetts, are relatively strong party states where we might expect stronger party loyalty among voters. However, in all six of these states it is relatively easy to shift from one party primary to the other. The region with the lowest average proportion of independents is the South; its eleven states average only 30 percent. One reason may be that the act of voting in a party primary probably reinforces a voter's sense of identifying with a party, and primaries (particularly Democratic ones) traditionally have been important in southern states.

Perhaps in the states where you have to register with a party to vote in the party's primary, the act of registering as a partisan may make voters more likely to identify as a Democrat or Republican rather than as an independent. If we look only at northern states, we find that there is a slightly higher proportion of persons identifying with a party than in open primary states. We have seen that in the southern states, however, there is a high proportion of party identifiers (70 percent,) even though these states do not require party registration to vote in a primary. The reason is probably, as we have noted, because voting in a primary reinforces party identification.

Party Registration

Twenty-seven of the states require voters to register as Democrats or Republicans if they want to vote in primary elections for one or the other of these parties (see Chapter 4). In states with that requirement, records of party registration are kept, providing a different way of measuring state partisanship. Table 2-4 compares the distribution of Democratic, independent, and Republican registered voters in the years 1982 and 1994. These years are chosen because they were late in the two time periods for which we have data on party identification. The table also shows the Democratic or Republican margins for each state, calculated in the same way as the margins of party identification.

Eighteen states had a plurality of Democratic registrants in both time periods; five had more Republicans in both periods; Arizona and Colorado shifted from Democratic to Republican; Iowa shifted from a tie to Republican; and Alaska was Republican in the second period but there are no previous data. A more important change is that the Democratic margin shrank in sixteen of eighteen consistently Democratic states, and the Republican margin grew in four of five Republican states.

In states with party registration, how does the balance of party identification compare with registration? Before making any such comparisons, we should make

Table 2-4 Party Registration in the States (percentages)

	1982				1994			
State	Democratic	Inde-pendent	Republican	Party Margin	Democratic	Inde-pendent	Republican	Party Margin
Louisiana	87	6	7	80 D	71	10	19	52 D
West Virginia	67	2	31	36 D	65	4	30	35 D
Kentucky	68	3	29	39 D	65	4	30	35 D
Maryland	69	8	23	46 D	61	10	29	32 D
Oklahoma	72	2	26	46 D	63	3	34	29 D
Massachusetts	46	40	14	32 D	40	47	23	17 D
North Carolina	71	5	24	47 D	59	9	33	26 D
New Mexico	63	7	30	33 D	57	9	34	23 D
New York	47	19	34	13 D	47	22	31	16 D
California	53	12	35	18 D	51	11	38	13 D
Connecticut	39	35	26	13 D	38	36	26	12 D
New Jersey	33	46	21	12 D	29	49	22	7 D
Delaware	44	23	33	11 D	43	21	36	7 D
Florida	64	6	30	34 D	49	9	42	7 D
Oregon	50	14	36	14 D	43	21	36	7 D
Pennsylvania	53	6	41	12 D	50	7	43	7 D
Maine	32	39	29	3 D	33	38	29	4 D
Nevada	53	8	39	14 D	43	15	42	1 D
Colorado	32	37	31	1 D	33	33	34	1 R
Iowa	32	36	32	0	35	28	36	1 R
Arizona	51	7	42	9 D	43	12	45	2 R
Alaska					18	59	23	5 R
New Hampshire	33	27	40	7 R	32	30	38	6 R
South Dakota	45	9	46	1 R	41	10	49	8 R
Nebraska	46	6	48	2 R	40	11	50	10 R
Kansas	24	44	32	8 R	31	25	44	13 R
Wyoming	37	14	49	12 R	33	10	57	24 R

Sources: Michael Barone and Grant Ujifusa, *The Almanac of American Politics, 1984* (Washington, D.C.: National Journal, 1983); Barone and Ujifusa, *The Almanac of American Politics, 1996* (Washington, D.C.: National Journal, 1995).

clear how these two indicators differ. Party identification data are based on answers given by voters to pollsters; figures for registration come from official state records. The identification data come from the periods 1976 to 1982 and 1989 to 1996; the registration data come from 1982 and 1996, single years late in each period.

In almost all of the states (twenty-five of twenty-seven) a larger proportion of voters—often much larger— *identify* themselves as independents than are registered as not affiliated with either party. Voters, including independent identifiers, have a strong incentive to register with a party in order to be able to vote in a party primary. For example, 22 percent of voters in Kentucky during the period from

1989 to 1996 considered themselves to be independent, but only 4 percent were unaffiliated with any party. In a state like Kentucky, which until recently was heavily Democratic, the closest competition was in the Democratic primary, not in the general election, and the most interested voters wanted to participate in the primary. This also explains why the ratio of Democratic to Republican registrants was much higher than the ratio of Democratic to Republican identifiers in Kentucky.

Several of the states with a relatively high proportion of nonaffiliated registrants are those in which highly competitive primaries are relatively rare, including Connecticut, New Jersey, and Colorado, or where unaffiliated voters may shift registration to a party on primary election day and thus have little incentive to register with a party.

There are some similarities between the scores for identification and for registration. In the 1989–1996 period in thirteen states a plurality of voters identified and were registered as Democrats, and in eight states a plurality identified and were registered as Republicans. Four states had more Republican identifiers and more Democratic registrants, one state was just the reverse, and one had identifiers who were evenly split and more registered Republicans.

Although in three-fourths of the states the party with the most identifiers also had the most registrants during 1989–1996, there were often large differences in the size of Democratic or Republican margins, depending on which measure of party is used. During the most recent period the Democratic margin was smaller, or the Republican margin was larger, among partisan identifiers than among registrants in twenty-two of the twenty-seven states.

Data on party identification and registration both show that in most states the Democrats were losing ground and the Republicans were gaining between the early 1980s and the mid-1990s. But the data also show that this Republican trend is more pronounced if we look at party identification than if we look at registration. We have said that, in areas like the South where one party is gaining, persons are likely to begin voting for the minority party—particularly in national elections—for some time before they consider shifting party identification.

It is also true that voters are more likely to shift identification than registration. A change of party registration requires making a trip or sending a postcard to the registrar's office. It may also seem to some voters to be a more traumatic or enduring change than just telling a pollster about a new party identification. In several southern, border, and southwestern states this lag in changing registration is particularly clear; in eight southern states, however, it cannot be measured because party registration is not required. This means that, if we want to predict voting trends over the next few years, we should look at trends in party identification more than trends in registration in those states where party registration is required for primary voting.

Two-Party Competition in the Fifty States

All the states are different, as we constantly remind our readers. Some states are more competitive than others, and some have been competitive for a much longer period than others. But with the Republican growth throughout the South, we can say that there are no longer any states where one party holds a monopoly of power. From 1961 through 2000 (the elections of 1960 through 1999) every state in the Union had at least one Democratic governor, and every state except Georgia and Hawaii had a Republican governor and also had divided government.

During these years every state legislature except Idaho had a Democratic majority at least once in one or both chambers. Only twelve states (plus nonpartisan Nebraska) in that period never had a Republican majority in either chamber, including six southern states, four border states (Maryland, West Virginia, Missouri, and Oklahoma), and Massachusetts and Rhode Island. In all of these states except Arkansas, the Republican minority was more than one-third, and often considerably higher, in at least one chamber at some time. Republican gains in southern legislatures made it seem almost certain that Republicans would win at least modest majorities in several more chambers early in the new century.

Because national political trends have a powerful effect on state politics, we should keep in mind how competitive the national parties have become. The ten presidential elections from 1960 through 1996 produced five Republican and five Democratic victories. In 1964 Democrat Lyndon Johnson carried every state except five in the Deep South plus Arizona. But in 1972 and 1984 Republicans Richard Nixon and Ronald Reagan each carried every state but one.

Old political loyalties of the voters are changing, particularly in the South. About two-thirds of the voters identify with one party or the other, party identification has been growing stronger in recent years, and such identification has a major effect on how votes are cast (Bartels 2000). Many voters are splitting their ticket, nevertheless, and making judgments about the candidates rather than just voting the party line. Most candidates who hold statewide office, such as governors or senators, have enough political skill, visibility, campaign funding, and support from their party organization that they can very often win reelection even if their state party is in the minority or if national trends do not favor their party.

Because party loyalty of voters has faded somewhat, incumbents have so much political strength, and most states have competitive parties, both party organizations are finding it necessary to establish strong organizations, make use of more advanced technologies, and raise more money for campaigns than in the past. Neither parties nor candidates can rest on their laurels or depend completely on their traditional supporters. We turn now to an examination of state political party organizations.

3 State Party Organization

In the introduction we described several characteristics of modern state political parties. They are changing in many ways. They have larger, more complex organizational structures. They have different functions to perform, with much more emphasis on serving the needs of candidates and raising money. They offer different incentives to attract loyal party workers. They operate in a more partisan and competitive environment, as we have seen in Chapter 2. Although all state parties are affected by most of the same national trends, and although they have similar structures, at least on paper, there are many differences among the state party organizations—including differences in how strong and effective they are.

In this chapter we will develop these themes in much greater detail, explaining why these changes are occurring and what impact they have on state party organizations and their ability to play a major role in political campaigns.

THEORIES OF PARTY ORGANIZATION

The theories designed to help us better understand the role of party organizations are also changing as political scientists struggle to articulate theories that fit the real world of party politics. Political parties today are "institutions responding to changes and searching for roles," as Maisel (1994, 383) describes them. Political parties differ from most other institutions because their fundamental purpose is to elect candidates to a variety of offices. Joseph Schlesinger (1966) has described party organizations as being made up of many units, or "nuclei," each of which is "a collective effort devoted to the capture of a single public office." The strength and effectiveness of a party depend on its ability to establish strong linkages among the nuclei.

Theories have been developed about the changing relationship between a political party and its candidates. John Aldrich asserts that modern campaign technology has made it possible, for the first time, "for the ambitious candidate to create a personal campaign organization rather than relying on the party" (1995, 269). Nevertheless state as well as national party organizations continue to exist and function, and they show many signs of being stronger, more complex, and better financed than they were a generation ago. If this is true, it must be because the parties are doing a better job of serving the needs of the candidates.

If candidates for office can get along without the state party organization, why are many of them relying on it in their campaigns? Aldrich (1995, 292–295) believes that candidates make use of party organizations because these are durable organizations that help candidates deal with three of their major needs. First, because there are sometimes several candidates seeking the same office, parties are needed to try to regulate competition through the nominating process. Second, candidates need parties because they can provide a cadre of campaign workers, access to valuable resources and services, and assistance in mobilizing voters, particularly those who have some degree of loyalty to the party and its principles. Third, once a party's candidates get elected, it is parties that represent coalitions of interests and have basic differences on issues. Therefore they are able to produce policy majorities, consisting largely of the party's officeholders in the legislative and executive branches.

Politicians not only make use of the party organizations but have reshaped them to serve their particular interests. The state party no longer exercises control over those who seek office, as the traditional urban machines often did, but rather it serves their needs:

> The party is in service to its candidates and officeholders, it is structured to advance the needs and interests of ambitious politicians. . . . A party in service can only help the candidate, who in principle has other sources for finding such help. The more effective and extensive the services the party offers, however, the more important they are to their ambitious candidates as they seek continual election and reelection. (Aldrich 1995, 289–294)

Aldrich and others (Bibby 1998; Stone and Rapoport 1998; Frendreis and Gitelson 1999) who write about the nature of parties and elections often describe modern election campaigns as "candidate-centered," partly because today's technology makes it possible for candidates to create and operate their own campaigns, even for a major office such as a congressional seat. But Aldrich also points out that a well-organized, well-financed party organization has many ways to help its candidates. It can offer them lists of voters, lists of campaign contributors, and the results of its public opinion polls. It can provide experts in media relations, fund raising, and advertising. And it can mobilize loyal party activists to perform a variety of campaign chores.

Political party organizations, national and state, have not only survived but have become more important because of the services they can provide to candidates. One example is the use of political consultants. Candidates for major offices have found that they need to hire campaign consultants, who are specialists in a wide variety of areas, from raising funds to conducting polls and creating television commercials. Increasingly the political parties are training their own consultants or hiring them to do specialized work for the party or to work directly with candidates. The parties also recommend which consultants their candidates should hire (Bibby 1999, 80).

Although Aldrich and many of the other political scientists writing about parties and elections are specialists in national politics, their descriptions of modern party organizations apply to state parties as well as national parties, and their theoretical analyses help us better to understand state parties and political systems.

Candidates running in state elections are not quite the same as candidates in national elections, however. Many candidates for the presidency, for U.S. senator or representative, or for state governor have the experience, skill, and resources to run their own campaigns, as Aldrich suggests, and to choose how much they want to rely on help from the party.

But candidates for other statewide offices, for state legislative seats, and for major local offices like mayor may be much less able to organize and run their own campaigns. There are some legislative and local candidates running in districts and towns or counties so small that a low-key, low-cost, door-to-door campaign is possible. But a large proportion of statewide, legislative, and local candidates—particularly nonincumbents—need the kinds of help that they may not be able to afford but that a state party organization can provide, such as political consultants and computer resources. Therefore it can be argued that state party organizations have the opportunity and responsibility to play a larger role in state election campaigns than the national parties have for national campaigns.

THE FUNCTIONS OF STATE PARTY ORGANIZATIONS

The major function of political party organizations is to contest elections, and they are judged by their success or failure in winning elections. The authors of the most comprehensive study of state party organizations, undertaken in the late 1970s and early 1980s, measured the strength of the one hundred state party organizations by calculating how well they performed a number of specific functions that the authors considered important. They showed that state party organizations were becoming better organized and more effective in performing these functions than had been the case earlier (Cotter, Gibson, Bibby, and Huckshorn 1984).

These data have been updated to describe the functions performed by state party organizations in the late 1990s. The new data show that state party organizations are continuing to develop, becoming considerably stronger and more effective than they had been twenty years earlier. The parties are now much more professional, with more resources and a much wider range of activities. A number of activities that used to be carried out by half or fewer state parties are now done by almost all of them, such as financial contributions to major candidates and major fund-raising programs (Aldrich 2000).

Now, as in the previous period, state Republican Party organizations are stronger, more professional, and better funded than Democratic Parties. For almost every one of the specific party functions and activities that were surveyed, a larger proportion of Republican than Democratic Parties is actively involved. The only important exceptions are such things as direct mail fund-raising and get-out-the-vote drives in which virtually every state party is active. In the early 1980s, when the previous survey was conducted, Republican Parties in southern states, which had long been moribund, were making dramatic progress. By the late 1990s Republican Parties in southern states were among the strongest and best financed parties in the country and among the most active in recruiting and providing funding and services to candidates.

We can divide party functions into a few broad categories. First, in order to function effectively, the state parties must be well organized. They need to create a headquarters with a large, competent staff and updated computing and communications equipment. The state leaders and staff must communicate frequently and work closely with local party organizations, public officeholders, and candidates—because they share the responsibility for carrying out many party functions. Most important, the state leaders and staff must raise enough money to maintain the headquarters and to pay for the functions that the state party should be carrying out.

Second, it is the party organization's responsibility to run a slate of candidates for state and local public offices throughout the state. This means that the political party must actively recruit candidates, particularly in areas where good candidates are hard to find. They must do the research necessary to target those positions and districts where the race is likely to be close and more effort is needed to recruit and support candidates. If possible the party needs to make an effort to see that the best candidate is actually nominated.

Third, after the nominating process is completed, the party must provide the services most needed by its candidates. We have stressed that parties are increasingly becoming service agencies for candidates. Some of these are general services that are helpful to all candidates: getting individuals registered to vote and getting out the vote (also referred to as GOTV). Some are services tailored to meet the needs of specific candidates: contributing funds to them or helping them to raise funds; providing research material on their opponents; giving them pertinent polling data; assisting them in preparing advertising (from brochures to television ads); giving advice on how to deal with the media; running phone banks for the candidates; and helping them to get brochures and letters mailed out to voters.

In describing and evaluating the functions performed by state political parties, we must remember that much of the actual work is done by the local parties in the counties, cities, and towns, supporting candidates running for statewide and congressional offices as well as those running for local and legislative offices. They are largely responsible, for example, for getting voters registered and getting out the vote, turning out crowds to hear and meet major candidates who visit the area, and mobilizing party activists to work for local and legislative candidates.

When we discuss how the party recruits, supports, and advises state legislative candidates, we should remember that these functions are performed not only by the state organization but also by legislative party campaign committees, with the division of responsibility varying from state to state.

Organizing Party Headquarters

There is no single model of a party headquarters. How large the staff and how well equipped the headquarters are depend largely on how much money the party has been able to raise. The staff is likely to be largest during political campaigns. In addition to an executive director, the staff is likely to include a political director, someone who oversees the money-raising efforts, a public relations director, and someone to program and run the computers. During the campaign season there may be staff members to provide services for candidates and very often a "field staff" of persons who directly help candidates to run their campaigns. In election years some of the stronger parties in larger states may have a professional and secretarial staff numbering twenty-five or more. The average state party has nine full-time staff and seven part-time staff members in election years and at least half that many in nonelection years (Aldrich 2000).

Unless a political party sets up a well-staffed, well-equipped headquarters, it will be seriously handicapped in carrying out its major functions. To accomplish this, the party needs strong, imaginative leadership and it also needs funding. What this means of course is that political parties need to give very high priority to fund raising, not only to supply cash, services, or both to local party organizations and to candidates but also to create a first-class party headquarters. Some party chairs are selected in part because they have demonstrated skills in raising funds and recruiting other fund raisers. Some state parties have several experts in fund raising on their staff. Surveys of state parties show that virtually all of them, Republican or Democratic, raise funds through direct mail programs and hold fund-raising events during the year. We will say more about raising funds to support the work of the state party later in this chapter.

It is difficult to imagine a state party headquarters operating efficiently without modern computer and communications technology. A recent study (Goodhart 1999), based on a large-scale survey of state parties conducted in 1996, found that almost all had some form of computerized voter database. The parties used these databases particularly for direct-mail fund raising, mailings about party candidates and election-day reminders, voter registration, and solicitation of volunteers. The Republicans gave highest priority to fund raising, and the Democrats stressed recruiting volunteers. The Wisconsin Republican Party provides an example of using technology for fund-raising purposes. The party headquarters in the late 1990s had a twelve-station computerized marketing center, staffed from time to time with as many as thirty-five telemarketers, designed primarily to expand the base of financial contributors and to increase the number of relatively small donations.

A very large proportion of the state parties that responded to this survey had e-mail addresses, and about two-thirds had Web sites. By the end of the 1990s these figures were doubtless close to 100 percent. Anyone who has examined state party Web sites, however, knows that some are much more detailed and useful than others, and some are not kept up to date.

The mere presence of up-to-date technology does not mean that it will be used efficiently to stay in contact with local organizations, party activists, and political contributors. But modern technology makes it possible to send messages of various kinds to large numbers of party members quickly and relatively cheaply. It makes possible the targeting of particular subgroups with the most appropriate messages. It enables a party to conduct public opinion polls more quickly and accurately and to interpret the results more successfully. Computers make it possible to analyze voting data more accurately and comprehensively and thus to target those districts that the party has a realistic chance of winning or a serious risk of losing.

Recruiting, Targeting, and Nominating Functions

To win elections, or even to run close races, a political party needs to run a slate of candidates—not just any candidates but the ones who have the best chance of being elected. In any election year the party will have a number of incumbents who have decided to run for reelection. In some races where the party does not have an incumbent running, individuals may decide to run without any coaxing from the party, particularly in areas that are usually safe for the party. In particular, the party needs to recruit candidates in two kinds of situations: where no candidate has entered the race or where the only candidate or candidates running are those who have little chance of winning or might be an embarrassment to the party.

Recruiting is a difficult job, and it is not consistently done well by state and local parties. Maisel and his colleagues (1994, 147) point out that many parties "have limited incentives to encourage prospective candidates to run" and "even fewer sanctions to protect their preferred nominee from a primary challenge."

Another problem is that "parties may find themselves with either an embarrassment of ambitious candidates or a dearth of willing contenders."

It is particularly important for the political party to recruit candidates where it is most difficult to find them—in localities where the party has relatively few loyal voters and often very little organizational strength. Unless the party becomes involved in recruiting, it may have no candidate running in a district or county, or at least not a viable one. It is likely to be difficult to find anyone who has any interest in running or any obvious qualifications as a candidate.

Recruitment may also be important in districts where the two parties are almost evenly balanced and the race is likely to be close. Although the party may have several candidates available to challenge the incumbent or to run for an open seat in such a swing district, the party needs to identify and encourage the strongest candidate it can find. Recruitment is usually least important for a party that has a comfortable margin in a district. But if the party does not have an incumbent running, it may need to recruit the strongest candidate it can find to block other potential candidates who may be outside the party mainstream or who might precipitate a divisive and expensive primary race.

Local party organizations have most of the responsibility for recruiting candidates at the local level. But many counties, particularly in rural areas, have been dominated for many years by one political party. The majority party has no shortage of candidates and little need to recruit, and the minority party is often not well enough organized to recruit candidates. The job of recruiting state legislative candidates is done either by the state party organization or the state legislative campaign committees, depending on the relative strength of the two organizations and the priority that each gives to recruiting. In some states the two party bodies work closely together, dividing up specific recruiting jobs. They may get assistance from local party leaders in the district in identifying potential candidates. Surveys of party chairs show that 88 percent of state Republican Parties and 72 percent of Democratic ones are actively involved in legislative recruiting (Aldrich 2000).

The most important state races are those for governor, U.S. senator, and other statewide offices, such as attorney general, and the races in individual congressional districts. Surveys show that roughly half of the state parties are actively involved in recruiting for these races (Aldrich 2000). The party that controls an office does not need to recruit if the incumbent is running for reelection. Almost every race for governor and senator is contested but, because of the importance of these races, the party that does not control the office must find the strongest possible candidate to run, particularly if the incumbent of the other party is seeking reelection. Parties face a similar problem in congressional districts they do not control, and in some districts they fail to run any candidate, strong or weak.

We would expect that a political party that was reasonably competitive at the state level would be able to run a full slate of statewide candidates, but this is not always the case. In 1998 the Kentucky Republican Party elected a senator (giving it control of both Senate seats) and five of the six House seats. But one year later, in 1999, it was unable to recruit a viable candidate to run against the incumbent Democratic governor, leaving the field to a couple of obscure candidates. Nor was it able to recruit anyone for any of the other statewide offices, such as attorney general, secretary of state, and auditor.

About two-thirds of the voters identify with a party, and on the average 75–85 percent of them vote for their party's candidate in most races. But that leaves roughly half of the voters who do not necessarily vote a straight party ticket. Therefore in many statewide races and in some congressional districts, the outcome of the election depends heavily on the voters' perceptions of the candidates. The chances of defeating an incumbent or other front-runner depend very much on the ability of the state party leaders to recruit a candidate with enough political strength, name recognition, experience, and other assets to run an effective campaign.

Persuading a potentially strong candidate to challenge the incumbent for a major office can be a difficult job. This is particularly true if the incumbent is well entrenched, has already raised lots of campaign money, and is doing well in the polls. The potentially strong candidate you are trying to recruit faces a daunting task of raising at least as much money as the incumbent does. Your candidate recognizes that there is a real risk of suffering a defeat that might jeopardize his or her political future. Sometimes there is the risk that some other candidate in your party, who is less likely to win, may insist on running and forcing a primary contest. The party may have to help its preferred candidate raise enough money to be competitive and try to discourage other candidates from running and forcing a primary.

The task of recruiting candidates to run for the state legislature is different in some respects. Because successful recruiting takes time, effort, and resources, the party will set priorities about the districts where it will make the greatest effort to recruit candidates to run against incumbents or for open seats. Such efforts will be least necessary in districts where the party usually wins. It may sometimes be impossible to find a viable candidate in a district where the party consistently loses. The districts in which it is most important to have a good candidate are those in which the outcome of the election is in doubt. In such cases the party runs a serious risk of losing a district it has controlled in the past, or it has a reasonable chance of winning control of a seat if it can find a good enough candidate. To set recruiting priorities, the parties often make a careful analysis of voting trends in each of the legislative districts, a process described later in this chapter.

When they are seeking potential candidates in a legislative district, state and legislative party leaders consult with local party leaders and officeholders in the district and with legislators in nearby districts. We have surveyed leaders who try to recruit legislative candidates based on the qualities that will suit their needs.

Most of all they want potential candidates who have a strong commitment to run and will work hard. It is important to locate those who know how to raise money. Party leaders seek out candidates who are well known and have a good reputation in the community, who have a record of organizational leadership, and who know the district well and share the views of its people. Personal qualities like judgment, intelligence, integrity, and a record free of scandals are also important.

One legislative leader summed up the views expressed by many others: "The candidate's philosophy must fit that of the citizens in the district they are to serve. They must be willing to dedicate their time—and have the time—to do the job. They need to understand the needs of the district and be willing to address these needs and to work to accomplish them. We look for intelligent, honest, hard-working individuals as candidates." This describes not only the qualities of a good candidate but those of a good legislator. It reminds us that the ideal candidate is one who not only stands a good chance of being elected but will do a good enough job in office to be reelected.

Political parties must make some choices about where to concentrate their recruiting efforts, particularly in state legislative races. Priorities are necessary because a thorough recruiting job takes valuable time and effort and because the party must often promise that it will help raise money for potential candidates to persuade them to run.

For these reasons political parties are using sophisticated techniques to target districts—that is, to collect information on district voting patterns in order to identify districts that are likely to be close if both parties run viable candidates. Targeting is designed to estimate a "normal party vote" in the district. This means not only recording the vote cast in previous legislative elections and the electoral margins of incumbent legislators but also the votes cast in the district in recent races for other partisan offices, such as those for president and U.S. senators and representatives. The normal vote is estimated by averaging the vote in several such races.

Voters increasingly cross party lines to vote for incumbents, particularly those who are politically skillful and work hard, and the most effective and experienced legislators are likely to attract only weak opponents. Therefore a Democratic incumbent might win 65 percent in a district where the normal Democratic vote was only 55 percent. If the Republican Party could recruit a really strong candidate and provide financial support, that person might be able to run a close race; and, if the incumbent were not running again, a strong, well-financed Republican candidate might have a good chance of winning.

How extensively do political parties use sophisticated targeting techniques in legislative races? We surveyed leaders in state party organizations and legislative leaders and found that almost all of them had made some use of such targeting data. A large majority of them had found the data to be useful, although they often stressed that other factors had to be taken into consideration before recruiting or investing resources in a district. One study (Bullock and Shafer 1997) has shown that in Georgia nonincumbent Republican candidates for the legislature were much more likely to be elected if the scores on a targeting system indicated a better than 50–50 chance of winning.

The growing use of targeting techniques is important for several reasons. The political party has a better chance of recruiting a good candidate if it can provide evidence that he or she has a realistic chance of winning the seat. Both political parties have learned how to target accurately, and therefore both parties are likely to concentrate their heavy spending—in any given election year—on the same legislative districts.

Another important implication of the targeting strategy is that state political parties, particularly those that are in the minority, usually do not make a serious effort to recruit and support candidates in every legislative district. Some legislative seats may go uncontested unless candidates in those districts decide on their own to enter the race. It can be argued that state parties should make more of an effort to encourage candidates to run in districts that appear hopeless because in the long run this may strengthen the local party and develop better candidates. On the other hand, some state parties may discourage candidacies in such districts to avoid siphoning off funds or stirring up counter-mobilization efforts by the other party that will hurt its statewide or congressional candidates. Republican Parties often avoid contesting African American or Hispanic majority districts to prevent turnout of these voters from affecting statewide elections the Republican Party hopes to win.

In recent years the Republican Party in most southern states has been winning an increasing number of legislative seats, and the increase in seats won has often been greater than the increase in the seats contested by Republicans because they have followed a targeting strategy. (See Chapter 7 for more details on Republican gains in southern legislatures.)

There is an obvious connection between the recruitment and nomination of a party's candidates. If party leaders recruit the best candidate they can find for a statewide, congressional, or legislative office, they want that candidate to get nominated. In fact, it may be difficult to persuade someone to run for office if the party cannot help that person to defeat any primary challenger and win the nomination. But of course the party's ability to influence the selection of nominees is seriously limited by the primary elections used almost exclusively for nomination in the American states. Recruitment used to be the job of state and local party organizations, which were often powerful enough to pick the candidate they wanted and make sure that person was nominated. Today very few state and local party organizations have the political power or resources to control nominations.

It is most important, and most difficult, for a state political party to influence the nomination in statewide and congressional races. Sometimes the party may persuade someone who is challenging its preferred candidate to drop out of the race by refusing to provide any funding. But this is not an effective weapon when the challenger has enough funding to finance primary and general election campaigns without any help from the party. The party leadership may have little influence when the party is divided into ideological factions and a candidate insists on running who is unlikely to be elected because of his or her extreme views on issues.

In our discussion of nominations in Chapter 4, we will describe the process by which some state parties make preprimary endorsements of candidates, and we will evaluate the effectiveness of that technique in gubernatorial races.

Services to Candidates

We have said that a major function of today's political parties is providing services to candidates, and once its candidates have been nominated, the parties concentrate on helping the candidates get elected. Candidates for major offices may hire their own campaign experts and commission their own advertising, whereas those running for less important offices are more heavily dependent on the party for assistance. But all candidates can benefit from some services, such as voter registration and a reservoir of party activists who are willing to work in campaigns. Candidates for major offices may also benefit from the linkages between parties and their interest group allies. Although the state party organization may plan and financially support many of the services to candidates, much of the day-to-day work during a campaign is done by members of the local parties.

Registering and mobilizing the voters. Registration drives and get-out-the-vote campaigns are examples of functions that need to be performed by the state and local party organizations on behalf of all candidates. It would make no sense for a candidate who is running for governor and another who is running for a congressional seat to make separate efforts to get voters registered or to get them to vote. No matter how skillful a candidate's television advertising, these ads are wasted on some potential voters—those who have not bothered to register or do not bother to go to the polls. Even persons with some interest in politics may forget to change registration when they move to another county or state or may be too busy on election day to make it to the polls. Political parties have learned that the failure to register and mobilize those voters likely to support the party's candidates can be disastrous. About 60 percent of state party organizations work with county parties on registration drives, and almost all of them work with the counties on GOTV drives (Aldrich 2000).

What difference does it make if the party contacts potential voters to get them to register or go to the polls? Survey data show that, from 1972 through 1990, between 20 percent and 30 percent of the population reported having been contacted by a political party, with the percentage gradually dropping from 30 percent to 20 percent. A more important figure is the difference in voting between those who were contacted and those who were not. In elections between 1974 and 1990 voter turnout has been 20 to 30 percentage points higher for those contacted than turnout for those not contacted. The gap has been greater in nonpresidential election years, perhaps because in those years the elections usually stir up less interest and therefore prodding by the party makes more of a difference (Wielhouwer and Lockerbie 1994). One reason for this gap, however, is that the parties were more likely to contact persons who were already registered voters and those who had voted in the previous election. In other words, they were trying to mobilize potential voters who had shown some previous willingness to participate, rather than wasting time on those who were much less likely to respond to a contact (Wielhouwer 1995).

Assisting specific candidates. The services that a party provides to candidates vary with the needs of the individual candidates. A candidate for senator or governor may have hired several experts in the various phases of campaigning, and may have a large number of volunteers at the state and local levels, but may still benefit from specific services, such as access to a statewide poll. A candidate for the state legislature, who often has no campaign experts and a modest number of volunteers in the district, may have several needs. The state party organization or the legislative party campaign committee—or both—will usually provide more help to those legislative candidates facing close races, following the targeting strategy we have described.

All candidates want, and most candidates need, lots of money for their campaigns. The political party may provide funding directly to particular candidates or urge political action committees of allied groups to make such contributions. It may arrange for major party leaders, such as a governor or House speaker, to attend a fund raiser for the candidate. It may make available to the candidate lists of those who have supported the party and its candidates in the past. It may make available a staff member who can provide expert advice on how to set up a fundraising operation. Almost all state Republican Parties and 70 to 80 percent of state Democratic Parties report making contributions to statewide and congressional candidates and slightly more give to state legislative candidates (Aldrich 2000).

Although candidates want as much financial help as possible, state political parties sometimes prefer to provide candidates with services rather than simply giving them money. The parties may fear that some candidates will waste funds. A former House Speaker once told us that his legislative party had given a candidate $200 to be used as seed money to help get his campaign under way. Instead the candidate bought 200 straw hats with his name on them to pass out to supporters! Thereafter that candidate received some services but no more money.

The party may believe that it knows what services can be most valuable to a particular campaign and believes that its staff members will do a better job than anyone the candidate can hire with additional money. The party may share the results of a statewide or regional public opinion poll with the candidate or may help the candidate to organize a poll in the district using volunteers. The party can provide research assistance, particularly pertaining to the voting record of the candidate's opponent, and perhaps some public statements the latter has made that can be used to criticize the opponent.

Candidates who have not held public office or dealt with the media in other jobs usually need help with media relations. How can you get a newspaper to print a press release or conduct an interview with you? If you are running for one of ten or twenty legislative seats in a metropolitan area, how can you get the newspaper serving that area to pay any attention to you? Can you get local clubs or interest groups to invite you as a speaker during the campaign? If the local radio station runs a talk show, how can you be invited as a guest and how do you answer when callers attack you on the air? If some organization sponsors a debate between you and your opponent, how can you gain rather than lose from the event?

For years one of the traditional tasks for campaign workers has been stuffing envelopes, a job that requires no particular talent by many people. If the candidate is short on volunteers, the state or local party should be able to recruit workers who are willing to put in an afternoon doing such routine jobs. Political parties, like other telemarketers, are increasingly using phone banks to contact voters, asking them how they are going to vote, urging them to vote for a particular candidate, or reminding them to go to the polls on election day. Hiring temporary help to run the phone bank is expensive, and therefore the state and local parties must be able to enlist volunteers in this work.

Most candidates running for office prepare some kind of brochure or flyer to be mailed (or sometimes delivered by volunteers) throughout the state or district. Most of them also need some help designing such a brochure so that it will at least attract the recipients' attention and that ideally will be informative and make a favorable impression. Candidates running statewide, in a congressional district, or in a large legislative district need—and can usually afford—some advertising on television and perhaps radio. Designing an effective television advertisement takes great skill and experience. If done by an amateur, it may be worse than useless. We have all seen political ads on television that were very effective and some that were a waste of money. Candidates need professional help in designing effective advertising and in making decisions about the timing and placement of such ads on television stations. Even a form of advertising as primitive as a yard sign requires a certain amount of skill in design (for example, the candidate's name should be large enough to be readable as you drive by).

A party gains another advantage if it provides staff members to help its candidates prepare advertising. It may be able to influence the policy content of advertisements, stressing the issues that the party believes need to be emphasized in the campaign. For example, the governor may be planning to propose a reform of health care after the election and wants party members to mention the issue in the legislative campaign.

There are new developments that give political parties much greater influence over the campaigns of their candidates. Judicial decisions have given both political parties and interest groups the right to run "issue advocacy" advertisements that are directly related to a campaign without any restrictions, as long as they do not explicitly urge viewers and listeners to vote for or against a candidate. During the 1996 and 1998 congressional elections national parties frequently ran advertisements in particular congressional districts emphasizing issues that the party considered important, praising their congressional candidate and record, or attacking the opponent.

A study of congressional elections in 1998 went so far as to conclude:

> There is a fundamental shift under way in competitive congressional elections from a candidate-centered system of elections to an interest group–and party-centered system of elections. With the stakes so high and resources available, the parties and interest groups now fight for control of Congress in a relatively few districts or states and the 'outside campaigns' can overwhelm the candidate campaigns. (Magleby and Holt 1999)

The candidates had no control over such advertisements run either by an interest group or the party. An antiabortion group, for example, might run an ad attacking the Democratic candidate for being pro-choice, even though the Republican candidate might be trying to avoid that issue because it was one that caused deep divisions in the district. The Democratic Party might run an attack ad aimed at the Republican member of Congress, although the Democratic candidate might be concerned that such sharply negative ads will backfire and hurt her own campaign because voters will not distinguish between the ads run by the party and those run by the candidate.

One way of describing the range of campaign activities carried out by the political parties is to look at data on the activities of local Democratic and Republican Parties in 1992, 1994, and 1996. These data were reported by the chairs of several hundred county parties in nine states scattered across the country (Frendreis and Gitelson 1999). In most years at least three-fourths of the counties report organizing fund-raising events and contributing funds to candidates; distributing campaign literature; organizing campaign events (such as visits by state or congressional candidates); and distributing yard signs and posters. At least half of the county parties report organizing telephone campaigns to reach voters; issuing campaign press releases; mailing literature to voters; conducting door-to-door voter canvassing. At least one-third conduct voter registration drives, and at least two-thirds conduct GOTV campaigns as the election approaches.

CAMPAIGN FINANCE

All of the tasks of state party organizations require money, and lots of it. The last section discussed the functions of the party. But first party headquarters need a competent staff who can use modern computing and communications equipment to communicate instantly with their candidates, officeholders, and local party organizations. Therefore the party must raise money to maintain a first-class headquarters.

The party's major function is to recruit and support candidates for office. Most of these candidates will be in competitive districts where the opposition has a lot of money to fight back. Candidates need services from the state legislator to the governor, and parties are increasingly becoming service agencies for candidates. Even major statewide candidates can benefit from party registration and GOTV efforts and phone banks. Most candidates need special services such as fund raising, research, polling, advertising, media advice, and phone banks.

Because the governor is the most important statewide officer, we will concentrate on what candidates for governor need to win office. When the only way to reach people was by speeches in public places, torchlight parades, whistle-stop tours from the back of the train, newspaper ads, and other publicity events, candidates could manage their campaigns with the aid of the party's minions. But now candidates need specialized help. Specialized commercial firms with politics as their business charge huge fees. The modern gubernatorial campaign needs at least two political consultants, and political consultants are expensive.

Gubernatorial candidates need to know many things about their voters. Professional campaign consultants who specialize in public opinion polling can conduct an initial benchmark survey to determine the candidate's own strengths or weaknesses as perceived by the electorate. Follow-up telephone polling; panel surveys, which measure shifts in attitudes; small focus group interviews of typical voters; and tracking surveys, which measure the impact of advertising and other campaign events on different groups of voters, are all services the polling consultants may offer to provide.

In addition to TV ad production and public opinion polling, commercial firms handle many other activities. Direct mail can now be used to raise funds as well as to persuade voters to vote a certain way. Computers have replaced loyal party workers (traditionally women) who used to address envelopes for direct mail purposes; in fact, they can spin out thousands in short order. Technology makes it possible to identify past contributors and appeal to them again. Phone banks identify voters and try to persuade them. Bumper stickers, campaign buttons, and other traditional items are also designed and produced by campaign firms.

The foregoing litany of the need for campaign consultants makes it obvious that these services are provided to single candidates rather than to parties, which tend toward an atomized politics with little joint activity between candidates running on the party's slate. Parties have begun to fight back by assuming the role of a management firm that contracts the services of professional consultants and specialized firms. The consultants are mostly partisan and work within the party of their choice. Parties direct candidates to consultants often as a condition for obtaining party support. An example of this type of linkage can be found in New Jersey, where one office building houses a complex of interlocking organizations that are all tied to the GOP and its candidates. These organizations include the Committee for Responsible Government, a political action committee (PAC) controlled by Gov. Christine Todd Whitman that gives money to candidates; a political consulting firm headed by the political director of Whitman's PAC; and four "political consulting, advertising, accounting, graphic design/printing companies with interlocking and overlapping leadership structures and ties to Whitman's PAC" (Bibby 1999, 80).

In several states, political action committees have become partners with parties. Party leaders can match their candidates with the appropriate PACs, outline the needs of the campaign, and determine the magnitude of support that would be required to win. A team concept emerges, with the PAC as the financial backer, the party as the initiator and strategist, and the candidate as the focus (Jones 1984, 197). A former executive director of the Washington Democratic Party spoke of the "Big 7" funding partners for the party including the Washington Labor Council, American Federation of State, County, and Municipal Employees, Washington Education Association, Machinists, Washington Conservation Voters, Firefighters, and the Washington Trial Lawyers Association. In a recent election for the state legislature, the state party, the Legislative Campaign Committee, and the "funding partners" got together and advertised for media consultants, interviewed them, and chose three or four who could be assigned to various candidates in targeted districts.

Financing the Campaigns

Where does the money come from to finance such expensive campaigns? Are candidates who are independently wealthy more likely to win because there is no limit to the amount of their own money that they can spend? Are those who must obtain their money from groups likely to be beholden to these backers? As we shall see, some states try to limit the power of groups and individuals by prohibiting or limiting contributions. But first, where does this money come from?

Figure 3-1 diagrams the sources and flow of money in state elections. The major sources of campaign funds in state politics are individuals and PACs. However, in half the states, corporations and labor unions may contribute directly to candidates and parties, although there may be limits on their giving. Two of the largest states—Illinois and Virginia—have no limitations on corporate or union giving, and New York and Texas do not limit corporate contributions for administrative purposes, therefore allowing unlimited contributions to the party overhead account. In addition to, or instead of, making political contributions, corporations may encourage their executives to make contributions to political campaigns. They also may give indirectly through attorneys and public relations firms who have been provided with large fees for that purpose.

In the states that prohibit direct giving, corporations and labor unions must form PACs to distribute campaign money. Businesses may, however, directly pay the overhead cost (personnel solicitation, administration) of the political action committees that they must form to distribute campaign money. In these states, their identity is often hidden behind a legal pseudonym—such as BWH-PAC, standing for Beer Wholesalers—and their contributions are more difficult to categorize. In some states, public money is given to candidates for primaries or general elections or directly to the political parties ("State," in Figure 3-1), a development that is described later. Candidates are not limited in their own contributions to their campaigns and may incur personal debts through bank loans to finance their candidacies.

Individuals provide most of the money for gubernatorial campaigns, usually

Figure 3-1 Sources and Flows of Money in State Election Campaigns

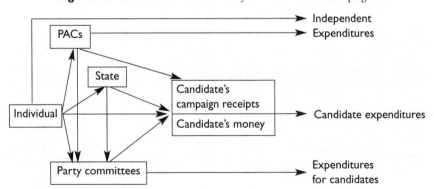

Source: Sarah McCally Morehouse, *The Governor as Party Leader* (Ann Arbor: University of Michigan Press, 1998), 69.

more than 50 percent. Some of these individuals give very large amounts. In New York, Gov. George Pataki received 31 percent of his early 1998 campaign money from Manhattan, which has long been a bountiful source of money for incumbents, particularly Republicans, because it is home to many Wall Street executives, developers, and other wealthy supporters. He received forty-four donations of $20,000 or more, with $28,000 being the contribution limit (Levy 1998). This example indicates that incumbent governors can raise vast sums of money.

Recently some state parties have been collecting huge sums of money from wealthy individuals and interest groups and giving the money to gubernatorial and state legislative campaigns. In twenty-six states, money given by parties to candidates is not limited, and thirteen of these have no limitations on what individuals or PACs may give to parties. In Florida, for instance, some interest groups make in-kind contributions to the parties—especially if the contributions can be identified while the gift passes through the party organization. The party then gives the in-kind contribution to the candidate. The Florida Lawyers Action Group pays for polls and gives the polling results to the party. The poll costs more than the limit on interest group contributions to the candidate. The party gives the poll to the candidate, and the candidate knows where the poll came from (Malbin and Gais 1998, 93).

Candidates and their families give personal money to their own campaigns, sometimes in huge amounts. We suspect that personal money plays more of a role in primary campaigns than in general elections. A study of nominating campaigns in ten states indicates that several candidates contributed more than 40 percent of their total receipts to fund their own nominating campaign. Four of these were successful business executives who had not held public office and needed to spend huge amounts to become known (Morehouse 1998, 68–69). As the California 1998 gubernatorial election season began, Al Checchi, a demibillionnaire Democratic businessman, had spent $7.25 million on the primary race by December 31; he broke the record for state primary spending (previously $9 million) with a total expenditure of $40 million (Scott 1998, 12). Checchi hired experienced campaign consultants and ran advertisements that portrayed him as the self-made grandson of immigrant grocers. He had never been involved in appointed or elected office before deciding to take on the leadership of the most populous state and the world's seventh-largest economy. In his own words: "No amount of money is going to get people who want to do something to do something they don't want to do. You can't buy votes, you can only disseminate information" (Purdum 1998). He was correct because the primary voters voted for Gray Davis, who spent $9 million on his campaign.

Finally the flow of money reaches the spending stage. Both individuals and PACs may spend as much money as they desire to urge the election or defeat of a candidate. State political parties may spend money on behalf of their gubernatorial candidates, but in many states spending is limited by law. Candidates are constitutionally permitted to spend as much money as they wish, which is limited only if they accept public funding.

Campaign Regulations: Prohibitions and Contribution Limits

Figure 3-1 has shown us where money comes from and where it goes. We learned that the major sources of campaign funds in state politics are individuals and PACs, although political parties have greatly increased their spending recently, partly in response to an infusion of money from the national parties. In some states, corporations and labor unions may give directly to candidates and parties. Also in some states, public funding is given to candidates for primaries or general election campaigns or directly to the political parties. Candidates are not limited in their own contributions to their campaigns and may incur personal debts through bank loans to finance their candidacies. Only thirteen states do not limit what political parties may receive from individuals or PACs or what they may contribute to candidates, and these are listed in note 2 of Table 3-1.

This is not the whole picture. Although money comes from individuals and PACs and parties, states have very different rules that govern "how much." This is called "state money." Whereas corporations and labor unions may give directly to candidates and parties in some states, the amounts they may give range from "unlimited" to $500. Table 3-1 lists contribution limits to state parties from individuals and PACs and the amounts that state parties may give to their candidates for governor. There are twenty-four states in which contributions by individuals and PACs to political parties are limited, and twelve of these have the same or stricter limits than the federal ones. (Federal limits are $20,000 for individuals and $15,000 for PACs.) This means that candidates for state office in these states cannot receive or spend money that has not been raised according to the laws of the state, that is, "state money."

In twenty-four states, parties are limited in what they may contribute to statewide candidates. Table 3-1, in the last column, lists the contribution limits for these states as well as the states where parties are unlimited in what they may contribute to candidates for governor. The last thirteen states in the table have no limits on what individuals or PACs may contribute to the parties. Eleven of these states without contribution limits to parties have limits on party spending for candidates. We will see in Chapter 9 how the national parties make use of this opportunity.

The fact remains that twenty-six states have no limitations on what state political parties may spend for their state candidates. These include the states detailed in note 2 of Table 3-1 for which there are no limits on money into or from the parties. Included in this group of 26 states are five of the most populous states: New York (except the primary), California, Texas, Pennsylvania, and Illinois.

Table 3-1 Contribution Limits to State Parties and from State Parties

State Parties	Annual Individual Contributions to Parties	Annual PAC Contributions to Parties	Contributions from Parties to Candidates for Governor
Alaska	$500	$1,000	$100,000
California	5,000	5,000	Unlimited
Colorado	25,000	25,000	400,000
Connecticut	5,000	5,000	Unlimited
Delaware	20,000[a]	20,000[a]	Limited by office
Hawaii	50,000	50,000	50,000
Kansas	15,000	5,000	Unlimited in general election
Kentucky	2,500	2,500	1,000 per slate
Louisiana	100,000[a]	100,000[a]	Unlimited
Maryland	4,000[b]	6,000[b]	Unlimited
Massachusetts	5,000	5,000	100 for publicly funded; 35,000 in-kind; 3,000 for non-publicly funded
New Hampshire	5,000	Unlimited	Unlimited for publicly funded
New Jersey	30,000	30,000	2,100 per primary and general election
New York	69,900[b]	69,900[b]	Primary-prohibited; general election-unlimited
Ohio	15,500	15,500	515,000 per primary or general election
Oklahoma	5,000	5,000	5,000
Rhode Island	1,000 (Limit: 10,000)	1,000 (Limit: 10,000)	25,000; in-kind unlimited[c]
South Carolina	3,500[b]	3,500[b]	50,000
South Dakota	3,000	Unlimited	Unlimited
Vermont	2,000	2,000	400
Washington	Unlimited	2,875[b]	0.58 per voter
West Virginia	1,000	1,000	1,000 per primary or general election
Wisconsin	10,000 (Limit: 10,000)	6,000	Unlimited
Wyoming	25,000 (Limit: 25,000)	Unlimited	Primary: prohibited; general election: unlimited
Arizona	None	None	None for publicly funded; 68,144 for non–publicly funded[d]
Arkansas	None	None	2,500
Florida	None	None	50,000 for publicly funded; in-kind unlimited[c]
Georgia	None	None	5,000
Idaho	None	None	10,000 per primary or general election

Table 3-1 (*continued*)

State Parties	Annual Individual Contributions to Parties	Annual PAC Contributions to Parties	Contributions from Parties to Candidates for Governor
Maine	None	None	None for publicly funded; 500 for non–publicly funded
Michigan	None	None	68,000
Minnesota	None	None	20,000
Missouri	None	None	10,700
Montana	None	None	15,000
Nebraska	None	None	750,000 for publicly funded
Nevada	None	None	5,000 per primary or general election
New Mexico	None	None	None in primary; unlimited in general election

Sources: U.S. Federal Election Commission, *Campaign Finance Law '98: A Summary of State Campaign Finance Laws with Quick Charts* (Washington, D.C.: FEC, 1998); and Jennie Drage, research analyst, legislative management, National Conference of State Legislatures.

Notes: (1) Corporations and labor unions are prohibited from contributing in Alaska, Ariz., Conn., Mich., Minn., N.C., N.H., N.D., Ohio, Ore., Pa., R.I., S.D., Wis., Wyo. Corporations only are prohibited from contributing in Iowa, Ky., Mass., Mont., Okla., Tenn., W. Va. Corporations and labor unions are limited the same as PACs in Calif., Colo., Del., Hawaii, La., N.J., S.C., Vt., Wash. Labor unions only are prohibited from contributing in Okla., W. Va. In Kan., corporations and unions are limited like individuals. In Ky. and Mass. labor is limited like individuals. In Ala., Ind., Miss., and N.Y., there are varying limits on corporate and labor contributing.

(2) Thirteen states do not limit individual or PAC contributions to or contributions from the parties: Ala., Ill., Ind., Iowa, Miss., N.C., N.D., Ore., Pa., Tenn., Texas, Utah, Va.

[a]Delaware contributions are for a two-year cycle and Louisiana contributions are for a four-year period.

[b]Md., N.Y., S.C., and Wash. limit cash contributions but not contributions to overhead expenses, therefore allowing unlimited contributions to the party administrative and housekeeping account.

[c]In R.I. and Fla., cash contributions are limited but in-kind contributions are not. Therefore, they are treated as if they permit unlimited party contributions.

[d]Total from political party and all political organizations combined.

Apparently their lawmakers agree with Edward W. Nottingham, U.S. District judge in Colorado, who has said that "the message of the party and the message of the candidate are unified" and hence that placing limits on what parties may spend on their candidates strikes at core First Amendment rights (*Colorado Republican Party v. Federal Election Commission, 1999*). We will see shortly how the national parties make use of this opportunity as well.

In New York, where parties may spend as much as they want to back candidates in the general election, Governor Pataki's fundraising for reelection had reached $12 million by February 15 of the 1998 election year. Of that total, $6.5 million were from the state Republican Party and $5.7 million were from Pataki's own efforts. The Pataki campaign asked large donors—both interest groups and individuals—to give to the state Republican Party, which then funneled the money to the campaign. That strategy allowed the campaign to get around individual and interest group limits for gubernatorial candidates since the state party is unlimited (Levy 1998). This generous funding to the governor's reelection campaign by the state Republicans was unprecedented in New York as well as the other states and may be a predictor of the future. It may have accounted for the fact that the governor set a record by spending nearly $20 million for his reelection. There are big stakes in reelecting the governor, and parties are more experienced fund raisers than ever before.

A recent development that affects state party contributions to candidates is the role of "soft money." In a series of advisory opinions beginning in 1978, the Federal Election Commission (FEC), the government agency that set the regulations in the first place, handed down the following ruling. When a state or national party spends money on generic party activities that affect both federal and nonfederal elections like overhead expenses, GOTV drives, voter registration, issue advertising, and television commercials, it can use combination of money raised according to federal limits and prohibitions (hard money) and funds unregulated by federal laws (soft money). This combination is based on a formula that reflects the proportion of federal and nonfederal candidates on the ballot. The flow of soft money from national parties to state parties for party-building activities has evolved since 1980. Soft money is subject to the laws of the state in which it is spent. Some state laws are more restrictive than the federal ones (see Table 3-1). In other states, funds from corporate treasuries, union dues, and generous individual donors are legal, and the national parties collect them for distribution to their state affiliates.

Although it was assumed that soft money would flow generously to the state parties during presidential election years and subside during the midterm election years when most governors are elected, this has not been the case. Soft money raising by both the Democratic National Committee and the Republican National Committee increased 300 percent from 1992 to 1996. It may have reached a saturation point in 1996, because the national parties decreased their soft money raising by 14 percent between 1996 and 1998, the first time there was a drop since 1992. So in both presidential and gubernatorial election years, state parties and national parties engage in party-building activities according to the formula. What is not generally known is how much of the fund raising for both the federal (hard) and nonfederal (soft) money the states do themselves. On average, states raise most of the hard money and 40 percent of the soft money for this joint spending.

The states originally benefited from audio and video equipment, computers, voter lists, fax machines, and high-tech phone systems that were brought in to build up the party for the presidential campaign. In 1996, however, a significant amount of money was spent on issue advocacy ads designed to promote national party issue positions. In 1998 these ads were run in state and congressional districts promoting party positions without urging people to vote for or against any candidate. For example, if the national and state Republican Parties want to run an "issue" ad in Illinois ("The Republican Party Is the Party of Fiscal Responsibility") they use a mixture of funds—the soft money portion raised according to Illinois campaign finance laws (which allow unlimited corporate, labor, and individual contributions) and the hard money portion raised according to federal campaign finance laws. Soft money is raised by both the state and the national parties to pay for these ads. We will further discuss this money relationship between the state and national parties in Chapter 9.

Public Financing of Elections

One of the most important recent developments in state campaign financing is the trend toward public funding, supported by tax dollars, for election campaigns—through contributions either to state party organizations or directly to candidates. Normally this funding is financed either through a check-off system or an add-on system on the state income tax form (the difference being that for the add-on, taxpayers must increase their tax by a few dollars for this purpose), though this may be supplemented by other appropriations. In this section we will describe the impact of public funding on party organizations, and in Chapters 5 and 7 we will describe the effect on gubernatorial and other statewide races and on state legislative races.

As of 1998 there were fourteen states in which the political party organizations received public funds. In eleven states the funds are allocated to Democratic or Republican Parties based on the choices indicated by those taxpayers using the check-off or the add-on. In the other three states the funds are either distributed evenly between the two major parties or divided on the basis of party registration in the state. A number of states have provisions for allocating funds to minor parties, specifying what proportion of the vote (such as 10 percent) or what proportion of party registration they must have to be eligible for public funding. In four of these fourteen states public funding also went directly to candidates. In some states the state party committees that receive these funds must share them with the local party committees. The state parties normally can use them for administrative purposes, to pay for services to candidates, or as direct contributions to candidates.

The minority party organization in a state sometimes complains that, if the wishes of those using the check-off determine how funds are allocated between parties, the majority party simply gains another financial advantage over its rival. But in some states where the minority party has more difficulty raising funds than does the majority party, it may actually be more dependent on public funding than is the majority.

Whether this public funding significantly helps the political parties depends on whether the parties receive a significant amount of funding or just a token amount. As Malbin and Gais (1998, 66–67) point out, there are huge variations in the funds transferred to parties. One major problem is that half of the states contributing to parties have used the add-on system, but because it requires tax-payers to pay this amount as a small additional tax, very few taxpayers do so. In 1994 an average of less than one-half of 1 percent of those filing tax returns agreed to add-on taxes in the seven states using that system (all of them were states that fund parties). In the thirteen states using check-offs (including seven funding par-ties), an average of almost 11 percent of filers checked off such funding. In that year the two parties divided public funds amounting to $73,000 in Virginia, $42,000 in Massachusetts, and only $10,000 in Alabama. But among the check-off states, the parties received $146,000 in Iowa and $838,000 in Ohio (Malbin and Gais 1998, 67). It is possible that some taxpayers are less willing to support political parties than candidates, but the key to larger support of parties would appear to be abandoning the add-on requirement.

THE STRUCTURE OF STATE PARTY ORGANIZATIONS

The one hundred state parties are organized in approximately the same way. The purpose of the party is to win elections, and all of the state parties are organized around the electoral districts in the state. The state party organization is responsi-ble for elections to state offices, like governor and attorney general. There are party committees in those counties, cities, and towns where at least some of the officials are elected on a partisan ballot. The Republican county committee, for example, might help to recruit candidates for county offices and then provide various kinds of support to the candidate during the campaign. It might also have the legal responsibility for filling a vacancy if a candidate resigns between the primary and the general election. There may also be party committees in state legislative dis-tricts, particularly those that include more than one county or city. In most states the county committee is the most important local organization, except in those northeastern states where cities and towns are the basic unit of local government.

Figure 3-2 depicts the formal structure that would be typical for a state party and its local branches. All state parties have a state chair, which may be a full-time or part-time job, and a state central committee, which might meet every month or so. The state convention is a much larger body that meets about every two years

Figure 3-2 Diagram of Typical Formal State Party Organization

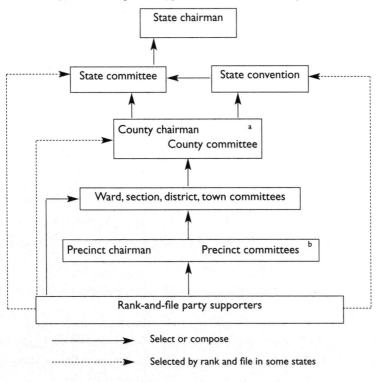

Select or compose

------------------> Selected by rank and file in some states

[a]3,000 in each party in the United States
[b]100,000 in each party in the United Sates

(in some states more often). At each level of local government the party is likely to have a committee and someone to chair it. Each precinct has a voting place, and each precinct may have a committee to work at the polls and perhaps perform other functions.

As Figure 3-2 indicates, state parties use a variety of means for choosing the membership of these party units. Rank-and-file Democrats and Republicans, meeting in caucuses or voting at the polls, may elect precinct or city or county committees, which in turn choose members to the next highest level. Chairs of county or city committees might be ex officio members of the state committee and might choose members from their unit to be delegates to the state convention. In some states the voters may directly elect members of the state convention from their locality. The convention in turn may choose some or all members of the state committee. The state party chair is almost always chosen by the state committee.

In reality, the party structure may not be as democratic, or as complete, as the diagram suggests. On the one hand, there may be very little competition for some of these positions. (One of us got elected as a precinct member when only four people showed up at the meeting and only two of them wanted the two available positions.) In theory, delegates to the state convention are elected from localities around the state, but often any active party member who has the time and inclination to go to the convention can do so. However, if the state convention is electing delegates to the party's national convention or is voting to endorse candidates running in a contested primary, there may be contests between would-be delegates to the state convention. In some state parties the leadership may be able to hand pick members of the state committee to make sure that they maintain control over the party.

The diagram of formal party organization in Figure 3-2 may exaggerate the level of party activity at the local level. In theory, both parties are organized in every voting precinct in the country. In reality, in localities dominated by one party the other party may have difficulty filling precinct positions and even developing and maintaining an active membership on county, city, and town committees. Southern Republican Parties are much better organized than they used to be, but still there are many gaps at the local level.

A diagram of the formal party organization at the state and local level is also incomplete because in reality some of the most important and active members of the party work through a variety of groups and committees that are closely associated with the formal party organization. Later in this chapter we will describe these related groups.

State Party Leadership

The formal leader of the political party is the state chair. The chair is the most visible party leader, the one most likely to be interviewed by the media, and therefore it is important to have someone who is articulate and has some skill in public relations. The chair presides over the meetings of the state central committee and bears much of the responsibility for keeping the party operating. In about half of the state parties the job of party chair is a full-time job; in the other half the job is likely to go to an elected official or to a lawyer or businessperson who is not a full-time chair. Almost all of the state parties have an executive director who would have heavier responsibilities if the chair worked less than full time (Aldrich 2000).

The actual power structure of the party depends very much on whether the party holds the governorship. Governors differ in the role they play in party affairs, but a governor who chooses to play an active role is almost always the most powerful party leader. Such a governor usually chooses the party chair, and this choice usually will be ratified by the state central committee or the party convention. The governor may pick the person who has run his or her election campaign, or perhaps an officeholder or party leader who has been a loyal ally in the campaign. In Kentucky the control of a Democratic governor over the Democratic Party is such a well-established pattern that the transition to new party leadership sometimes occurs very shortly after the Democratic gubernatorial nominee is chosen in the primary, late in May.

A party chair who has been selected by the governor is likely to be powerful for that very reason and to remain powerful as long as the governor continues to provide support. Bibby (1992, 99) quotes the comments of a New England state chair on his relationship to the governor: "I'm the governor's agent. My job is to work with him. If I look good—he looks good because I'm his man. I don't bother him with messy stuff. He expects me to handle it my way. I meet with the leaders on his behalf. I'm the liaison to the city and town leaders."

To be an effective party leader, the governor needs to be very much involved in party affairs, and a chair who is close to the governor should be able to depend on the governor's active participation. The governor needs to be accessible to local party leaders, to help in recruiting candidates for public office (such as legislative seats), and above all must be personally involved in fund raising. The Michigan Republican Party is a good example of one that was run by the governor during the term of John Engler in the 1990s. He was active in fund raising and recruiting and played a key role in picking the party chair. One staff member said, "We're part of the governor's team. This place lives and dies with John Engler" (Weissert 1997).

Governors do not always succeed in picking the party chair without a struggle. Florida is an example of a state where a Democratic Party chair frequently "serves as the political arm of the governor and looks out for the governor's political interests" (Kelley 1997, 63). Gov. Lawton Chiles, however, on one occasion failed in his effort to have the central committee select his choice—the lieutenant governor—to be party chair. But in 1995 Chiles succeeded in getting a law passed by the legislature that increased the voting power of the governor and other public officials on the central committee from 2 to 42 percent (Kelley 1997). In Kansas the governors of both parties have sometimes had difficulty picking the party chair. Democratic governor Joan Finney, elected in 1990, got her choice as party chair only by agreeing to keep the party executive director in his post. She continued to face a struggle for power with some leaders of the state party and leaders in the legislature. On the Republican side, Gov. Bill Graves, elected in 1994, was unable to pick the party chair; the central committee, controlled by the Christian right, chose a chair who disagreed sharply with the governor on the conservative social agenda (Aistrup and Bannister 1997).

In some cases, the governor does not seek to select the party chair. For example some party chairs have served for several terms and are well entrenched in office. The incoming governor may decide that it is better to take advantage of the party chair's experience and skills rather than using up political capital trying to find a replacement—particularly if the chair has proved to be helpful and effective in the governor's campaign for election. John Bailey dominated the Connecticut Democratic Party for many years, serving as its chair from 1946 until his death in 1975 and exercising power independent of the governor.

Some governors have been nominated and elected with little help from the party and may have won nomination over the opposition of party leaders. They are likely to believe that there is little to be gained from trying to work with the established party leadership and no point in trying to win control over the party organization.

Massachusetts is an example of a state in which both parties are rather fragmented and governors of both parties have sometimes taken little interest in them. Democrat Michael Dukakis, elected as governor in 1974 and 1982, was unable to choose his own party chair in either term, and Democrat Edward King, who defeated Dukakis in the 1978 primary and was elected governor, never tried to control the party. Republican William Weld, elected in 1990, had a good but not close working relationship with the state committee and deliberately stayed out of the selection process for a new chair after his reelection in 1994 (Mileur 1997).

In Louisiana there has seldom been a strong relationship between the governor and his party. The state's unusual nonpartisan primary helps to explain the gap between the party and the governor, but it also results from the personality and strategy of various governors. Democratic governor Edwin Edwards, who served four terms between 1972 and 1996, built his own electoral coalitions without party involvement and took no interest in the party or party organization building. Recent Republican governors have also remained largely aloof from the party organization (Parent 1997). During Republican governor Mike Foster's first term (1996–1999), he often feuded with Mike Francis, the state party chair. Foster had the support of many elected officials and party activists who were fiscal conservatives, but a majority of those on the state party central committee were social conservatives, some of whom were linked to the Christian Coalition. Early in 2000, at the start of Foster's second term, his supporters launched a campaign—with his approval—to win control of the central committee, whose members are chosen by the voters.

A party chair who is not the governor's choice, or the chair of a party that does not control the governorship, has to build a base of support. In parties that are divided into factions, and particularly those split into ideological factions, the chair's job may be very difficult. A party out of power lacks the unifying leadership usually provided by the governor, and it has no state-level patronage to distribute. As the next election approaches, the chair may have difficulty handling the various demands of party leaders who are running for various offices. If the party loses ground in an election, it is easy to blame the party chair.

The success of state chairs, like that of any political leader, depends largely on their ability to build a strong base of political support. If they have been chosen by the governor, their success is of course heavily dependent on the governor. About three-fourths of the state party chairs are elected for two-year terms, and the rest are elected for four years; but the average tenure is less than three years (Bibby 1992, 98). Party chairs often step down before their term is up. This may be involuntary if they are being blamed for the party's election losses or if the governor wants a different chair. The chair may resign voluntarily to devote more time to his or her other occupation or sometimes to run for public office. An extreme example of turnover can be found in the Kentucky Democratic Party, which, over a period of seventeen years (1979–1996), had thirteen different chairs, all chosen by governors (Miller and Jewell 1990, 1997). None of them stayed in office long enough to build their own base of support or even to learn much about how to do their job.

The success of party chairs depends on a wide range of political skills. Chairs must learn how to build the trust of a wide variety of officeholders and other politicians. They must work to unify the party and overcome whatever factionalism exists. They must hire a capable staff, master modern campaign technology, and become effective spokespersons for the party.

Perhaps the highest priority for a party chair is to raise lots of money, or to find others who know how to raise money, for the party. The chair of the Minnesota Republican Party going into the 1998 election was Bill Cooper, a banker with close ties to other bankers and businesspersons who knew how to raise money. This was a major reason why Cooper was able to persuade all of the candidates running for statewide office to sign a pledge that they would support in the primary whichever candidates were endorsed by the Republican convention (a topic covered in more detail in Chapter 4).

The state central committee, which generally meets every month or so, is the governing body of the political party, although basic changes in party rules and bylaws must usually be approved by the state convention, which meets every couple of years. As we have seen, the central committee formally chooses the party chair and other party officials, although in practice the governor may select the party chair. There is a lot of variation from state to state in the size and makeup of the central committee and its selection. Most central committees have about fifty members. The larger the committee, the more likely it is that the committee will meet less often and most of the work will be done by an executive committee. The New York and Pennsylvania parties both have central committees of three hundred members or more. The California central committees each have over one thousand members, and the committees meet only every year or two. The most important function of the California Democratic central committee has been to endorse state and legislative candidates before the primary.

Members of the central committee are chosen by a wide variety of methods in the state parties. Some public officeholders such as members of Congress and statewide officials, along with some party officials such as the chairs of county committees, may serve ex officio on the central committee. State conventions, perhaps voting by districts, may elect members. County, state or district committees often choose some members. In some states, party voters at the local level choose members to the central committee, often in a primary election.

Legal Regulation of Party Structure

In thirty-eight states some aspects of the legal structure of state and local party organizations are specified by law, often in considerable detail. These laws often mandate the composition of the state party central committee, the required number of meetings, and the method for selecting central committee members, including whether they are to be chosen by voters or by other party committees or conventions. Most state laws specify what party unit is authorized to fill vacancies if a person who has won nomination dies or resigns before the election. Seven of the twelve states that do not regulate party organization are in the South or border areas where there has traditionally been less state control over the parties (Appleton and Ward 1997, 372–376).

State regulation of political parties began at the turn of the century as a result of the Progressive movement. Progressive reformers criticized the state parties for not being operated in a democratic manner and for being under the control of state and local bosses. Leon Epstein describes political parties as being regulated like "public utilities" (1986, chap. 6). The laws that specified, often in great detail, how the parties were to be organized and operated were designed to make them more democratic and to minimize boss control. The Progressives were also committed to the direct primary, to replace caucuses and conventions for nominating a party's candidates. The laws in virtually all the states today require the use of the direct primary and specify in some detail how candidates who appear on a party ticket are to be nominated (discussed further in Chapter 4).

California is a good example of a state where the law specified party organization in great detail. The membership of the state central committee was carefully spelled out in a fashion that gave state legislators a large voice in it. The time and even the place of committee meetings were specified; the state chair was limited to a two-year term, and the position was even required to rotate between northern and southern California. After a group of local party committees and political scientists challenged the California law in the courts, the U.S. Supreme Court in 1989 decided that it was unconstitutional for the state to dictate how political parties should be organized (*Eu, Secretary of State of California v. San Francisco County Democratic Central Committee* 1989).

We might expect that state party organizations would rush to take advantage of this newly won freedom to organize however they choose, but there are only a few signs that state parties are doing so. A limited number of changes were made in California law. Oregon changed its laws to provide that the parties could choose whether or not to follow state laws regulating party organization, but the parties have generally followed these laws (Karp and Banducci 1997). Both parties in New Jersey responded to the *Eu* decision by making a number of changes in party structure and explicitly describing the party's role in providing services to candidates. The *Eu* decision also legalized the New Jersey counties' practice of making endorsements in state and local contests for nomination (Salmore and Salmore 1997).

The laws in about two-thirds of the states still specify how members of the state central committee are selected, and in almost one-third of the states the timing of central committee meetings is specified (Appleton and Ward 1997). Some parties may be satisfied with the system they are using, and some have developed informal ways of avoiding some of the problems imposed by state law. In the long run, however, we will probably see greater variety and perhaps some streamlining of party organizations.

Party Organization at the Local Level

The basic unit of local party organization is usually the county committee, although in some northeastern states where counties are less important, the city or town committee plays this role. The county committee traditionally has been very important because there are a number of elected county officials, usually elected on a partisan ballot. These men and women are usually powerful figures in the local party organization, and the county courthouse is still an important source of patronage and contracts in most states. The county is also the basis for defining some congressional, state legislative, and judicial districts (though the latter may have nonpartisan races).

The county committee is often made up of persons who chair committees at the township, ward, or precinct level; in some cases party voters may directly elect the town committee. County committees are much smaller in rural, sparsely populated counties and are much larger in major urban areas. To give an extreme example, in Bronx, New York, the Democratic county committee has 3,750 local committee members, elected by the state Assembly district leadership. The chair of the county committee, elected by its members, is usually a powerful figure in local politics—whether in a rural or metropolitan area. The county chair is usually the contact person between the state party organizations and local leaders and constituents. Sometimes if there are factional divisions on the committee, those members who are most loyal to the governor will try to elect a chair who will have a similar loyalty. For the party in power a county chair who has the confidence of the governor is likely to have more influence in county politics and will be in a better position to hand out patronage. The county chair may benefit personally from legal fees, contracts, or other perks of the job.

For the party that holds power at the county level, the persons holding major elective county offices, such as the county clerk and sheriff, will try to play major roles in the county committee and use the organization primarily to assure their reelection. County officials are usually able to hire staff members without having to worry about civil service procedures, and these staff members can also be expected to work for the party and its local and state candidates. For the party out of power, the county committee has the responsibility of trying to recruit a full set of candidates for elective county offices in an effort to gain control of offices that can control patronage and contracts.

From the viewpoint of the state party organization, it is important, in as many counties as possible—and not only safe counties, to have organizations that are capable of campaigning effectively for statewide, congressional, and state legislative candidates and not just for the county clerk and sheriff. When there are contested primaries for statewide or congressional office, candidates will try to cultivate allies among the party leaders and activists in each county. Even if the leaders are not willing to make a preprimary commitment to a candidate, they may be willing to take them around the county, introducing them to local leaders and activists, some of whom might be willing to work in the campaign. It is worth remembering that, even when campaigns are dominated by television advertising, efforts to build a local group of activists in order to register voters, hand out leaflets, and get out the vote are still important, particularly in close elections.

Surveys of local party leaders in a number of states indicate that many local organizations are well organized at the county level and generally were better organized and more active by the late 1990s than they had been in the early 1980s. As we would expect, the level of organizational activity was greater during election campaigns. They were particularly active in distributing campaign literature, organizing fund raisers and campaign events, distributing yard signs, and conducting registration drives and GOTV efforts. Local candidates considered these last two activities the most valuable ones performed by local organizations (Frendreis and Gitelson 1999; Gibson, Frendreis, and Vertz 1989).

In theory, the precinct is the basic building block of the party organization, and in every precinct each party will have a group of several activists who are prepared to work hard for the party. In practice, as we have suggested, there may be many gaps in the precinct structure, particularly for the party that is in the minority in the county or city. Precinct members may sometimes be elected by voters, are sometimes elected in a party caucus in the precinct, and in practice are probably often recruited by the chair of the county or city committee.

If a party is well organized down to the precinct level, particularly in urban areas, the precinct captain may work hard to stay in touch with residents. In an election year the captain may also distribute some literature door to door and make sure residents are registered and that they can get to the polls. This kind of personalized leadership is becoming much less common in the precinct. It is even more rare for precinct leaders to help individuals solve problems in dealing with local government—an important function that was performed by the traditional party machines.

At a minimum a precinct leader might be expected to serve as a contact person with the party organization during a campaign, finding persons to hand out leaflets, getting yard signs put up, and helping individual candidates who want to campaign door to door in the precinct. In many precincts even these functions are not consistently performed by anyone. It can be very helpful for an individual candidate running for a local or legislative office who wants to campaign personally in the neighborhoods to be able to contact someone who is familiar with the areas and perhaps can even recruit a couple of helpers.

If precinct organizations are declining in effectiveness and even in existence, one reason is that very few persons have the time and the commitment to work at the precinct level, probably without any tangible reward. Party activists who are committed to a campaign would probably prefer to work at county or city campaign headquarters. If the party has a comfortable majority in the area, the closest races may be in primary elections, and precinct activities likely are organized by individual candidates.

A major reason for the decline in precinct activity is the change in campaign style. Campaigns for national, state, congressional, and sometimes state legislative office are dominated by television advertising, which appears to be the most direct way of influencing voters. There seems to be a growing recognition, however, that television advertising—sometimes called the "air war"—needs to be supplemented by a "ground war"—the effort to get voters registered and get out the vote. But it is becoming more impracticable to reach voters by going door to door—it is hard to find voters at home, they won't come to the door after it gets dark, and it is hard to gain access to those living in apartments and condos. The warriors in the ground wars are those persons—volunteers or paid workers—who work the phone banks or stuff and stamp the letters and leaflets to be mailed out. Phone banks, in particular, can be used to remind persons to register, to give a brief plug for a candidate, to conduct polls of voters, and to get out the vote on election day.

Organizational Linkages to Party-Related Groups

Up to this point we have described the state and local party organizations simply in terms of their formal structure of committees and the persons who serve on them. But a number of other groups are directly involved in party affairs and are frequently important to the party's success, and many individuals have significant influence on the party's activities and decisions, whether or not they are a member of any party committee. For example, at the state level, there is likely to be a Young Democrats Club, a Republican Women's Club, and perhaps clubs representing some ethnic or racial groups that are prevalent in the state.

Those persons who hold elective public office are important to a party's success: the governor and other state officials, U.S. senators and representatives, and the leaders of the legislature. Similarly, in the local party, members of the state legislature and those holding partisan office in the county, city, or town are usually important figures. The mayor of a large city often plays a major role in the party organization at the state level.

We have already talked about governors and the fact that they often have the opportunity to select the party chair and to play an active role in party affairs if they choose to do so. Whether or not a governor chooses to exercise that role, he or she is widely regarded as the spokesperson for the party and the one who sets its policy agenda.

We might think that U.S. senators and representatives would focus most of their attention on the national party and developments in Washington, but this is not necessarily the case.

By definition, members of Congress have their roots in the state. Many of them have served in a statewide office like attorney general, in the state legislature, or as mayor of a city before going to Washington. Some have even served as governor before being elected to the Senate. They return to the state every week or so, even when Congress is in session, meeting with groups and individuals and often speaking at party meetings. Although they are often ex officio members of the central committee, their party influence does not depend on this but on their position as a member of Congress.

If their party does not control the governorship, members of Congress are the most important and visible elected officials the party has, and they are likely to have an even greater influence over party affairs. Members of Congress have assets and resources that are important to the party. Each has a substantial number of party activists who regularly work in their campaigns and may be willing to work in other party campaigns. Each has a long list of persons who have contributed funds to their campaigns, a list they may or may not be willing to share with party headquarters. When the party does not control the governorship, sometimes rivalries develop among its members of Congress, rivalries that can be damaging to the state party. The Kentucky Republican Party has had considerable success in electing their candidates to the U.S. House and Senate but has not elected a governor since 1967. At times it has appeared that the Republicans in Congress have been much more interested in protecting their fiefdoms than in helping to elect a governor (Miller and Jewell 1990).

Some senators in recent years have become de facto the dominant figure in their party. In 1994 the New York Republican Party was in a slump. It had not elected a governor since 1970. Its last two challengers to Democratic governor Mario Cuomo had been dismal failures, with the 1990 candidate barely able to beat out a third-party candidate for second place. When the party leaders started the search for someone who might be able to beat Cuomo, Sen. Alfonse D'Amato took charge. Once he became convinced that a relatively obscure state senator, George Pataki, was the best prospect, D'Amato worked vigorously and skillfully to win over the other party leaders and then engineered Pataki's endorsement by the party convention. D'Amato's choice defeated Cuomo for the governorship. In Louisiana, a very different state, there was a vacuum in Louisiana Democratic leadership in the 1990s because Edwin Edwards, who dominated state politics during four terms as governor, built his own political coalition and paid no attention to the Democratic Party organizations. Sen. John Breaux stepped in, building a faction of supporters within the Democratic Party and putting together a party staff and establishing a party platform that reflected his own centrist position in the national party (Parent 1997).

The state legislative leaders are another source of leadership in state parties. Several of the leaders often have seats on the state central committee. Occasionally a legislative leader is picked as chair of the state party committee. One reason for legislative leaders to develop strong linkages with various elements of the party is that they often run for statewide offices such as governor or senator. By virtue of their leadership position, they have a major influence over the record on issues compiled by the legislative parties, particularly if their party does not control the governorship. They also develop close contacts with some of the interest groups most closely allied with the party.

Legislative leaders are also important figures in the state party because, in almost all states, they play crucial roles in the legislative campaign committees that raise funds and distribute them to legislative candidates. The legislative campaign committees (described in detail in Chapter 7) are an important component of the state party's campaign funding effort. The campaign committees are run by the legislative party leaders, who play a large role in raising the funds, very often from interest groups, and who usually play a decisive role in allocating the funds among legislative candidates.

Among the state party systems, there are some variations in the division of responsibilities for financial support of legislative candidates between the legislative campaign committees and the state party headquarters. In some parties the legislative campaign committees support legislative candidates while the state party is raising funds to support other candidates, such as those for statewide office. In some parties the two groups divide up the responsibility for legislative candidates, often coordinating closely. In a few parties the state party handles this responsibility almost entirely. Capturing control of the state legislature is almost as important a priority for the state party as winning the governorship, and therefore fundraising for legislative candidates is an important component of the party's total fund-raising effort; however, the responsibility may be divided between particular party units.

Finally there are the Democratic and Republican Party activists. Not everyone who has ever worked on a campaign can be considered an activist. We would use this term to describe persons who work in political campaigns with some regularity over a period of several years, working directly with state and local units of the party and working directly for candidates. Most candidates have some workers who are personally loyal to them and perhaps never work for any other candidate. But many of those who join a primary or general election campaign for a Republican candidate have worked for other Republican candidates in the past and will do so in the future. Some of these serve on a party committee, but there are more activists than there are members of party committees, and effective work on a campaign is really more important than simply sitting on a party committee—state or local. The delegates, usually a thousand or more, who attend the state party convention held every couple of years represent a good cross section of party activists. Later in this chapter we will say more about party activists: what motivates them to become active in politics and work in campaigns, what are their characteristics, and what are their viewpoints.

A political party tries to win support from a number of interest groups, but a few of these groups are so important to the party that they might be considered allies or compatriots. Close linkages between the national parties and a variety of interest groups became increasingly important during the 1990s. A similar, though less publicized, trend is occurring at the state level as state governments are dealing with more economic and social issues of direct concern to these groups.

In most states where labor unions have any political strength at all, they have been closely aligned with the Democratic Party for many years. Unions usually endorse Democratic candidates and provide funding to the party, to its candidates, or both. Many of the delegates to Democratic conventions and similar meetings belong to labor unions, and union members may have seats on important party committees. The unions run television ads supporting Democratic candidates and sometimes opposing Republicans. A candidate for governor or for a seat in Congress needs union support to have a good chance of being nominated and elected. In addition to labor unions, teachers' organizations, feminist and prochoice groups, and environmental organizations are developing linkages to state Democratic Parties. These groups have considerable input into the writing of the state Democratic Party platforms, and Democratic governors and legislators must take seriously their legislative demands.

In similar fashion the Republican Party has some close alliances with interest groups. In a number of states the Christian right is strong enough that its loyalists win substantial numbers of seats on Republican committees, help write the platform, and may have veto power over candidates who fail to support their position on key issues. State Republican Parties are developing closer ties to business groups such as state branches of the National Federation of Independent Businesses and close ties to state branches of the National Rifle Association, as well as to antiabortion groups and organizations working for lower taxes.

PARTY WORKERS

If a political party is going to be effective, it needs a large number of activists willing to work for the party at the state and local levels and it must have incentives to attract and keep them. Traditionally the political parties attracted workers by offering them various forms of patronage, and they maintained party discipline by the threat of reducing or removing such patronage. In recent years, as patronage has become less available and less important, parties have had to find new incentives.

In most party organizations today the incentives most likely to attract workers are purposive ones—the opportunity to influence policy by working for a party's candidates who share their views on public issues. The fact that the party's most committed workers are usually strongly issue oriented has an impact on the stands the party takes on issues and the types of candidates it is likely to nominate. This may also be a source of factionalism within the party.

Party Machines and Patronage

The state and local party organizations operating today are fundamentally different from the party machines we would have found fifty to one hundred years ago, largely because the incentives offered to those who work for the party have changed. The traditional rewards for party workers in the late 1800s and the first half of the twentieth century were material incentives, particularly the large numbers of patronage jobs provided by local and state party machines. Because party workers were primarily motivated by the desire to get and keep jobs, they could be disciplined by the machines. The harder a person worked, the better job that person could get. If a worker did not do what was expected, such as failing to carry a precinct for the party's candidates, that person was either demoted or fired.

At a time when governments provided few social services, the party machines provided a variety of services to lower income voters and particularly to immigrants.

They provided assistance when people were short of funds or needed rent money, helped some of them find jobs, and intervened if they got in trouble with the law. In return for such services, the machine expected them to vote regularly for that party's candidates. They also worked to develop strong personal and ethnic loyalties among the voters and often discouraged voting by persons who were not loyal to the organization. The machines exercised political power because they were able to deliver the votes, in both primaries and general elections, to those candidates who were loyal to the organization (Sorauf and Beck 1988, 83–90).

Local urban machines were in their heyday at the end of the nineteenth century. The most powerful organizations were in northeastern and midwestern cities: Tammany Hall in New York, the Hague Machine in Jersey City, and the Pendergast Machine in Kansas City, for example. In the past few decades, machine politics has declined and almost disappeared. Some of the most corrupt party machines have been decimated because the party bosses have ended up in jail. In some cities reform movements defeated political machines at the polls. Most states have adopted civil service laws that sharply reduce the number of jobs that can be given to loyal party workers.

The last major political machine, which remained strong until the 1970s, was the Cook County Democratic Party organization in Chicago, which was run by Mayor Richard J. Daley from 1955 until his death in 1976. Daley inherited a machine that dated back to the turn of the century, and he developed it into one of the best-organized and most powerful machines the nation had ever seen. It was estimated that Daley's organization controlled 35,000 patronage jobs and had access to 10,000 more in the private economy (Green 1997; Sorauf and Beck 1988, 83–90; see also Rakove 1975).

Neale Peirce (1972, 347) describes how Daley's machine operated at the peak of its power:

> Under this authoritarian, hierarchical organization, some 500 patronage jobs are allotted to each ward. Virtually every precinct committeeman has a city job; the public, in effect, subsidizes the system by salaries paid to patronage workers. Many ward committeemen own insurance agencies and do a land-office business with retailers and real estate owners who see an obvious way to get access to City Hall. But the ward and precinct committeemen, in turn, are under tremendous pressures to contribute and work on election day, or they can expect to be thrown out on the street. The machine knows what they are doing, and it brooks no election day inefficiency—or dissent.

Mayor Daley not only ran the city of Chicago, but he also played a powerful role in state Democratic politics, choosing candidates to run for statewide and congressional offices. He was actively involved in the nomination and election of Democratic presidential candidates, most notably John Kennedy's election in 1960.

During this same period a few other political leaders played powerful roles in state political party organizations. Earlier in the chapter we mentioned John Bailey, who dominated the Connecticut Democratic Party as its chair from 1946 until his death in 1975. During this time Bailey was instrumental in nominating and electing four Democratic governors, who served for twenty-four years. He also worked effectively to get their bills passed in the legislature. Bailey owed much of his success to his skill in building alliances with labor unions and ethnic minorities and particularly with the mayors and other political leaders of the cities and towns. Bailey was a skilled political negotiator who made effective use of patronage to keep these leaders loyal to him (Lockard 1959, chap. 9; Lieberman 1966).

The collapse of political machines has not made party workers insignificant in political campaigns. But patronage plays a much smaller role in attracting workers, and it is much more difficult for a party organization to discipline this new breed of campaign workers.

Incentives to Work for the Party

At a time when the outcome of elections often seems to be determined by the air war—which candidate has the best advertisements on television and enough money to run them repeatedly—it is easy to forget that the success of campaigns depends in no small part on the effectiveness of the ground war. There is a lot of work to be done: staffing party headquarters, raising campaign money, turning out voters when the candidate comes to town, putting up yard signs, mailing out flyers by the thousands, getting potential voters registered, calling voters in the closing days of the campaign. Lots of work requires lots of workers, most of whom are volunteers because there is not usually enough money for large paid staffs.

How can the party attract enough volunteers to get the jobs done, particularly during election campaigns? Every volunteer organization finds it increasingly difficult to attract individuals who have the time, energy, and interest to play an active role in the organization. Most adults under age sixty-five are employed, and many couples are trying to bring up children while both husband and wife hold full-time jobs. Campaign work is often boring and sometimes discouraging. Who wants to spend the evening making phone calls to voters, night after night, while the spouse or a grandparent looks after the children?

As a practical matter, we know that individuals are more likely to play some role in a campaign if someone from a political party calls them and asks them to do so. They are more likely, for example, to work for a political party, to attend a campaign rally or meeting, or to agree to display yard signs if they have been contacted and asked to do so (Wielhouwer 1999). It is likely that, if the party headquarters is trying to find active workers, they will call someone who has worked in some campaign in the past; but such persons may not volunteer to work unless they are contacted. On the other hand, campaign workers who are trying to find someone to display a yard sign, which involves a much smaller commitment of time and effort, may simply drive up and down the street looking for someone who might be willing to have a sign put on their front lawn.

What kinds of people are willing to do significant amounts of work for political parties and candidates, and what kinds of incentives attract them? We know what kinds of people become party workers from a number of studies (Abramowitz, McGlennon, and Rapoport 1986; Miller and Jewell 1990, chap.6). Roughly half are men and half are women, and most are between thirty and sixty years old. Over half are college graduates and about one-third have done postgraduate work, a higher proportion than was true a generation ago. Party workers, and particularly Republican workers, have incomes well above the national average, partly because of their higher education levels. A large majority of party workers have lived in the state for more than twenty years, though the figure would be lower in some western states that are rapidly gaining population. Better-educated, higher-income persons, ages thirty to sixty, should be particularly valuable workers for the party; but almost by definition, they also should be the busiest group of people with the least time available for party work.

To attract busy people to work in politics, a party must offer strong incentives. These incentives are changing, as American society is changing, and these changes have important implications for the party system. Many kinds of incentives attract persons to work in politics, and they are not entirely different from the incentives for other voluntary organizations. Some persons, for example, may be persuaded by a friend who is already involved in such an activity. But because politics is a different kind of enterprise, certain kinds of incentives are particularly important for those working in politics.

Kinds of incentives. Material, solidary, and purposive incentives are the three most important ones motivating persons to work for the party and its candidates (Clark and Wilson 1961). *Material incentives* are tangible rewards, such as jobs and contracts. *Solidary incentives* are intangible and perhaps psychological rewards that result from participation in a group. *Purposive incentives* are related to policy; party activists work in campaigns to elect officeholders who are committed to policies they agree with. Over the past fifty years or so, as patronage has dried up and material incentives have become less important, purposive incentives have grown more important in attracting and keeping individuals who are willing to work in party politics and campaign for candidates.

Declining importance of material incentives. We have explained how patronage, in the form of jobs or other benefits, has steadily declined in importance as traditional party machines have faded away. The kinds of patronage jobs that may be available in some states and localities are low-level and sometimes part-time jobs (like the highway repair crew or toll booth personnel) that are of little interest to today's upper middle class party volunteers. The most important development has been a series of decisions by the U.S. Supreme Court from 1976 to 1990 declaring that it is unconstitutional for a government to hire, promote, or fire a person for political or partisan reasons. Only high-level policy-making positions remain exempt from this principle (*Elrod v. Burns,* 1976; *Rutan v. Republican Party,* 1990).

Some kinds of patronage are still available and may interest the most valuable party workers who help manage campaigns and raise money for elections. Sometimes businesspersons who have worked for the party may be able to get special consideration when contracts are given out or when government regulations are being drafted that might affect their company. Lawyers may be hired to represent a government agency in a judicial hearing.

The governor has the opportunity to fill hundreds of positions on various boards and commissions, positions that do not pay anything but that may be interesting or prestigious or that satisfy the person's yearning to perform a public service. A position on the board of trustees of a university is a good example. There may even be a few "harmless" fringe benefits. Until a few years ago, the governor frequently appointed political allies and big campaign contributors to the University of Kentucky Board of Trustees, whose members receive choice seats to all of the home basketball games—an important benefit in Kentucky.

In states where some forms of patronage still exist, its practical value to the governor and the governor's party varies with circumstances. Some governors scorn the patronage system, and some do not have the skill or patience to make effective use of it. A skillful governor may use some forms of patronage to strengthen his or her position and the party organization. Where patronage has some importance, a party may be severely handicapped in rebuilding its political fortunes by losing the governorship and its access to patronage.

There remain some differences among the states, not only in how strictly contracts and appointments are regulated but also in the traditional norms and public attitudes. There is more tolerance of various kinds of patronage in Illinois, Indiana, and Kentucky than there is in Minnesota or California.

Continuing importance of solidary incentives. Most of us join a club or a service, religious, or professional organization because we are interested in the purposes and activities of the group but also because we enjoy participating in a group with others who share our interests. We gain a sense of belonging and accomplishment from our joint efforts. The solidary incentives to work in politics are very much the same, and there is the special sense of accomplishment that comes from working in a winning election campaign. Long ago the traditional party machines used to run a clubhouse and organize social events for their members. Today's party organizations try to get party loyalists involved through cocktail parties, barbecues, fish fries, picnics, and annual dinners where awards are presented to star performers in the organization. Whenever we attend state party conventions, we realize how much the delegates, some of whom have been attending for years, enjoy the chance to renew old acquaintances and make new friends, while attending the dinners and enjoying the hospitality suites maintained by candidates. Solidary incentives alone may not be enough to keep people active in political activity, but they help to reinforce other motivations.

Growing importance of purposive incentives. As material incentives decline in importance, it is clear that those who become political activists are increasingly motivated by purposive incentives. Because they have a strong interest in public policies, they are willing to work for the party and help elect the candidates who are committed to the policies they support and share their ideological beliefs. A survey was conducted in eleven states of delegates to party conventions that chose delegates to national conventions; they were asked about their reasons for being actively involved in the campaign. The most common responses were "to work for issues I feel very strongly about" and "to support a particular candidate I believe in" (Abramowitz, McGlennon, and Rapoport 1986). Kentucky Democrats who were actively involved in gubernatorial primaries (1979–1987), responding to questions about their motivations, also emphasized supporting a particular candidate and working for issues they felt strongly about. Even in a state with a strong tradition of patronage, few of these Kentucky Democratic activists mentioned state jobs, contracts, or careers (Miller and Jewell 1990, 139–144).

Some party activists first became actively involved in interest groups supporting particular causes and interests and then became active in parties to advance those causes and interests. At the national level, many persons first became involved in political campaigns because of a particular presidential candidate, like Dwight Eisenhower, John or Robert Kennedy, Barry Goldwater, George McGovern, or Ronald Reagan. Many of them held strong ideological beliefs and supported presidential candidates who espoused those beliefs. It is not uncommon for persons who began as supporters of presidential candidates to become party activists, working in state and local as well as national campaigns.

Impact of Ideologically Oriented Activists on Parties

Aldrich (1995) argues that the approach to politics taken by activists with purposive motivations is fundamentally different from that taken by those with material motivations. "Policy-motivated activists are typically under less pressure to support any particular candidate or party, . . . deriving benefits only from the policies espoused or enacted. As a result they are more nearly true volunteers—free to offer their time, effort, and services, or to withhold them, as they see fit" (182). These activists often will choose to work only for particular candidates they closely agree with rather than work in a broader range of party campaigns (270).

Party activists who have strong ideological commitments may be a source of both strength and weakness for the political party. They may be dedicated activists, willing to work harder and longer than the average party worker, particularly in races where the party's candidate shares their ideological commitment. But if such a candidate is defeated, these party workers may not be willing to work in campaigns for other party candidates who do not measure up to their ideals. We have noted that some activists with such a motivation have come into partisan politics from an interest group and, if there is a conflict between party and group, their first loyalty may be to the group. V. O. Key, Jr. (1958, 241) pointed out this problem: "The top party leadership must try to restrain the extremism within party ranks . . . [and] must seek to hold together the divergent and often conflicting elements."

Most persons who are active in parties—working in campaigns and attending conventions—have strong ideological beliefs and commitments, according to a number of studies (Erikson, Wright, and McIver 1993, chap. 5; Aldrich 1995, 171–173, 186–17; Green, Jackson, and Clayton 1999). This leads to a situation where Republican activists are more conservative on a number of policy issues than the average Republican voter and Democratic activists are more liberal than the average Democratic voter. This is not an entirely new development in state politics. One 1972 study (Montjoy, Shaffer, and Weber 1980) of the county party chairs in the fifty states showed that on some issues there were larger differences between the views of Democratic and Republican chairs than there were between Democratic and Republican rank and file. The gap between the party chairs and rank and file was larger in the Republican Party than among Democrats.

Table 3-2 illustrates this point. The data compare the views on ideology and issues in 1996 of Democratic and Republican delegates to national conventions (based on surveys conducted by John Jackson) and Democratic and Republican voters (surveyed in the National Election Study) (Green, Jackson, and Clayton 1999). Because most delegates to national conventions are activists in their own state parties, the data presumably also reflect differences at the state level between activists and voters.

The data on ideology and the data on the four issues in the table both show large gaps between Democratic and Republican delegates and smaller gaps between voters identified with the two parties. The rank order from the most liberal to the most conservative position always runs from Democratic delegates to Democratic voters to Republican voters to Republican delegates.

Table 3-2 Comparing the Views of Party Convention Delegates and Voters Identified with a Party on Ideology and Issues (percentages)

Issues	Democratic Delegates	Democratic Voters	Republican Delegates	Republican Voters
Ideology				
Liberal	51	37	0	4
Moderate	45	46	18	26
Conservative	4	17	82	70
Health insurance				
Government insurance	71	49	4	16
Private insurance	14	27	90	62
Government services				
Continue present level	79	37	5	13
Reduce level	9	19	88	60
Government aid to minorities				
In favor	68	25	11	5
Opposed	17	43	76	73
Abortion				
Pro-choice	82	52	19	32
Pro-life	8	31	68	51

Source: Based on data in John C. Green, John S. Jackson, and Nancy L. Clayton, "Issue Networks and Party Elites in 1996," in *The State of the Parties,* 3d ed., edited by John C. Green and Daniel M. Shea (Lanham, Md.: Rowman and Littlefield, 1999).

Note: Figures on policy issues do not add to 100% because those who are neutral, take an intermediate position, or have no opinion are omitted.

Within each party, the gaps between delegates and voters are relatively small on the liberal-conservative alignment. Republican voters are more strongly conservative than Democratic voters are liberal on three of the four policy issues. The exception is the abortion issue, on which Democrats are more pro-choice and Republicans more pro-life, both by margins of roughly five to three.

Bibby (1999, 1998) believes that because of these trends both state and national political parties are undergoing fundamental changes and becoming networks of issue-oriented activists. In many state party organizations there is a wide gap between the activists, who are strongly committed to ideological principles, and elected officials, who have to take more moderate, pragmatic stands on issues to represent the views of their constituents and get reelected. A study of opinions on policy issues held by elites and voters in each of the states shows that in each party elected officials have viewpoints that are more moderate and closer to those of the voters than are the viewpoints of party activists (Erikson, Wright, and McIver 1993, chap. 5). These differences become evident when state convention delegates, including elected officials, are trying to agree on a party platform.

In Chapter 4, where we explore the politics of the nominating process, we will point out that party activists play a particularly active role in contested primaries that will choose the party's candidates and in conventions, held in some states, that endorse candidates before the primary election. If they are supporting candidates who are closest to their (sometimes extreme) ideological views, party activists may help to nominate a candidate who is not moderate enough to win the general election.

All political parties face the potential problem of factionalism. In the past, intraparty factions were based on ethnic, racial, or religious groups or on loyalty to individual candidates. Increasingly, serious factional divisions are based on ideological and policy differences. In the 1960s and 1970s some state Democratic Parties had serious splits between liberals and conservatives; except during the 1964 Goldwater campaign, Republicans were less likely to be split over ideology.

But since the mid-1980s state Republican Parties have had more serious splits over ideology and policy. There are often deep divisions over the issue of abortion policy. In a growing number of state Republican Parties one faction is led by the religious right, which has a strong moral and social agenda, while the other faction is likely to be more concerned with economic issues. In a number of states it is Republican officeholders, sometimes including the governor, who lead the more moderate, fiscal-conservative wing, while the party chair and a majority of the state central committee are aligned with the social conservatives and the Christian right.

Earlier in this chapter we described such ideological conflicts in both the Kansas and Louisiana Republican Parties that made it difficult or impossible for the governor to control the state committee. In Chapter 4 we will describe how a similar split in the Minnesota Republican Party undermined the party's efforts to endorse a strong gubernatorial candidate. The more conservative wing of the Republican Party in Washington State gained a dominant position in the party organization in the mid-1990s (Appleton and Depoorter 1997). In Iowa the religious right began making inroads into the Republican Party in 1988 and gained control of the state central committee in 1992. But Terry Branstad, the Republican governor from 1993 through 1998, was closely allied with this coalition and therefore was able to control the central committee (Trish 1997).

In Virginia conflicts between supporters of the Christian right and more traditional economic conservatives within the Republican Party date back to the 1980s. In both 1993 and 1994 the more conservative wing mobilized huge numbers of supporters to dominate the state Republican nominating conventions, where they nominated some very conservative candidates who failed to get elected. However, George Allen, who had a broader base of support in the party, was nominated and elected governor in 1993 (McGlennon 1997).

In Colorado, where most Republican activists are clearly conservative, splits have occurred between the Christian right and more moderate conservatives. These differences came to a head during the 1998 election cycle. For many years moderate conservatives ran the party organization, but in early 1997 Steve Curtis, a leader of the Christian right wing, became the Republican Party chair. Critics charged that Curtis used his position as chair to mobilize party activists in his faction to attend party caucuses that endorse candidates before the primary and that he worked for the nomination of candidates associated with the Christian right, particularly in legislative primaries. The struggle within the party continued during the fall campaign, and a few weeks before election day Curtis announced that he had doubts about supporting Bill Owens, his party's candidate for governor, because of ideological differences. Owens was elected governor nevertheless, and a few months after he took office Curtis was replaced as party chair.

MEASURING PARTY STRENGTH

In view of the discussion so far, it is clear that parties are not decomposing as was predicted but have been adapting to the technology-driven society in which they find themselves. Candidates make use of the party organizations because they can help them with three of their major needs, as we have seen. A party can groom and help the candidate of its choice win the primary and become the party's nominee. Second, the party can help the candidate win electoral office by providing campaign workers, access to valuable resources and services, and assistance in mobilizing voters. Third, once a party's candidate gets elected, the party provides the organizational strength to govern, consisting of the party's officeholders in the legislative and executive branches.

Parties differ across the states in the degree to which they can perform those functions just listed. Not all parties are strong, and the states offer "little political laboratories" to study the differences between the strong and the weak. Fifty different political systems operating within a common national framework offer a cross-state comparison of party strength.

At first it was assumed that parties would be strongest and most cohesive in states where there was close competition between them. V. O. Key, Jr. (1964, 289–304) claimed that each party would be united to fight the opposition party that threatened to take over the government in the next election. Accordingly the more competitive the state, the stronger the parties would be. Key formed his hypothesis after observing the noncompetitive one-party states of the South, where the parties were weak and divided into factions. Key believed that competition determines party strength. He stated that two-party competition produced cohesive parties that would translate election promises into policy for fear of retribution at the polls. When Key turned his attention to the competitive northern states, however, he noted that two-party competition was not uniformly producing the cohesive parties he predicted. He tried to show why the hypothesis was not predicting with accuracy, but his findings were not heeded.

Competition was used as an indication of party strength (see the section on Measuring Partisanship and Two-Party Competition in Chapter 2). However, some researchers found that there was not a very high correlation between the two (Morehouse 1981, 145–148; Cotter, Gibson, Bibby, and Huckshorn 1984, 83–95). Cotter and associates traced the relationship between competition and their measure of party organizational strength from 1960 to 1980. They used the Ranney index of competition and concluded that the relationship between competition and party strength from 1960 to 1980 showed a strong relationship in the earliest and no relationship in the most recent period. "Whatever causes the party's electoral fortunes to vary does not cause the strength of party organizations to vary as well"(1984, 91).

Competitive states appeared to encompass a variety of party structures based on a rivalry between the "ins" and the "outs," or programmatic differences between the middle-of-the roaders and the wings or rivalries between upstate and downstate or between suburbs and farms. In some competitive states the governor and the party leaders may attempt to suppress internal strife so as to present a united front in the election, as Gov. John Engler did for the Michigan Republican Party in the 1990s. In other competitive states, no such attempt is made; the factions slug it out in the primary, and the leaders acknowledge the results and back the nominee with whatever effort they can muster. The Kentucky Republicans who in 2000 have two Republican U.S. senators, indicating that they can win statewide elections, were not cohesive enough to recruit and endorse a candidate for governor in 1999.

If competition cannot be used as a measure of party strength, what other measures can we use? The strength of the state party bureaucracy can be used as a measure to compare parties. The Party Transformation Study, which was the work of four political scientists (Cotter, Gibson, Bibby, and Huckshorn 1984), documented the growth in strength of state and local organizations over a twenty-year period (1960–1980). They found that state budgets had grown and that more than 90 percent of the parties had either full-time state chairs or executive directors. The state party bureaucracies ran campaign seminars for party candidates, and a majority of them had mobilization programs through which to identify and turn out their party's likely voters. Many parties were increasingly active in providing campaign services to candidates. The indicators of party organizational strength were combined into a composite party organizational strength score (by factor analysis, 27–29).

The relationship between bureaucratic strength and winning elections needs more proof. The authors of the Party Transformation Study documented the fact that state Republican Party bureaucracies were considerably stronger than their Democratic counterparts. In several southern states the Republicans built up the party apparatus in anticipation of more favorable conditions as the region's white voters realigned with the GOP. Therefore we would not expect an immediate correlation between bureaucratic organization and electoral strength. Leaving out the southern states for that reason, the authors tested for party organizational strength (POS, as they call it) and party electoral success in contests for governor. This measure of competition is related to the specific office of governor and tests for the relationship between the state party organizational strength and success in winning gubernatorial elections. Their findings show that the state party with an organizational strength advantage over the other is more successful on election day (1984, 93–104). This is a modest finding but in the right direction.

A related measure of party strength is county bureaucratic strength, measured much the same way as state-level bureaucratic strength, and it is getting stronger over time (Gibson, Frendries, and Vertz 1989). To test the relationship between county party organizational strength and competition, researchers developed a statewide average measure of county party strength that aggregates the county-level scores (Patterson and Caldeira 1983; Barrilleaux 1986). They used the Ranney index of competition, which is an appropriate measure for it incorporates partisan strength in both houses of the legislature and thus may be related to local party effort. Patterson and Caldeira concluded that the organizational strength of county parties is a factor of major importance in understanding partisan competition. Barrilleaux discovered a modest effect of county party organization on change in partisan competition in the United States during the 1970s.

Measuring county party effort on the county level, one researcher found that strong county party organizations affected public attitudes toward parties. Party strength can help build supportive partisan attitudes in the county, particularly when parties are competitive (Coleman 1996).

Over twenty years ago, Cotter and associates conducted research that measured the party bureaucratic strength discussed earlier. In 1999, twenty years later, John Aldrich conducted a mail survey of state party chairs, replicating their efforts. Although the results of the survey have not been fully analyzed or correlated with competition, Aldrich makes two major points. First, he finds that state party organizations throughout the nation have become stronger over the past two decades, continuing the trend discovered by Cotter and associates. Second, the South has developed the most strongly organized parties on average in the nation. In particular the southern Republican Parties are among the strongest. Aldrich concludes that, "It may have been long and slow in coming, but heightened and sustained competition between the two parties has gone hand-in-hand with the development of partisan organizations that are comparable to, if not exceeding, those in the rest of the nation"(Aldrich 2000).

The question "Which comes first, the chicken or the egg?" may be appropriate here. Cotter and associates did not find competition to be associated with party organizational strength in the 1970s. During the 1980s and 1990s, as the states became increasingly competitive, many parties became bureaucratically stronger. They anticipated victory and organized to fight the opposition. Their efforts began to make a difference in closely contested elections. As Aldrich says, party competition and party organization go hand in hand.

In spite of the relationship between competition and organizational strength, there is wide variation among the one hundred state parties in their degree of bureaucratic strength. The typical Republican Party is stronger, more professional, and better funded than its Democratic counterpart. The Democratic Party is reputed to relish diversity, dissent, and fractiousness. Cotter and associates ranked the state parties by organizational strength, and it is apparent that in most states the Republican Party is stronger than its Democratic Party rival. Exceptions are Pennsylvania, where both parties are strong; Michigan, California, Virginia, Georgia, and Florida, where they are both moderately strong; and Kentucky, Massachusetts, Rhode Island, and North Dakota, where the Democratic Party is stronger than the Republican Party (Cotter, Gibson, Bibby, and Huckshorn 1984, 28–29). To conclude this discussion, it appears that, while most state parties have responded to increasing competition by strengthening their operations, diversity still exists between the parties within each state.

So far, party strength has been measured by the degree of party bureaucratic organization, which is considered to be basic to the performance of the party's functions of nominating, electing, and governing. However, party bureaucratic strength has not proved to be convincingly related to the functions mentioned above. Organizational strength does not necessarily mean that a party will recruit the best candidates and help them win the nomination and election. You cannot measure the strength of a football team by the size of its locker room.

We will consider another indicator of party strength that measures one of the most important party functions—that of recruiting and nominating strong candidates for public office. The coalitions that candidates build to receive the party nomination may be related to the party's bureaucratic strength. We do not know how this increased organizational capacity matters to candidates for the gubernatorial nomination, for instance. Most state parties, even those with ample budgets, hold back on campaign contributions and fund-raising assistance until a candidate emerges from the primary process. We predict that strong party leadership can commit effort and resources to their favored candidate for the endorsement and following primary.

Lucky is the candidate who has the backing of a party leadership with money to bestow and activists to mobilize. In the states that make use of a preprimary endorsing system, we hypothesize that the parties are cohesive in the nominating process. The following conditions would apply. The party leaders in counties and towns are unified under a state chair. They can control the nomination for a gubernatorial candidate, for instance, by sending local delegations to the convention who will back that individual. The candidate may not be challenged, but if a challenge does occur, these party leaders build a coalition for the candidate that will ensure a primary win. The gubernatorial candidate wins by a large percentage (80–100 percent). The coalition carries over into the election campaign and works to elect (or reelect) the candidate.

This measure of party strength is based on the primary vote for governor, who is the most important state officer. The primary reflects the factionalism within the party and hence the primary vote indicates the degree to which the party is unified or divided. The measure is the average percentage of the party primary vote received by gubernatorial candidates over a certain time period. Although the measure can be applied to a single party over time, it can also be applied to the governors who hold office during a time period and can tell us to what extent the state's governors have come from parties that are unified or divided.

In Table 3-3 party coalition strength can be estimated from the magnitude of the governor's vote in the primary. If the average primary vote for all of a state's governors serving for the last twenty years is 80–100 percent, we predict that coalition building for the nomination is not episodic. We believe that a steady corps of party leaders exists within both parties who outlast individual gubernatorial candidates and can recruit and help each prospective candidate. This pattern is typical of New York, Colorado, Connecticut, Michigan, Illinois, and Ohio, to mention a few of the nineteen strong parties shown in Table 3-3. If the average primary vote is between 60 percent and 79 percent, both parties may be making modest efforts, or one may be strong and the other weak, thus producing a modest average. Twenty-two states fall in this category including California, Pennsylvania, Texas, Florida, and New Jersey. The weakest category, 35–59 percent, indicates that there is no steady corps of party leaders in either party. Factions within the party fight it out in the primary, and party leaders make no effort to influence the nomination contest. This is typical of several southern states including Georgia, Louisiana, Mississippi, and the border state of Kentucky.

The matching of party coalition strength with the strength of preprimary endorsements provides striking proof that preprimary endorsements occur only in states that have strong or moderately strong parties. We call a strong nominating system one in which preprimary endorsements are made by law and apply to both parties. A moderately strong system is defined as one in which preprimary endorsements are permissive and are used by political parties. A weak nominating system is defined as having no provision by law or party regulations for preprimary endorsements for major or competitive parties. (Chapter 4 provides a complete discussion of the nominating process.)

Table 3-3 Gubernatorial Nominations and Party System Strength

Party System Strength (1978–1998)	Party Gubernatorial Nominations (Preprimary Endorsements by Law)	Party Gubernatorial Nominations (Preprimary Endorsements by Party Rule or Practice)	Party Gubernatorial Nominations (No Party Endorsements by Major Parties)
Strong (19)	Colorado North Dakota Connecticut New York Rhode Island Utah	Delaware (R) Virginia[a] Ohio Michigan (D) Illinois Iowa (post)[c]	Vermont Indiana (pre–1976)[b] Tennessee South Carolina Idaho (1963–1971)[b] North Carolina Oregon
Moderate (22)		Massachusetts Pennsylvania California (D) (1990–1994)[b] Minnesota	South Dakota New Hampshire Wisconsin (R) (pre–1979)[b] Maine Florida Missouri Wyoming Oklahoma Arkansas New Jersey Hawaii Nevada Texas Maryland Arizona Alabama Montana Washington
Weak (9)			West Virginia Kansas New Mexico (1964–1966, 1978–1982, 1994–1998)[b] Georgia Nebraska Alaska Mississippi Louisiana Kentucky

Note: Party system strength is measured by averaging the governors' percentage of the primary vote in gubernatorial primaries, 1978–1998 (inclusive). In states with strong party systems, the average primary vote received by the governors-to-be was 80–100 percent. In moderately strong party systems, it was 60–79 percent. In weak party systems, it was 35–59 percent. The five most recent elections were used with the following exceptions: Alaska; Conn.; Minn.; Maine (4), which went back to the 1978 election and did not use elections in which an independent won; and ten elections apiece for the states with two-year terms: N.H.; Vt.; R.I. Ariz. (6) changed to a four-year term in 1986, R.I. in 1995.
[a]State party officials may by law choose either the primary or the convention.
[b]Dates in parentheses indicate years preprimary endorsements were used.
[c]Postprimary nominating convention if no candidate receives at least 35 percent.

Eleven of the nineteen states with the strongest parties have preprimary endorsing conventions, and Iowa has a postprimary convention to endorse a candidate if no candidate receives a majority in the primary. Four additional states with moderate party strength practice preprimary endorsements. For these sixteen states, party leaders make a practice of controlling the nomination to ensure that an electable and loyal candidate is nominated. For the vast majority of states no such process exists, and the party leaders must live with the results of the primary, which may give them a self-selected candidate who owes them nothing.

Interestingly, Democratic Parties in all sections of the country are more likely than Republicans to report that they engage in preprimary endorsements. They are almost twice as likely to engage in this practice (Aldrich 2000, Tables A3 and A4). Preprimary endorsements are informal in some of the states that endorse by party rule or practice. They may come about as agreements within state party committees or by county leaders' associations. States most likely to have strong or moderate systems for preprimary endorsements are in the Midwest or East (see Table 3-3). Parties in these states have long histories as organizations competing against each other. Most of these states were slow to adopt the primary, and many of them mandated preprimary endorsements when they were required to adopt direct primaries during the Progressive era. They discovered that recruiting and endorsing candidates for the nomination is necessary to ensure that candidates loyal to the party will carry its banner in the general election. Thus this index of party system strength measures the extent to which the party performs its most important function: grooming and offering candidates for election. Later we will use this index to predict the ability of a party to govern by supporting the governor's program in the legislature.

PARTY ORGANIZATION MATTERS

By almost any criterion state political parties are better organized than they used to be. They have larger, more professional staffs and many of the modern tools of communication, such as computers, fax machines, and Web sites. More important, they have recognized the importance of providing a variety of services to their candidates. They are much more aggressive and skillful than in the past in raising funds so that they can maintain a party headquarters and provide services to candidates. Some state parties have leaders who are more skillful and imaginative than others.

We have discussed some of the handicaps in which state party organizations operate. In many states the parties have little influence over the nominating process and have been helpless to prevent the growth of open primaries. Party leaders often fail to understand the importance and the feasibility of finding, endorsing, and supporting the strongest candidate for nomination to high-level state offices, such as governor or senator. Parties, like many other organizations, are having trouble attracting capable, committed activists to work in campaigns. In some state parties the activists who are most willing to work are committed more to an ideology or a particular cause than they are to the party. The resulting factional divisions can tear a party apart.

Political scientists have difficulty in measuring exactly how much the outcome of elections is affected by various components of party organization. But the political trends in southern states over the past few decades provide convincing evidence that party organization matters. Southern state Republican Parties during the 1950s and 1960s (and often later) failed to take advantage of the gains being made by Republican presidential candidates in the South, largely because they were poorly organized. The spectacular gains of Republican candidates for congressional, state, and local office in more recent years are in large measure a product of much stronger Republican Party organizations. In the years ahead in most states, the level of two-party competition is likely to be high enough so that a party organization that fails to perform effectively runs a high risk of falling behind in the electoral arena.

4   The Nominating Process

In almost every American state the voters directly choose the nominees for their party in a primary election. The president of the United States is chosen in a national convention, but in a large majority of the states the voters directly choose convention delegates committed to particular presidential candidates. In almost every foreign country, on the other hand, the voters play no direct role in party nominations.

The nomination of candidates for public office is one of the most important steps in the political process, so we must understand how the nominating process varies in practice from state to state if we are to understand the infinite variety of politics among American states. A study of state nominations can tell us a great deal about many significant characteristics of state politics, including (1) the character and level of two-party competition; (2) the nature and strength of party organizations; and (3) the elements or factions that make up the two parties.

Nominating systems differ in various ways, but the basic dimension for comparing nominations among the states is the breadth of participation in the selection of nominees. At one extreme is the case in which a few party leaders select the nominee and their choice is not challenged in any primary election. At the other extreme is a primary election in which there are several candidates, there are no efforts by the party organization to influence the choice, a large proportion of the eligible voters turn out to vote, and the outcome is close.

To analyze participation in the nominating process, we need to collect information on the following:

Laws that define who is eligible for a primary.
Laws and practices for party organizational endorsements in primaries.
The extent of competition, specifically whether several candidates are running and
    the closeness of outcomes in such a race.
The proportion of voters who turn out for primaries.
The factors that explain the outcomes of nominating contests.

V. O. Key, Jr. provides some historical perspective on the nominating process: "Throughout the history of American nominating practices runs a persistent attempt to make feasible popular participation in nominations and thereby to limit or destroy the power of party organizations" (1964, 371).

During the Jacksonian period (1829–1837), the legislative caucus, in which members of each party in Congress nominated presidential candidates, was replaced as a nominating device by the convention attended by popularly elected delegates. The convention system in turn came under attack at the end of the nineteenth century because too often the selection of delegates and the decisions of the convention were tightly controlled by the party organization, which often was made up of a small group of bosses.

The Civil War had created a pattern of Democratic control in southern states and Republican control in many of the northern states, a pattern that was reinforced by the 1896 election. Even in those northern states that were more competitive, many counties and cities were dominated by one party. The effect of tight organizational control over nominations in a dominant party was to deny voters any real choice in the elections.

The primary election first came into use late in the nineteenth century in the area where the one-party system was strongest—the southern states. This occurred initially as a result of party rules and later as a result of state law. The major purpose and effect of the primaries in southern states was to guarantee Democratic control of southern politics. Democratic leaders believed that public primaries would "legitimate the nominees, settle intraparty differences before the general election, and greatly reduce the power of opposition voters" (Kousser 1974, 74). The Democrats were concerned about opposition from both Republican candidates and third parties and about the possibility that such challengers would seek support from black voters.

Outside the South the campaign for direct primary elections was an important ingredient in the Progressive movement, and it represented a direct challenge to the conservative political leaders who dominated one or both parties in most states. The speed with which this movement spread across the states is impressive. Wisconsin adopted the first relatively comprehensive statewide compulsory primary law in 1903. Within five years similar laws had been adopted in most of the plains and western states where the Progressive movement was strong, and by 1917 the direct primary had been adopted in all but a handful of states (Key 1964, 371–376; 1956, 87–97).

Most of the states that were slow to adopt the primary or did not use it consistently were eastern or midwestern states with relatively high levels of two-party competition and strong party organizations, such as New York, Connecticut, Rhode Island, Delaware, and Indiana. When Connecticut adopted a limited form of the direct primary in 1955, no state remained that relied entirely on the convention system. In the past four decades a number of states have enacted laws that changed the number of offices covered by the primary or the authority of party conventions to endorse candidates running in the primary. However, no clear legislative trends have developed toward either greater organizational control or greater popular influence in the nomination process.

To understand differences among the states in the nominating process, we must first look at differences imposed by law. We are particularly concerned with statewide nominations because of our interest in statewide political systems. We will first examine the procedures that have been established in the states to determine what persons can vote in primary elections—the distinction between open and closed primary elections. Most of these rules have been written into state law, although in some southern states the law permits the parties to establish the criteria for participating in their primaries.

We will then examine the laws that establish requirements for primaries and party conventions. Most state laws now require the major political parties to nominate statewide candidates by primaries. But Alabama and Virginia laws permit parties to use either primaries or conventions, and both the Republican and Democratic Parties in Virginia have made some use of conventions in recent years in an effort to unite the party behind one candidate. In the past, several other southern states permitted the parties to choose the method used for nominations. The Republican Parties in some of these states used the convention system but shifted to primaries when the party became more competitive.

The laws in several states require the political parties to hold preprimary conventions to endorse candidates; in some of these states candidates must get a minimum percentage of convention votes to enter the primary or to get on the primary ballot without getting petitions signed by voters. We will examine how the laws and party practices affect the nominating process.

REQUIREMENTS FOR VOTING IN PRIMARIES

One aspect of the law on nominations that significantly affects the primary system is the definition of voter qualifications for participation in the primary. The basic distinction is between closed primaries—which are limited to voters registered with a party, and open primaries—which are open to anyone qualified to vote in the general election. The practical difference between the two major categories is that it is relatively easy in open primaries for voters to shift from one party primary to the other, whereas such shifts are usually more difficult in closed primaries. A closer examination of primary laws discloses wide variations in the qualifications for voting in a party's primaries. Not all primaries are equally closed or open, and no consensus even exists on how to classify primaries. As we shall see, there are several variations of both closed and open primaries (summarized in Table 4-1).

Table 4-1 State Requirements for Voting in Primary Elections

Type of Primary	Northeastern States	Midwestern States	Southern and Border States	Western States
Completely closed	Delaware Maryland New York Pennsylvania	South Dakota	Florida Kentucky Oklahoma	Arizona Nevada New Mexico
Closed, but some voters may shift on election day	Connecticut[d] Maine[a] Massachusetts[a] New Hampshire[a] New Jersey[a] Rhode Island[a]	Iowa[c] Kansas[a] Nebraska[a] Ohio[c]	North Carolina[a] West Virginia[b]	Colorado[a] Oregon[b] Wyoming[c]
Open, but voter must select primary publicly		Illinois Indiana	Alabama Arkansas Georgia Mississippi Missouri Tennessee Texas Virginia	
Completely open	Vermont	Michigan Minnesota North Dakota Wisconsin	South Carolina	Hawaii Idaho Montana Utah
Open, blanket primary				Alaska Washington California[e]

Sources: Malcolm E. Jewell and David M. Olsen, *Political Parties and Elections in American States* (Chicago: Dorsey Press, 1988), 89–92. Data also supplied by John Bibby.

[a]Unaffiliated voters or persons who have not previously voted in a party primary (depending on the state) may change party registration on election day.

[b]Unaffiliated voters may vote in Republican primaries.

[c]Any voter may change party registration on election day.

[d]An unaffiliated voter in Connecticut can register with a party the day before the primary election.

[e]The U.S. Supreme Court has declared that the California, open blanket primary is unconstitutional.

Types of Closed Primaries

The most rigid form of closed primary, found in eleven states, is one in which a voter must be registered with a party in advance of the primary election. A record is kept of that partisan registration, and anyone who wishes to change to the other party primary must shift party registration a certain period of time before the primary. The deadline for making that change is less than two months in half of these states but up to almost a year in the others. The earlier the deadline, the more difficult it is for a voter to shift primaries.

Fifteen states have a closed primary system but permit some degree of flexibility by letting voters make a change in their status on primary election day. (See notes at the bottom of Table 4-1 for details on these states.) The greatest flexibility occurs in several states that keep a record of party registration but permit anyone to shift registration from one party (or nonaffiliated status) to another on primary election day (or in one case the day before the primary). Some states permit a new voter or one who has not previously voted in a partisan primary to register with a party on primary election day. A few states permit only unaffiliated voters to change their status by shifting to registration with a party on election day. A few state parties permit unaffiliated voters as well as those registered with their party to vote in the primary. There is little practical difference between some of these systems and some forms of open primaries except that a record is usually kept of each voter's party registration.

Types of Open Primaries

In ten states, mostly in the South, a voter need not register with a party in advance, no permanent record is kept of party preference, and there is no real obstacle to a voter who wants to change party primaries in each election. But the voter is required to express a choice or request a primary ballot of one party at the polls. Sometimes the request must be made in writing, and in a few states it is noted on a registration form for that election.

In ten states the voters are not required to make public their party preference. They can vote in either primary, and the mechanics of the election permit them to keep confidential in which party primary they voted. Voters in such states can move freely from year to year from one party primary to the other. Washington, Alaska, and until recently California have used the blanket primary, which gives voters even greater freedom. In a single election they can participate in the primaries of both parties; for example, they can vote in the Democratic primary for governor, the Republican primary for senator, and so forth.

What is often referred to as a nonpartisan primary election is simply a two-stage election in which voters and candidates of all parties participate. In the first stage any candidate who receives a majority of the votes wins the election; if no one has a majority ,a runoff is held between the top two candidates. This system is commonly used in a number of states for nonpartisan judicial elections and some local elections. Louisiana does not really have partisan primary elections but uses this two-stage election system for statewide and congressional races.

If this wide variety of primaries seems confusing, keep in mind that some voters may not fully understand the primary system in their own state, particularly if they have moved from a state with a different system. Do many voters in closed primary states know how many months before a primary election they must change party registration? In states where voters may change their registration on election day, how many voters are aware of this and how many take advantage of it? There is evidence in Massachusetts that the numbers of voters making that switch are sometimes quite high. W do not know how many voters understand the blanket primary system or use the option of jumping back and forth from one party to the other as they go down the primary ballot.

Regional Variations in Types of Primaries

Table 4-1 lists by region the states using various types of primaries. The variations in primary voting requirements reflect the strength or weakness of party organizations at the time the laws were adopted, the influence of habit or tradition in state politics, the recent strength of party organizations, and pressure to liberalize primary voting requirements in the states. Many of the states with closed primaries are in the Northeast or Midwest, regions where the traditionally strong parties have been able to keep primaries closed.

Some of the states with open or blanket primaries are in the midwestern or western states where the Progressive movement was strong. Most of the southern states have open primaries because only the Democratic Party used to have competitive primaries and state law often allowed the Democratic Party to establish requirements for participation if it so chose. In eight of these open primary southern states, however, voters must publicly specify the party primary in which they want to vote. The growth of competitive Republican primaries in most southern states has caused most primaries to remain open, although Florida and North Carolina, along with several border states, have closed primaries.

Most southern primaries are distinct from those in most other states in another respect. In the southern states (all but Tennessee) if no candidate gets a majority on the first ballot (or at least 40 percent in North Carolina), a runoff primary is held between the top two candidates. This is done to ensure that the winner will have majority support among primary voters. When the Democratic primary was the only important one in southern states, it often attracted many candidates, which usually reduced the chances of anyone attaining a majority unless a runoff was used. Two border states—Kentucky and Oklahoma—along with South Dakota, also use runoffs. They apply in Kentucky for the governor's race if no one wins at least 40 percent and in South Dakota if no one gets 35 percent on the first ballot. In Iowa, if no candidate wins at least 35 percent on the primary ballot, a party convention makes the nomination.

Differences between Types of Primaries

The rationale for a closed primary is that the selection of candidates should be limited to persons who are willing to be identified with the party through registration and that this identification should remain reasonably stable over time. It is argued that in an open primary the party is vulnerable to being "raided." Voters who normally vote in one primary might enter the other primary to vote— either for the candidate whose personality or views are particularly attractive or for a candidate they believe is less likely to win the general election. In reality, it appears that voters who cross over to the other party are rarely trying to pick a weak candidate but usually support the candidate whose views or record and personality are appealing to them.

The basic argument for an open primary is that voters should be able to participate freely in primaries without having to reveal their political preferences or to give up their status as independents. The open primary preserves the secrecy of political choice and thus the secrecy of the ballot.

We know little about how many voters shift back and forth from one party primary to another in an open primary state, or how many voters take advantage of the opportunity to make a last-minute change in party affiliation in those closed primary states where it is possible. We will return to this question of how voters select a primary later in the chapter when we discuss levels of participation in primaries.

CANDIDATE NOMINATIONS AND PARTY ENDORSEMENTS

The development of the direct primary as the vehicle for nominating candidates in the states has taken from the political party its most important function: making nominations. As a consequence, many observers believe that the organizational vitality of the parties has been eroded. They believe that they have lost the ability to screen potential candidates and to present to the voters a slate of candidates who represent the major interests and viewpoints of the party and who have a good chance of winning. Yet there are a number of state parties that try to influence the nominating process by using some procedure for endorsing candidates before the primary elections.

Types of Endorsements

In some states the political parties have persuaded the legislature to establish a legal foundation for preprimary endorsements, which are made by a party convention. Currently these legal endorsements are made by both parties in Connecticut, Rhode Island, New York, North Dakota, Colorado, Utah, and New Mexico. Several of these states—including Colorado, New York, Rhode Island, and Connecticut—had strong political parties that used to make nominations directly. They were able to get endorsement systems written into the law in return for accepting the passage of direct primary legislation.

Legal endorsements in such states usually provide some formal advantage for those endorsees who obtain a certain percentage of convention votes. In Utah and Connecticut the only way to get on the primary ballot is to win a certain percentage of the votes at the convention. In Utah the party must endorse two candidates for the primary unless one candidate gets a large majority—70 percent in the Republican convention, 60 percent in the Democratic convention. In Connecticut the endorsee is nominated unless challenged by a candidate who gets at least 15 percent of the convention vote. In three states any candidate qualifies for the ballot who gets a specified percentage of the convention vote (30 percent in Colorado, 20 percent in New Mexico, and 25 percent in New York). Other candidates can qualify by petition, but in New York the petition route is a very expensive and time-consuming process. In Rhode Island and North Dakota the endorsee automatically gets on the ballot and others must qualify by petition.

A second category consists of state parties that make endorsements based on party rules, with endorsements made by a public convention. Candidates endorsed under this system usually do not gain any advantage of ballot access or position. But in Massachusetts both parties require a candidate to win at least 15 percent of the convention votes to get on the primary ballot, a requirement that has been upheld by the courts. In addition to the parties in Massachusetts, both parties in Minnesota, the Republicans in Delaware, and (for some offices) the Democrats in California make endorsements under their rules. In the Massachusetts parties and the Delaware Republican Party the endorsements by party rule replaced legal endorsement systems that once were in effect.

A third category of endorsements includes state parties whose leaders or party committees make informal endorsements, usually meeting behind closed doors. This kind of endorsement may be done intermittently, and records of such actions are usually obscure. (For that reason, we will not examine these state parties in any detail here.) Examples of such parties are those in Illinois, Pennsylvania, Ohio, Michigan, and Louisiana. Both parties in Virginia have sometimes held conventions instead of primaries to make nominations as permitted by state law. In some states preprimary endorsements are made by groups, such as the California Democratic Council, which consist of party activists but are not officially connected to the party.

How Does the Endorsement Process Work?

Endorsements are made by party conventions that usually meet several months before the primary election. Some delegates are appointed by local party organizations, and others are elected at local caucuses, which are attended by voters who are interested and active enough in politics to show up. If the election of delegates is contested, those who are running may be asked to identify the candidate they support for endorsement in major statewide races. In the New York party conventions, which number about three hundred, all delegates are members of the state central committee. In recent years roughly half of the delegates to party conventions have held some local or state position in the party, such as a county Democratic chair, or else hold elective public office, such as a state legislator.

Delegates are usually party activists, persons who work frequently in local, state, or national political campaigns. We would expect them, as party loyalists, to recognize the importance of nominating the candidate with the best chance of winning the primary—if there is a contest—and the general election. They should also be experienced enough to make accurate judgments about the strengths and weaknesses of potential candidates. On the other hand, delegates are likely to hold strong views on issues. There is extensive evidence that delegates to both state and national party conventions who are Democrats are likely to be more liberal than the average voter who identifies as a Democrat. Likewise delegates who are Republicans are likely to be more conservative than the average Republican identifier (Erikson, Wright, and McIver 1993; Miller 1988; Miller and Jennings 1986).

The political background of delegates also helps to explain their viewpoints. Some of them started out as active members of an interest group and became active in politics in part to advance the goals of that group. Republican delegates, for example, may belong to a Christian right or right-to-life group. Democratic delegates may be active in a feminist or environmental group or a teachers' union. Some party activists seek election as convention delegates because they are strong supporters of one of the candidates seeking endorsement, often because of that candidate's stand on issues.

State party endorsing conventions meet, usually over a weekend in a large arena, with television and print media coverage. Large signs promoting one or another candidate hang from every available space in the hall. Delegates listen to speeches, particularly those by candidates seeking endorsement for a statewide office. Before or after a candidate's speech, there may be a floor demonstration for the candidate. In their spare time delegates socialize and politick, sometimes visiting hospitality suites maintained by the candidates. In short, the endorsing conventions closely resemble the national presidential nominating conventions we see on television every four years, except that in many of these state conventions there is often considerable suspense about which candidate will win the convention's endorsement.

The high point of these conventions is the roll calls on endorsements. Usually the chair of each county or district, after having polled its delegates, announces the results, with some of the announcements being greeted by loud cheers from the hall. Some parties take on a single ballot on endorsement but most of them have successive ballots until a candidate receives enough votes to be endorsed. This is usually a majority but in a few parties consists of 60 percent of the delegates. Sometimes a deadlock develops, and a party may conduct as many as ten ballots, each generally taking at least an hour to complete. Sometimes a convention adjourns without any candidate in one of the major contests having succeeded in getting the number of votes necessary for endorsement.

What Is the Impact of Endorsements on the Nomination?

For an endorsement to be effective, the endorsee must win the nomination, either because that person has no primary opposition or because the endorsee is able to defeat anyone else who runs in the primary. Table 4-2 shows the success of endorsees in gubernatorial primaries over the period from 1960 through 1998. We are particularly interested in the more recent period, 1982–1998, and we are comparing the success rates for legal and party rules endorsement systems.

Table 4-2 Success of Endorsed Candidates in Primaries, by Time Period, Legal and Party Rule Endorsements, and Party, 1960–1998

Years	Party	No Primary Contest	Contested Primaries	Contested Primaries: (%)	Contested Primaries: Endorsee Wins	Contested Primaries: Endorsee Wins (%)	Percentage of All Primaries Won by Endorsee
Legal:							
1960–1980	Democrat	20	13	39	11	85	94
	Republican	17	16	48	13	81	91
	Total	37	29	44	24	83	92
Legal:							
1982–1998	Democrat	17	15	47	7	47	75
	Republican	20	12	38	6	50	81
	Total	37	27	42	13	48	78
Party rules:							
1960–1980	Democrat	1	5	83	4	80	83
	Republican	3	5	63	4	80	88
	Total	4	10	71	8	80	86
Party rules:							
1982–1998	Democat	1	10	91	6	60	64
	Republican	5	9	64	4	44	64
	Total	6	19	76	10	53	64
All parties							
1960–1980	Total	41	39	49	32	82	91
1982–1998	Total	43	46	52	23	50	74

Source: Data compiled by the authors over many years and from various sources.

The best outcome for an endorsee is to have no primary opposition. The table shows that in states with legal endorsements less than half of the endorsees are challenged in a primary, with little change over time. For state parties with endorsements by rules, the proportion of contested primaries is higher and has increased to just over three-fourths. The most significant finding is that when there was a contested primary the endorsee won over 80 percent of the time in the 1960–1980 period and only half the time in the 1982–1998 period. This means that the overall success of endorsees, including both primaries that were uncontested and those they won, dropped from 91 percent to 74 percent. In the case of contested primaries the figures are about the same for both legal and rules endorsements.

Factors that Determine the Success of Endorsements

In recent years gubernatorial endorsees have been running into more serious obstacles when they have to face one or more opponents in the primary. There are a number of reasons why some endorsees win gubernatorial nominations and others fail, and there are some clues as to why the success rate has been dropping. We can illustrate these points with examples from some of the endorsing conventions held in recent years.

In 1994 and 1998 we studied seventeen endorsing conventions held by state parties. We selected state parties that held contests for the gubernatorial nomination. In most cases we were able to observe the conventions firsthand, and we collected information from the press on the conventions and primary campaigns that followed them. Our major source of data on the conventions came from questionnaires sent out to a large sample of delegates, using the same types of questions in the two years. We received, coded, and analyzed almost 2,500 questionnaires from the delegates over the two years.

Much of the analysis of the endorsement process that follows comes from these questionnaires. Delegates are a particularly good source of information about endorsements. Most of them have had considerable experience in politics. More than half serve on local party committees or hold public office. Many of those attending the 1998 conventions had been delegates to their party convention in 1994—from about one-half to two-thirds, depending on the state. Their answers to our questions were perceptive and informative, particularly their assessments of the endorsement process in their party and its strengths and weaknesses. The following sections discuss the topics addressed in our questionnaire.

The party's commitment to the endorsement principle. The preprimary endorsement is a much more established tradition in some parties than it is in others, and convention delegates are much more strongly committed to endorsements in some states than in others. This is best illustrated by comparing the Connecticut Republican and California Democratic conventions in 1994.

The Connecticut parties have been making preprimary endorsements since the direct primary was established in 1955 and the law provided for such endorsements. The 1994 Connecticut Republican convention pitted former member of Congress John Rowland against Secretary of State Pauline Kezer. Everyone knew that Rowland, a strong conservative, was going to be endorsed. The only question was whether Rowland and the party leaders supporting him could keep Kezer from getting the 15 percent of the convention vote that she needed to be able to challenge Rowland in a primary.

The roll call went on for hours, with some 1,300 delegates voting one by one. When it concluded, the totals were not announced, but in fact Kezer had only twenty-one more votes than the 15 percent that she needed. The chair announced that the delegates had the right to change their votes and kept repeating this invitation as he held the voting open for more than an hour. Rowland and Kezer scurried around the hall, trying to change votes or hold delegates in line. Every few minutes, a delegate came down the aisle to a microphone and announced a shift from Kezer to Rowland. A mixture of cheers and boos greeted each conversion, and many of the delegates were chanting, "Shift, shift, shift! No primary, no primary!" Finally the procession ended, no one else came to the microphone, and the chair reluctantly announced the end of the roll call. Kezer had held 15 percent of the delegates, with three votes to spare. There would be a primary election (which she lost).

The story of the 1994 California Democratic endorsing convention could not be more different. After a judicial decision had overruled a state law banning party endorsements, the Democrats endorsed a gubernatorial candidate for the first time in 1990, but the margin was very narrow and the endorsee lost the primary. Thus in 1994 the convention delegates had very little experience with making endorsements, and some doubted its value.

The 1994 convention endorsed candidates for a number of statewide races but not for governor. If the California delegates had been chanting anything, it would have been "Unity, unity, unity! No endorsement!" Before the state convention met, the state chair, Bill Press, with the apparent support of Democratic leaders, decided that to preserve unity in the party there would be no endorsement for governor, and there would be no debate among the gubernatorial candidates at the convention. Press stressed that the party should not emphasize its differences but instead should concentrate on beating Republican governor Pete Wilson. The delegates evidently agreed with Press; two-thirds of those who answered our survey opposed any effort to endorse for governor.

Endorsing a strong candidate. There is an old adage in politics that "you can't beat a somebody with a nobody." The chances of the endorsee winning a nomination are greater if the party has endorsed the strongest available candidate. A "strong" candidate usually means one who has political skills, some experience as a campaigner, a record in public office, and preferably some demonstrated ability to raise campaign funds.

One category of candidates who are usually strong consists of incumbent governors, and they are almost always endorsed by party conventions. As we would expect, they are highly successful, and in the 1982–1998 period three-fourths of endorsed incumbent governors had no opposition in the primary, and more than half of the endorsees who had no primary opposition were sitting governors.

One of the arguments in favor of using conventions to make party endorsements is that most delegates are party activists who are experienced in politics, knowledgeable about candidates, and concerned about picking the strongest possible candidate. But we have pointed out that delegates often are persons who have become active in politics because they have strong views on issues and may judge candidates at the convention on the basis of their viewpoints and not just their potential for winning nomination and election.

The 1998 Massachusetts Republican convention provides a good example of a party that endorsed its strongest candidate. The convention had a clear choice between acting governor (and former lieutenant governor) Paul Cellucci and Treasurer Joseph Malone. The major theme of Malone's campaign was that Cellucci was too liberal and as lieutenant governor had worked too closely with Gov. William Weld, whom he also accused of being a liberal. But, though his title was only acting governor, Cellucci skillfully used his position to build support, won endorsement by a 7–3 margin, and beat Malone by a 58–42 percent margin in the primary. Cellucci's reputation as a moderate Republican helped him win the general election in a state with a relatively liberal electorate.

In 1994 the Minnesota Republican convention did not select its strongest candidate. The delegates faced a choice between two major candidates: the incumbent governor, Arne Carlson, and a relatively obscure former legislator supported by the Christian right, Allen Quist. Many of the delegates were critical of Carlson for not being conservative enough and for being pro-choice on abortion. Our survey asked delegates whom they were supporting and what were their reasons; a very small proportion of Quist supporters said he had a better chance of being elected, but this did not weaken their support from him. Although the convention endorsed Quist by more than a two-thirds vote, he was defeated in the primary by a similar margin by Governor Carlson, who went on to be reelected. This reversal in the primary also indicated that, with regard to viewpoints on issues, the delegates to the convention were not representative of Republican primary voters.

In 1998 the Minnesota Democratic-Farmer-Labor (DFL) convention did not face the problem of deep divisions over issues, but it had to make a choice among six serious candidates for the gubernatorial nomination. The two strongest candidates were Attorney General Hubert Humphrey, III (son of the former vice president) and Mike Freeman, a district attorney and son of a member of President Kennedy's cabinet. On the tenth ballot the closely divided convention endorsed Freeman, who had worked very hard for a long time to win delegate support, instead of Humphrey, who consistently held a large lead in the public opinion polls and appeared to be the stronger candidate. Humphrey won the primary decisively over Freeman and other candidates.

The importance of unity. If a large majority of convention delegates are able to unite behind the endorsee, whatever candidate is their first choice, the endorsee has a good chance of being nominated. This kind of unity is difficult to achieve if the delegates are deeply split over ideological issues or have very strong commitments to different candidates, but it sometimes is possible.

The Minnesota Republicans, who were so sharply split in 1994, achieved unity in 1998. In that year Bill Cooper, the chair of the Republican Party, persuaded the three gubernatorial candidates seeking endorsement to sign a pledge committing them to support whichever candidate was endorsed. The endorsee by a two-thirds vote on the fourth ballot was Norm Coleman, mayor of St. Paul. He defeated Lt. Gov. Joanne Benson and Allen Quist, the Christian right candidate who was endorsed but defeated in the primary in 1994. Surprisingly, Quist willingly took the unity pledge, and our survey showed that the delegates supporting him were strongly supportive of the pledge. Coleman was virtually unopposed in the primary and appeared to be the favorite in the general election until Reform candidate Jesse Ventura, a former wrestler, defeated both major party candidates in November.

The 1994 New York Republican convention provides another example of the importance of achieving unity. Under the leadership of Sen. Alfonse D'Amato, Republican leaders held a number of meetings before the convention and finally agreed to unite behind D'Amato's choice, state senator George Pataki. Consequently Pataki was able to win the endorsement on the first ballot. The leaders not only prevented his only opponent at the convention, George London, from getting the 25 percent vote necessary to get on the primary ballot automatically but also talked London out of running for governor on a third-party ticket by offering him the Republican nomination for controller. Pataki beat his only remaining primary opponent and went on to upset incumbent governor Mario Cuomo in the general election.

The 1998 New York Democratic convention not only was unable to achieve unity; it proved incapable of endorsing a gubernatorial candidate. A candidate needed a majority of votes to be endorsed, but the party changed its rules to permit only a single ballot. With four serious candidates running, this made it more difficult for anyone to win a majority. The strongest vote-getter was Peter Vallone, Speaker of the New York City Council, but his 44 percent of the vote fell short of a majority. The party had failed to unite behind anyone or discourage any of the other three candidates from entering the primary. Vallone won a solid 56 percent of the primary vote, but he was handicapped by the necessity of contesting in the primary and lost to Gov. George Pataki by almost one million votes in the general election.

The importance of funding and other tangible resources. A candidate who wins the endorsement of a party convention may in the short run gain some publicity and name recognition, as well as some campaign momentum. But if the endorsee faces opposition in the primary, the endorsement will be a significant advantage only if it brings substantial tangible advantages to the endorsee.

In both 1994 and 1998 we asked convention delegates whom we surveyed what advantages, if any, the party's gubernatorial endorsee would gain from that endorsement. Almost three-fourths of the delegates thought that there were some specific advantages. Of those responding positively, almost half mentioned tangible resources that the endorsee would get, such as the backing of state and local party organizations, participation by party activists in the campaign, and funding—both from party organizations and from individuals. More than one-third mentioned less tangible advantages such as good publicity and greater name recognition for the endorsee and a boost to the campaign momentum. Less than 10 percent believed that the endorsement would have a direct effect on how voters cast their ballot.

The state party organization may provide the endorsee with campaign funding and advisers who can assist with organization, polling, media relations, and other essential services. Local party organizations may mobilize their resources in support of the candidate. In only a handful of states—the most important being New York—does the law prohibit party organizations from contributing funds to candidates in contested primary elections. Party activists may be more willing to campaign and raise money for the candidate who has been endorsed. Delegates whom we surveyed were more likely to mention the importance of tangible resources in states where the political parties are well organized and there is a long tradition of endorsements, such as New York, Connecticut, and Minnesota.

In recent years there has been an increasing number of candidates for governor or other statewide office who are either very wealthy or very successful in raising large sums of money. They are able to outspend and often defeat candidates who have much more experience and better credentials for public office. Supporters of the endorsement system often argue that it can help to prevent nominations from being bought by candidates with the biggest campaign fund. For this to happen, however, the party that endorses a candidate must be able to raise funds and mobilize workers in support of the endorsee. Critics of the endorsement system, particularly in states without strong party organizations, often argue that endorsement is meaningless because it is not translated into much tangible party support for the endorsee. A California delegate in our survey complained, "The endorsement is not 'self-enforcing'—that is, it does not have any value other than what the candidate is able to make of it. *The party does not have any resources to publicize its endorsements.*"

The political parties in Minnesota provide the endorsee with a number of services, such as fund-raising assistance, computer services, phone banks, access to lists of voters, and campaign workers. But in 1998, because many of the Minnesota Democratic leaders thought endorsee Mike Freeman was a weaker candidate than Hubert Humphrey, there were disagreements about how much funding the party should provide to Freeman. The Minnesota Republican Party had similar problems in 1994, when the party rejected the incumbent governor and endorsed Allen Quist. Obviously a united party is better able to provide tangible aid to the endorsee than a badly divided party.

In New York and Connecticut the local party organizations, particularly in the larger cities, usually provide organizational support to the endorsee. In 1994 the Connecticut local Republican Party organizations united behind endorsee John Rowland at the convention and in the primary, helping him win the nomination. But in the Democratic Party, the urban organizations that had delivered the endorsement to John Larson were unable to match the campaign efforts of Bill Curry, who lost the endorsement but defeated Larson in the primary.

Back in 1982 the endorsement system faced a challenge in both New York parties. The Democratic contest was between New York City mayor Edward Koch and Lt. Gov. Mario Cuomo. Koch, who had the support of most party leaders in New York City, won endorsement by a 3–2 margin. But Cuomo won the primary. He almost broke even in New York City, mobilizing the support of labor unions and minority groups to counter the efforts of party leaders, while upstate, where Democratic organizations were weak, Cuomo won comfortably. Cuomo won the election and served twelve years as governor.

In 1982 the New York Republican Party was confronted with a wealthy outsider, Lew Lehrman, a multimillionaire who ran a chain of drugstores but had never held political office. By the time the convention met, Lehrman had spent almost $3 million on advertising and was far better known than his three opponents, all of whom were experienced party leaders. The convention delegates, recognizing that Lehrman would outspend his rivals in the primary and almost certainly defeat them, accepted the inevitable and endorsed him. Lehrman easily outspent and defeated his remaining primary opponent and almost spent enough to defeat Mario Cuomo in the general election. In effect, Lehrman used his millions to buy both the endorsement and the nomination from the Republican Party.

The Future of Endorsements

What is the future for preprimary endorsements of candidates by political parties? Is this the wave of the future or a relic of the past? Earlier in this chapter we provided evidence that slightly more primaries were contested during the 1980s and 1990s than in earlier years. Only half of endorsees won contested primaries compared with over 80 percent in the past; and the percentage of endorsees winning with or without a contest fell from just over 90 percent to 74 percent. We know that those who challenge endorsees are often well financed and that political parties sometime fail to provide their endorsees enough tangible support to make the endorsement really meaningful. For endorsements to be a success, we have learned that the convention delegates and the party organization must do a lot of things right.

Convention delegates should be good judges of endorsement systems. Our surveys of 1994 and 1998 endorsements show surprising support among delegates for the continued use of endorsements by the party. The percentages in Table 4-3 are an average of the results of the 1994 and 1998 surveys; in most cases there were only small differences between the answers in the two surveys.

The most important finding is that almost three-fourths of the delegates agreed that their party should continue to make endorsements. We would expect that delegates who had voted for the endorsee at the convention would be more enthusiastic than those supporting someone who failed to get endorsed, and the table

Table 4-3   Viewpoints of Delegates to 1994 and 1998 Conventions on Endorsements

Delegate Viewpoints	Percentage Agreeing
Party should make endorsements	74
Delegates supporting endorsement	
Supported endorsement winners	82
Supported endorsement losers	65
Most frequent reasons given for supporting endorsements:	
It enhances role of activists and it has a grassroots base	46
It strengthens the party	44
It produces better candidates	12
Criticism of primaries	12
It helps voters decide	8

Source: Data taken from authors' surveys of convention delegates conducted in 1994 and 1998.

shows that this in fact occurs (by a margin of 82–65). But it is worth noting that almost two-thirds of those who supported losers at the convention still favored endorsements.

We also asked those who were supporting endorsements the reasons for this support and combined their answers into several major categories. The figures in Table 4-3 are the percentages of those favoring endorsements who mentioned each reason; the numbers add to more than 100 percent because some gave more than one reason.

Almost half (46 percent) emphasized the grassroots character of the endorsement process starting at the local level or said that it gives the party delegates more opportunity to learn about the candidates and more influence over the nomination. A Minnesota delegate stated, "The endorsement procedure is the best result of grassroots politics. Delegates are extremely well informed on candidate views and backgrounds, so they can make the right choices."

Almost an equal number (44 percent) favored endorsement because it strengthens the party by helping party unification, making candidates more responsive to the party, and emphasizing the party's position on issues. It is worth noting that the proportion of delegates mentioning party strength rose from about one-third to a little over half between 1994 and 1998. Another delegate said, "Having the power to endorse gives the party power. It allows us to hold candidates accountable to the principles outlined in the party's platform."

About 12 percent of delegates stressed that endorsements lead to the selection of better candidates and those more likely to win election. Another 12 percent were critical of the primary system and particularly of the great influence of money in primaries. According to one Minnesota delegate, "If we give up the endorsement system, we forfeit any power we have to the big boys who raise money and make television commercials." A relatively small proportion of the delegates (8 percent) thought that voters, at least those with strong party loyalties, are likely to take their voting cue from the party endorsement.

Most political parties that have been making endorsements for many years are continuing to do so. In both Massachusetts and Delaware the laws that provided for party endorsements were repealed, but both parties in Massachusetts and the Delaware Republicans now make endorsements under party rules. After the U.S. Supreme Court ruled in a California case that states could not prohibit parties from making endorsements, only the Democratic Party in California began doing so; it has now stopped endorsements for statewide races. No other state parties took advantage of the judicial decision. One southern party, the Republican Party in Louisiana, has made some gubernatorial endorsements in an effort to prevent Republican candidates from being shut out of the nonpartisan primary runoff used in that state.

We have to conclude that there are no great changes in the use of endorsements. Most parties that have been using them continue to do so despite occasional controversy. But most other parties show no interest in endorsements. Increasingly two-party competition is becoming closer in most states. This means that parties need to nominate the strongest candidates they can find; very few can coast to victory with weak candidates. A party that is deeply divided, particularly over ideological issues, faces an uphill battle in an election; and party disunity, particularly among Republican Parties, seems to be a growing problem. We might think that the need for stronger candidates and more unified parties would move some political parties to begin experimenting with endorsements, but there is little evidence of such a trend.

LEVELS OF COMPETITION IN PRIMARIES

The purpose of primary elections is to enable voters rather than a party organization or leaders to choose the nominee. That purpose is thwarted if the voters find only a single candidate's name on the primary ballot (or if no primary votes are cast because only one candidate is running). The choice has already been made by the potential candidates who decide not to run and possibly also by the party organization that supported and encouraged one candidate and discouraged others. A relatively close primary would be an even stronger indication that voters had a choice between at least two strong candidates.

Why are some primaries more competitive than others? The answer depends on the reasons that potential candidates decide to run or not to run. At the individual level, these decisions may be affected by a person's education, occupation, wealth and ability to raise money, and interest in a political career—among other reasons. But we are concerned with influences on potential candidates that are characteristic of certain states or electoral situations. Do some states have a higher level of primary competition than other states, and if so why? Why does one party in a state often have more competition in its primaries than the other party?

The simplest way to measure primary competition is by measuring the proportion of primaries that are contested, that is, the proportion with more than one candidate. We measured the proportion of gubernatorial primaries that were contested for each of the parties in the elections from 1968 through 1998, and the results are shown in Table 4-4. The percentages in the table are averages of the percentage for each state. Because most states elect governors only every four years, we needed a thirty-year period to have at least eight elections for each state. We have compared the proportion of election contests in the four regions of the country. (Louisiana is omitted because its primaries are not comparable to those in other states, and Virginia is omitted because its parties often nominate in conventions rather than in primaries.)

Table 4-4 Contested Gubernatorial Primaries, 1968–1998

	Total (%)	Democratic Incumbent (%)	Democratic Nonincumbent (%)	Republican Incumbent (%)	Republican Nonincumbent (%)
All states	69	61	84	49	79
Regions					
Northeast	58	54	83	29	67
Midwest	68	58	78	54	81
West	75	64	84	63	87
South	75	68	91	56	80
Endorsements					
Used in state	48	37	71	27	58
Not used	75	68	87	56	85
Party balance					
Heavily Democratic	77	75	92	59	79
Competitive	63	51	81	38	79
Heavily Republican	68	51	69	64	86

Sources: Congressional Quarterly's Guide to U.S. Elections, 3d. ed., 1994; recent data from issues of CQ Weekly.

Everything being equal, we would expect more candidates to run and more primaries to be contested in circumstances where a candidate has the best chance of being nominated and elected. In Table 4-4 we make the distinction between elections with and without incumbents because incumbents are usually harder to beat and often are able to discourage anyone from running against them in their party's primary. Because state parties making preprimary gubernatorial endorsements should have fewer contests, we have compared state parties with or without endorsing systems during at least part of this period. Because more candidates should run in the primary of the party more likely to win the election than in the other party, we have compared primary contests for the majority and minority parties (and parties that are closely balanced) in each state.

On average, for all states and all types of electoral situations, 69 percent of primaries are contested, but Table 4-4 shows that there are some wide variations among the states and among particular electoral patterns. For every category in the table we find that there is a larger proportion of contested primaries when there is no incumbent governor running in that party's primary, and most of the differences are large ones. For Democratic primaries in northeastern states, for example, there were contests in only 54 percent of primaries with the Democratic governor running but in 83 percent of primaries when there was no Democratic governor running.

There are differences among the four regions, with the least competition in the Northeast and the most in the West and South. In southern states the proportion of contested primaries is greater for the Democrats than for the Republicans, but the gap is smaller than it was twenty years ago, when the Republicans sometimes had trouble finding one serious candidate to run for governor and so primary competition was infrequent. Now, in the absence of a Republican governor running, four out of five southern Republican primaries are contested.

In the ten states where parties made some use of endorsements during this period, only half of the primaries were contested compared with three-fourths in the other thirty-eight states. This is what we would expect to find based on our discussion of the impact of endorsements on primaries. The proportion of contested primaries with a governor running is even smaller in an endorsing state where a challenger would almost always be taking on an endorsee governor.

A careful examination of the last section in Table 4-4 shows that there is a much larger proportion of contested Democratic primaries in states dominated by Democrats than in the small number of states dominated by Republicans. (The state partisan categories are the ones used in Table 2-1.) There are more contested Republican primaries in the small number of Republican states than in the Democratic ones, but for some reason the differences are much smaller. Candidates are more likely to run in states where winning the primary is likely to lead to victory in the general election.

It is harder to predict what might happen in more closely balanced states, and the pattern is inconsistent from one party to the other. Where the parties are closely balanced, candidates have a better chance of being elected than where their party is weak, but party leaders may be more likely to put pressure on candidates to avoid costly and divisive primaries. We should also remember that a state that is counted as having a partisan balance over a thirty-year period may have had one or the other party dominant during part of that time period.

Another measure of competition is the number of serious candidates (those winning more than 5 percent) running in a primary. Incumbency is a very important factor in reducing the number of candidates who will compete in the primary. In the party that controls the governorship, the number of primary candidates running is highest if the governor is prohibited by law from running, somewhat lower if the governor is permitted to run but does not do so, and lowest if the governor runs. In the party not controlling the governorship, there might be more candidates running, but the number would be reduced if the governor in the other party were running because the winner of the primary would probably have to face the governor in the general election. If there is one dominant party in a state, there are likely to be more candidates running in that party's primary because the primary winner is very likely to be elected. If the dominant party holds a runoff election when no one wins a majority in the initial primary contest, this feature is likely to attract more primary candidates (Berry and Canon 1993).

VOTER PARTICIPATION IN PRIMARIES

Who votes in primaries? In what conditions is voter turnout in primaries likely to be high or low? We are going to look at two types of variables that affect turnout for primary elections: those that vary from state to state and between the parties in a state and those that vary from one individual to another. The decision to go to the polls or stay home on primary election day is an individual one. But there are characteristics of primary elections in a particular state or party that either encourage people to vote or discourage them. We will begin by looking at variations in primary turnout from one state party to another over a period of years and try to explain them. Then we will attempt to explain what types of persons are more or less likely to vote in primary elections and find out whether and how they differ from those who vote in general elections.

Variations among State Parties

We would expect turnout to be higher in a state party in a particular primary election if:

The election laws and procedures make it relatively easy to vote in general and to vote in a primary in particular.

Voters get accustomed to voting in a party's primary because there are more frequent contested primaries and many of them are closely competitive.

Voters think that their individual votes will affect the outcome, perhaps because the primary election is close or because the party is likely to win the general election.

The primary is well publicized probably through television and radio advertising, or campaign workers are active in mobilizing supporters, or both of these are true.

There are a number of contested primary races on the ballot.

One or more candidates in the primary and the issues they raise attract voter interest and support.

What is the best way to measure variations in primary election turnout among the states and parties? It is more difficult than it sounds. There is no point in trying to calculate turnout for uncontested primaries because voters have little incentive to vote in them, and in some states the race does not even appear on the ballot if only one candidate is running. When both parties have a primary contest, we could compare the total vote in the two party primaries but that ignores turnout in one party's primary when the other party has no contest.

We really want to compare the two parties in each state over a period of time by calculating what proportion of Democrats and what proportion of Republicans vote in their party's primary. But how do we calculate the number of Democrats and Republicans in each state? It is simple to do in the states (roughly half) that have closed primaries requiring voters to register with a party if they want to vote in its primaries. But in open primary states anyone who is registered as a voter can vote in either party primary, and therefore voters cannot be classified by party. We would have to leave out of our calculations about one-half of the states that have various forms of open primaries.

We will use another method of calculating turnout in primaries, one that can be used in all states and that can include all contested primaries. We will calculate the votes cast in a contested Democratic gubernatorial primary as a percentage of the votes cast in the general election for the Democratic gubernatorial candidate, and we will make the same kind of calculation for Republican primaries.

We should be clear about what this measure of turnout does and does not mean. It does not mean that everyone voting Democratic in a general election can be considered a Democrat. Some are Republicans and some are independents, and in a closed primary state neither group would be eligible to vote in the Democratic primary. Nor does it mean that everyone voting in a Democratic primary will vote Democratic in the general election. For example, some might change their minds if the candidate they voted for in the primary did not win the nomination.

But the relationship between the vote cast in one party's primary and the vote for that party's candidate in the general election provides us with some useful clues about how the two-party system is operating. In a state where parties have considerable influence over the nominating process, such as states where endorsements are used, the number of voters in each party's primary may be much lower than the votes cast for that party's candidate in the general election. In states where one party has been dominant for many years, the proportion of primary to general election turnout in the two parties may be related to changes over time in the two-party balance.

The data in Table 4-5 on the ratio of primary to general election voting turnout provide us with some clues to the reasons for variations in voting turnout and the linkages between turnout and two-party competition. We would expect states in which one party is dominant and usually wins elections to have a higher turnout in the majority party primary for several reasons.

There should be more contests and more closely competitive races in the primary of the majority party because the primary winner is likely to win the general election as well. We see in Table 4-4 that there were, in fact, more contested primaries in the majority than in the minority party. Voters are more likely to get in the habit of voting in their party's primaries if they usually are contested. When

Table 4-5   Average Gubernatorial Party Primary Vote as Percentage of
Party Vote in General Election, 1968–1998

States	Democratic	Republican
All States	68	47
Party balance		
Two-party competitive	50.5	50.6
Heavily Republican	45	72
Heavily Democratic—northern	78	38
Heavily Democratic—southern and border	107	28
Individual southern-border states		
Florida	62	40
North Carolina	72	21
Tennessee	108	51
Kentucky	95	31
South Carolina	92	25
Georgia	99	30
Oklahoma	116	43
Texas	99	22
Alabama	135	29
Arkansas	118	11
Mississippi	184	16

Sources: Congressional Quarterly's Guide to U.S. Elections, 3d. ed., 1994; recent data from
issues of *CQ Weekly.*

their party has a closely competitive race, voters are particularly likely to become interested enough to vote.

In the twenty states with a relatively close two-party balance on average from 1968 through 1998, Table 4-5 shows that the ratio of a party's gubernatorial primary vote to the vote for its gubernatorial candidate in the general election was almost identical: 50.5 percent for Democrats and 50.6 percent for Republicans. In both parties roughly half as many persons vote in the primary as vote for the party's candidate in the November election. We might consider 50 percent as the norm in states with balanced parties.

We also see that in the eight states dominated by Republicans during this time period, the ratio of primary to general election vote was 72 percent for Republicans and 45 percent for Democrats. In nine nonsouthern states dominated by Democrats, the difference in the ratio was somewhat larger: 78 percent for Democrats and 38 percent for Republicans. These data support the theory that, in a state where one party usually wins statewide elections, the number of voters in that party's primary as a proportion of those voting for the party in the general election will be substantially higher than it is in the party that usually loses elections.

When we look at the figures for the eleven southern and border states, we find a huge gap between the primary to general election ratios: 107 percent for Democrats and 28 percent for Republicans. To understand what has been happening in the South in recent years, we must remember that until the mid-1960s the Solid South was overwhelmingly Democratic. Except for presidential races, the Democrats won almost every statewide office, and in the Deep South Republicans failed consistently to run statewide candidates. Republican primaries were rare, Democratic primaries were often very competitive, and the winner of the Democratic primary almost always was elected. Consequently the primary election that almost everyone voted in was the Democratic one.

Since the 1960s the Republicans have won major gains in statewide (and legislative) races. In every southern state except Georgia the Republicans have elected at least one governor, and in most states they held the governorship for at least six to eight years during the 1990s. Despite these gains, in most southern and border states—particularly in the Deep South— voters have been slow to shift from the Democratic to the Republican primary. This is so even though most of these states continue to use the open primary, which would make it easy for voters to shift primaries.

Table 4-5 compares the average primary to general election turnout ratios for Democratic and Republican primaries; the states are listed in order from the smallest to the largest difference between Democratic and Republican ratios. In many of these states the number voting in the Democratic primaries remains about as large or larger than the number voting for a Democrat for governor. This suggests that many voters stick to the Democratic primary, although they often vote for the Republican gubernatorial candidate. This also means that if there is a contested Republican primary, the nominee is often chosen by a small proportion (often one-fourth or less) of those voting Republican in November. The Republican Party thus is hurt in two ways. Republican primary voters are unlikely to be representative of the larger Republican electorate and may fail to nominate the candidate in a contested primary who would have the broadest appeal to potential Republican voters. Moreover, a voter who gets in the habit of voting in Republican primaries is more likely to vote for a Republican in the November election.

If we compare the southern and border states in the table, we find that the two with the smallest gap between Democratic and Republican ratios, Florida and North Carolina, are among the very few using closed primaries. Florida in particular has experienced dramatic growth in Republican registration, and once voters are registered as Republicans they are unlikely to slip back into Democratic registration. In Florida in 1994 more persons voted in the Republican gubernatorial primary than in the Democratic one—a very rare event in the South. The next two states—Tennessee and Kentucky—have had relatively strong two-party competition for many years, and this is also true of Oklahoma.

In South Carolina, Georgia, and Texas, the Republican Party has made major gains in recent years after slow starts. These gains have been reflected in a growing ratio of Republican primary to general election turnout. In 1974 James Edwards became the first South Carolina Republican in the twentieth century to be elected as governor. He was nominated in the first contested Republican primary, which drew 35,000 voters, or 13 percent of Edwards's general election vote. In 1994 when the Republicans elected David Beasley as governor, the Republican primary had 257,000 voters, or 58 percent of Beasley's vote for governor. In 1978 when William Clements, the first modern Republican governor of Texas, was elected, the party's primary drew only 13 percent of Clements's general election vote. In 1990 the Republican gubernatorial primary drew almost half as many voters as the party's nominee, Clayton Williams, won in the general election.

Although they elected Republican governors at least twice during the 1990s, Alabama, Arkansas, and Mississippi have lagged behind in almost every respect, particularly in winning legislative seats. In 1991, when Mississippi Republicans elected their first twentieth-century governor, Kirk Fordice, only 64,000 votes were cast in the Republican primary, which was only 8 percent of the vote cast in the Democratic primary and only 18 percent of Fordice's vote in the general election. And in Arkansas in 1980, when Republican Frank White beat Gov. William Clinton at the end of his first term, only 8,000 votes had been cast in the Republican gubernatorial primary, which was 2 percent of White's vote in the general election. In some respects political change comes slowly to Mississippi, Arkansas, and Alabama.

Individual Participation in Primaries

Voters who stay at home cannot affect the outcome of primary elections, so we want to know whether certain types of voters are more likely than others to vote in primaries. We have seen (in Table 4-5) that about two-thirds as many persons vote in Democratic primaries as vote Democratic in general elections and that for Republicans the figure is just under half. But this is probably because Democratic primaries are more often contested and more likely to be competitive and because the Democratic primary in southern states still attracts many more voters than does the Republican primary. When the political situation is comparable in the two parties, there is no reason to expect persons who consider themselves Democrats to be more likely to vote in primaries than Republicans. We found that in states with a party balance, average turnout in primaries was about half the turnout in general elections for both Democrats and Republicans.

Generally speaking, turnout for primary elections is lower than for general elections (although in southern states in the past the Democratic primary turnout was often higher than the total turnout in the general election). Therefore we may think of persons who vote often in primaries as a subset of those who vote often in general elections. We want to know how those who vote in primaries differ from those who vote only in general elections.

There is substantial evidence that voters are better educated, have higher status occupations or professions, are older, and have a greater interest in politics and a greater sense of civic duty than nonvoters (Beck 1996, 181–188). The more of these qualities a voter possesses, the more regularly that person votes. It is not surprising to find that those who vote in primary elections are likely to rank even higher in these qualities than persons who vote only in general elections (Jewell 1984, chap. 6; Scheele 1972, chap. 3).

Are there additional characteristics that separate these two types of voters? Primary voters are far more likely to have a strong sense of party identification; they are more likely to be strong Democrats or Republicans and less likely to be independents (Jewell 1984, chap. 6). We are not surprised to find that strong party loyalists have more interest in party nominations than do other voters. Moreover, persons who consider themselves to be independents—as many younger persons do—may be reluctant to register with a party, thus making them ineligible to vote in primaries in those states with closed primaries. Voters who identify with the minority party may be less motivated to vote in the primary if they assume that the eventual nominee has little chance of being elected because the majority party dominates the elections.

Is there any reason to believe that voters with strong ideological viewpoints—strong conservatives or strong liberals—are disproportionately represented in the primary electorate? To the extent that this is true, these voters might nominate a candidate who reflected their preferences but would have trouble in the general election because they were not moderate enough to win votes from independents and members of the other party. Surveys of voters taken in a few states have failed to provide any consistent pattern of liberal or conservative overrepresentation in primaries. Anecdotal evidence suggests that this may occur in some state primaries. The presence of a candidate prominently identified with a strong ideological viewpoint (like the presence of a black, ethnic, or female candidate) probably attracts voters to the primary who are strongly interested in seeing such a person nominated.

Although in a book on state parties we are mainly interested in state-level primaries, we should not ignore the connections between state and local primaries. In states where party registration is required for primary voting, voters who are particularly interested in local politics may register with the party that is strongest in their county or city, even though it may be the minority party at the state level. Turnout in state primaries may sometimes be affected by the level of interest in local primaries in various sections of the state.

In Kentucky, for example, where a majority of voters are registered as Democrats, Republican registration is particularly heavy in the traditionally Republican sections of the state, where local officials are usually Republican and local Republican primaries are often competitive. In a statewide Republican primary for governor or senator, turnout may be particularly heavy in the traditionally Republican rural counties. Heavy turnout could lead to nomination of a candidate who can easily carry these safe Republican counties but who has less appeal to independent and even Republican voters in the metropolitan areas of the state.

Who Votes in Which Primary?

It is easier to determine which kinds of voters are more likely to vote in primaries than to figure out who is likely to vote in which party primary and how often. It is also easier than determining the reasons voters shift back and forth from one primary to another—particularly in open primary states where that is easy to do.

We can begin by assuming that persons who consider themselves Republicans usually vote in Republican primaries and those who identify as Democrats usually vote in Democratic primaries. National surveys suggest that only 6 or 7 percent of those who identify with a party report voting in the other party's primary (Scheele 1972, chap. 2). Why would anyone vote in a primary other than the one with which they identified? In a state where one party is usually dominant (as the Democrats used to be in southern states) persons who identify with the minority party may vote in the majority party primary because it is the only real contest in the state and the winner is likely to get elected.

How do voters who consider themselves to be independents choose between a Democratic or Republican primary? As we have pointed out, independents are less likely to vote in either party primary, particularly if voting requires registering with that party. Those who do vote are more likely to pick the primary of whichever party seems most likely to win, partly because it is more likely to have close competition (Finkel and Scarrow 1985). In most closed primary states it is not easy to change party registration, and most voters presumably vote consistently in one party primary, usually the one with which they identify.

The behavior of voters in open primary states is more difficult to measure. How often do voters take advantage of their opportunity to cross over from one party primary to the other in successive elections? Is this unusual or do many voters shift back and forth year after year? More important, what factors motivate a shift? After the 1982 election voters in Michigan—an open primary state— were asked in a survey whether they always voted in the same party's primary or shifted from time to time. About one-fourth said they always voted in the same primary, and slightly more said they usually voted consistently; but almost half said they shifted back and forth between party primaries. When asked how they decided which primary to enter in 1982, the frequent shifters usually mentioned a particular candidate or issue or said it was time for a change in parties (Jewell 1984, 202–204).

Voters in California, Washington, and Alaska have had a so-called blanket primary, which gives them even more choice than an open primary. In a blanket primary voters can vote for Democratic primary candidates for governor, Republican candidates for senator, and so on down the list. Recent studies (Kousser 1999; Cohen and Sides 1998) of the blanket primaries in California give us some clues about what motivates voters when they vote for candidates in a primary of a party they do not consider their own. Voters in these states are particularly likely to shift from a less competitive primary to one that has closer competition. Voters who cross over from their normal partisan preference are likely to vote for a more moderate candidate. For example, a Republican might vote for the least liberal Democrat who is running for governor. This tendency might encourage both Democratic and Republican candidates running in an open primary, and particularly a blanket primary, to emphasize that they are moderates in an effort to attract voters who would normally vote in the other party's primary. In fact, supporters of the blanket primary argue that it would encourage more moderate candidates to run. The blanket primary has been overruled by the U.S. Supreme Court.

These studies also suggest that relatively few crossover voters are trying to "raid" the other party. That is, they do not try to help nominate the weakest candidate in the other party in order to help their own party win the general election. There are probably several reasons why raiding is seldom attempted. Most voters do not have the strong level of party loyalty or the skill in judging candidates' political strength that would be necessary to become effective "raiders."

FACTORS EXPLAINING PRIMARY ELECTION OUTCOMES

What determines the outcome of primary elections? We have seen that, in the state parties making endorsements, the party organizations sometimes have considerable influence over the outcome of primaries, but in most other primaries the organization has relatively little influence.

The party loyalty of voters plays a big part in the outcome of general elections, but it cannot explain the outcome of a party's primary. The other factors that influence general elections can be expected to have a greater effect on primary outcomes: the candidates, the issues they stress, and their skill in running a campaign. Because television and radio advertising is so important in campaigns— particularly at the statewide level—a candidate's ability to raise enough funds to pay for commercials becomes even more important in primary campaigns than it is in general elections.

The Assets and Liabilities of Incumbency

An incumbent governor (or any other visible officeholder) usually has a great advantage in primary elections. The governor is almost always better known than any opponents in the primary because of the experience and greater opportunities to get what is often called "free TV" that go along with holding office. These include media coverage of the governor's speeches, press conferences, and other activities. A skillful governor can use these opportunities to build a favorable image, not just during the campaign but over four years in office. These advantages often discourage really strong candidates from challenging the governor in a primary. Moreover, if there is strong two-party competition in the state, candidates do not want to be accused of hurting the party's chances of winning by forcing the governor to undergo an expensive and possibly divisive primary campaign.

In the 157 state elections that took place from 1988 through 1998, the governor sought reelection in ninety-one of them. In only forty-three of those did the governor have a primary race with more than token opposition (that is, in which the incumbent won less than 90 percent of the vote). In thirty of those forty-three contested races the governor got more than 60 percent of the primary vote, usually much more. Only two of these governors lost their bid for renomination.

In addition to having name recognition and an image, the governor has a record of performance, although this is not necessarily an asset. Voters will likely support a governor whom they perceive as having a good record, but they may vote against the governor if they hold that person responsible for raising taxes, tolerating scandals, or doing other perceived misdeeds.

The risks of being an incumbent who has to run on a previous record of achievements are illustrated by two successive Massachusetts Democratic governors who were defeated by each other in primaries. In 1978 Michael Dukakis (the 1988 Democratic presidential candidate) was finishing his first term as governor and seeking renomination. But he was under attack by many liberal Democrats because he had decided it was necessary to cut back levels of spending for a number of their favorite economic and social programs. He was also under attack by conservative Democrats, including his primary challenger, Edward King, who opposed funding for abortions and favored capital punishment and tougher treatment of criminals. King defeated Dukakis and was elected governor. Four years later, in 1982, Dukakis attacked King for being too conservative on both taxing and spending policies and social issues and in addition blamed him for a number of scandals during the King administration. This time it was Dukakis who was nominated and elected.

Even if the governor is not running again, a candidate who has served in the administration—like a lieutenant governor or one running with the governor's support in the primary—may gain or lose votes because of such a linkage to the governor. In 1982, for example, Michigan Republican governor William Milliken announced that he would not run again and endorsed Lt. Gov. James Brickley in the Republican primary. But Brickley was handicapped because Governor Milliken had persuaded the legislature to pass a temporary increase in the income tax. He was beaten in the primary by a conservative businessman, Richard Headlee, who had attracted attention as the originator of a tax-cutting initiative adopted by the voters in 1978 and who argued it was "time for a change." A Democrat was elected that year.

Candidates, Issues, and Campaigns

When the primary campaign does not center on the record of the incumbent administration or a recent governor, public attention is likely to focus on the candidates and the issues they raise. Their skill in campaigning may determine how voters perceive the candidates and how positive they are about the issues raised by each candidate.

Sometimes candidates who have enough name recognition to get nominated do not turn out to be strong enough candidates to get elected. The 1998 Democratic gubernatorial primary in Michigan was narrowly won by Geoffrey Fieger, who had little experience in politics but who was known to the voters as the attorney who often represented Jack Kevorkian in his court appearances. Leaders of the state Democratic Party and the United Auto Workers worked for other candidates but were unable to stop Fieger. It would have been difficult to find a Democratic candidate who could have beaten John Engler, the popular Republican governor. But Fieger embarrassed the Democratic Party with his frequent personal insults of the governor (at various times he called Engler a moron, a liar, fat, and ugly), and he won only 38 percent of the general election vote.

Tennessee Democrats also had a difficult job trying to find a candidate who could seriously challenge Don Sundquist, the popular Republican governor. The candidate favored by Democratic leaders had little name recognition or financial support from the party, and so voters in the primary chose John Jay Hooker, someone whose name they recognized because he had lost five previous campaigns for senator and governor. Once nominated, he lost again, tallying less than 30 percent of the vote against Sundquist.

Although candidates running in the same party primary often have similar viewpoints on many issues, each is likely to define or emphasize issues in a way that will appeal to voters. They may, for example, promise to cut taxes in general or to cut particular taxes that appear to be most unpopular, such as property taxes. They may try to convince voters that their opponent is making such expensive promises that taxes will have to be raised. Candidates may try to appeal to particular groups of voters—union members, women voters, small-business owners, or environmentalists, for example—whose support they believe may be crucial.

Some issues generate more disagreement within political parties than most. One example is the continuing disagreements between right-to-life advocates and those who support some or all forms of abortion. Gun control may be another issue that divides parties. For example, the 1998 Illinois Democratic primary for governor was eventually won by Rep. Glenn Poshard, who represented a relatively conservative downstate district where his antiabortion views and opposition to gun control were popular. In his statewide race for governor, Poshard faced considerable opposition from other candidates on issues such as these, yet he eventually won the nomination.

Some Republican primaries in recent years have featured not only disagreements on specific issues but more basic ideological splits, mostly over social issues. Christian right organizations have often supported candidates taking very conservative positions on such issues as right-to-life, prayer in schools, and tougher penalties for criminals. Two Republican incumbent governors in southern states were defeated for reelection in 1998 after each had faced strong primary challenges that focused on ideological differences in the party. Alabama governor Fob James gave high priority to issues stressed by the Christian right, particularly the question of school prayer. His major opponent was Winton Blount, a wealthy businessman who argued that James should give higher priority to attracting new business to the state. James won the primary but lost the general election. Republican governor David Beasley of South Carolina was first elected in 1994, following a primary in which his major opponent argued that Beasley was a captive of the Christian Coalition. Beasley won both nomination and election, but in 1998 he was defeated for reelection.

Can the Nomination Be Bought?

There are many examples of candidates winning primaries after spending much more than the losing candidates. Some of these are candidates who can raise much more campaign funding because they have held public office or have demonstrated other political strengths so that contributors believe they can win. Other candidates may not have much political experience or be well known, but they are able to gain name recognition and credibility as candidates because they are wealthy or know how to raise large sums of money.

The impact of campaign spending on the outcome of primaries is similar to its impact in general elections (discussed in the next chapter). Incumbent candidates for governor and those who have held other major offices are already well known and have less need for huge amounts of campaign funds. Nonincumbents who are not well known throughout the state need lots of campaign funds to gain name recognition and develop a public image, but because they are underdogs it is usually hard for them to raise money.

A study of campaign spending in 1982 in fifty of the fifty-six contested gubernatorial primaries shows that in thirty-seven of these races the candidate who spent the most money won the primary. In thirty of these thirty-seven cases the winner's proportion of total spending was larger than the proportion of the primary vote. All of the incumbents who won in the primary were also the top spenders in their race; the only incumbent governor who lost, Democrat Edward King of Massachusetts, was also the top spender. Often candidates who won by large margins spent more on their races than seemed necessary to win. A regression analysis of the 1982 primaries shows that the level of experience of the two candidates who are running and the amount that each spends in a campaign go a long way toward explaining the outcome of the primary (Jewell 1984).

Tables 4-6 and 4-7 show the relationship between the proportion of the votes won by the winning primary candidates and the proportion of the total primary funds that were spent by these winners. Both tables include a large number of contested primaries for three election cycles from 1988 though 1998. Included are those contests in which the data make it possible to distinguish between funding for the primary and funding for the general election for all of the candidates.

Table 4-6 covers 35 races in which an incumbent governor was running , and Table 4-7 covers 115 races in which no incumbent was running. The tables are organized in similar fashion. The columns show the percentage of the vote won by the winner of the primary, clustered into several groups. The rows show the percentage of the total funds spent by the winner. Incumbents won all 35 of the primary races that they entered (although two governors lost other primary con-

Table 4-6 Comparison between Proportion of Votes that Incumbent Governors Received and Proportion of Campaign Funds that They Spent in Contested Primary Elections, 1988–1998 (number of elections)

Funding Proportion	Proportion of Votes Cast for Incumbent Governor				
	86+%	71–85%	56–70%	55% or Less	Total
95+%	7	7	2	0	16
86–94%	1	1	1	0	3
71–85%	0	3	3	0	6
56–70%	0	0	1	5	6
55% or less	0	0	1	3	4
Total	8	11	8	8	35

Sources: Congressional Quarterly's Guide to U.S. Elections, 3d. ed., 1994; recent data from issues of *CQ Weekly.* Data on funding were provided by Thad Beyle.

Table 4-7   Comparison between Proportion of Votes that Winning Gubernatorial Candidates Received and Proportion of Campaign Funds that They Spent in Contested Primary Elections without Incumbents Running, 1988–1998 (number of elections)

Funding Proportion	Proportion of Votes Cast for Winning Candidate					Total
	86+%	71–85%	56–70%	45–55%	Under 45%	
95+%	9	6	2	1	0	18
86–94%	3	3	2	1	0	9
71–85%	1	4	8	5	0	18
56–70%	0	2	4	8	5	19
45–55%	0	0	2	8	4	14
30–44%	0	0	1	13	7	21
Under 30%	0	0	1	3	12	16
Total	13	15	20	39	28	115

Sources: Congressional Quarterly's Guide to U.S. Elections, 3d. ed., 1994; recent data from issues of *CQ Weekly.* Data on funding were provided by Thad Beyle.

tests during this time period). Because incumbents have such an advantage in fund raising, we need to analyze the impact of campaign funding on the outcome of elections separately for primaries with and without incumbents running.

Table 4-6 shows that more than half of the governors won by a very comfortable margin (over 70 percent and often over 85 percent), and less than one-fourth won with 55 percent or less, even though primaries often have more than two candidates running. Although most governors won easily, a large number had a share of spending that was even greater than their share of votes. Just a handful of governors spent proportionately less than their share of votes.

Governors do not often face serious challenges in their party's primary. The odds against beating a governor in the primary are much higher than the odds against doing so in a general election. Therefore the primary challengers are usually politically weak and inexperienced, they seem unlikely to win, and so they have great trouble raising money. The governor can usually raise money easily, and it is not surprising that twenty-five of the thirty-five governors for whom data are given in Table 4-6 were able to raise at least 70 percent—and often much more—of the total funds. The huge imbalance in spending may not be crucial to the governor's renomination, but it helps to ensure that the margin will usually be large. The fact that relatively unknown candidates who cannot raise much money sometimes get one-fourth to one-third of the vote or more suggests that some voters are casting protest votes.

One example, in 1998, of a governor winning nomination by a relatively narrow margin (58–42 percent) was Massachusetts acting governor Paul Cellucci, who had only a 55–45 lead in spending and who had the endorsement of the

Republican Party convention. In 1998 one Republican governor, Fob James of Alabama, was outspent by his closest opponent by $2 million in the primary but won with less than a majority; he won the runoff primary despite being outspent again by more than $2 million. At the other extreme, David Beasley of South Carolina outspent his primary opponent by $814,000 to $15,000 but won by a much smaller margin, 72–28 percent. Oddly enough, James and Beasley were the only two southern Republican governors who lost in the 1998 general election.

Because governors can usually raise as much money as they need, and because governors have so many other advantages that they often do not need a large financial advantage, campaign funding may have a more direct impact on primary elections in which no incumbent is running. Table 4-7 includes 115 such races. We have excluded completely lopsided contests that were won by 95 percent or more.

The absence of an incumbent in the race is likely to attract stronger, more experienced candidates in the primary, particularly if the party has a reasonable chance of winning the seat. Several of these candidates may be capable of raising enough money to be competitive. Only about one-fourth of the winners had more than 70 percent of the vote, while almost 60 percent won by 55 percent or less.

It is difficult to generalize about 115 different primary races, but several patterns emerge. The winners in the upper left-hand corner of Table 4-7 won landslide victories, and almost all of them had huge advantages in funding. Although not incumbents, most were probably experienced politicians—perhaps holding visible elective offices—who were capable of raising plenty of money. Most of their opponents probably were much less well known and unable to raise enough money to be competitive.

An obvious example is Sen. Pete Wilson of California, who decided to run for governor in 1990 and won 66 percent of the vote against a scattering of opponents who spent virtually nothing. In that same year in Michigan John Engler, an experienced and well-known legislative leader, won 88 percent of the vote against two obscure candidates who spent virtually nothing; he went on to beat the incumbent governor in the general election. George W. Bush won his first election as governor of Texas in 1994 after a 93 percent primary victory against an opponent who spent nothing.

The winners who cluster in the lower right-hand corner generally won half or less of the vote and raised half or less of the money. We should keep in mind, however, that such races often had at least three or four viable candidates. Except in a few southern states that hold runoff elections, it is possible for a candidate to win with less than 50 percent of the vote, and the winner may not need to spend as much as half of the total. For example, in a Tennessee Democratic primary the winner got only 53 percent of the vote and spent that same proportion of all funds in the primary. Yet he beat his closest opponent in a five-person race by a comfortable margin of 53–20 percent and had about the same lead in financing.

The bottom row of Table 4-7 includes sixteen candidates who won, however narrowly, while raising less than 30 percent of the funding. A few examples may explain how this is possible. Generally these candidates had experience and visibility that outweighed their financial disadvantages.

In the 1998 Democratic primary in Minnesota Mark Dayton was the big spender (55 percent), but he was the least well known among five candidates and was one of three who each got about 18 percent of the vote (including Mike Freeman who was endorsed by the Democratic convention). The winner, who spent only 15 percent of total funds but got 37 percent of the vote, was Hubert Humphrey III. Humphrey had been attorney general for many years and had played a well-publicized national role in forcing tobacco companies to reimburse the states for health care costs.

In 1994 Fob James, the winner of the Alabama Republican primary in a runoff, spent less than $700,000 in the primary against two candidates, each of whom spent close to $3 million. But James was a former governor, and his opponents were less well known. In the 1996 West Virginia Republican primary, Cecil Underwood, the winner with 41 percent of the vote, came in third in the spending derby, but he was a former governor who was well known throughout the state.

The 1998 Democratic gubernatorial primary in California provides a classic example of how experience may be more important than campaign funds, even in a state where it is enormously expensive to campaign. For most of the 1998 Democratic gubernatorial campaign in that state the best-known candidate, Al Checchi, ran television ads that dominated TV airwaves for six months. Checchi (with a net worth of some $800 million) owned a substantial share of Northwest Airlines; he had never run for political office or even voted consistently. Checchi eventually spent almost $40 million to campaign and won only 21 percent of the Democratic primary vote. Jane Harman, a member of Congress who also qualified as a millionaire, spent about $16 million and gained another 20 percent of the vote. The winner of the primary, however, was Gray Davis, who was not wealthy but was the incumbent lieutenant governor and a veteran officeholder. He worked hard to raise $9 million, hoarded the funds until barely six weeks before the primary election, and then launched his television campaign with the slogan "Experience money can't buy." The slogan made sense to the voters, and Davis won 58 percent of the Democratic primary vote and was elected governor.

Occasionally spending a lot of money in a campaign seems to accomplish almost nothing. In a West Virginia Democratic primary a candidate who spent almost $700,000 (14 percent of the total) won only 1 percent of the vote. Sometimes raising and spending money can become an embarrassment to a candidate and a party. John Lindauer, winner of the 1998 Alaskan Republican primary, was able to spend $1.7 million on the race, which is a lot of money in Alaska. But questions were raised about the sources of his funds. After repeatedly denying that much of the campaign money came from his wife, he admitted once the primary was over that the allegations were true. The Republican state central committee withdrew its support from him and supported a write-in candidate. Lindauer lost to the incumbent Democratic governor by almost a 3–1 margin.

We can draw a few conclusions from the wide variety of primary elections without incumbents running. Candidates who win by very large margins and raise most of the money in the campaign are usually much better known than the other candidates and attract relatively weak opponents. Candidates who get nominated despite being significantly outspent are usually better known than their opponents and do not need as much advertising. If there are three or four viable candidates in the race, which frequently happens in contests without incumbents running, the person who spends the most is not necessarily the winner. But those who fall way behind in money raising are very unlikely to win.

Earlier in this chapter we described the endorsement process used by a number of state parties and pointed out that convention delegates who support the endorsement system often argue that it reduces the impact of money on the nominating process. An examination of 20 primary elections in endorsing parties (of the 115 without incumbents in Table 4-7) fails to prove that money is less crucial in these nominations. In about one-third of the cases, the winners had a proportion of votes that exceeded their proportion of spending, but in another third the winners had a larger proportion of spending than of votes. In several cases the endorsee lost the primary despite having more money, and in other cases the endorsee lost to a higher-spending opponent. We noted that in the 1998 Minnesota Democratic primary the endorsee was beaten not by the highest spender but by a better known, more popular candidate.

The success of endorsement systems cannot be judged by the ratio of votes to spending. When a party endorses a candidate, it hopes that this action will encourage contributors to send checks to the endorsee; in some parties either the state or local organizations, and sometimes both, usually contribute funds to the endorsee. In other words, a successful endorsement should give the endorsee at least enough funding to match what the strongest challenger can raise. If an endorsee is outspent in the nomination race, it suggests that the party and its contributors are not doing their job well enough. If an endorsee loses the nomination despite having a financial advantage, it suggests that the party has failed to endorse its strongest available candidate.

THE IMPACT OF PRIMARIES ON GENERAL ELECTIONS

The primary election can have a number of effects on the general election that follows: some are obvious and some are difficult to discover and measure. We begin by examining the reasons why the voters in a primary may fail to nominate the best available candidate, that is, the one with the best change of winning. Next we explain how a divisive primary may damage a party and hurt its chances of electing its nominee, and we consider why it is difficult to define and measure what we mean by a divisive primary. We conclude by summarizing what we have said about the primary and its relationship to the general election.

Searching for a Winning Candidate

The primary election can have a number of effects on the general election; some are obvious and some are difficult to discover and measure. As we have noted, primary voters do not always vote for the candidate who would have the best chance in the general election. The Democratic Party in southern states used to be divided sharply between liberal and conservative wings, and if a more liberal candidate won the primary, conservative Democrats might vote for the Republican candidate in the fall election. Although differences remain in some southern Democratic Parties, so many conservative Democrats have shifted allegiance to the Republican Party that the Democrats are more united and if they nominate a moderate candidate they may win in the November election.

It is the Republican Parties in some states that are now more divided along ideological lines. Republican Party activists are likely to be very conservative on economic issues and, where the religious right is strong, on social issues, particularly in western and southern states (but not so much in northeastern states). These Republican activists work hard in primary elections to mobilize voters who share their ideological views. The result may be the nomination of a very conservative candidate who in some cases may have difficulty winning the support of the independent and moderately conservative Democratic voters who are sometimes needed to win an election.

A relatively recent study (Schneider 1997) shows that the proportion of Republican statewide primaries in southern states that pitted a candidate supported by the Christian right against a social moderate candidate increased from only 16 percent in the 1980–1985 primaries to 50 percent in the 1991–1996 elections. The proportion of contested Republican primaries won by Christian right candidates compared with social moderates increased from less than one-half to two-thirds, but these Christian right candidates were less likely to win general elections than the smaller number of socially moderate candidates.

There may be other reasons why primary voters make a poor choice. They may know little about the strengths and weaknesses of candidates and simply pick a familiar name—perhaps someone who has run for various offices in the past without winning—rather than a candidate who may have a better chance of winning in the fall campaign. One of the strongest arguments for party endorsements is that the convention delegates are likely to make a better judgment about which would be the strongest candidates with experience, political skills, and the ability to appeal to a wide range of voters.

Divisive Primaries

Regardless of whether voters in a party's primary pick the candidate who would have the best chance of winning, the candidate who is nominated may have more difficulty winning the general election if the primary is very divisive. How do we define a "divisive" primary, and how do we measure divisiveness in practice? Political scientists interested in this question have had difficulty in determining what kinds of divisions in a primary are likely to hurt the primary winner's chances of winning the general election and finding ways to measure such divisions.

We might expect that a candidate who wins the primary by a narrow margin will have trouble winning the general election, but studies do not show that this is consistently the case (Kenney and Rice 1984; Kenney 1988; Carlson 1989). Just because a party's nominee has won the primary by a small margin and many voters preferred other candidates does not mean that the candidate will be handicapped in the general election. One factor to consider is whether both party primaries appear to be divisive (Kenney and Rice 1987).

We look for other aspects of the primary that may be damaging to the winner. If the party is sharply divided into factions or split along ideological lines, the primary may be divisive. Supporters of the losing candidate may be more likely to stay home on election day or vote for the other party's candidate than they would if there were no ideological or factional conflict. Even in the absence of serious ideological splits, a party primary can be divisive if the campaign is a bitter one, with the leading candidates making sharp attacks on one another. Even if we recognize that a primary has factional conflicts or bitter disputes between candidates, it is difficult to measure the intensity of these.

One indication of the divisiveness of a primary is the behavior of party activists who have worked for a candidate in the primary. If most of those who have worked for losing candidates in the primary campaign are willing to work for the winner in the general election, this suggests that the primary was not very divisive. If most are unwilling to work for the winner in the general election, this is an indication of divisiveness that may cost the party the election. A study of Democratic gubernatorial primaries in Kentucky found that two-thirds to three-fourths of those who worked for a losing candidate in the primary worked for the winner in the general elections, and those most likely to do so had strong loyalties to the Democratic Party and a long-term record of sustained activity in party politics (Miller, Jewell, and Sigelman 1988; see also Johnson and Gibson 1974).

If a closely contested primary election is very expensive, the winner may be seriously handicapped in the general election campaign. The victor may have raised and spent $1 million to win the Republican primary, while a Democratic candidate without a primary opponent was raising $1.5 million and putting most of it in the bank. The Republican starting the general election campaign almost $1.5 million behind in funds may never catch up.

The winner of a competitive primary election almost certainly may be handicapped in the general election if the primary was characterized by ideological divisions, bitterness between the candidates, unwillingness of party activists to work for the winner in the general elections, very high campaign spending, or some combination of these. But these aspects of a primary election are difficult to measure accurately, and therefore studies of this issue usually measure divisiveness simply by the closeness of the primary outcome. These studies do not consistently show that candidates who win a primary by a narrow margin are likely to do poorly in the general election.

A recent study (Hogan 1999) of state legislative elections found that, after other variables were taken into account, the *smaller* the margin of the primary winner, the *larger* the margin that the candidate won in the general election. The explanation for this, as Hogan concludes, is that more candidates are likely to run in the primary of the party that seems most likely to win. This situation produces closer competition and means that candidates who win the primary by only modest margins have a good chance of being elected.

In our discussion of primary competition earlier in this chapter, we pointed out that there was more likely to be a contest in the primary of the party that seemed most likely to win the general election, particularly if no incumbent was running in that primary (see Table 4-4). When a party's chances of winning appear to be small, the party might have difficulty finding one serious candidate willing to run. The same logic would lead us to expect more candidates in the primary of the favored party. This is not a new finding; it was emphasized long ago by V. O. Key, Jr. (1956). It does not mean that divisive primaries cannot be damaging to a primary winner, even in a party that is strong. But divisiveness must be measured by more than simply the margin of victory in the primary.

The Problematic Primary

If all voters were either Democrats or Republicans, and if they all voted consistently for their party's candidate, the outcome of the primary election would have no effect on the outcome of the general election. But this is not the case. Although a high proportion of partisans (often around 80 percent) vote the party line, others do not; roughly one-third of the voters identify with neither party and vote more independently. Therefore it makes a great deal of difference what candidate a party nominates. In a two-party system each party represents a coalition of interests. The party needs to nominate a candidate who has campaign skills and personal appeal but who also can appeal to most of the interests represented in the party—and to at least some of those outside the party.

Primary elections are not the most efficient, dependable method for nominating a political party's candidate, for a number of reasons that we have discussed. The primary campaign may be so divisive and bitter, or so expensive, that the winner's chances of winning the November election are reduced. As the costs of primary campaigns increase, there is greater risk that the best-financed candidate will win, though that candidate may not be well suited to win the general election where partisanship is important. Turnout in primaries is usually lower than in general elections, and those who do turn out in the primary may be unrepresentative of the interests and viewpoints in the party as a whole. This is particularly a problem if the political party is sharply divided along ideological lines.

It is important for the political party to nominate a mainstream candidate, one who can appeal to the broadest range of interests and viewpoints in the party. But in most states the law permits persons to vote in a party's primary, even though they do not have much of an allegiance to that party. In twenty-three states each party's primary is open to any registered voter, and in fifteen other states unaffiliated voters (and in a few of these states any voter) can shift their registration to a party on primary election day. Only eleven states have a completely closed primary. If it is easy for voters to enter any party's primary, this may help moderate candidates who can appeal across party lines. However it can also mean that the balance of power in a party's primary may be held by voters who do not share the interests and viewpoints of the mainstream partisans, and the candidate who is nominated may have difficulty winning the votes of party loyalists.

We have described the endorsement system used by a number of parties to support one of the candidates running in its primary. This system is far from ideal. The delegates, though knowledgeable about the candidates, may not choose the stronger candidate. This is a greater risk if the party is divided into ideological factions, and some delegates are more interested in winning a factional victory than nominating a candidate who can get elected. Even an endorsee who is the strongest candidate may not be able to win the primary if the state and local party organizations fail to provide significant tangible support to the endorsee. Despite these imperfections, political parties might improve their ability to nominate the strongest candidate if more of them experimented with some form of endorsements.

5 General Elections: Candidates, Campaigns, and Issues

Every four years the voters in most states elect their governor and a number of statewide officials such as lieutenant governor, attorney general, and secretary of state. (Vermont and New Hampshire elect governors for only a two-year term, as many other states did until the 1980s and 1990s.) State House members normally serve a two-year term and state senators a four-year term. A few states have four-year House terms and a few others have two-year Senate terms.

In thirty-six states the elections for governor and most other statewide officials are held when members of Congress, but not the president, are elected (such as 1994, 1998, and 2002). In eleven states these elections are in presidential–congressional election years (1996 and 2000). Where governors serve two-year terms they are elected in all even-numbered years. In five states (Kentucky, Mississippi, Virginia, Louisiana, and New Jersey) governors are chosen in odd-numbered years.

In this chapter we will concentrate on gubernatorial elections because they are more important than the election of other state officers. The gubernatorial campaign is on a larger, more expensive scale and attracts more interest and turnout than other statewide campaigns (except U.S. Senate races). In Chapter 7 we will analyze the election of state legislators.

One of the most important trends in gubernatorial elections during the last half of the twentieth century was the growing independence of these elections from national trends. There was a gradual shift of gubernatorial elections to non-presidential election years. This change was motivated in part by the desire to insulate gubernatorial elections from presidential politics, but this cannot completely explain the denationalization of gubernatorial elections because large-scale shifts in partisan voting sometimes occur in nonpresidential election years such as 1966, 1974, and 1994.

There is some tendency for a party to gain or lose a gubernatorial seat when there is a national partisan trend in that direction. But this does not happen consistently, and it occurs less frequently than was the case in the 1940s through the

1960s. This means that many voters are not voting a straight Republican or Democratic ticket in gubernatorial, congressional, and presidential races. (We will discuss voting patterns in more detail in the next chapter.)

If voters are acting more independently in gubernatorial races, it suggests that the outcome of these elections depends very much on the candidates who are running for governor, the character of the campaigns they run, and the issues they stress while campaigning. Gubernatorial candidates spend enough money and run visible enough campaigns that many voters are able to make judgments about the candidates, their records in office, and the issues they emphasize. Basing their decisions on these judgments, they may cast a vote that does not always reflect their identification with a party or the impact of national partisan trends.

CANDIDATES

Because gubernatorial campaigns are usually more visible than most other races (except presidential elections), the voters are likely to be relatively well informed about the candidates. Therefore the outcome of the race depends heavily on the qualifications and political skills of the candidates. We begin our examination of candidates by discussing who runs for governor. How much experience have they had, and what specific offices have they held? We then examine how candidates decide whether to run, a decision very much affected by the status of the incumbent, who may or may not be eligible and willing to run for another term. An incumbent who is running again usually has a large advantage over other candidates, but we shall see that there are often both liabilities and advantages to being an incumbent candidate.

Who Runs for Governor?

Where do gubernatorial candidates come from? What kinds of offices or positions have they held before running for governor? It is difficult to compile such information on losing gubernatorial candidates, but we know much more about the backgrounds of those who become governor.

If we examine all the governors who served between 1981 and 1999 (counting each only once) and look for the position they held immediately before being elected governor, we find the following (based on Beyle 1999, 193–195):

30 percent held a statewide office (such as secretary of state).
20 percent served in the state legislature.
15 percent served in the U.S. Senate or House.
10 percent served in some law enforcement position.
6 percent served in a local elected office (usually mayor).

6 percent held an administrative position in government.

13 percent were not in government but in private positions, very often business.

Holding a statewide elective position immediately before being elected governor is not only the most common career path (30 percent) but also one that is becoming increasingly common. A person who has run a successful statewide race gets broader exposure to the voting public than does a state legislator or even a member of Congress because those candidates are elected from only a single district. Moreover, some of those who hold statewide elective positions such as lieutenant governor, secretary of state, treasurer, attorney general, or state auditor have various opportunities during their term of office to attract attention in the media. An attorney general may have negotiated a settlement with tobacco companies or sued businesses for consumer fraud. An auditor may have recommended reforms in state or local government operations that result in lower spending. The secretary of state may have initiated steps that make it easier for people to register and vote.

A recent study (Squire 1992) examined the previous experience of all the candidates in gubernatorial elections (1977–1989). The highest profile candidates were former governors and U.S. senators because they had won high statewide office and therefore were better able to attract contributors. Next came U.S. representatives and statewide elected officials. Peverill Squire found that former governors and members of Congress are just as likely to run against incumbents as for open seats, but only former governors demonstrated much ability to unseat incumbents. Statewide officeholders are more strategic in choosing when to run. They are twice as likely to run in open seat contests than in those with an incumbent running, probably because members of the incumbent's party wait their turn to move up the ladder. All three categories of high-profile candidates win regularly in open seat contests.

One-fifth of the governors moved directly from the state legislature to the governorship. Perhaps more important is the fact that 40 percent got their political start in the legislature, and almost half served at some time in the legislature. This experience gets governors off to a running start in working with the legislature and helps them engineer legislative support for their program. When a governor has served recently in the legislature, those legislators who have known the governor as a peer and feel comfortable and familiar with that person are more likely to cooperate.

The third most frequent, and an increasingly common, route to the governorship is from the U.S. Congress (15 percent). Members of Congress, though they may not have served in the state legislature, have learned a lot about the legislative process and policy making. Why do members of Congress want to return home to run for governor? The governor of a state exercises more power and has great influence over a much broader field of policy than a relatively junior member of the

U.S. House. Even U.S. senators occasionally run for governor. Dirk Kempthorne, U.S. senator from Idaho who returned home to run for governor in 1998, put it this way: "I relish the chance to be at the center of that action." California governor Pete Wilson, who quit his U.S. Senate seat in 1990 to win the governorship and who faced a two-term limit in 1998, said regretfully, "I wish, frankly, that I could have another term." Thanks to devolution of power to the states, being governor is "an even more attractive proposition today than in 1990" (Chen 1997, A5). Another factor may be that as Congress has been returning power to the states governors now have the authority to manage high-profile issues like welfare reform and expanded health insurance for children in low-income families.

One career route to the governorship that has been declining in importance is law enforcement, down from almost 20 percent to 10 percent in the more recent period. Perhaps as the range of issues handled by state government has increased, law enforcement has become a less important aspect of the governor's job.

Some persons get elected and many more probably run without any experience in elective public office. After the 1998 election eight governors could claim previous "outsider" status; all were businesspeople. Candidates who have become successful in business before running for governor can sometimes contribute a substantial amount of their own funds to the campaign and also know how to raise money from other businesspeople. One of the most famous of these was Lewis Lehrman, a multimillionaire executive of the Rite Aid drugstore chain that is found all over the country. His personal contributions of funds played a crucial role in his winning the Republican gubernatorial nomination in New York and almost defeating Democrat Mario Cuomo in the 1982 governor's race. The gubernatorial election year of 1998 put two "outsider" businesspeople named George W. Bush and Jeb Bush into the governorships of Texas and Florida, respectively. The fact that eight of the governors in late 1998 had been businessmen before winning the governorship may attest to the increasing role of money in the election process to buy political exposure through television advertising.

Deciding Whether to Run

The first question a prospective candidate for governor thinks about is whether the incumbent governor is running again. Sometimes the answer is negative because the state has a two-term limit and the governor is finishing a second term. The number of states without a two-term limitation has decreased from twenty-one to nine in the past twenty years. On the other hand, governors have to run less often than in the past. Only two states have a two-year term for governor. In 1960 sixteen states had two-year terms, and thirty-four states had four-year terms.

If there is no term limit, a governor is sometimes undecided about running, and potential candidates may have to wait and see what happens. If your party's governor is running again, you have to face the reality that it is very tough to beat an incumbent in a primary. As we saw in Chapter 4, relatively few governors are challenged by serious candidates in the primary and even fewer lose to them.

Candidates in the party out of power have to realize that about three-fourths of the governors who run in the general election are successful. Why would a state legislator or secretary of state choose to run against the governor of the other party? They might prove their ability to run a good campaign and be in position to run in an open race if the governor retires in four years.

The overall result of longer and limited terms is that only about once in a decade is the governor's chair empty. The only other circumstance in which a seat is open is if a governor does not run after one term or is defeated. States with no term limits may reelect the governor for a third term or more, thus closing out any real chance for gubernatorial hopefuls for twelve or more years. And sometimes a former governor with nostalgia runs again after his or her successor has served a term or two, thus keeping out a gubernatorial hopeful who was prepared to step in. During the 1970–1994 period twenty former governors waited for a term or two before running again for the governorship (Beyle 1996b).

Lest all this appears to be a counsel of despair for the gubernatorial hopeful, the fact remains that about 20 percent of governors decide not to run for reelection or "quit," to use the current term. In modern times (1978–1996) on average 60 percent of governors run for an additional term. A study of quitters found that they are more likely the governors who perceive themselves to be vulnerable because they have presided over the state's poorly performing economy or put into place a number of tax increases. Hence governors who have performed poorly avoid voters' punishment for the tax increases and economic misfortune that have taken place during their last term of office (Winters 1998). It does mean that those with better political-economic records will run in the ensuing open election and that usually neither will be scarred by the former incumbent's performance.

What Advantages and Disadvantages Do Incumbent Governors Have?

Gubernatorial elections have incumbents running more than half the time, and their success rate is about 75 percent. Why do they win so often, and what causes incumbent losses? First, and most obviously, governors have been highly visible to their citizens for four years. The media covers their activities more fully than it covers anyone else at the state level, and they have many opportunities to appear on television and to speak at meetings across the state. Although some candidates who run against the governor have held important public offices, it is rare for them to be as well known as the governor.

Second, incumbent governors share the advantages that all incumbents have.

They have run for governor before. They know how to run a successful campaign in their state. They know the state very well—its political makeup; its major interests, organizations, and companies; and its needs. They know how to raise money and have a long list of contributors to the last campaign. Some of these contributors are hoping to gain some particular benefit from government for themselves or their business, and they believe a contribution to the governor will help.

Governors have no choice but to run on their record; sometimes this is a major asset and sometimes it is a burden. The governor who has kept his or her promises, who has been able to develop or expand popular programs, who has cut taxes or at least avoided tax increases stands a very good chance of being reelected. But a governor who has not been able to keep important promises may be in trouble at the polls. This might be the case, for example, if new programs have been blocked in the legislature, or have been abandoned because funding was not available, or above all if the governor has found it necessary to recommend substantial tax increases—particularly if the campaign promises included one not to raise taxes.

The political success of a governor is often dependent on positive or negative trends in the national economy over which the governor has no control. There is little a governor can do to mitigate the effects of national economic trends in the state, at least in the short run. If the prices for hogs and corn collapse, the governor of a midwestern state cannot restore them. If the bottom falls out of the oil market, the governor of Texas is helpless to change the international supply and demand situation for oil. A booming economy may enable the governor to get new programs adopted and even lower taxes, whereas an economic slump may force the governor to postpone new programs and ask for tax increases to balance the budget.

There is evidence that voters are more likely to vote for a governor running for reelection if the state's economy is doing well. The more taxes have been raised during a governor's administration, the less likely they are to vote for an incumbent. This clearly shows that voters hold the governor at least partially responsible for the health of the state economy and changes in the level of taxation (Niemi, Stanley, and Vogel 1995). If the governor has been forced to recommend a tax increase because the sluggish state economy has produced a drop in tax revenue, the governor would appear to be more vulnerable in the election. (We discuss this issue in greater detail in the next chapter, where we examine voting behavior.)

Governors and U.S. senators are the two major officials who are chosen by a statewide electorate. Incumbent governors, though they win 80 percent of the time, are still more vulnerable than incumbent U.S. senators, who win 85 percent of the time. Voters hold governors responsible for the state's economy but appear to hold senators far less accountable for the health of the national economy.

In 1974 Gerald Wright provided an explanation that is still pertinent for why governors are so vulnerable to criticism about public policy issues:

The state chief executive is a central figure in virtually every controversial policy issue that arises in state politics. The reason for his prominence is the high visibility of his office coupled with public perceptions that he has considerable if not enormous power in *all* state-level policy areas and conflicts, although in fact gubernatorial powers are limited. (1974, 97)

Governors who seek reelection now are more likely to face serious competition than existed in many states two decades ago. This is because almost all of the states have two-party systems, in the sense that both Democrats and Republicans seriously compete for the office of governor, and each party has held the governorship some of the time since the beginning of the 1980s. Refer to Chapter 2, where we describe the growth of two-party competition for control of government, particularly the major gains made by Republican Parties in the southern states.

CAMPAIGNING FOR OFFICE

Do campaigns make a difference in the outcome of a gubernatorial election? The answer is that they do; a candidate who seems to be far behind at the start of the election does sometimes win. It is true that governors win four-fifths of the time and that candidates with a huge advantage in fund raising are very likely to win. Moreover, when candidates run who are perceived to be strong—including most governors—they sometimes scare away potentially viable candidates, leaving only candidates who are relatively unknown, widely perceived as hopeless, and unable to raise enough money to run a serious race.

But if four-fifths of governors win, that means that one-fifth of them lose. The perceptions of experts at the start of the races about who will win often turn out to be wrong. If both parties have viable candidates and the fund-raising disparity is not too large, upsets are quite possible. Therefore campaigns do make a difference.

We can illustrate this point easily by taking a brief look at two California gubernatorial elections, described in more detail later in this section on campaigns. In 1994 Republican governor Pete Wilson was running for reelection against Democratic treasurer Kathleen Brown, daughter of one former governor and sister of another. Despite his position as governor, Wilson entered the race as an underdog, having trailed in polls against Brown since the beginning of 1993. But during the campaign Wilson was much more successful then Brown in focusing the attention on those issues where his position was closer to the voters than Brown's was. Wilson defeated Brown by more than a million votes.

In the 1998 California gubernatorial race, when the state's term limits prevented Wilson from running, Democratic lieutenant governor Gray Davis faced Republican attorney general Dan Lungren. Davis was the underdog twice—in the

Democratic primary and in the general election. Davis defeated two millionaires in the primary election, one of whom outspent him by a margin of $40 million to $9 million, using the effective slogan "Experience money can't buy." Despite his primary success, Davis started the general election campaign widely perceived as the underdog. But he was much more successful than Lungren in focusing on issues that concerned the voters, particularly education, and he won by a surprising margin of 20 percentage points.

Television advertising plays a major role in gubernatorial campaigns because the voters get most of their information and perceptions about the candidates from this source. Many prospective voters spend little time reading the political coverage in newspapers. Particularly in a large state such as California, Florida, or Ohio, relatively few citizens attend a candidate's rally or meetings where one or both candidates speak in person, and even fewer have a chance to meet and talk to the candidates. Both Democrats and Republicans view television commercials, while campaign rallies are usually attended only by voters who are loyal to the candidate's party. Therefore television has a greater potential for persuading voters to cross party lines when they vote. A candidate who cannot afford to run many television commercials or cannot afford high-quality commercials is at a serious disadvantage, no matter how many hours a day are spent traveling around the state.

A skillful, large-scale television campaign is essential, but it is not enough to ensure victory. There is a growing recognition that the "ground wars" can be crucial to a campaign. The ground wars include the visits a candidate makes in cities and towns across the state attending rallies, meeting with groups, holding press conferences, and meeting with local newspaper editors. These activities are more feasible and more productive in smaller states than in larger states. Perhaps more important, they also include efforts by local party leaders and campaign workers to get voters registered and to get them to the polls; to staff the phone banks, calling voters in the closing days of the campaign; and to distribute campaign literature door to door. How well this works depends on the party's ability to organize party activists across the state and on the gubernatorial candidate's ability to make use of the local organizations and perhaps to build organizations for individual interests or concerns.

Organizing the Campaign

Candidates for governor (and other statewide and congressional offices) usually organize their own campaign, although they may rely on the state party organization for various kinds of help. They recruit their own staff, hire campaign consultants, establish a state headquarters, and try to set up a local headquarters in as many cities or counties as possible. Incumbent governors, of course, have the advantage of experience. They know how a campaign should be run; they have ideas about strategy and tactics that were tested in the previous campaign. They may even hire some of the same campaign consultants they used before. How large the candidate's staff is, how many consultants are hired, and how well equipped the headquarters is depend on how much money has been raised or can be expected to be raised. It also depends on what proportion of this funding the candidate chooses to devote to these administrative costs as well as how large the state is.

Candidates running for governor or U.S. senator, and often those running for U.S. representative, usually give high priority to finding the best campaign consultants that money can buy. There are hundreds of persons working as campaign consultants, most of whom work either for Democrats or Republicans, but not both. If you are running for governor you want consultants who are experienced in major statewide races, who have a good won-lost record, and who have the reputation of being first rate. Not surprisingly the consultants who are perceived to be the best often are the most expensive and the most in demand. Campaign consultants perform a variety of specialized functions. A large-scale, well-financed campaign may hire four or five consultants for these various jobs. A smaller scale, less expensive campaign might hire one or two consultants and perhaps use other staff members to perform some of the chores.

Regardless of how the campaign is organized and staffed, there are several essential jobs to be done. Someone must be in charge of running the campaign, planning strategy, and coordinating the work of other individuals. The campaign must have an experienced press secretary to write press releases, deal with reporters, and make sure the campaign is getting coverage in newspapers, television, and radio. The campaign needs a skilled, experienced person in charge of advertising, primarily for radio and television. This means working with the candidate and campaign manager on the themes to be emphasized in campaign ads, creating the ads (or hiring a specialist to create them), and developing a schedule for putting the ads on the air—all highly technical, and increasingly important, jobs.

If the campaign budget is large enough, a pollster must be hired. Polling is important for a number of reasons. Of course it is used to determine whether the candidate is ahead or behind but also to find out how much name recognition the candidate has, which segments of the voting population support the candidate, and what issues being raised by the candidate or the opponent are having the most impact on voters. A small-scale campaign may try to accomplish these objectives by having staff members prepare questions and having volunteers poll voters on the phone. But polling is a highly professional and complex process, and candidates get what they pay for. If the questions are poorly prepared, if the sample is too small or the polling operation cuts too many corners to save money, the poll may not be worth the paper the results are printed on. A poorly prepared poll is worse than having no poll at all because it can provide the candidate with misleading results.

Very early in the campaign the candidate needs to find someone to assume responsibility for fund raising; if adequate funds are not raised there is little chance of running more than a minimal campaign. Although a consultant might be hired for a specific task such as organizing a mass mailing to solicit funds, the chief fund raiser is likely to be an active party member with considerable experience raising campaign money.

An incumbent governor, a member of Congress, or the mayor of a large city can make use of staff members who have worked with him or her in the office, persons who would take a leave of absence during the campaign. This is a big advantage because the candidate has worked with these individuals and knows what jobs they can handle. Many of the staff members in the office of a major elected official have had considerable experience in politics; their day-to-day work on the staff brings them into contact with other political leaders; and many of them originally worked in the campaign that first got the candidate elected to office.

Not every gubernatorial candidate is able to build a staff—including consultants—that is large enough and capable enough to run an effective campaign. Some candidates cannot raise enough funds to provide the staff and headquarters organization that they need. Some candidates try to control many of the details of the campaign themselves—usually a mistake. Some candidates simply do not understand the importance of an experienced, skillful professional staff. Republican Dan Lungren entered the 1998 gubernatorial campaign as a clear favorite over Democrat Gray Davis. He lost to Davis by a large margin partly because of Davis's skill in developing issues in contrast to Lungren's ideological rigidity—a factor described below. But at least one close observer attributes the outcome to Lungren's failure to rely on experienced professional advisers for making major strategic decisions and his choice of a "homegrown campaign inner circle consisting of his brother, his father, his wife and himself" (Scott 1998, 9).

The Role of the Party in the Campaign

The role of the state political party in gubernatorial campaigns is usually much smaller that its role in some other campaigns, such as U.S. House and state legislative races. Most gubernatorial candidates have enough experience running for office and access to enough financial resources that they are not heavily dependent on the party. Gubernatorial candidates usually develop their own organization, hire their own staff, establish a funding operation, and plan their own campaign strategy.

But gubernatorial candidates may rely on the state and local party organizations for help with such activities as staffing phone banks, getting voters registered, and getting out the vote at election time. The state party organization may provide the candidate with lists of persons who often contribute funds to the party, and the state and local organizations may help with funds for the candidate.

In Chapter 3 we discussed the conditions in which a state party organization is likely to be more or less involved in a gubernatorial candidate's campaign. Sometimes a gubernatorial candidate wins nomination by defeating a candidate who is supported by most of the party's leaders. The nominee may not have much confidence in the party organization. An incumbent governor seeking reelection, on the other hand, is likely to control, or at least to work closely with, the state party organization and will be able to determine what kind of role it will play in the gubernatorial campaign.

From the viewpoint of the state party organization, the gubernatorial election is the most important race in the election cycle. Winning the governorship usually enhances the state party's power more than winning a U.S. Senate race. A skillful, committed governor who understands the importance of party building is in a position to strengthen the state and local parties in a variety of ways, such as providing help with raising money. In Chapter 3 we explained that party patronage is less important than it used to be. We also said that a governor (unlike a member of Congress) is in a position to make a lot of appointments, not all of which are regulated by civil service rules and many of which are unpaid memberships on state boards that are often in demand. This is a major reason why electing a governor is so important to a party. For these reasons the party organization will usually be willing to offer as much assistance as possible to the gubernatorial candidate—particularly if the candidate has a realistic chance of running a competitive race.

We noted in Chapter 3 that in recent election campaigns some political parties have run independent television advertisements in support of one of their candidates or in opposition to the opponent. This may be of considerable help to the candidates, but they often have little or no influence over the content of the advertisement and may believe that it will do more harm than good. For example, if the party's advertisement is a personal attack on the opponent, it could backfire by casting blame on the candidate for the attack.

Candidates for governor and other major offices in some states find that they have to rely primarily on their own efforts to run a campaign. David Price, a political scientist and a Democratic member of Congress from North Carolina, provides a good example. Despite the fact that he is a former chair of the North Carolina Democratic Party, Price has been able to get only limited help from the state party. Although he is describing his campaigns for Congress, gubernatorial candidates in that state would probably have similar experiences:

> We gained numerous foot soldiers and saved scarce campaign dollars by combining forces with other Democratic candidates, in our canvassing and

turnout operations, but even here, we gave as much as we got. Party precinct structures were spotty at best, and the cadres of volunteers often needed shoring up. So activists from the Price campaign helped make the party efforts work, as well as the reverse.

In other facets of the campaign, the party role was far less prominent. The state party organized a rally in each congressional district for all Democratic candidates. . . . But most of my campaign appearances and fundraising events were organized by our campaign alone. The state party had an able research director on whom we drew. . . . But by and large, in devising a press strategy, in formulating a message, in putting together an advertising campaign, and in raising the money to pay for it, we were on our own. (Price 1992, 80–81)

The Role of Interest Groups in Campaigns

Interest groups are playing an increasingly important role in campaigns for governor and other offices. They can influence the campaigns in a variety of ways. Interest groups often submit questionnaires to candidates and hold candidate forums to make the candidate pay attention to and perhaps support the group's concerns. They sometimes distribute to their membership voting records of candidates who have served in Congress or a state legislature on bills that are important to the group. Sometimes state interest groups formally endorse a candidate in a gubernatorial race and publicize this endorsement to their membership. Interest groups engaging in such activities are not necessarily regular supporters of one party or the other but are trying to get candidates of both parties to support their viewpoints on issues.

Candidates find that there are a growing number of single-issue groups who demand that candidates explicitly support their cause and threaten to oppose them at the polls if they fail to do so. There are also more broadly based ideologically oriented groups, both liberal and conservative, applying similar pressure on candidates.

Interest groups that have sufficient resources are increasingly running television advertisements supporting one candidate or attacking the other. Some of them also run so-called issue-advocacy advertisements that do not explicitly urge viewers to vote for or against a candidate but that strongly support or criticize the viewpoint or voting record of a candidate. This technique is employed because campaign finance regulations give groups that run such advertisements much more freedom to spend money on them without restrictions.

When an interest group independently runs advertisements supporting a candidate or criticizing the opponent, this can be either an asset or a liability to the candidate. The candidate may benefit from favorable advertising that costs the campaign nothing and that may appeal particularly to voters who are loyal to the group running the advertisement. The independent advertisements by interest groups may be a liability to the candidate, however, particularly if they take the form of an attack on the opponent. For example, an interest group supporting the Republican candidate for governor might run an advertisement criticizing the Democratic governor for making too many concessions to "greedy" teachers' groups that were making "unreasonable" demands for pay increases. This might undermine the Republican candidate's efforts to capture the support of at least some teachers in the state.

The interest groups that are most likely to be valuable to gubernatorial candidates are those that are closely allied with a political party. Republican candidates can usually depend on the support of some business groups, organizations opposing gun control (like the National Rifle Association), groups that promote tax cuts, and some antiabortion and Christian right groups. Democratic candidates can usually count on support from labor unions, teachers' groups, African American and Latino groups, feminist and pro-choice groups, and environmental organizations.

It is true, as we have noted, that these groups often press the candidates to endorse their positions so completely that a candidate might be portrayed by the opponent and perceived by voters as an extremist or as too fully committed to a particular group. We have also said that interest groups may run independent advertisements on television that do their preferred candidate more harm than good.

But interest groups that are closely aligned with a political party usually want to help the party's candidates to win election and may be realistic enough to realize that if they force a gubernatorial candidate, for example, to endorse the group's positions totally, that candidate may be defeated. This is particularly likely to happen if the interest group is basically satisfied with the candidate and believes it is very important to defeat the opponent. Over the long run, the political party can play an important role in maintaining good working relationships with its allied groups.

One of the most important functions the party performs in this relationship is to give the interest groups and their political action committees accurate and realistic information about the chances of electing particular candidates and to suggest priorities for PAC funding of candidates. If, for example, a party was running candidates for both governor and senator in the same year, and a friendly interest group was supporting both, in the closing weeks of the campaign the party could tell the group which race was closer and therefore which campaign needed the most funding from PACs and other sources. The party may also be able to persuade an interest group to run commercials that are best able to help the party's candidates that they favor.

Some interest groups are valuable because they have large number of voters who may be persuaded to vote for candidates the interest group favors. If some of these potential voters go to the polls only irregularly, the interest group may be able to mobilize them and get them to the polls. For example, Christian right groups will support those candidates—usually Republicans—who are willing to support much of their social agenda. Particularly if church pastors use the pulpit to urge support for particular candidates, serious churchgoers may follow their advice and get to the polls.

African American organizations often mobilize their members to support particular candidates—very often Democrats—who support their agenda. Although these voters are more likely to turn out for African American candidates, they are an important source of votes for Democratic candidates whatever their race. The Democrats have also had considerable success in winning votes in alliance with Latino organizations, although some Republican candidates have been able to get a substantial share of this vote as well.

The other interest group that has large numbers of members and has considerable success in mobilizing them to support Democratic candidates is the labor unions. They work very hard at trying to get out the vote, though with more enthusiasm for some Democratic candidates than others. Of course, the unions are a much greater Democratic asset in states where they are well organized and have many members. In most southern states, by contrast, labor unions are relatively weak.

Campaign Strategy and Tactics

During the course of a campaign a great many decisions must be made about strategy and tactics. Ultimately these are the responsibility of the candidate, although he or she may take advice from the campaign manager and other consultants. Decisions have to be made about allocating resources. How much should be spent on television commercials and how much on various aspects of ground wars such as running telephone banks and getting voters registered? How much can be spent on paid staff for routine jobs and how much should the campaign try to rely on volunteers?

Another important campaign resource is the candidate's time. Some candidates spend a large proportion of their time, particularly in the early months, raising money by making endless phone calls and attending money-raising events. Should the candidate spend much of the time touring the state, speaking to groups, meeting with local journalists, perhaps occasionally walking the streets trying to meet people? The larger the state, the less a candidate can accomplish by trying to meet voters one by one. It may be more efficient to spend the afternoon that is allocated to a particular county by appearing on a local call-in radio show, calling on the local newspaper editor, and meeting with local party activists in an effort to motivate them to work harder.

Decisions about timing can sometimes be crucial in a campaign, particularly if not enough money has been raised to run a campaign that is both intensive and very long. There is plenty of evidence that voters pay relatively little attention to an election campaign until the last month or so. This is one reason why candidates often spend the early part of a campaign raising money, creating an organization, and winning the active support of party leaders and activists across the state.

If the candidate is not well known, or if the opponent has started running television commercials relatively early, the candidate may find it necessary to start running advertisements early even if the voters may not be listening. An example from the 1998 California Democratic gubernatorial primary is equally pertinent for general election campaigns. The polls showed that Lt. Gov. Gray Davis was running behind his two millionaire opponents in the polls, both of whom were spending huge amounts of money on television commercials, many of which attacked each other. Davis was busily trying to raise money, but he was not entering the television air wars and his campaign seemed to many observers to be dead in the water. A number of his strongest supporters were pleading with him to enter the fray, and some were threatening to abandon him. But Davis held his ground and hoarded his advertising funds. The approval ratings of the two millionaires were dropping as they continued to attack each other, while Davis's approval rating remained relatively high. Then, on April 20, barely six weeks before the primary, Davis launched a full-scale television campaign describing his record and accomplishments under the slogan "Experience money can't buy." The strategy worked, and Davis was nominated by a comfortable margin.

The California primary example also illustrates one of the most difficult campaign decisions that candidates often face: whether and in what conditions to run television commercials attacking the other candidate. A related question is how to respond to attacks by an opponent. In their answers to pollsters, voters often are critical of candidates who attack their opponents; but pollsters often find that attack ads are effective in weakening public approval of the candidate being attacked. Sometimes, if two candidates begin trading charges against each other, they are both hurt in the polls, as in the California example.

Part of the dilemma that candidates face is determining what the voters may consider to be an unfair attack. A personal attack, like revealing that an opponent has been arrested for drunken driving, may backfire, particularly if voters think it is unfair or not relevant to the election. Apparently some voters disapprove of candidates who criticize their opponents' records in public office or their position on issues. But presumably this is what candidates should be doing—letting the voters know how they differ on their records and issues. It is true, of course, that candidates may exaggerate or oversimplify when discussing records and issues, and they may try to portray themselves as moderates and their opponents as extremists.

Candidates do not, however, have complete freedom to develop whatever strategy they want; nor can they make strategic decisions in a vacuum. We have already made it clear that the financial resources available to the campaign establish the parameters within which decisions are made. Incumbents and other candidates who raise a lot of money early in the campaign not only have the advantage of being able to have a larger campaign budget but of being able to plan a campaign knowing approximately what resources will be available. They can, for example, reserve time on television for commercials relatively early.

The limit on funds available for the campaign is not the only aspect of the political environment that affects the campaign. If the state or local party organizations are weak, candidates will have to do more campaigning on their own. If the state usually votes Republican in statewide races, the Democratic candidate for governor must develop a strategy that might realistically win some votes from independents or even Republicans. If a candidate has never held elected office but has been successful in business, the candidate must try to persuade voters that "government should be run more like a business" or "it's time to give an outsider an opportunity." If labor unions are strong in the state, a Democratic candidate needs to pay serious attention to the issues raised by unions and must enlist union members in the campaign. The state's economy is an aspect of the political environment that candidates cannot ignore. As we discuss campaign issues in more detail, we will note that a serious slump in the state's economy may force the governor to recommend raising taxes or cutting programs; if so, the governor is limited on what claims can be made about his or her record.

The Role of the Media

Newspapers, television, and radio play an important role in state campaigns in addition to being the vehicles used by candidates for paid advertising. The candidates are heavily dependent on the media to cover their campaigns, and this is particularly important for nonincumbents, who are usually not well known to the voters. Candidates regularly complain that the media do not provide enough coverage of their campaigns. Sometimes reporters reply that the candidate gives the same speech at every appearance, and so there is nothing new to report. Candidates also complain that the press often pays more attention to the "horse race" aspects of the campaign—who is ahead and who is gaining or losing ground—than the substantive content of candidates' speeches.

It is more difficult than in the past for candidates to attract crowds at rallies, and therefore they are more dependent on the media to provide coverage of their campaign. Newspapers, particularly the major metropolitan daily newspapers, usually provide more frequent and detailed coverage of campaigns than television and radio do. If the candidate is spending a day in a city with perhaps 50,000 residents, it is likely that the candidate will actually meet only a few dozen of them and be heard in person by only a few hundred. This is if the candidate speaks to a gathering of campaign workers and to some organized group like schoolteachers or a business organization and then spends an hour shaking hands outside a factory as workers are leaving the plant. The candidate may hold a press conference that is attended by a handful of reporters. A newspaper that may be published only twice a week is likely to cover the candidate's visit. The candidate may go to a local radio station and spend a couple of hours answering questions on a call-in show.

The larger the state, the more dependent candidates are on the media. It may be possible, during a four-month campaign, to go door to door in a large number of towns and cities in Vermont or Delaware, but it is impossible to accomplish much by that technique in Ohio, Texas, or California. Candidates who travel around in large states must plan their schedule mostly around events that are likely to attract some media attention.

Candidates sometimes come up with gimmicks in an effort to attract media attention. Candidates for statewide office have been known to "walk across the state," stopping in towns and cities to talk to people and, they hope, attracting coverage from the media wherever they go. Candidates have sometime worked in various jobs across the state—the more mundane the better—to show that they have the common touch and understand the needs of working people.

Candidates will hold press conferences in various settings—usually outdoors—that are designed to make a political point. A candidate running against the governor may stand in front of an empty, decaying factory to dramatize the governor's failure to attract new businesses in the state. The challenger may stand in front of a polluted river that has been neglected by the governor. The candidate may be shown outside an ancient-looking public school to emphasize the importance of a program to build more new schools and renovate others.

Joint appearances on TV by candidates, loosely described as debates, are becoming an increasingly important part of campaigns. These are often covered by public television and sometimes by commercial stations. Often the challenger, or at least the candidate who appears to be trailing, will insist that there should be more televised debates than the incumbent or front-runner prefers, but candidates find it is essential to make at least a few such appearances. These events give both candidates a chance to emphasize their issues as well as a chance to criticize their opponent. The debates often attract a sizable number of viewers and the highlights are reported by the media, which of course increases the impact of the event. The viewers not only learn something about the issues but also get an opportunity to judge the personalities and political skills of the two candidates.

The media can also have an effect on the campaign in several ways. Most newspapers endorse candidates for major offices like governor a week or so before the election, but there is little evidence about how many voters are influenced by such endorsements. Major newspapers often commission public opinion polls. Their publication of findings about who is ahead or behind and what issues are influencing the voters, as well as their interpretation of these findings, may have some influence on the outcome of the campaign. Newspapers may also influence the campaign by the tone and substance of their coverage. If they report that one candidate is losing ground, is running a poorly organized campaign, or has failed to find issues that matter to the voters, this report may be damaging to the campaign, thereby discouraging party workers and driving away potential campaign contributors.

ISSUES IN THE CAMPAIGN

It is not enough to have a well-organized campaign and plenty of funding to buy television time if a candidate does not have a clear message to present to the voters. An important part of that message must deal with public policy issues.

The Incumbent: Running on the Record

Earlier in this chapter our discussion of candidates emphasized that incumbents cannot escape the record of their administrations, but they should be able to present a defense of that record and have the opportunity to describe what they plan to accomplish if reelected. Winning reelection depends in large part on the skill with which the governor explains what he or she has done and why, and focuses the attention of voters on the issues most important to the governor and the party.

If things are going well in a state, it is easy for the governor to claim credit. If the economy is doing well and employment levels are growing, the governor can claim that his or her policies have made a difference. There is no question that governors work hard to improve conditions in their states. They recruit businesses to their communities through tax incentives and the availability of inexpensive land and skilled labor. They work to provide job retraining to reduce unemployment. But it often takes several years for such policies to bear fruit; for a governor to claim much of the credit for state economic growth at the end of the first term may be an exaggeration. In fact, very often much of a state's economic growth is caused by the strength of the national economy. A growing state economy also helps the incumbent governor by producing enough tax revenue that the governor can get new programs adopted and funded without asking for a tax increase (and perhaps even propose tax cuts).

If incumbent governors want to claim credit for state economic prosperity largely caused by factors beyond their control, it seems only right that they should have to bear the burden of an economic slump in the state also largely caused by national factors over which they have little control. It is difficult to determine to what extent voters blame governors for a drop in the state economy (a question we examine further in the next chapter). But the resulting slump in state tax revenue creates problems that the governor cannot escape. It may be necessary to postpone new and expanded programs that the governor had been supporting; it may be necessary to raise taxes, often forcing the governor to break a campaign promise; or it may be necessary to do both.

What determines the electoral fate of a governor who raises taxes? The political climate in the state, the mood of the voters, and the skill of the opponent in using the tax issue may all have an effect. But the most important factor has been the governor's ability to defend the tax increase—to prove that it was necessary, to show what was accomplished with the new revenue, and to mobilize interest groups' support of the governor's taxing and spending programs. If the tax increase resulted from a slump in tax revenues and did not make possible new or improved programs, interest groups may still support the governor if they believe that the tax increases prevented cuts in programs they favor.

Even when a state faces a serious financing problem, the governor may risk reelection by recommending a tax increase. In 1986 the Texas state government was facing a $3.5 million deficit because the oil industry was reeling from a collapse in prices. Gov. Mark White, a conservative Democrat, called a special session of the legislature and recommended that it cut spending and increase the sales tax. The legislature adopted part of the governor's proposals with reluctance. White's opponent, former Republican governor William Clements, opposed any tax increases and offered no specific solutions to the budgetary crisis. The voters threw out Governor White and returned Clements to office.

A skillful governor, however, may be able to take advantage of a financial crisis to justify a tax increase. A classic example occurred in Vermont a number of years ago when Gov. Dean Davis, who had initiated the adoption of a sales tax, used a dramatic television commercial as the focus of his campaign:

> The governor's pants were rolled up, he was put in a rowboat half filled with water in the middle of the pond, and he was set to bailing. The audio hammered away at the theme that Davis had bailed the state out of economic disaster. The commercial was short and was broadcast incessantly around the state. With one theme the Republicans had justified the sales tax. (Bryan 1974, 120)

In Iowa in 1986 incumbent governor Terry Branstad, a three-time taxer, faced long-time Democratic legislative leader Lowell Junkins. Iowa citizens were hurting in 1986; the economy was depressed and Branstad's recent tax increases did not help. Branstad won the election in what was considered a classic Republican victory. The governor was able to claim that he understood Iowa economic development and taxes. He knew the agonies of the Iowa farm community because, as an Iowa farmer, he had lost half his net worth since 1980. He also enjoyed one common advantage of incumbency—the ability to outspend his opponent two to one.

Sometimes a tax increase spells disaster for the governor's party as well as for the governor. In 1990 Jim Florio, the newly elected Democratic governor of New Jersey, faced several serious problems. The state, like many others at that time, was in an economic slump and losing jobs. On taking office Florio faced a $3 billion budget deficit. There was a need to spend more money on education and to redistribute educational funds so that poorer districts would receive considerably more funding than they had been getting—as the New Jersey Supreme Court continued to insist must be done. Florio also saw a need to reform the tax structure to reduce dependence on the property tax. He persuaded the Democratic legislature to increase the sales tax from 6 to 7 percent and to increase the state income tax significantly. The public reacted angrily to the tax increases, and two years later the Republican Party won two-thirds control of both houses of the state legislature, winning a total of thirty-two seats from the Democrats. Florio's effort to defend his tax increases and reforms fell short, and he lost the 1993 election by a narrow margin to Republican Christine Todd Whitman, who promised a 30 percent cut in the income tax over the first three years of her term. In 1999, when the Democrats began looking for a strong candidate to run against Whitman for an open seat in the U.S. Senate in 2000, Florio entered the race. Many Democratic leaders quickly urged him to drop out because they thought the tax issue would doom him to another defeat by Whitman.

Nonincumbents and Issues

Nonincumbents running for governor do not have a record in that office that they have to defend. But a gubernatorial candidate who has served in some other elective office, as have three-fourths of those elected to the governorship, may be criticized for some aspect of that record (for example, a vote on a particular bill). Such a candidate may be able to claim credit for votes cast that are likely to be popular with some of the voters.

A good example of a candidate who had represented a congressional district but was out of step with many of his party's supporters in other parts of the state was Glenn Poshard, a member of Congress from southern Illinois. Poshard was the 1998 Democratic gubernatorial candidate. He was opposed to abortion, gun control laws, and government programs to protect the environment. His generally conservative position on these and some other issues made him popular in southern Illinois but weakened him in the Chicago area, where Democrats usually have their greatest strength. Republican George Ryan had a two-part strategy. In his bid for conservative voters, he emphasized that Poshard had voted for numerous tax increases during his years in Congress; at the same time, he reminded liberal Democrats about Poshard's opposition to gun control and abortion. Ryan's strategy worked. Although Poshard won the support of Chicago mayor Richard M. Daley and the state AFL-CIO, his lack of appeal to many liberal Democrats contributed to his defeat by Ryan in the gubernatorial race.

In recent years it has become increasingly common for gubernatorial candidates (as well as those running for other offices) to try to create an image of themselves as moderates and their opponents as extremists of the left or right who are out of touch with the people of the state. Often both candidates will use the same tactic, with the Democrat accusing the Republican of being much too conservative and the Republican painting the Democrat as much too liberal. In the 1994 Illinois governor's race the incumbent, Jim Edgar, had the reputation of being a moderate as a result of his balancing of liberal and conservative positions on various issues. He succeeded in portraying his opponent, Dawn Clark Netsch, as much too liberal because, among other things, she favored large increases in income taxes (with some property tax cuts) to pay for improved education and she opposed the death penalty (favored by 79 percent of voters in the state).

It is said that some issues help Democratic candidates and others help Republicans. This means that many voters favor the Democratic Party's commitment to better and more affordable health care, better education, and clean air and water, for example, while many voters (often the same ones) favor the Republican commitment to get tough on crime and maintain the death penalty. This may be an oversimplification, but gubernatorial candidates usually find that there is more voter support for some of their positions than there is for others. Thomas Carsey (1996) argues that the salience of issues among voters is volatile and that candidates may be able to engineer a short-term influence on voting behavior if they can alter the salience of particular issue dimensions during the election process. In these conditions, candidates during the campaign will try to find ways of focusing attention on those issues where there is greater support for their position. This strategy sometimes involves redefining an issue or suggesting a new way of trying to solve a problem.

In 1994, as we noted, Republican governor Pete Wilson of California was running for reelection against Democrat Kathleen Brown, the state treasurer and the sister of former governor Jerry Brown. Brown was a more charismatic figure than Governor Wilson, and she entered the race well ahead of Wilson in the polls. But she had difficulty explaining her basic beliefs and defining a set of issues on which to focus. Wilson placed heavy emphasis on issues of law and order and focused attention on Brown's opposition to the death penalty. In an effort to neutralize the law and order issue, Brown's campaign devoted a great deal of attention to it, essentially fighting the campaign for many weeks on Wilson's turf instead of paying more attention to issues such as education (Lubenow 1995).

Wilson also focused attention on illegal immigration, an issue of great concern to many citizens in California. He strongly endorsed a popular initiative on the ballot, Proposition 187, which would require the state's schools, hospitals, and other government institutions to deny services to illegal immigrants. Because Proposition 187 was going to be on the November ballot, it was easy for Wilson to make a major issue of it. Brown's strong opposition to the proposition weakened her position in the race. She lost the election to Wilson by a margin of 55–41 percent.

Four years later, in 1998, it was the California Democratic candidate for governor, Lt. Gov. Gray Davis, who focused more skillfully on issues in defeating Republican attorney general Dan Lungren. Davis gave top priority to improving education, an issue that clearly was of great concern to California voters who had watched the quality of the state's educational system decline for years. Davis also attacked Lungren's rigidly right-wing position on issues and his conservative voting record in Congress (prior to his term as attorney general). Lungren was strongly antiabortion and anti–gun control, positions that were out of step with the majority of California voters.

Lungren's efforts to paint the pragmatic, moderate Davis as an extremist failed. In attempting to paint Davis as an opponent of the death penalty, he distorted Davis's voting record in the legislature and got caught doing it. Lungren tried for weeks to demonstrate that Davis was "weak on crime" until the California Peace Officer's Association endorsed Davis and spent money in behalf of his campaign. Gray, who had upset two millionaires to win the Democratic primary, defeated Lungren by a surprising margin of 20 percentage points (58–38 percent), the largest margin in an open contest in forty years (Scott 1998).

The 1986 Wisconsin gubernatorial election provides another example of how a candidate can change the focus of an election. Democratic governor Anthony Earl could make a strong claim for his return to office. Endorsed by the *Capital Times,* he had restored the state's fiscal stability, improved the workings and benefits of the unemployment compensation fund, and claimed credit for adding 190,000 jobs to the state's economy. He was strongly supported by his party and its officeholders. He had worked with the state's business community on economic development. But a veteran Republican legislative leader, Tommy Thompson, defeated Governor Earl, 53 percent to 47 percent. How did Thompson win? Thompson shifted voters' attention to spending. He attacked welfare spending, which he said was a magnet for Illinois migrants. Thompson said: "Earl has Madison myopia, and we all know that Madison is the liberal laboratory for social engineering" (Winters 1996, 20–21). Thus Thompson turned the spending issue to his advantage.

Sometimes a candidate can develop a relatively new issue that has not previously been debated in a campaign. One such issue that is becoming increasingly effective in gubernatorial campaigns is a proposal to establish or expand state lotteries or other forms of gambling. It is popular with many voters who want to be able to play the lottery in their state, who think it will ward off tax increases, or who favor the programs for which lottery revenues are earmarked.

Democratic candidates used the lottery issue in 1998 to defeat incumbent Republican governors in Alabama and South Carolina. These incumbents, who had been favored in their races, were the only two Republican governors who lost in southern states. In Alabama Democratic lieutenant governor Don Siegelman proposed a state lottery that would be used to pay for college scholarships, prekindergarten programs, and school computers. A poll showed that the lottery was favored by a margin of 61–34 percent in Alabama. Gov. Fob James attacked the lottery as being a "deceitful tax," but this made little impression on the voters. In South Carolina Republican governor David Beasley was defeated by Democrat Jim Hodges, who proposed a lottery to improve funding for education. A poll in that state showed the lottery had the support of two-thirds of the respondents.

In 1994 George W. Bush, the son of the former president, was elected governor of Texas by defeating the incumbent, Democrat Ann Richards. Polls showed that Richards's popularity was high, and she had succeeded in getting a state lottery tax and avoiding a state income tax. Bush's moderately conservative views were closer to the mainstream of Texas voters than were Richards's more liberal positions. But a contrast in campaign styles may have hurt Richards's chances even more. Her campaign included a number of personal attacks on Bush ("some jerk who's running for public office"). On the other hand, Bush was careful to treat her with respect in his own comments (Barone and Ujifusa 1995, 1258–1259).

THE ROLE OF MONEY IN GUBERNATORIAL ELECTIONS

The starting point for a study of the role of money in gubernatorial races is to find out what it costs to run for governor. Next we try to clarify the relationship between being an incumbent and having a large campaign fund and the effect of both incumbency and campaign funds on the outcome of races. Finally, in this section, we look at the trend toward public funding of a large portion of the cost of gubernatorial campaigns, if candidates choose to accept this option.

The Costs of Campaigns for Governor

The gubernatorial elections of 1998 cost more than they had four years earlier. Governors' races in thirty-six states officially reported spending a total of $469 million compared with the total of $418 million in 1994—a 13 percent increase

(Beyle 2000). Although these seem to be staggering figures, gubernatorial election costs adjusted for inflation have not risen that much recently. Professor Thad Beyle has compared the spending in gubernatorial races since 1977, and the following statistics come from his study. For the thirty-six states, 1994 spending was only 6.5 percent more than the amount spent in 1990. In turn, that 1990 figure increased just 7.2 percent over the cost of the gubernatorial elections in 1986. The real increase was that of 32 percent between 1982 and 1986 (Beyle 1996a, 1999). The 1982 gubernatorial election year was the first in which state campaign finance data were widely available for comparative research, so we cannot make comparisons before that. The early 1980s also marked the beginning of the modern gubernatorial electoral politics, which features television, polling, direct mail, telephone banks, and consultants. After 1986 spending stabilized, perhaps indicating a saturation level in campaign advertising.

What can explain the rise in 1998? The California race cost more than twice the golden state's expenditure in 1994. It rose from $61 million to an unprecedented $125 million, close to one-fourth of all state gubernatorial spending in 1998. So the 13 percent rise may be explained by looking at the most extravagant state. Perhaps we can get a clue from California. It was an open election, meaning that there was no incumbent running. And we have already noted that Al Checchi spent $40 million out of his pocket in the Democratic nominating contest. (He lost.) Perhaps incumbency depresses overall spending in gubernatorial elections. This may be true because incumbents win 80 percent of the time and are able to raise enough money to discourage challengers. The odds are not good for intrepid challengers, talented and capable though they may be, and they do not raise or spend as much money.

The test of the incumbency theory rested on comparing the spending in 1994 and 1998 in the twenty-four states that ran incumbents in the 1998 election (a slight increase in incumbents over 1994). This rough comparison showed that $51 million less was spent in these twenty-four states for the incumbent contests compared to those states' spending in 1994. Two of the largest states had incumbents: Texas and New York. As expected, Texas spent 12 percent less in 1998. But New York governor George Pataki spent 24 percent more as an incumbent in 1998 than he had as a challenger in 1994. Perhaps he wanted to improve his vote percentage, which was only 49 percent in 1994. He improved it to 55 percent. Perhaps New York's great wealth gives it a campaign finance momentum that cannot be retracted even in years where it is not needed. Perhaps there is an expectation that the governor must raise money for the under ticket even if the election is secure.

There are other ways to look at campaign spending. Common sense tells us that it costs more to run in a large state than in a small one. Clearly California, with the largest population, spends the most, and Texas, with the second largest, spends nearly as much. California's gubernatorial races from 1982 to 1994 averaged $51 million, which makes the $125 million expenditure in 1998 all the more remarkable. Texas races averaged $44 million from 1982 to 1994. The 1990 and 1994 races in California cost more than $60 million each, and the 1990 race in Texas exceeded $57 million. Although more populous states such as California, Texas, and New York might be expected to have expensive races, four of the twelve most expensive races in 1998 were in southern states, where one-party Democratic dominance is declining and races are competitive between the parties. Some states spend very little to elect a governor; in Wyoming and Vermont, for example, races average less than $2 million.

Because there are such wild variations among the states in population size and density, total dollars spent convey little information about the impact of money. For instance, in 1998 the amount spent per general election voter was highest in Nevada ($22.97). In three of the largest states—Texas, New York, and Florida—the cost ranged from $3 to $8 per voter. It costs more per voter in states where voters are spread out geographically, but this still does not tell us what we need to know about the impact of money on waging a campaign.

We mentioned the advantages of incumbency and the fact that gubernatorial incumbents can win 80 percent of the time and that percentage is rising. It is clear that incumbents do not have to spend as much to win. Races involving incumbents cost $6 per voter, while open seat races cost about $10 per voter. (Beyle 1996a). Ironically, incumbents can raise money very easily because they have control over the awarding of contracts and services, and groups that stand to benefit are eager to contribute. Apparently challengers to incumbents are not strong and generally not able to raise or spend as much as the incumbents themselves, who can raise as much or more than they need to win.

The degree of competition also dictates how much money needs to be spent. Races with a winner clearly predicted by the polls cost less than half the amount per voter ($4.21) than races that were unpredictable or toss-ups ($8.78) (Beyle 1996a). Does the candidate who spends more money invariably win? No. Texas governor George W. Bush beat the incumbent Ann Richards, who outspent him ($14.5 million to $11.9 million). California governor Gray Davis beat Al Checchi in the 1998 Democratic primary. Checchi outspent him $40 million to $9 million.

After increasing dramatically in the 1980s, the costs of gubernatorial campaigns did not rise as rapidly in the 1990s. There are several reasons why this may be so. First, the money spent on media ads and polling and consultants may have leveled off after the initial rise in expenditures. This type of campaign is commonplace in almost all states now (except for Vermont, New Hampshire,

Wyoming, and South Dakota). Second, more incumbent governors are able to run again, thus cutting the cost of campaigns.

Campaign Funding, Incumbency, and Election Outcomes

Can gubernatorial elections be bought? There is no simple, direct answer to that question. What we really want to find out is how frequently and in what conditions the outcome of a gubernatorial election is significantly affected by the amount of money spent by the candidates. We can begin by emphasizing an obvious point: Spending by the two major candidates on a gubernatorial campaign is not the only variable that explains the outcome. Most incumbents have a major advantage in a campaign above and beyond the fact that they can usually raise more money than their opponent. The party balance in a state is also important, reflecting the normal voting patterns of those who go to the polls. This means that any effort to systematically measure the impact of money on the outcome of gubernatorial elections must take into account some of these other factors.

One of the most comprehensive and systematic studies of gubernatorial elections covers 250 elections from 1977 through 1994 (Partin 1999b). Taking into account other variables, such as incumbency and state partisanship, Randall Partin finds that the more candidates spend, the larger the share of votes they get. In races with an incumbent running, the more the incumbent spends and the less the challenger spends, the greater share of the vote the incumbent will get. The challenger's ability to mount a serious challenge to the incumbent depends heavily on his or her ability to raise substantial amounts of campaign funds. The stronger the challenger's party and the more experienced and qualified the challenger, the more the challenger will be able to raise and spend and the more the incumbent will have to spend. Controlling for incumbency, Partin finds that the effects of campaign spending on the number of votes won is essentially the same for Democratic and Republican candidates. This study also finds that there is a law of diminishing returns at work in campaign funding; for example, the first $2 million a candidate spends is likely to have more impact than on the vote than the second $2 million. Samuel Patterson (1982) reached a similar conclusion from a study of the 1978 gubernatorial elections.

We have compared the amount of campaign money spent by candidates with the share of the vote that they get. Our information comes from the gubernatorial elections from 1987 through 1998, a period covering three four-year election cycles—three elections in most states and six in those electing a governor every two years. (Only a handful of elections are omitted because of missing data.)

We will analyze separately the ninety-two elections in which an incumbent governor was running and the sixty-two elections without an incumbent because the differences between the two types of elections are so important. We know that gubernatorial incumbents win about four-fifths of the time, in part because they usually can raise much more money than the challenger and in part because they usually have many advantages besides money. Money may not play a larger role in races without incumbents, but it may play a different role. Races without incumbents are very often closer than those with an incumbent running.

Table 5-1, comparing races with incumbents, and Table 5-2, comparing those without incumbents, are organized almost the same way. Elections are clustered. In Table 5-1 the columns show how many winning incumbents got 71–85, 56–70, and 45–55 percent of the vote, and how many lost. (None got more than 85 percent, and a few won with less than 50 percent when more than two candidates were running.) The rows show the incumbent's share of the total amount spent by the two top candidates; only one incumbent spent less than 30 percent.

Table 5-2 is organized the same way for nonincumbent races except that the percentages refer to the votes and the spending of the winning candidate. No nonincumbent winner got more than 70 percent of the vote. (There is, of course, no column for losers.) In this table the percentages of spending include only the two candidates with the largest vote, usually but not always candidates of the two major parties. When the third candidate gets at least 15 percent of the vote, the winner's vote percentage is based only on the top two candidates.

It is important to recognize that in these two tables the spending percentages include the total amount spent in both the primary and the general election by the top two candidates running in the general election. (By contrast, Tables 4-6 and 4-7, on primary elections, used only the spending for primaries.) Whenever a candidate spends campaign funds for organization, advertising, or other reasons, it has an effect on the general election. Candidates with little or no primary opposition

Table 5-1 Comparison between Proportion of Votes that Incumbent Governors Received and Proportion of Campaign Funds that They Spent in General Elections, 1978–1998 (number of elections)

Funding Proportion	Proportion of Votes Cast for Incumbent Governor					Total
	86+%	71–85%	56–70%	45–55%	Lost Race	
86+	0	4	6	0	0	10
71–85	0	4	21	1	3	29
56–70	0	2	14	6	5	27
45–55	0	0	6	6	6	18
30–44	0	0	4	1	2	7
Under 30	0	0	0	0	1	1
Total	0	10	51	14	17	92

Sources: Congressional Quarterly's Guide to U.S. Elections, 3d. ed., 1994; recent data from issues of CQ Weekly. Data on funding were provided by Thad Beyle.

Table 5–2 Comparison between Proportion of Votes that Winning Gubernatorial Candidates Received and Proportion of Campaign Funds that They Spent in General Elections Without Incumbents Running, 1978–1998 (number of elections)

Funding Proportion (%)	Proportion of Votes Cast for Winning Candidate			
	71+%	56–70%	45–55%	Total
71+	0	3	4	7
56–70	0	7	13	20
45–55	0	8	17	25
30–44	0	2	7	9
Under 30	0	0	1	1
Total	0	20	42	62

Sources: Congressional Quarterly's Guide to U.S. Elections, 3d. ed., 1994; recent data from issues of *CQ Weekly.* Data on funding were provided by Thad Beyle.

often spend substantial amounts of money during the primary campaign to get a head start on the election. It is true that candidates who have a tough primary battle sometimes spend a lot of money battling their opponents, and these funds might have less effect on the general election than if the same amount could be spent on the election in November. No measuring system is perfect, but we believe spending for both the primary and the general election needs to be included in the total calculations.

Large differences in spending between two candidates probably have some influence on the outcome; small differences are unlikely to have any effect. There were eighteen races for which the governor spent slightly more or slightly less than the opponent (where his or her spending ranged from 45 to 55 percent); we assume money had little impact on the outcome of these races.

Two-thirds of the governors won by substantial margins; fifty-one of ninety-two of them had 56–70 percent of the vote, and ten more won by 71–86 percent. Fourteen won narrowly with 55 percent or less of the vote, and seventeen were defeated. Those governors who had substantial winning margins usually had a large advantage in funding. Ten of them had an overwhelming lead in funds—at least 86 percent. Another twenty-five had a very comfortable lead—71–85 percent. Running against an incumbent governor who, in addition to the other advantages of incumbency, is able to outspend you by more than two to one (and sometimes more than four to one) must be a very discouraging experience.

Although a large spending advantage over opponents is helpful to governors and other candidates, the advantage does not translate into votes on a one-to-one basis. In a relatively competitive state a governor might have a two-to-one lead in spending because, for example, major contributors recognize that the incumbent's reelection is likely, but then the incumbent wins by only a 54–46 percent margin because almost half of the voters support the party out of power. Govs. Tom Ridge of Pennsylvania, Tommy Thompson of Wisconsin, and George W. Bush of Texas, all of whom ran for reelection in 1998, were perceived as sure winners and thus were able to outspend their opponents by huge margins. Each won by comfortable margins—between 58 and 69 percent of the vote—in two-party states where the losing candidates could count on getting 30 to 40 percent of the vote from loyal partisans. Then there was Republican Don Sundquist's reelection the same year in Tennessee, where he outspent his Democratic opponent, John Jay Hooker, by almost $5 million to $9,000; but Hooker got 29 percent of the vote. Hooker got votes because there are many Democrats in the state and because he had name recognition, having lost many statewide races over the years.

There were eighteen governors who were able to spend about as much as their challengers, in the 45–55 percent range; twelve won and six lost. Only eight governors spent less than 45 percent of the total; five won and three lost. The fact that five governors could win, despite lagging well behind in spending, reminds us that most governors have many political advantages other than funding. One example was Gov. John Engler of Michigan. Engler had a successful record in office and won 62 percent of the vote against a Democrat who lacked the support of the Democratic organization and whose personalized attacks on Engler embarrassed many Democrats. Democratic governor Parris Glendening of Maryland was reelected with 56 percent of the vote in 1998, although he was trailing in the polls earlier in the race. His Republican opponent, Ellen Sauerbrey, was an outspoken conservative who had almost beaten him four years earlier and therefore was able to get strong financial support from conservative contributors. Sauerbrey outspent the governor by a 70–30 margin.

Given the fact that seventy-five of ninety-two governors (82 percent) won, it is interesting to look more carefully at the cases of those who lost. Eight of the seventeen losers had a substantial funding advantage, while the other nine had a modest advantage or none at all. How did three governors lose despite spending from 71 to 80 percent of the total funds in the race? Jim Folsom narrowly lost in Alabama in 1994 to a former governor who was more successful in developing popular issues. Democrat Ray Maubus of Mississippi had a tough primary fight in 1991 and narrowly lost the general election to Kirk Fordice, the first Republican elected governor in over a hundred years. Maubus may have been too liberal for the state, and he was caught in the rising tide of Republicanism in a state that used to be solidly Democratic. Mike Hayden, a Republican governor in Kansas, lost narrowly in 1990, in large part because of his role in raising property taxes.

Three of the governors who lost spent less than 40 percent of the total. Why did they fall so far behind in raising money, and did this shortage of funds explain their loss? Gov. Edward DiPrete lost the 1990 Rhode Island governor's race by almost a three-to-one margin. He spent over $1 million, which is a substantial amount in a small state, but was outspent by Bruce Sundlun, who had the advantage of great wealth. But DiPrete was probably hurt more by the slumping economy and by personal scandals, for which he was eventually convicted in the courts. Arch Moore, a veteran governor of West Virginia, was defeated in 1988 after being outspent by a seven-to-three margin. The monetary disadvantage was probably less important than the state's weak economy, Moore's difficulties in getting programs passed, his tough primary battle, and the general feeling in the state that it was time for a change.

The third governor who lost after being heavily outspent was Gov. Mario Cuomo of New York in his run for a fourth term in 1994. Cuomo lost to George Pataki by a 49–45 percent margin, which is less than 200,000 votes of almost five million votes cast. He was believed to be slightly ahead until election day. Cuomo was outspent by a 64–36 margin, but he was able to spend over $8 million, a significant amount even in New York. As in any close race, we can imagine that Cuomo might have won if he had another million or two to spend, but we cannot prove that. Cuomo was handicapped by his liberal position on issues in a period of rising conservatism, by the feeling that it was time for a change, and by his lackluster campaign. Why was Pataki able to outspend Cuomo by such a large margin? Perhaps many potential Democratic and Republican contributors were convinced that Cuomo was losing political strength and could be beaten. If so, Democrats would be less willing and Republicans more willing than in the past to contribute generously to their party's candidate.

If we look at the winners' margins of victory in Table 5-2, we find that no winner got more than 70 percent of the vote, and two-thirds of the winners got 55 percent of the vote or less. By contrast, ten governors won more than 70 percent, and the two-thirds of the winning governors got 56–70 percent of the vote. In other words, winning governors usually win by comfortable margins, but the winning margin is usually quite narrow when there is no incumbent in the race.

Table 5-2 also shows us that the winner seldom has a huge advantage in funding. Only seven winners spent more than 70 percent of the total funds, while twenty spent 56–70 percent, and twenty-five spent approximately as much as their opponent, in the 45–55 percent range. Ten nonincumbent winners spent significantly less than the loser. Because there were twenty-five races in which there was a relatively small difference in spending and relatively few in which there was a huge difference, and because there were relatively few lopsided victories, it is difficult to prove that there were many races in which differences in funding were the key to the outcome.

Democrat Wallace Wilkinson enjoyed the largest spending advantage by far in the 1987 Kentucky gubernatorial race. He spent almost $10 million (two-thirds of it in the hotly contested primary) compared with Republican John

Harper, who spent almost $300,000. The leading Republican candidate had dropped out of the race before the primary, leaving a large gap that Harper, a state legislator, tried to fill. No one expected him to win, and he had virtually no support from the state party. But Harper won 35 percent from loyal Republicans and some voters who had supported losers in the Democratic primary.

How do we explain the ten races where the winner spent substantially less than the loser (under 45 percent)? In several of these cases the winner fell only slightly below the 45 percent spending figure, or the winner won by a very small margin. In the 1994 Tennessee race Republican Don Sundquist won with a 54 percent majority (spending $7 million) over a Democrat wealthy enough to fund most of his $16 million campaign. Both candidates were strong and experienced. This is an example of a case where even a large funding gap between the candidates may not be decisive if both candidates are able to spend plenty of money (by the standards of the state). In the 1990 Texas gubernatorial race, Democrat Ann Richard beat Republican Clayton Williams by barely 100,000 votes out of 3.8 million, even though she was outspent by him by a 63–37 percent margin. The race was extremely close. Williams was hurt in the closing days of the campaign by making some controversial remarks and by failing to shake Richards's hand after a debate. Richards was able to spend over $11 million dollars—enough for an extensive campaign—and once again the funding gap was not crucial.

Finally there is the unusual case of Jesse "The Body" Ventura, a former professional wrestler and talk-show host who won the Minnesota governorship in 1998. Ventura ran on the Reform Party ticket and won 37 percent of the vote, compared with 34 percent and 28 percent, respectively, for the Republican and Democratic candidates. The Republican and Democratic candidates spent almost $6 million between them. Ventura spent about $200,000 (3 percent of the total). Ventura had a message that many voters wanted to hear, and he got it out to voters largely through participating in numerous debates on television and around the state. He was running against the established parties, and that message played well in the campaign. The Democratic and Republican candidates discovered too late that Ventura had to be taken seriously. This is by far the most dramatic recent example showing that money does not always win gubernatorial elections.

It is difficult to make simple generalizations about the effect of campaign funds on the outcome of gubernatorial elections. No two elections are exactly the same: the issues are different, the candidates have different strengths and weaknesses, the political traditions in each state are different, and national trends vary from year to year. By looking at some races that do not fit the pattern we might expect, we can illustrate the importance of factors other than campaign spending in individual cases.

Governors usually win reelection, they usually can raise more money than challengers, and this monetary advantage helps them to win. They often seem to spend more than they need to for a victory. Even when they lose, challengers often win a larger share of the vote than their share of spending. Challengers have trouble raising money because the experts and potential contributors expect them to lose; however, many voters will support a challenger representing their party whether or not that person has a realistic chance of winning. The outcome of races without incumbents is likely to be closer than those with incumbents. The winners of such races seldom have as large an advantage in spending as winning incumbents do.

If we know that one candidate has spent much more than another, we can usually predict who will win the race. Examples like Jesse Ventura's win are very rare. To run a race that is at least competitive, almost any candidate has to raise a substantial amount of money. How much must be raised depends, of course, on the state: how large is its population, how much does it cost to run television commercials across the state, and what are the spending norms in campaigns? To be competitive and to have at least an outside chance of winning, a candidate probably needs to raise enough to run an adequate campaign based on the conditions in the state. If possible a candidate should raise at least half as much as his or her opponent. But if that candidate is spending much more than seems necessary, running an adequate campaign may be enough to compete.

Public Funding for Gubernatorial Candidates

In Chapter 3 we introduced the topic of public funding for political campaigns and described how the system worked when public funds in fourteen states were distributed to state political parties. We found that the effect on party organizations was rather limited in several of the states because the level of funding was relatively modest.

In this chapter we examine the fifteen states where public funding is made available directly to candidates for governor—and sometimes to candidates for a number of other statewide offices. These states are those in which public funding was available to candidates as of 1998, as well as several states in which a new or fundamentally changed system of funding for state candidates has been adopted, scheduled to take effect in 2000 or 2002, depending in part on the outcome of challenges in the courts (Maine, Vermont, Massachusetts, and Arizona). In Chapter 7 we will examine the effects of public funding on legislative elections in Minnesota and Wisconsin, where it has already been used, and the possible impact in other states where it will take effect in the 2000 elections.

All states that provide candidates with public funding provide funding for gubernatorial candidates (or in some states the governor–lieutenant governor ticket). Some states extend lower levels of funding to other statewide candidates, though others have decided that it is unnecessary because those other races usually are much less costly.

One purpose of public funding for candidates is to reduce the cost of running for office and the candidates' need to solicit funds from PACs and wealthy supporters. Another purpose is to keep elections from being "bought" by reducing the disparity between candidates who are wealthy or who—like incumbents— can raise a lot of money and candidates who are neither incumbents nor wealthy.

A state cannot require candidates to accept public funding, and under existing judicial rulings a state cannot impose an absolute limit on the amount a candidate can spend on a campaign (though it can limit the size of contributions). The state can, however, require candidates who accept public funding also to accept spending limits on their campaigns. Candidates who have difficulty raising adequate campaign funds can be expected to accept public funding under these conditions. But why should a candidate who has enough funds, or who can raise enough funds to run an expensive campaign, agree to limit spending? One way to persuade such a candidate is to set the spending limits high enough to make it tempting. If the limit is set too high, however, the goal of lower cost campaigns will not be achieved. Some states have dealt with this problem by providing that if one candidate accepts a spending limit (such as $3 million), and another refuses it and spends $4 million, for example, the first candidate will get an additional $1 million from state funds.

The way the public funding system usually works is that a gubernatorial candidate is expected to demonstrate that his or her campaign is legitimate (particularly in a primary) by raising a certain amount of funds in relatively small individual contributions (perhaps $100,000). Once that goal is accomplished, the candidate is permitted to raise a total of $2 million (including the first $100,000), for example, which the state will match dollar for dollar. The result is a total limit of $4 million that the campaign can spend.

In the late 1990s so-called clean election laws were adopted in several states (including Massachusetts, Maine, and Arizona), usually by public initiative. These laws greatly expanded the role that state funds would play in a campaign. They established total spending limits for campaigns and provided that a very large proportion of the money would be paid for by state funds. The laws made it both unnecessary and impossible for candidate to raise funds beyond an initial threshold. For example, a candidate in the Massachusetts governor's race has to raise contributions of $100 or less from 6,000 registered voters, but the maximum that can be raised from private contributions is $450,000. The state will then provide $2.55 million in public funds (85 percent of the total) with an overall spending limit of $3 million. In Massachusetts this covers both primary and general election expenditures, and a candidate who was unopposed in either the primary or the general election would get a reduced amount of state funding for the campaign.

Because these clean election laws are just beginning to take effect, it is too early to tell what their impact will be. Some laws may not be approved in the courts because judges in some other states have disapproved of very low limits on individual contributions, arguing that voters have a right to participate in campaigns by contributing money. But the U.S. Supreme Court has avoided specifying how low a state may set limits on contributions; see *Buckley v. Valeo* (1976) and *Nixon v. Shrink Missouri Government PAC* (2000).

What have been the consequences of public funding with spending limits for a governor's race in those states where it has been used? Does such a change result in lower levels of spending? One dramatic example is found in Kentucky, where the total cost of primary and general election campaigns for governor in 1991 was $20 million. In the 1995 elections, after adoption of a public funding law with spending limits, the total cost dropped to $9.4 million. Moreover, the margin of Democratic victory in the governor's race dropped from 30 percent to 2 percent. In 1999, for the first time in many years, the Republicans failed to run a serious candidate for governor. One of their excuses was that the spending limit prevented them from running the large-scale campaign that would be necessary to give them a chance of defeating the incumbent governor.

How often do gubernatorial candidates participate in public funding plans with spending limits? A study of gubernatorial elections in 1993–1996 in eleven states found that four out of six incumbents and eleven out of sixteen nonincumbents accepted the funding with limits. Nine out of eleven Democrats, but only six out of eleven Republicans, did. Both candidates in Minnesota, Michigan, New Jersey, Kentucky, and Rhode Island participated. In the first three of these states public funding was a long-established practice that had bipartisan support. Neither candidate took funding in North Carolina, where the limit on spending was much lower than the usual costs of a campaign in that state. There was no apparent connection between accepting public funding and winning. Incumbent governors who did not accept public funding beat challengers who did in Massachusetts and Wisconsin. An incumbent who accepted funding beat one who did not in Florida. When two nonincumbents were running, only one of whom accepted public funding, one who did so won and the other lost (Malbin and Gais 1998, 62–65).

It is difficult to forecast the long-term future of programs to provide public funding for gubernatorial candidates. Some programs that have been in effect for a number of years may be in jeopardy for a couple of reasons. The proportion of taxpayers using the check-off on state income tax forms has declined steadily to about 10 percent, and taxpayers' willingness to pay small add-on taxes has almost evaporated. To provide enough revenue for public funding, it is becoming increasingly necessary for the legislature to appropriate additional funds. But in some state legislatures many Republicans are opposed to public funding, and where they have gained a majority in the legislature, they have sometimes reduced or abolished public funding of elections (as occurred in Florida).

At the same time, in some states at least, there appears to be much stronger public support for public funding. It was the voters, acting through public initiatives, who adopted the "clean elections" laws going into effect in four states in the 2000 elections; these greatly increase the proportion of campaign costs paid for by public funds. How far this movement may spread through initiative or legislative action remains to be seen. It is also unclear whether some courts will reject the very low individual contribution limits incorporated in these laws.

GOVERNORS: STRONG BUT NOT INVINCIBLE

Gubernatorial elections have many of the same characteristics as other statewide and congressional races. Incumbents are usually reelected, although governors are vulnerable to attack on policy issues such as taxes and spending. The growing level of party competition—particularly in southern states—that we described in Chapter 2 is evident in governors' races. Closer competition means not only that every state except Hawaii and Georgia had at least one Democratic and one Republican governor between 1965 and 2000 but that in every state in almost every election the party out of power is able to run a serious candidate for governor.

National trends have some impact on gubernatorial elections, and Republicans increased their share of governors significantly in the 1994–1998 elections. But governors are often strong enough to win reelection despite a national trend favoring the opposite party. Governors who are skillful politicians are often able build a base of public support that crosses party lines and makes them difficult to defeat.

In describing how gubernatorial campaigns are run by the candidates and parties, we have had to generalize about the fifty states. But it is important to remember how much variation there is in actual campaigns from state to state, particularly the differences between the larger and smaller states. Campaigning is fundamentally different in California, New York, Ohio, and Texas from what it is in New Hampshire, Delaware, Idaho, and Arkansas. Remember how presidential candidates are able to campaign in the New Hampshire primary, speaking to small groups and meeting thousands of voters face to face, compared with their overwhelming reliance on television advertising in California. The contrast between gubernatorial campaigns in those two states is just as dramatic. There are other differences in campaign styles among the states. Political party organizations can provide gubernatorial candidates with more support to in some of the northeastern and midwestern states. Ethnic and racial factors are more important in some states than others. Moreover, there are many differences in the voting patterns that prevail in the various states.

6 Voting Behavior in Gubernatorial Elections

In the previous chapter we described gubernatorial elections from the perspective of the candidates and other participants in the campaign and analyzed candidates, how campaigns are run, and the role of issues in campaigns. In this chapter we focus on voters and the factors that appear to determine what decisions they make in gubernatorial elections.

The main questions are what factors determine the choices voters make; in what conditions does one or another factor assume greater importance; and has the relative importance of these factors been changing over time? Most studies of voting behavior in this country have dealt with presidential and congressional elections. Is voting behavior fundamentally the same at both the national and state levels, and if not what are the differences?

Much of our analysis of voting behavior is based on aggregate voting data—that is, the actual votes cast in various state gubernatorial elections over a period of years. The advantages of aggregate voting statistics are many. They are available at the state and county levels for all states for long periods of time. We can generalize from such data about all states and measure trends over the time periods in which we are interested. We can sometimes estimate the voting pattern of ethnic or racial groups or urban and rural dwellers, for example, but we cannot draw conclusions from such data about the perceptions and motivations of individual voters.

Data from voting surveys can provide much more specific information about the variables associated with voting and can make possible a number of inferences about motivations. If we had enough data from surveys of state elections, we could be much more confident about answering our questions. Which types of voters participate in state gubernatorial elections? How consistently do they vote according to party identification? How frequently do they split their tickets, and which ones do so? How much do voters know about the candidates for state office and their positions or records on major issues? Most of the survey data on gubernatorial elections come from a limited number of states and are relatively recent, making it difficult to generalize to all states or over time.

ARE STATE ELECTIONS AUTONOMOUS
FROM NATIONAL ELECTIONS?

There are differences of opinion among political scientists about how much state elections are influenced by national factors and how autonomous they are. One school of thought considers gubernatorial elections as national referendums in which voters use their votes to express their approval or disapproval of the sitting president and his policies. This school argues that if the voters are satisfied with the economic policies of the president, candidates of the president's party (incumbents as well as challengers) will benefit from his success. If, on the other hand, things are going badly in domestic or international relations, gubernatorial candidates of the president's party will lose in November. Inversely candidates who are not of the president's party will see their electoral fortunes rise and fall depending on the electorate's approval of the president (Simon 1989). A variation on this theme says that only the incumbent candidates of the president's party are rewarded or punished based on prevailing economic conditions (Chubb 1988; Stein 1990).

On the other hand, scholars hypothesize that voters consider the performance of the incumbent governor, and if they think the economy is doing well that is who they vote for. The voter who feels better off financially will reward the incumbent officeholder. This theory stresses state-level accountability. The difference between these two theories lies in the notion of state autonomy. The national referendum theory posits the states as dependent upon the national economy and state elections as referendums on national performance. On the other hand, the state economic voting hypothesis views the states as separate economic units with independent policymaking choices that affect state elections (Atkeson and Partin 1995; Partin 1995). One question is to what extent do voters distinguish between state and federal level responsibility for economic conditions when they vote for governor? We will more carefully examine questions about the impact of the strength of the national or state economy on state elections later in this chapter when we discuss ideology and issues.

Influence of National Forces on State Elections

There are several reasons for thinking that state elections may respond to national electoral forces. It is argued that the media have been increasingly nationalized with national news dominating the airwaves. Governors hire nationally based consultants with sophisticated national strategies. Because campaigns are becoming more expensive, governors depend on national fund raisers. Most state parties do not have the funds to counterbalance these trends, and the extra funds they receive may come from the national parties. Direct primaries have replaced state nominating conventions, and few (sixteen) states have attempted to control the nomination by making endorsements.

A strong case has been made that evaluations of the president operate as an influence in gubernatorial elections. Approval of the president's performance will increase the probability of voting for the candidate of the president's party. Although Dennis Simon's research does not deny that party preference and incumbency have an impact on voting behavior, he concludes that "public satisfaction or dissatisfaction with conditions in the national and international environment register an impact on state politics" (1989, 301). Researchers of this school assert that state elections reveal referendum voting and hence are coherent national events (Simon, Ostrom, and Marra 1991; Stein 1990).

Differences between State and National Elections

What differences exist between elections held at the state level and those at the national level? Do some states have closer competition at the national level and less at the state level? Within some states are there differences in the voting patterns for president and for governor, for example? Various forms of evidence indicate that voting patterns in state elections are quite different from those in national elections, though the differences are more obvious in some states than others.

It is well understood that fewer voters have strong party loyalties than existed in the 1940s and 1950s. This means that compared with that earlier period, a smaller proportion of voters identify with a political party and a larger proportion consider themselves independent; those who do identify with a party vote for candidates of that party less consistently than used to be the case.

We know that for a number of reasons there is more split-ticket voting than there used to be, although this phenomenon is more common in some states than in others. Substantial partisan gains and losses in congressional races do not consistently coincide with similar changes in the proportion of Democratic and Republican governors. We know that incumbent governors as well as members of Congress are difficult to beat when they run for reelection, and this contributes to split-ticket voting. When voters split their tickets, it is usually because they vote for an incumbent of the other party who is seeking reelection; this is partly because incumbents who are politically strong are not very often challenged by relatively strong candidates from the opposite party. A Democratic voter might, for example, vote to reelect a Democratic governor and a Democratic U.S. senator but vote for an incumbent Republican state legislator.

In almost four-fifths of the states, the governor is chosen in a year when there is no presidential election. In a way this makes it even easier for voters to vote Republican for president and two years later to vote Democratic for governor.

Political scientists often describe both national and state election campaigns as being candidate centered, a term that has several meanings. It suggests that although candidates often get assistance from their political party they usually run their campaigns rather independently. It also suggests that elections are not necessarily determined by traditional voting patterns in a state or by national partisan trends. A skillful, hard-working, well-financed gubernatorial candidate can sometimes win in a state that is usually carried by the other party.

In Chapter 5 we described how elections can be won or lost depending on the characteristics of the candidate, the type of campaign he or she runs, and the issues that are developed during the campaign. In a state that is reasonably competitive between the two parties, it is very possible that some of the party's candidates will win and some will lose in the same election year because some are better candidates than others and run better campaigns. Similarly it is possible that the Democratic candidate for governor for example will win by getting support from voters who usually vote for the Republican presidential candidate, while the Republican gubernatorial candidate will fail to run the kind of campaign that will win votes from enough of those voters—whatever their party affiliation—who usually support a Republican for president.

State and National Party Systems

James Gimpel defines autonomous state party systems as "those where the local party coalitions are consistently different from the national party coalitions" (1996, 3–4). (He is using the term *local* to include gubernatorial and other statewide races.) Gimpel says that there are states where

> state and national [political] cleavages do not neatly match. It's not just that elections in one state are cleaved differently than those in other states, although that phenomenon is clearly both common and important. Individual state elections are cleaved differently from one another. One formulation of the notion of incongruence, although not the only possible one, is that partisans of one party at the local level, say, in gubernatorial races, will be different from partisans of that party in that same state in adjacent presidential elections. (1999, 134)

In such states partisanship is a less consistent predictor of voting patterns than in other states. This, in turn, weakens the political party and forces candidates for both state and national office to identify and mobilize their own coalition of voters and to build their own group of activists because they cannot be sure that party activists are willing to work consistently for their party's candidates (Gimpel 1999, 135).

Although we generally expect that states with close two-party competition will have relatively strong, united parties, Gimpel argues that in states where electoral incongruence exists parties may be relatively weak and disorganized even though they are competitive. Gimpel (1996) finds that since the early 1950s the political parties in most western states have been reasonably competitive but weakly organized, at least in part because of their electoral incongruence. While most western states have been voting Republican in presidential races, they have been electing some Democratic governors—in some states more often than Republican governors.

From the 1950s through the 1980s most southern states had incongruent voting patterns. Beginning in 1952 Republican presidential candidates began to carry an increasing number of southern states because conservative, traditionally Democratic voters were willing to vote Republican in presidential races, often because they believed the Democratic presidential candidates were much too liberal. But the Republican Party had difficulty electing candidates in state elections, ranging from governor and senator to state legislator, in large part because most of the Democrats running for those offices were conservative enough to satisfy the voters. When the southern states were known as the Solid South, neither party was very organized, and it took many years to develop viable party organizations, with the Republicans often moving more rapidly than the Democrats. It was not until the late 1980s and the 1990s that both parties in many southern states were able to develop more congruent electoral bases as voters became more likely to vote in a consistent pattern in state and national elections.

The northeastern and midwestern states have had the most congruence between national and state elections and the strongest political organizations. But Gimpel (1996) sees some signs of greater incongruence between state and national elections in the Northeast, particularly in the Republican Party. He believes that as national Republican politics has become more conservative—beginning with the Reagan elections—Republican leaders, and particularly governors in a number of northeastern states, have established a more moderate base for the state Republican Party. This lays the groundwork for differences in national and state elections in these states.

PARTY LOYALTIES OF VOTERS

In Chapter 2 we described how pollsters have measured the party identification of individuals through the years as an important factor because repeated studies have shown that party identification is usually the strongest predictor of how voters will vote. We also emphasized that the impact of party identification on how individuals vote for presidential and congressional candidates has been growing since the early 1970s.

There are various ways to measure the impact of partisan identification on the vote cast for governor. The first step is to find out what proportion of voters who identify with a party are likely to vote for the gubernatorial party of that governor. Of course, other factors, such as incumbency and national political trends, would affect this. Given such differences, what proportion of Democrats vote for Democratic candidates, and what proportion of Republicans vote for Republicans?

Gubernatorial elections were held in thirty-six states in 1986, 1990, and 1994. In all these states except Alaska, surveys of voters were conducted in one or more of these years, showing that 79 percent of those voters who voted for a major party gubernatorial candidate and who identified with a party voted for that party's candidate for governor. The figure for Democrats was only one-half of one percentage point higher, and the figure for Republicans was one-half of one percentage point below 79 percent. Independent voters preferred Republicans by a 53–47 percent margin (Partin 1995, 1999a).

These figures were comparable to those in the 1982 election in a sample of twenty states. The proportion of Democrats who voted for a Democratic gubernatorial candidate ranged from 87 percent when the incumbent was a Democrat to 77 percent when the incumbent was a Republican. Republicans gave 84 percent to Republican incumbents and 64 percent to Republicans challenging Democratic incumbents (Jewell and Olson 1988, 191).

The record of party loyalty is somewhat similar in congressional races. In the ten elections for 1980 through 1998 in races for the U.S. House, polling data show that voters identifying with a party voted for candidates of their own party almost 80 percent of the time. Data also show that those who defected from their party's candidate were usually doing so to vote for the incumbent (Jacobson forthcoming).

By comparison, we can look at how Democratic and Republican identifiers voted in six presidential elections from 1976 through 1996. (In elections when third-party candidates got a substantial vote, we are calculating only the percentage of the vote for the two major parties.) In three elections won by Republicans, 91 percent of Republican voters voted for the Republican candidate, and only 75 percent of Democrats voted for the Democrat. In three elections won by Democrats, 88 percent of Republicans and 85 percent of Democrats voted from the presidential candidate of their party (with the low Democratic vote for Jimmy Carter in 1976 pulling down the Democratic average) (*New York Times* 1996).

Erikson, Wright, and McIver conducted the most thorough study of gubernatorial elections in their work *Statehouse Democracy* (1993). They examined exit polls conducted by CBS/ *New York Times* in a number of gubernatorial elections in thirty-three states from 1982 through 1988. Their first conclusion was acknowledging "the dominant role of party identification at the individual level" (p. 199). They also found that the ideological position of voters had an important effect on that vote.

The party identification of voters in a state was most likely to be important when the campaign tapped traditional partisan issues. This included elections in some of the states where the two parties stand for quite different policies on major issues, such as California, Illinois, Massachusetts, Michigan, Minnesota, and Ohio. But partisanship was sometimes very important in contests in such states as Florida, North Carolina, Tennessee, and Texas, where we would not expect partisan differences on issues to be so clear-cut. It is obvious that the campaigns waged by the two candidates play a large part in determining how much voting is affected by the partisanship of those who go to the polls. The 1986 elections in California and Illinois both pitted liberal Democrats against conservative Republicans, and in both cases the same two candidates had run against each other four years earlier. Perhaps in a rerun election the voters are particularly familiar with the differences between candidates and vote a party line. In 1982 in Massachusetts Mike Dukakis, well known as a liberal, defeated a conservative Republican in a race where party identification was very important. Partisanship had a minimal effect on Georgia's race in 1986, when both candidates were very conservative (Erikson, Wright, and McIver 1993).

In the final analysis, political parties remain influential in determining the voter preferences for governor (Partin 1995). Separate studies found that party identification was the most important variable in the gubernatorial races of 1982, 1986, and 1990 (Svoboda 1995; Atkeson and Partin 1995, 104). State politics has become independent from national politics, and state issues are independent of national issues. Only eleven states force the governor to stand for election at the same time as the president. Parties in most states are closely competitive, and traditional party identification can account for voting outcomes when the state economy is stable. Of course, short-term factors such as tax increases or unemployment may affect the outcome of an election, thereby reducing the importance of the traditional party loyalty of voters in a state.

THE IMPACT OF GUBERNATORIAL INCUMBENCY

In Chapter 5 we described the advantages that incumbent governors enjoy when they run for reelection. We pointed out that a governor must run on his or her record in office and that, although the incumbent's record may be a major asset, it is sometimes a liability. This is true particularly if the state is in an economic slump and if the governor has been forced to raise taxes and perhaps cut back on programs. We also explained why voters are more likely to hold the governor accountable for his or her record than to hold accountable a U.S. senator seeking reelection.

Squire and Fastnow (1994) have explained some of the reasons why voters pay more attention to the record of governors than of senators during a campaign. They note that the media pay more attention to governors than to senators during a campaign as well as at other times. Also voters are more likely to recall the name of their governor than of either senator, but when asked by pollsters they are likely to rate governors as favorably as they do senators. Governors are more likely than senators to face a relatively experienced, fairly well known challenger. There is some evidence that voters are less likely to cross party lines to vote for a governor than for a senator.

The beginning point in analyzing the impact of incumbency on voters is to examine the record of gubernatorial elections. Table 6-1 covers the elections in the 1980s and 1990s. Each row covers a two-year period, such as 1993–1994. Most states elect in the even-numbered years, but a very few elect in odd-numbered years. For each election period the table shows in how many states the governor was running and whether he or she was reelected or defeated. It also shows how many elections had no incumbent running and in how many of these there was a turnover in party control of the governorship.

We find for the twenty-year period that an incumbent was running more than half of the time (58 percent) and that the incumbent lost in only 19 percent of these races. When no incumbent was running, there was a change in party control of the governorship 56 percent of the time, compared with only 19 percent when the incumbent ran. This is a pretty good indication of how much difference the incumbent governor makes.

Over time, governors have become more successful in seeking reelection. In the 1940s and 1950s about two-thirds of governors who ran were reelected. From 1963 through 1978, 75 percent of governors won; from 1979 through 1988, 78 percent won. And in the 1990s (from 1989 through 1998), 82 percent won. (These figures do not include the very small numbers of incumbent governors who were defeated in primaries; in the table those are counted as general elections without incumbents running.)

State elections are primarily state-specific. Incumbents usually win them because they have built a record and have been highly visible to the citizens. But most states have term limits now, and even the most successful governors must retire after eight years in office. Hence nearly half of the contests are open and the competition is intense. In the thirty-six gubernatorial contests in 1998, 64 percent featured incumbents (twenty-three), and all but two governors won reelection. (Maine reelected an independent governor, Angus S. King Jr.) In an election that was predicted to be heavily influenced by a national level scandal involving President Clinton and a White House intern, the gubernatorial contests were decided by state issues of experience, education, crime, and taxes. The Republicans won four governorships in open races in former Democratic states, and the Democrats won four contests in former Republican states, making the net results nearly identical with the line-up in the beginning: twenty-three Republican governors and

Table 6-1 Electoral Record of Incumbent Governors and Their Impact on Party Turnover

Years	Number of Elections	Elections with Incumbent				No Incumbent Running			Percentage of Elections with Incumbents Running
		Total	Incumbent Won	Incumbent Lost	Percentage Who Won	Total	Party Turnover	Percentage of Party Turnover	
1979–1980	16	10	7	3	70	6	2	33	63
1981–1982	38	24	19	5	79	14	8	57	63
1983–1984	17	7	4	3	57	10	6	60	41
1985–1986	38	18	16	2	89	20	12	60	47
1987–1988	15	10	8	2	80	5	2	40	67
1989–1990	38	23	17	6	74	15	9	60	61
1991–1992	15	6	4	2	67	9	4	44	40
1993–1994	38	22	17	5	77	16	10	63	58
1995–1996	14	8	8	0	100	6	3	50	57
1997–1998	38	26	24	2	92	12	7	58	68
Total	267	154	124	30	81	113	63	56	58

Sources: Congressional Quarterly's Guide to U.S. Elections, 3d. ed., 1994; recent data from issues of CQ Weekly.

eleven Democratic governors. Reform Party candidate and former professional wrestler Jesse Ventura won a three-way race in Minnesota over Hubert Humphrey III, the state's attorney general, and St. Paul's Republican mayor, Norm Coleman.

In addition to analyzing individual data on gubernatorial elections, Erikson, Wright, and McIver (1993) measured the effect of a number of variables on these elections, including the traditional partisanship of the state and the presence of an incumbent in the race. They found both to be very important in predicting the outcome of races in the 1976–1988 period, with incumbency having the greatest effect. They also found that short-term forces in addition to incumbency were important, a point we will return to in describing ideology and issues in campaigns.

A more precise way of measuring the impact of incumbency on voting for governor is to look at individual voting patterns. In discussing the effect of party identification on voting for governor (in 1982), we noted that among Democrats there was a 10 percentage point gap between the proportion voting for a Democrat who was an incumbent and one who was challenging an incumbent. For Republicans, there was a gap of 20 percentage points between those voting for Republican candidates who were incumbents and challengers.

In making a comparison with U.S. House races, we find that incumbency is a major factor in explaining defections by voters who identify with a party. At least one-third of voters defect from their party to vote for an incumbent of the opposite party. The data suggest the figure may be as high as 40 percent, although respondents tend to exaggerate the extent of their voting for incumbents. On the other hand, less than 10 percent of partisans defect to vote for a candidate who is challenging an incumbent.

Keep in mind that those who defect to vote for an incumbent in a congressional race are usually identified with the minority party in a district, and their party's candidate, running as a challenger, may be inexperienced and virtually unknown to many voters. By contrast, a candidate who is challenging an incumbent governor may be more experienced, better known, and therefore a better match for the governor.

THE IMPACT OF IDEOLOGY AND ISSUES

The study of individual voting in a number of gubernatorial elections from 1982 through 1988 (Erikson, Wright, and McIver 1993) found that the ideological position of voters, though a little less important than party identification, has a considerable impact on vote choice. Not surprisingly, the ideological factor assumes more importance when a strongly liberal candidate (usually Democratic) is running against a strong conservative (usually Republican). Ideology was important in some of the races where partisanship also was important, such as the

Dukakis victory in Massachusetts in 1983. Ideology had virtually no impact in a 1986 Pennsylvania gubernatorial race in which the Democratic candidate followed a more conservative position on cultural issues than did the Republican candidate.

Ideology and issues can both be thought of as short-term factors affecting the outcome of elections because individual candidates who belong to the same party often have different points of view on some issues as well as different strategies about the issues they decide to emphasize during a campaign. Over a period of several elections the balance between the two parties as manifested in the party identification of voters is not likely to change very much—creating what is often called a normal division of the vote. Whether an incumbent is running (obviously a short-term factor) and the issue positions of candidates and their campaign strategies are short-term forces that often make it difficult to predict the outcome of elections. Erikson, Wright, and McIver (1993) emphasize that such short-term factors are very important in gubernatorial elections. This has become increasingly the case as the normal two-party balance in many states has been growing closer.

One way to gain some perspective on the kinds of issues that are most likely to be crucial in gubernatorial elections is to examine what journalists and other experts have said about individual gubernatorial elections. We have drawn this information from press coverage, particularly from *The Almanac of American Politics* (Barone and Ujifusa 1979–1999), which is published every two years. We have selected the thirty general elections from 1979 through 1998 in which an incumbent governor was defeated. Because it is rare for a governor to be defeated, these should be among the elections in which issues were particularly important. Moreover, we have emphasized that the governor's record in office can be both an asset and a liability and that these elections should illustrate the ways in which a governor's record can be used against him or her in a campaign.

In Table 6-2 we have tried to distinguish between issues that appear to have had a major effect on the outcome of gubernatorial elections and those that appear to have been a contributing factor. The number of issues listed in the table add to more than thirty because in many elections more than one factor was listed. A total of forty-one issues explaining the governor's defeat were directly related to the record of the incumbent administration; at least one such issue was found in all but three of the thirty elections.

There were twelve elections (almost one-third of the total) in which the governor's record on taxes appeared important—usually very important—in the campaign. This generally meant that the governor had raised taxes, or tried to raise them, and ran into legislative resistance. Sometimes this action violated a campaign pledge not to raise taxes. Inevitably the challenger criticized the governor. In 1978 Charles Thone was elected governor of Nebraska on his promises to cut taxes, but his approval of increases in both the sales tax and the income tax con-

Table 6-2 Factors Affecting the Outcome of Incumbent's Defeat in Gubernatorial Elections

	Major Factor	Contributing Factor	Total
Record of incumbent administration			
Taxes	11	1	
State economy	3	1	
Scandals	2	1	
Time for a change	1	3	
Other major issues	3	15	
Total	20	21	41
Partisan factors			
Dominant party	0	2	
Governor's party divided	0	5	
Winning party very united	0	2	
Total	0	9	9
Personality of winner or loser	0	7	7

Source: Data compiled from authors' research.

tributed to his defeat in 1982. In 1980 John Spellman campaigned successfully for governor of Washington, promising not to raise taxes. But he did so, and the issue contributed to his defeat in 1984.

Occasionally a governor running for reelection has come under attack for refusing to promise no tax increases in a second term. In New Hampshire candidates were always under pressure to "take the pledge" promising not to recommend adoption of an income or sales tax. Gov. Hugh Gallen took that pledge in 1980 and abided by it, but he refused to renew the pledge in the 1982 election because he foresaw the need for new tax revenue. Gallen was defeated in his reelection bid. Sometimes governors have been defeated because they pushed through the legislature a tax restructuring such as cutting the property tax and raising the sales tax and came under attack for making that change. In 1990 New Jersey Democratic governor Jim Florio pushed through the legislature a tax increase that not only dealt with a revenue gap by raising taxes but restructured the income tax to make it more progressive, that is, substantially increasing taxes for residents with higher incomes. Angry citizens promised to defeat him, and in the 1993 election he was beaten by Republican Christine Todd Whitman, who promised a 30 percent income tax to be phased in over three years.

In four elections it appears that a state's economic slump was serious enough to contribute to the governor's defeat. In three of those four cases there was a direct link between the economic slump and the governor's demand for higher taxes.

There were probably several more states where a sluggish economy played an indirect role by increasing the need for more tax revenue.

Interestingly enough, there were only three elections in which scandals that arose in the governor's administration were serious enough to have contributed to the governor's defeat for reelection. Democratic governor Edwin Edwards lost the 1987 race in Louisiana after facing two trials for bribery and corruption during his term. He was not convicted in either case, but the trials were an embarrassment to the state and a major reason for his defeat. Republican Edward DiPrete of Rhode Island was reelected narrowly in 1988, despite a well-publicized scandal in which he appointed to a state job a local official who had approved a land deal in which DiPrete's family made $2 million. DiPrete was beaten by almost a three-to-one margin in the 1990 election, in part because he had agreed to higher taxes to cope with an economic slump and in part because the voters apparently had not forgotten the earlier scandal. DiPrete subsequently admitted to steering state contracts to friends and faced charges of accepting bribes for state contracts. Alabama Democratic governor James Folsom Jr. was narrowly defeated in 1994 in a campaign that focused partly on education issues, but he was hurt by assertions that he had steered a Medicaid contract to a firm set up by a relative.

In four elections the challenger's claim that it was "time for a change" appears to have impressed the voters. We have previously mentioned the 1994 election in New York in which Gov. Mario Cuomo lost his bid for a fourth consecutive term after failing to make it clear why he deserved it. The others were Bruce King in New Mexico, who was seeking his fourth nonconsecutive term in 1994; Rudy Perpich in Minnesota, running in 1994 for the fourth consecutive time (twice successfully); and Arch Moore of West Virginia, running in 1988 after having won three of four gubernatorial elections dating as far back as 1968. (Moore's most notable victory had been in 1972, when, as the incumbent, he defeated multimillionaire John D. Rockefeller IV. Moore's classic bumper sticker said, "Make him spend it all, Arch!")

In more than half of the elections (a total of eighteen) a wide variety of other issues played at least a contributing role in the incumbent governor's defeat. The Republican governor of Florida (Bob Martinez) in the 1990 election and the Democratic governor of Minnesota (Rudy Perpich) in the same year lost considerable support in their reelection bids because of their efforts to have stricter limits imposed on abortion.

One of several issues that hurt Gov. Mark White in the 1986 Texas election was his support of a "no pass, no play" proposal by an education committee (headed by Ross Perot) that would require students to meet higher academic standards before being eligible to compete in sports like football and basketball. In a state where high school football games take on the importance of college games in other states, this proposal aroused angry opposition.

In 1980, when Bill Clinton was defeated for reelection after his first term as governor of Arkansas, he was hurt for two main reasons. He had raised the fee for license plates, and he had failed to prevent President Jimmy Carter from sending a large number of Cuban refugees to camps located near the second largest city in Arkansas. (Some traditional Arkansas voters also grumbled because Clinton's wife was known as Hillary Rodham; when he regained the governorship two years later she called herself Hillary Rodham Clinton.)

Voters' expectations of their governor differ from state to state. In the 1984 governor's race in North Dakota Gov. Allen Olson was hurt because he had splurged and had his office redecorated and because he used state funds to purchase an airplane for his use in traveling around the state. Although these activities caused quite a stir, we do not believe they qualify for our category of "scandals."

There were sixteen elections in which factors other than or in addition to the governor's record in office appear to have a major impact on the outcome of the election. These include seven elections in which the governor's party was badly divided (such as a governor who won a very close primary race) or the other party was unusually united in the campaign. In a couple of states the candidate opposing the governor came from a party that generally dominated the state. There were seven cases where the outcome appeared to be affected by the fact that one candidate was much stronger or had a more attractive personality than the other.

The more controversial issues are among those most likely to have an effect on gubernatorial elections. One of the most controversial issues for a number of years has been the abortion question. Pro-choice groups try to persuade state government to lift some of the restrictions on abortions or to provide funding for abortions, while anti-abortion groups try to enact additional limitations. Both groups put considerable pressure on candidates for governor and other state offices to support their position.

Cook, Jelen, and Wilcox (1994) conducted a study based on exit polls in ten states in 1989 and 1990; they found that in all but one state the candidates' position on abortion had a significant effect on the election outcome. Most gubernatorial candidates in these states made their position on abortion clear. In most of the states between one-fourth and one-third of the voters said that the abortion issue was one of the two most important issues in determining their vote for governor. In six states—Virginia, Florida, Texas, New Jersey, Michigan, and Ohio—Democratic candidates for governor took a pro-choice stand, and the Republican candidates were pro-life. In all six states voters who said abortion should be legal were more likely, often much more likely, to vote Democratic than those who favored the opposite position. In Pennsylvania, Illinois, and Massachusetts it was the Republican candidate, not the Democrat, who took a pro-choice position; in Pennsylvania and Massachusetts pro-choice voters were more likely to vote Republican, but in Illinois the Democratic candidate drew evenly from both groups. Both candidates were pro-choice in California, but pro-choice voters were more likely to vote Democratic. In some states from one-fourth to one-third of partisan voters who disagreed with the abortion position of their party's candidate crossed party lines to vote for the other gubernatorial candidate. Pro-choice Democrats won in Virginia, New Jersey, Texas, and Florida; pro-choice Republicans won in Massachusetts, Illinois, and California. Pro-life Republicans won in Ohio and Michigan; a pro-life Democrat won in Pennsylvania.

Impact of Economic Conditions on Gubernatorial Elections

Are voters likely to give the governor the credit if the state's economy is booming and the blame if the economy is in a slump? Does the governor get credit for lowering taxes or keeping them steady and get blamed if taxes are increased? Although research on most aspects of gubernatorial elections is rather thin, political scientists have devoted considerable attention to analyzing the impact of these two issues on the outcome of gubernatorial elections involving an incumbent. We will try to explain the conditions in which these issues become important to voters in evaluating a governor running for reelection.

The issues of the state economy and taxation are separate yet closely related. If the state's economy is doing well, the governor can usually maintain and expand programs without raising taxes. But if the state is in a prolonged, serious slump, the governor may have to ask the legislature to raise taxes and perhaps even cut back services.

There is considerable evidence that state elections are based on the voters' evaluations of the governor's economic performance; since incumbents are reelected 80 percent of the time, the evaluations are generally positive. Governors today serve longer terms, have greater institutional powers, and are more publicly visible than those in the past.

In our discussion in Chapter 5 of the advantages and disadvantages facing a governor who must run on a past or current record, we made the point that in the short run the governor has little control over the economic condition of the state. National and international conditions and decisions made in Washington determine the strength of the national economy, which in turn causes the state economy to be strong or weak. Specific changes in national economic conditions affect states differently, depending on whether the state economy is heavily dependent on natural resources like coal and oil, agriculture, heavy manufacturing, or military contracts, such as the manufacture of airplanes or high-tech weapons.

Over a period of years the governor and legislature can take steps to strengthen the state's economy. One strategy is to lure new industry and other businesses to the state, which may require subsidies or tax breaks. Another is to improve the quality of the state's educational system at all levels so that it develops a higher caliber work force and to strengthen its research universities to attract research-oriented businesses. Governors often take credit for higher levels of employment and new businesses opening in the state. But most of these strategies, particularly improving education, take many years to produce visible results, and very few governors serve more than two terms in office. If the economy is growing significantly in a state, it may be the result of bold steps taken by the governor's predecessor.

Paul Brace, who has studied in detail the economic impact of state government policies, concludes that during the 1980s state government policies had an effect on per capita personal income:

> The capacity of state governments, the quantity of economic policies they adopted, and the amounts they spent on developmental policies all were positively related to growth in this new era. . . . In essence the institutionally more powerful, entrepreneurial state has been better suited to sustain income in the changing economic environment of the 1980s. (1993, 112)

However, higher income levels in a state could lead to a slowdown in job growth. Brace also cautions that during some time periods national economic policies and trends may overwhelm state efforts at economic development.

To understand how much the strength or weakness of the state's economy influences voters, we must be able to answer several difficult questions. If the state economy is doing well or poorly, do many voters give the credit or blame to the governor? Are voters more likely to blame a governor for a slump than to credit him or her with a thriving economy? There is some evidence that voters give the president credit for a booming national economy and blame him for hard times. But if the national economy was booming under President Clinton, for example, would a Democratic governor be more likely than a Republican to get some credit for the resulting gains in the state's economy?

Political scientists have devoted considerable attention to the effect that state and national economic conditions may have on the governor's chances of winning reelection. Using extensive public opinion data from eight states, Susan Hansen (1999) finds that the public's approval rating for governors drops when unemployment levels in a state grow. Unfortunately for the governor a drop in unemployment levels does not seem to help the rating very much. Presumably voters who give a governor a higher approval rating are more likely to vote for that candidate.

Research that tests these hypotheses shows that voters do indeed hold governors responsible for the health of their state economies, and their views are not subject to fluctuations in presidential approval (Tompkins 1988; Partin 1995; Atkeson and Partin 1995). In open races, without incumbents, candidates are not held responsible for past events. This finding indicates that voters are able to distinguish between the functional responsibilities of presidents and governors and vote accordingly. This is a reaffirmation of the ability of voters to assign responsibility where it is due.

A study of the 1990 gubernatorial elections, based on surveys of voters in the thirty-six states with gubernatorial elections that year, asked voters whether they thought that economic conditions in their state were better or worse than a year ago. In states where a Republican governor was seeking reelection, those voters who said conditions were much better than they had been a year earlier were more than twice as likely to vote for the Republican governor as those who said conditions were much worse (in an analysis in which many other pertinent variables were held constant). In states where Democratic governors were running, voters were one and a half times as likely to vote for the incumbent if they had a very favorable perception of the state's economy. This provides evidence that many voters do hold the governor responsible for the health of the state's economy. It is often suggested that voters may credit or blame both the governor and the president for the state's economy. The fact that Republican president George Bush was in office in 1990 may explain why Republican voters were more sensitive to the economic issue than were Democrats. In open races, with no incumbent running, the voter's perception of the state's economy did not affect their vote for governor, presumably because there was no incumbent to credit or blame (Partin 1995).

Another study of gubernatorial elections that covered thirty-six states in 1986 also found that the performance of the state economy is an important factor in the voters' choice of a governor. The study, based on ABC/*Washington Post* exit polls, found that when asked directly, "a third of the voters say that the governor is responsible for the state's economic performance (alone or along with the president)" (Niemi, Stanley, and Vogel 1995, 938). The study also found that voters were more likely to vote for the incumbent governor—whether Democratic or Republican—in states where the economy was growing more quickly. Another study (Svoboda 1995) of voters in the 1982 and 1986 elections found that they were considerably more likely to vote against an incumbent governor if they held him or her responsible for economic problems in the state and they were somewhat more likely to vote for governors who were given credit for state economic prosperity.

Voters can discriminate between the parties responsible for policymaking in a divided government scenario and reward or punish a political party when that party's responsibility for government performance is unified. One study explored the influence of unified and divided control of state governments on the outcomes of gubernatorial elections. The researchers found that state electorates are more likely to blame or credit the incumbent governor (and his or her party successor) for the performance of the state economy when that party has control of the state legislature. This result shows that voters reward or punish a party when performance can be traced to that single party. It also makes it more likely for governors from unified governments to be punished for poor state economic conditions. Undoubtedly opponents can pin the blame on the governor who heads a unified government (Leyden and Borrelli 1995). This accords with the claim made by advocates of responsible party government.

Impact of Taxes on Gubernatorial Elections

If voters often hold governors somewhat responsible for the strength of the state's economy, what judgment do they make about the governor's record on taxes? We can imagine that some voters have difficulty figuring out the extent to which the governor is responsible for the strength or weakness of the state's economy. But it is much easier to determine that the governor has initiated proposals for new taxes or higher tax rates and the legislature has approved it. And if the governor had promised no tax increases, the opposing candidate is sure to remind voters of this during the campaign.

According to the taxpayer retribution hypothesis, voters punish governors who implement new taxes or increase the rates of taxes. Taxes are more important to voters at the state level than they are to voters in national elections. Most states have legal or constitutional constraints on deficit spending, so they cannot use this method to finance new programs. Voters are especially sensitive to the most visible taxes such as the personal income and sales taxes levied in American states.

Kone and Winters point out some of the reasons why voters at the polls might hold governors accountable for raising taxes:

> Opponents of tax-raising incumbents question the worth of tax increases and endeavor to differentiate themselves from the office-holder's taxation policies. Tax opposition can prove politically lucrative in the short run because of the high political visibility of tax changes. Even in the long run, the tangible benefits of tax increase (e.g., new highways) take time to manifest themselves. (1993, 27)

A study of the 1986 election in thirty-four states shows that raising a visible tax such as the sales or personal income tax can cost the governor a considerable number of votes. Also the risk to the governor is greater if taxes have been raised several times during the governor's four-year term (Niemi, Stanley, and Vogel 1995).

The most comprehensive study of the effect of tax increases on gubernatorial elections was conducted by Kone and Winters (1993); it included 407 gubernatorial elections in the fifty states from 1957 through 1985. This study shows that the governors seeking reelection can be damaged by either new sales or income tax programs or increases in the rates of sales or income taxes during their term of office. It is riskier for a governor to establish a sales tax than an income tax, and increases in the sales tax are much more heavily penalized at the polls than are changes in the income tax. This finding is compatible with the finding by Hansen (1983) for an earlier period that 31 percent of new sales taxes and 22 percent of new income taxes were followed by defeat of the incumbent governor's party.

It is not obvious why raising the sales tax should arouse more voter resentment than raising the income tax. Kone and Winters (1993) suggest that the progressive income tax might be expected to evoke more electoral punishment since it places a greater burden on upper income citizens who are better educated, better informed, and more politically responsive and influential. On the other hand, the sales tax is encountered more frequently in daily life and that may be why it is more likely to draw electoral retribution. Raising rates—particularly for the sales tax—is riskier than establishing a new tax program, perhaps because governors underestimate the need to defend changes in tax rates. Finally, as we might expect, governors are punished at the polls for raising taxes, but they are not rewarded for lowering taxes.

Not every governor who presides over a tax increase loses the bid for reelection or even suffers a sharp drop in the margin of victory. Moreover, a governor has more control over tax policy than the state's economy. Therefore we need to take a closer look at the circumstances surrounding changes in the state's tax policy and the tax strategies used by governors during their terms so that we can figure out what makes a governor more or less vulnerable at the polls.

One study covered adoption of a variety of new state taxes over a period of some years between 1916 and 1991 (with the years chosen depending on the type of tax most likely to be adopted in that period). The study found that the reelection risk for a governor was least under three conditions: if the tax was adopted a long time before the next election, if the tax could be justified by a fiscal crisis in the state, and if the tax was already used in neighboring states (Berry and Berry 1992).

Many governors have learned that the best time to adopt or increase a tax is early in their term. In part, this is because voters get used to the higher tax in four years. But, in addition, higher taxes often make possible increases in spending (such as higher salaries for teachers), and the interest groups that benefit from these spending programs are more likely to support the governor's reelection. Similarly an increase in the gasoline tax may be better accepted by the public if the highways are significantly improved in the four years following the increase.

Because almost all states are constitutionally required to have a balanced budget, an economic slump may seriously cut tax revenues, and an urgent need for increased spending may require more revenue. In such cases the governor may be better able to defend a tax increase. Sometimes, in an effort to make a tax increase more palatable, the governor will propose a temporary tax increase, with the expectation that the increase will be repealed after the economic situation improves. In 1983, when the state of Michigan was facing a financial crisis, Gov. James Blanchard supported a 38 percent temporary increase in the income tax. But in 1986 Blanchard was able to announce that the increase had been repealed; this move helped him to win reelection by a landslide.

The tax policies of neighboring states may be relevant because voters may be aware of a trend toward higher taxes. More individuals and merchants living close to the state border may be willing to accept an increase in the gas tax or a general sales tax, for example, if higher rates already are in effect in gas stations or stores across the border.

Sooner or later, most governors find that they need to recommend an increase in taxes or a change in the tax structure in order to deal with pressing program needs or to cope with a sluggish economy. Taking such action is not equivalent to signing a political death warrant. Almost four-fifths of governors in the most recent years have been reelected, and many have found it necessary to make some changes in taxes. A governor who is cautious and realistic about the tax changes he or she seeks, who has accomplished a lot in office, who is a skillful politician, and who has learned how to be an effective communicator has a good chance of being reelected.

VARIATIONS IN VOTING TURNOUT FOR STATE ELECTIONS

There are significant variations among the states in the proportion of residents who turn out to vote in elections. We will begin by looking at the variation in gubernatorial elections for the 1990–1996 elections (see Table 6-3) and then discuss some of the causes for such differences.

The figures shown in Table 6-3 are the number of votes cast in gubernatorial elections as a percentage of the voting age population—those eighteen years of age and over. In states where the percentages are higher, there would seem to be a greater interest in state-level politics and perhaps a larger proportion of persons who believe it is their responsibility to vote. (We could measure voting totals as a percentage of the registered vote, but since registration itself is an indication of interest in politics, the use of the voting age population appears to be a more direct, accurate way of measuring voting turnout.)

Voter turnout is consistently higher in congressional, state, and local elections during a presidential year than in midterm years because the presidential election usually arouses interest and attracts more voters to the polls, many of whom (though not all) would vote in other races such as the governorship (Weber and Smith 1991). Therefore, in Table 6-3 we have distinguished between gubernatorial elections held at the same time as the presidential election and those held at other times.

Table 6-3 Turnout of Voters in Gubernatorial Elections as a Percentage of Voting-Age Population in Presidential and Nonpresidential Election Years, 1990–1996

State	Presidential Years	Nonpresidential Years
Montana	66.0	
North Dakota	60.2	
Utah	59.2	
Washington	58.4	
Missouri	57.7	
Maine		55.9
South Dakota		55.6
Wyoming		54.5
Minnesota		54.0
Louisiana		53.6
Oregon		52.7
Delaware	52.3	
Indiana	51.1	
Nebraska		49.8
Vermont	66.6	49.0
Massachusetts		48.8
North Carolina	48.8	
Idaho		48.7
Alaska		48.1
Iowa		47.2
Rhode Island	54.6	46.6
West Virginia	46.6	
Connecticut		45.6
Kansas		43.3
Ohio		41.8
Hawaii		41.1
Michigan		40.9
Colorado		40.8
Arkansas		40.8
Oklahoma		40.6
Mississippi		40.3
Alabama		40.1
New Jersey		40.0
Wisconsin		39.5
New Mexico		39.2
Arizona		38.8
Illinois		37.1
Virginia		37.0
Florida		36.8
Pennsylvania		36.3
New Hampshire	59.0	36.2
California		36.2

Table 6-3 (*continued*)

State	Presidential Years	Nonpresidential Years
Nevada		34.8
New York		34.5
Maryland		34.2
Texas		32.1
Kentucky		32.0
South Carolina		31.9
Georgia		30.3
Tennessee		29.8

Sources: Congressional Quarterly's Guide to U.S. Elections, 3d. ed., 1994; recent data from issues of *CQ Weekly.*

Note: La., Miss., N.J., Va., and Ky. elected governors in noncongressional, odd-numbered election years.

During the 1990–1996 period twelve states elected governors in a presidential year (1992 and 1996), and forty-one states elected governors in a nonpresidential year. Of these, thirty-six were in even-numbered congressional election years (1990 and 1994), and five were in odd-numbered years (1991 and 1995 or 1989 and 1993). New Hampshire and Vermont held elections every two years and so appear in both columns; Rhode Island also followed this practice until 1996 and is included in both. The states are listed in order from those with the highest to the lowest turnout. Where a state appears in both columns, its position is based on its turnout in nonpresidential years. Each figure is the average of the percentages in two elections.

It is obvious from Table 6-3 that turnout is usually higher for gubernatorial races in states that elect a governor in presidential election years, but that is not always the case. The top five states in the table—with the highest turnout—elected in presidential years; the next six states elected in nonpresidential years. Vermont and New Hampshire (states with two-year terms) had much higher turnout in presidential than in nonpresidential years, and these states would rank up with the top five states if we considered only their elections in presidential years. In New Hampshire, where the gap was largest, the gubernatorial races in 1990 and 1994 were very lopsided, which helps to explain the low turnout.

Among the states with the highest turnout are a number of western states, many of them relatively small like North and South Dakota, Wyoming, Idaho, and Montana. Other small states with high turnouts are Maine and Vermont. (A number of these states have also ranked high in previous studies.) The high turnout in Minnesota may be explained by the state's civic culture. Somewhat surprisingly, several of the large, metropolitan states rank below average in gubernatorial turnout, among them are New York, California, Pennsylvania, and Illinois, which ranged from 35 to 37 percent. Perhaps this is explained in part by the large number of racial and ethnic minority residents, some of whom may vote in below-average numbers and some of whom are not U.S. citizens.

Many of the states with the lowest turnout are southern or border states. Voter turnout is likely to be higher when there is close two-party competition, and we know that competition is getting closer in most southern and border states. Although southern and border states rank relatively low in this table, some of them (such as Virginia, Texas, Alabama, and especially Louisiana) have higher turnout rates than they did in a previous study covering the elections from 1960 through 1986. It is possible that the nonpartisan election that Louisiana uses may attract more voters. Kentucky and Tennessee, states where there has been little change in gubernatorial competition in recent years, have actually experienced a drop in turnout. There are large differences in turnout among the southern and border states, from 54 percent in Louisiana to 30 percent in Georgia and Tennessee.

It seems remarkable that there are such large differences among the states in turnout for gubernatorial elections. If we look only at the states holding elections in nonpresidential years, the proportion who vote range from less than one-third to more than one-half. We know that individual characteristics affect the vote; young persons and those with less education are less likely to vote, and there are clearly some interstate variations in education levels (though not many in average age). We are more interested in characteristics of the state political system, such as the level of two-party competition that might affect turnout.

Several systematic studies of gubernatorial turnout provide us with some clues to the state-to-state variations. One study of gubernatorial elections from 1980 through 1990 found that among the important political variables were registration deadlines and campaign spending (Weber and Smith 1991; see also Jackson 1997). There is enough difference among states in the lead time required for registering to vote, and enough potential voters are slow to register, that turnout is significantly higher in states where it is possible to register late. North Dakota does not require registration, and there are six other states (Maine, Wyoming, Minnesota, Idaho, New Hampshire, and Wisconsin) where a person can register to vote on election day, making registration as easy as possible. All of these rank relatively high on turnout except Wisconsin (counting presidential election years for New Hampshire). It is worth noting that in 1998, when Jesse Ventura, the former professional wrestler, was elected governor of Minnesota on a third-party ticket, much of his support came from young men, many of whom did not regularly vote. Apparently many of these voters took advantage of Minnesota's same-day registration rule to register at the last minute.

One obvious question is whether greater campaign activity by candidates and parties can have an effect on turnout by generating more interest in the gubernatorial election. In a classic study of the 1978 and 1980 gubernatorial elections,

Patterson and Caldeira (1983) found that higher campaign spending by the gubernatorial candidates did increase turnout. The authors explained the effect of spending: "Variations in spending represent variations in campaigning effort—candidates and parties spend money to advertise, canvass, hold rallies, promote, conduct polls, and otherwise endeavor to get out the vote" (p. 684). Writing today we would emphasize that most of the advertising is on television, where it can reach the supporters of both parties.

Jackson's (1997) study of the 1988 and 1990 elections drew somewhat different conclusions about the effect of campaign spending on gubernatorial elections. First, he found that a presidential election (1988 is one example) has such a large impact on overall turnout in the election that campaign activities in other races, such as that for governor, have a modest effect on turnout. But in a non-presidential year (such as 1990) campaign activities may have more impact. Specifically, the campaign of a candidate who is challenging the incumbent, as measured by that candidate's spending, is likely to increase turnout (while more spending by the incumbent has little effect). If the challenger has the finances necessary to run an aggressive campaign, the race is likely to be closer and to arouse more interest among the voters. Members of the challenger's party who might not bother to vote if a barely visible nonentity were running might go to the polls if their party had a viable, visible candidate. A study by Gross, Goidel, and Shields (1998) covering gubernatorial elections from 1978 through 1997 also found that campaign spending increases turnout only in nonpresidential elections. The study found that the impact of spending on turnout in those years does not depend on the incumbency variable.

Political scientists do not always agree about whether and how the closeness of an election might produce higher voter turnout. There is good reason to believe that if voters expect an election to be close rather than lopsided more of them will vote in an election, figuring that they are not wasting their vote. But statistical analyses done by political scientists often do not provide clear proof of this (Jackson 1997; Weber and Smith 1991). There is no easy way to measure whether voters expect an election to be close. If you measure closeness by the outcome of the race, you may be mixing cause and effect. It may be that an active, well-funded campaign by both candidates (and not just the incumbent) informs the voters about the challenger as well as the better known incumbent, arouses their interest, and perhaps incidentally makes some of them realize that the race is close and that their vote matters.

Patterson and Caldeira (1983) found that the closeness of the race had a modest effect on turnout but that the long-term pattern of competitiveness in the state had a greater effect. This would suggest that voters of both parties are more likely to go to the polls in a state where they realize that the parties are reasonably competitive year in and year out. Many of them get in the habit of voting whether or not their party has a strong candidate in the governor's race that year. We know that in many of the southern states until the mid-1970s or early 1980s turnout in state elections was low because the Republicans rarely elected a candidate and sometimes did not even run one. For that same reason turnout in southern Democratic primaries was high because the winner of the Democratic primary was usually elected. More broadly, we have found that turnout in a party's primary is higher in state parties that usually have rather close competition whether or not a close race is anticipated in a particular year. In other words, voters get in the habit of voting in that state party's primary. (See the analysis of primary competition and turnout in Chapter 4.)

THE VOTERS CHOOSE

In many respects, gubernatorial elections are like elections for other major offices. Party identification is the strongest predictor of voting, with roughly 80 percent of partisan voters voting for their party's candidate; this pattern is similar to what we find in congressional and presidential races. Voters are most likely to cross party lines to vote for an incumbent; but the 80 percent reelection rate for those governors who run again is a little lower than that for senators and much lower than the rate for U.S. House members. The record of a governor is much more visible to voters than that of a member of Congress; therefore, governors may be vulnerable if they have been ineffective or if they have had to take unpopular steps, such as raising taxes. Because the governor is visible, a skillful governor who works hard at building and maintaining public support is often very difficult to defeat.

Because of their political strength and visibility, governors are less likely to be swept out of office by national political trends than was the case fifty years ago. On the other hand, most states have relatively strong two-party competition, and if the other party nominates a strong candidate, the governor seldom has a free ride. The most dramatic example of change is in southern states, where Democratic governors no longer can coast to victory over weak or nonexistent opposition. In states where neither party dominates, the outcome of elections depends heavily on the quality of candidates nominated by each party, the record of the incumbent (if one is running), the extent of factionalism in each party, and the ability of each party and its candidate to build a coalition among party loyalists and other voters.

7   State Legislative Elections

Every two years (or in a few states every four years) when voters go to the polls, they find on the ballot the names of legislative candidates, often near the bottom of a long list. Every two years millions of voters cast a vote for these candidates (while millions of others do not bother), but we do not know enough about the reasons for these decisions. Rarely have pollsters asked voters any questions about their votes for state legislative candidates. We are entirely dependent on aggregate voting returns for such information, and only recently have political scientists begun to scrutinize these.

NOMINATING LEGISLATIVE CANDIDATES

The first step in getting elected or reelected to the legislature is getting nominated by your party. In every state except Nebraska legislators are elected on partisan tickets. When incumbents seek reelection, they often face little or no opposition in the primary and are rarely defeated. Data (Jewell and Breaux 1991) from a number of southern and border states in the early 1980s suggest that about two-thirds of incumbents are unopposed in primaries, and a larger proportion are likely to be unopposed in primaries in states with closer two-party competition. In most states incumbents seeking renomination win about 95 percent of the time, or about 85 percent of the time when they have an opponent.

If the incumbent decides not to seek reelection, perhaps because he or she is running for some other office, there is likely to be a scramble in the incumbent's party among several candidates. This is because that party often holds a majority in the district, and the primary winner can be expected to have an advantage in the general election. Potential candidates from the other party are also more likely to run when there is no incumbent running. Primary competition is likely to be least in the opposition party when an entrenched incumbent is running; sometimes the opposition has difficulty finding any candidate to run under those conditions.

There is evidence from a number of states (Breaux and Gierzynski 1998) that incumbents are able to raise much more money than the challengers they face in primaries. This is an important factor that not only makes incumbents difficult to beat but also discourages potential candidates from even challenging incumbents in the primary.

Most legislative candidates running for the nomination must campaign on their own—finding volunteers, raising money, developing an organization, and planning an advertising campaign. Those who have run for political office before can benefit from that political experience. Incumbent legislators, of course, benefit from the experience gained, the financial contributors located, and the organization that was built in their previous successful campaigns.

Generally speaking, local political parties stay out of legislative primaries, but there are exceptions. Connecticut, Pennsylvania, Ohio, Indiana, Minnesota, and Colorado are examples of states where local parties frequently endorse and work for candidates in legislative primaries. Public endorsements are provided by law in Connecticut and Colorado and by party rules in Minnesota. In other states the endorsements are made informally and intermittently, and the process often takes place behind the scenes. In all of these states incumbent legislators usually win endorsement with little difficulty, but there are occasional exceptions. Party caucuses in the state legislature, which are described in greater detail later in this chapter, seldom become involved in primary elections, but they may support an incumbent legislator who has a challenger in the primary.

ELECTORAL COMPETITION AND INCUMBENCY

When we turn our attention from nominations to general elections, we continue to find that incumbents usually have major advantages, particularly in states where the legislature is more professional, members serve more terms, and they have more resources. We begin by explaining just what these advantages are. Then we turn to the level of competition in legislative races and the reasons why there are more contests and closer contests in some states than in others. Often the lack of a serious contest results from the fact that the incumbent is well enough entrenched to discourage potentially strong candidates from running.

Incumbent Advantages

When incumbents seek reelection, they are almost as successful in general elections as in primary elections. We said that about 95 percent of incumbents seeking nomination are successful. In the elections from 1978 through 1988, 94 percent of incumbent state representatives and 92 percent of senators who were nominated won reelection. In other words nearly 90 percent of legislators who run again win both the nomination and the general election (Jewell 1994).

Of course, there are some differences among the states in the electoral success of incumbents. In the 1970s and 1980s a higher proportion of incumbents in southern states were reelected because most were Democrats and the Republican Party was too weak in most districts to run strong challengers. In the 1990s the growing strength of the Republican Party in southern states made the rate of incumbent success more nearly comparable to that in other states. In 1994 the general election rate of House incumbents who had been renominated was 90 percent in all states and 88 percent in southern states (National Conference of State Legislatures 1994). A number of studies show that incumbent electoral success is greater in the more professional legislatures, which tend to be in the larger, more urbanized states.

Why are incumbents so successful in winning reelection? One major reason is that many of them represent districts that are usually safe for either Democratic or Republican candidates. State legislative districts are almost always smaller than congressional districts (except the California Senate districts), and therefore they are likely to be more homogeneous, with a substantial majority of constituents sharing common interests, similar political views, and the same partisan loyalties. Even where there is close two-party competition at the state level, many legislative districts are likely to be dominated by one party. New York State has strong two-party competition. But most New York City districts are safely Democratic, while many small-town, rural upstate districts are safely Republican. When the legislatures draw district lines, they often try to create as many safe districts as possible, rather than trying to create competitive districts. It is true that American voters often vote independently in more high-profile national and statewide elections, but they are more likely to stick to their traditional party when voting for state legislators.

The success of incumbents cannot be explained entirely by the partisan safety of their districts, however. One study has shown that if one controls for district characteristics and election-year trends, incumbents in recent years in about three-fourths of the legislatures have had at least a 90 percent chance of winning (Carey, Niemi, and Powell 1997).

Even if they represent more competitive districts, incumbents have a number of advantages over challengers. Because they have campaigned in the district before and have represented it for one or more terms, they know the district well—its interest groups, its viewpoints on issues, and its political character. Incumbents know how to run a campaign that is well suited to the district.

Incumbents have spent endless hours meeting with organized groups and perhaps holding periodic "town meetings"; they have used opportunities to appear on local radio and television programs between election campaigns; and they have mailed out newsletters and questionnaires to constituents. They have also helped individual constituents and businesses to solve a variety of problems involving state—and even local—government. Most of them have staff assistance in doing these chores, particularly in the more professional legislatures.

Incumbents usually have a huge advantage in raising money for their campaign. They start out with fund-raising experience as well as a list of contributors from previous campaigns. Because incumbents are usually expected to win the elections, political action committees are much more likely to contribute campaign funds to them than to their opponent. Ironically the incumbent can raise more money but needs less money than the challenger because he or she is usually so well known in the district (Breaux and Gierzynski 1998).

Contested and Competitive Races

It is important to recognize that in some states a substantial proportion of seats in each election go uncontested and that proportion is higher in districts where there is an incumbent running rather than in districts where there is an open seat. The overall proportion of legislative seats that are contested has been steadily dropping for many years. It fell from almost four-fifths in the early 1970s to about two-thirds in the late 1980s and 1990s. The rate dropped in thirty-six of the states (Van Dunk and Weber 1997; Squire 1998). There is statistical evidence that in the 1990s there have been fewer legislative contests in legislatures that are more professional, presumably because incumbents have more resources available (Squire 1998).

The drop in contested races has occurred even though political parties in many states are making an effort to recruit more legislative candidates, an effort we described in some detail in Chapter 3. The fact that parties are working hard to recruit candidates does not guarantee that most seats will be contested, for several reasons. The uncontested seats are most likely to be in districts where one party is dominant and the other party is likely to be weakly organized. It is difficult to find any candidate, and particularly a viable candidate, to run in such a legislative district. Moreover, the major goal of a party's recruiting effort is to find good candidates in those districts where it has some chance of gaining a seat or some risk of losing one it holds. In those districts that it targets, the party will not only try to recruit a good candidate but will also provide tangible support. Parties spend much less effort trying to recruit candidates in districts that look hopeless because relatively few voters are loyal to the party, the party is weakly organized, and viable candidates are very hard to find. As a result many of these seats will be uncontested.

Table 7-1 provides information on two measures of competition in House races in the forty-six states for which the data are available. For most states this includes elections from 1984 through 1994; in a few states some years are missing and in most southern states we have also included the 1996 or 1998 elections because the level of competition increased rapidly in the South in the 1990s. The

Table 7-1 Percentage of Two-Party Contests and of Competitive Two-Party Races in Legislative Houses, 1984–1994

States	Two-party Contests (%)	Competitive Races (%)
New Jersey	98	41
Michigan	94	22
California	93	18
Washington	89	40
Ohio	88	21
North Dakota	86	63
Connecticut	85	36
Oregon	85	44
Nevada	83	44
New York	82	14
Maine	77	33
Alaska	75	44
South Dakota	75	47
Colorado	75	36
Utah	74	40
Montana	73	38
Indiana	72	31
Illinois	72	20
Pennsylvania	71	18
Kansas	71	34
Iowa	70	39
Wisconsin	70	25
Wyoming	66	36
West Virginia	65	36
North Carolina	65	41
Hawaii	64	18
Idaho	59	30
Maryland	58	20
Delaware	55	21
New Hampshire	54	29
Rhode Island	54	20
Oklahoma	52	25
New Mexico	50	24
Arizona	49	25
Missouri	43	17
Massachusetts	42	16
Virginia	40	22
Florida	40	20
Alabama	36	15

Table 7-1 *(continued)*

States	Two-party Contests (%)	Competitive Races (%)
Kentucky	32	14
South Carolina	32	15
Texas	31	15
Georgia	28	14
Tennessee	27	12
Mississippi	22	11
Arkansas	20	10

Source: Data from Bruce Anderson.
*States are in order from those with the highest to those with the lowest
proportion of contested races.

first column of figures shows what percentage of races were contested by both the
Democratic and Republican Parties. The second column of figures shows the percentages of races that were closely competitive, defined as races in which the
losing candidate got at least 40 percent of the vote; in other words the margin was
60–40 or closer.

The states that have the highest proportion of contested races include a number where both parties are strong and well organized, and thus are likely to be active
in recruiting candidates, and are usually closely balanced in the legislature—such
as New Jersey, Michigan, Ohio, Connecticut, and New York. Several other states
with these characteristics, such as Indiana, Illinois, and Pennsylvania, have a somewhat lower proportion of contests, presumably because a number of districts are
safe for one or the other party. California ranks very high on contests, in large part
because its districts with huge populations should have more potential candidates.
Half of the states in the table have two-party contests in less than two-thirds of the
districts. Some are states with relatively weak parties, and many are either border
or southern states where the Republican Party has until recently been weak.

The proportion of general elections that are contested by both parties has
been substantially lower in the South than elsewhere. Between the early 1980s and
the early 1990s the proportion of contested races in the House in ten southern
states (including Kentucky) rose gradually from 33 percent to 40 percent. This is
less than we might have expected, considering how rapidly the Republican Party
has become more competitive in the South. Between the early 1980s and the early
1990s the proportion of southern House seats the Republicans contested rose
from 48 percent to 62 percent, but the proportion Democrats contested dropped
from 85 percent to 78 percent. In other words Republican growth has become so
strong that the Democrats failed to contest over one-fifth of the seats, and by 1994
only 70 percent of winning Republican incumbents were opposed in these states

(Jewell 1995). In Florida, South Carolina, Texas, and Georgia close to 20 percent of seats were contested only by Republicans in the mid-1990s, and in Virginia more Republicans than Democrats won uncontested races.

Eleven of the thirteen states at the bottom of Table 7-1, with contests less than half of the time, are southern or border states. The two states where the Republicans were slowest to compete seriously for legislative seats are Arkansas and Mississippi (at the bottom of the table). Kentucky and Tennessee, though not in the Deep South, are states where both parties—not just the Democrats—have traditionally held substantial numbers of safe districts.

Not only has there been a decline in the proportion of legislative races that are contested, but there is also a trend toward larger margins of victory and fewer races that are really close. A study of all the states (except Vermont) shows that the proportion of seats that were closely competitive or "marginal" (defined as those where the loser got at least 40 percent of the vote) dropped from about 40 percent in 1968 to about 28 percent in 1988. Forty-one states had a drop in the proportion of marginal races (Van Dunk and Weber 1997).

The second column of figures in Table 7-1 shows the differences among the states in the proportion of closely competitive House races. A comparison of the figures in the two columns shows some interesting differences among the states. If the numbers in the two columns are close, it means that most of the contested seats have close races. California has a slightly higher percentage of contested races (93 percent) than North Dakota (86 percent); but only 18 percent of California races are marginal, compared with 63 percent of those in North Dakota. The party that does not control a seat in California has little difficulty in finding someone to run, but that person is not usually a strong candidate.

Pennsylvania and Iowa both have contests in almost 70 percent of the races, but Pennsylvania has close races in less than half as many districts as Iowa (18 percent to 39 percent). In Pennsylvania the two parties are usually closely balanced in the legislature, but a high proportion of the seats are very safe for one party or the other. The proportion of districts that have closely competitive races is less than half in every state but North Dakota, and it is less than one-fourth in twenty-two of the states, including the nine southern states in the bottom section of the table.

The more incumbents there are, the fewer contested races—and the fewer marginal races. This suggests that in individual districts the presence of an incumbent in the race either drives away any challenger or results in only weak challengers who are likely to lose by a large margin.

These findings raise an interesting question. Do incumbents win reelection in large part because their challengers are often very weak or nonexistent? Or do incumbents often face little or no opposition because they are so well entrenched politically that potentially strong challengers are unwilling to face them and the party has to scrounge around just to find warm bodies willing to run? We know that when a well-entrenched candidate decides not to seek reelection, the opposition party has a much better chance of finding a viable candidate to run.

We also know that if the quality of legislative challengers is higher, they are more likely to defeat incumbents, or at least they are more likely to run competitive races. When we speak of "quality challengers," we usually mean those who have experience. A record of having held another elective office is a good example of quality. A candidate might also benefit from having run for the legislature or some comparable office in the past, served on a legislator's staff, or at least been active in politics or campaign fund raising. A study by Emily Van Dunk (1997) of ten states in the 1988–1992 elections shows that quality legislative candidates are more likely than others to win election, presumably because experience has given them political skills and knowledge. Van Dunk found that another reason for their greater success is that quality candidates are more "strategic" in calculating when to challenge an incumbent. In other words they are more likely than other challengers to run when the prospects of winning are greater—for example, when there has been relatively close two-party competition in the state's legislative races and the incumbent's margin in the previous election was modest.

CAMPAIGNING FOR THE LEGISLATURE

The first feature of legislative campaigns that we have to recognize is the huge variation in the size and population of the districts. The larger the population of the state and the smaller the number of districts, the larger the population in each district. California has more than 30 million residents but only 40 Senate seats and 80 Assembly seats. Therefore the Senate districts average about 800,000 constituents (much larger than a congressional district), and the Assembly districts average about 400,000. Texas, New York, Florida, Illinois, have more than 600,000 constituents for each seat. At the other extreme are small states such as Vermont with about 4,000 and New Hampshire with about 3,000 constituents per House district. Vermont has 150 House seats, and New Hampshire has 400. Other states with fewer than 10,000 constituents per House district include Maine, Montana, North Dakota, and Wyoming (National Conference of State Legislatures 1994).

The differences between campaigning in large and small legislative districts is a little like the difference we described in Chapter 5 between campaigning for governor in large and small states—except everything is on a smaller scale. Campaigning in a heavily populated district requires the candidates to rely heavily on television and radio advertising. When candidates visit particular sections of the district, they will spend most of their time meeting with newspaper editors, appearing on talk shows, or speaking to organized groups where they might be able to meet with 50–100 people at a time. Campaigning door to door is simply too inefficient and time consuming, unless the candidate can get some media coverage of this personal-style campaigning.

Candidates who must rely on television and radio advertising face serious problems, not only because such ads are expensive but because most television and radio stations reach far more people than those living in a single district. This is not a cost-efficient way of reaching constituents. For example, in a large metropolitan area the television stations may reach 500,000 people living in twenty different legislative districts. A candidate running in one of these districts must pay the cost of televising a campaign commercial that will reach people in all twenty districts, most of whom cannot vote for that candidate. Candidates can also try to get what is called "free" media coverage, trying to attract the attention of the local media by the stands they take on issues and the appearances they make. This may be difficult to do, particularly if the candidate's district is only one of ten or a dozen districts located in a metropolitan area.

In smaller districts, and particularly those with 25,000 constituents or fewer, it is much more feasible for a candidate to campaign on a smaller scale. Even in small districts door-to-door campaigning is time consuming, but it is more feasible if the candidate concentrates on households where voting lists show that the residents usually vote. It is productive to talk to relatively small groups and to attend local debates that may attract a modest crowd and that will probably be covered in the press. The geography of a district influences campaign strategy. Wyoming and Rhode Island have legislative districts with roughly the same population (about 8,000–10,000), but most Wyoming districts are much larger if measured by square miles and much more sparsely populated than those in Rhode Island. As a result much more effort is required in Wyoming simply to reach constituents in their homes or in meetings.

Legislative elections have some of the same characteristics as gubernatorial races, on a smaller scale. The candidate needs an organization (usually of volunteers), help in raising funds, and a campaign strategy. In Chapter 3 we said that legislative candidates often rely more heavily on the party organization than do gubernatorial candidates, and the party is most likely to provide such help in close races.

A major difference between the two types of campaigns is that legislative races are likely to be low-visibility races. Some voters may not even be aware that there is a legislative election in their district until they get to the polls. A legislative candidate who is challenging an incumbent is handicapped because many legislators are skilled politicians who stay in touch with their constituents and become well—and often favorably—known. The challenger is starting from scratch in trying to gain name recognition and create a positive image unless he or she has held another local office. Some new candidates have been actively involved in helping to run election campaigns for other candidates, and this experience may be a big advantage. As well as learning the ropes, candidates can make contacts with other political activists who may provide help when they run for the legislature.

A challenger running for the first time in a district also has to learn as much as possible about the district. A Republican challenger, for example, needs to learn which groups are likely to provide political support and which geographic areas are most strongly Republican. The new candidate must learn which issues are of most concern to voters and the issue priorities of the groups most likely to support the candidate. Most candidates have previously been active in local public affairs and perhaps have belonged to groups concerned with problems in the district: schools, the environment, economic development, for example. The candidate may be able to build a base of loyal supporters from such organizations who can help with the campaign. One candidate in Colorado, for example, had been an active member in an organization opposed to gun control, and his core group of supporters came from that organization. Candidates who have been active in school affairs or who have served on a school board may be able to count on teachers as core supporters. A businesswoman who was active in the local Chamber of Commerce had strong support from members of that organization during her campaign. Candidates have sometimes been able to recruit supporters from nonpolitical groups in which they have been active, such as a church, a service club, or an athletic organization.

A survey of legislative candidates running in 1998 in Wisconsin, a typical medium-sized state (with House districts of about 50,000 and Senate districts of 150,000) gives some impression of how widely various campaign techniques are used. At least two-thirds of the candidates used each of the following techniques: distributing handbills, putting up yard signs, advertising in newspapers, advertising on radio, and sending out direct mail. Only about one-fifth had a full-time campaign manager, did some polling, or ran advertisements on television. At least three-fourths held large fund-raising events and asked individuals and PACs for campaign funds; half asked parties for funds; and two-thirds made some use of personal funds (Monardi 1999). We can assume that incumbents were more likely to use some of these techniques than were nonincumbents.

First-time legislative candidates learn that the campaign is a long, hard grind. One Washington State candidate, who campaigned for five months and put 18,000 miles on her car, said, "There is a feeling you should always be doing something else, something more." Another woman said she spent three hours a day making phone calls to raise money and then spent seven hours "walking the district." Another candidate, who said she worked on her campaign 80 hours a week in the summer and then 100 hours a week in September and October, said, "If you are really going to do this, it takes a huge commitment and a tremendous amount of time is involved."

FINANCING LEGISLATIVE RACES

The cost of campaigning is a major concern for any legislative candidate. A number of years ago most legislative candidates were on their own when it came to fund raising. But in recent years the political parties at the state and local levels and in the legislature have played an increasingly active role in providing funding and helping legislative candidates raise money. This is an important development that we examine in some detail. We then turn to the question of whether money buys legislative elections, or more precisely in what conditions does the amount of campaign funds that each candidate can raise determine the outcome of the election? Finally we look at two states where there has been partial public funding of legislative elections to see what difference that makes.

The Role of Political Parties

Money plays an important part in the outcome of legislative elections as it does in elections at all levels. The cost of running for election to the state legislature differs enormously from state to state, depending on the size and types of districts, the costs of media advertising, and the intensity of competition. The average spending for each House candidate in 1994 in competitive races (those won by 60 percent or less) was more than $400,000 in California, almost $200,000 in Illinois, more than $45,000 in Washington State, and less than $5,000 in Maine and Wyoming. The cost of legislative elections has been rising, particularly in the larger states with more professional legislatures. In 1998 the average cost of winning a California Assembly seat had risen to about $500,000. The average increase from 1986 to 1994 in fourteen states was about 70 percent but only about half that much adjusted for inflation (Moncrief 1998).

During the 1980s and 1990s political parties increasingly provided campaign assistance to legislative candidates, both incumbents and nonincumbents. This increase seems to have been motivated by both the increasing costs of campaigns and the larger proportion of legislatures with close two-party competition. The assistance has taken the form of direct financial contributions, help with fund raising, and a wide variety of campaign services. Political parties have been playing a more active role in recruiting legislative candidates, and when they do so it usually is necessary for them to offer financial assistance and campaign services as an enticement to persuade candidates to run.

Legislative candidates may get campaign financing and assistance from party organizations at the national, state, or local level or from the state legislative party. One study estimated that in 1992, for a sample of seventeen states, two-thirds of the funding received by Democratic candidates from party organizations came from the state party, one-fifth from the legislative party, and one-tenth from the local party. Republican candidates received slightly more from state and local parties and somewhat less from legislative parties. National party financial aid made up a very small proportion for either party (Gierzynski and Breaux 1998).

Contributions to legislative candidates from the national party are relatively rare and are most likely to occur in the elections leading to a new national census. The reason is that in most states it is the legislatures that draw district lines for both congressional and legislative districts; the way these lines are drawn may affect the partisan balance among the districts. Local party organizations probably provide less aid to legislative candidates now than they did in an earlier period when legislative district lines more often coincided with city, town, or county lines.

In most states the state party organizations or the legislative parties—or both—provide most of the party financing and assistance to legislative candidates. In a number of states the state parties had been helping to fund legislative candidates for many years before the legislative parties became active. In states where the legislative parties are weak, including some southern Republican Parties, the state party organization continues to provide most of the funding assistance.

In some other states the leaders of legislative parties began to play an important role in funding candidates because they believed that the state and local parties had failed to provide legislative candidates with enough support. Moreover, the leaders wanted to control the process directly instead of leaving it to the governor and state or local party officials (Gierzynski 1992).

In a number of states the state party organization and the legislative party work closely together to recruit and fund candidates. The division of labor between the two groups may depend on the sources of funds each group can tap. In the Minnesota Democratic-Farmer-Labor Party (DFL) the legislative party's campaign committee occupies space in the state party headquarters building, and day-to-day coordination is possible during a campaign. In New York formal responsibility for legislative campaign fund raising has been shifted from the legislative parties to the state party, but legislative party leaders still control this activity (Rosenthal 1997, 183).

Clearly the trend has been toward a larger number of legislative parties providing financing and other tangible forms of campaign support to legislative candidates. In the late 1970s only a handful of legislative parties made a systematic effort to raise funds and provide services to legislative candidates. For example, in California Assembly Speakers Jess Unruh and Willie Brown and in Ohio House Speaker Vern Riffe raised and distributed large sums of money for their Democratic colleagues.

By the early 1990s there were thirty-six states in which one or more of the four parties in the two legislative chambers had campaign finance committees or committees run by individual leaders (Jewell and Whicker 1994, 107). Cindy

Simon Rosenthal (1995) found that the legislatures with such campaign committees by the mid-1980s not surprisingly were likely to be more professional legislatures and ones with the strongest two-party competition. She also found that when one legislative party began raising more money the other party also increased its fund raising. By 1997 in forty-seven states some of the legislative parties, legislative leaders, or both were directly engaged in raising funds to support legislative candidates. The only exceptions were nonpartisan Nebraska and two states in the Deep South—Mississippi and Louisiana. In at least half of the states and probably more, both the Democratic and Republican Parties or leaders in both the Senate and House were involved in funding legislative candidates.

In addition to the funds that they raise for the party's campaign committee, some leaders have raised money for their own personal PACs and have had complete freedom to distribute PAC funds however they choose. In some legislative parties not only the top leaders but also others in a leadership position, such as committee chairs, are encouraged to raise funds because they are in a position to do so. They are then encouraged to distribute the funds to legislators or nonincumbent candidates who have stiff opposition and do not have the clout to raise much money themselves.

There are some trends, however, that in some states may reduce the role of legislative leaders and parties in campaign funding. In a few states the transfer of funds from leadership PACs or from legislative party campaign committees to candidates has been restricted or prohibited by law (Rosenthal 1997, 183). There are signs that the fund-raising role of legislative leaders is shrinking in states like Maine, which has strict term limits on members that seriously reduce the tenure of leaders. As a result the state party organizations are increasing their role in recruiting and funding legislative candidates.

Political parties raise funds and provide support for legislative candidates because they want to hold on to a legislative majority if they have it and gain a majority, if possible, if they are in the minority. Studies have repeatedly shown that, in an effort to accomplish these goals, parties concentrate their financial support on the races that are closest. One 1992 study of funding in seventeen states (Gierzynski and Breaux 1998, chap. 10) showed that two-thirds of Republican funds and almost three-fourths of Democratic funds went to candidates in competitive races (defined as those in which the winner got 60 percent of the vote or less). In half the state parties studied recipients in competitive races averaged at least three times as much as those in noncompetitive races. Legislative parties and state party organizations followed the same strategy. But local parties did not give such high priority to close races, presumably because they supported their local candidates for the legislature, even when the races were not so close.

The same study (Gierzynski and Breaux 1998) showed that 80 percent of Republican Party funding and half of Democratic Party funding in 1992 went to nonincumbent candidates. The differences are probably due to the fact that in 1992 the Democrats held a much larger proportion of seats and thus had more incumbents running than did the Republicans. If party leaders are asked about their funding priorities, they usually say that they would give more support to incumbents in close races than to nonincumbents in equally close races. But incumbents seldom are in close races in most states, and therefore the challengers and particularly those running for open seats usually average more party funding than do incumbents. These findings about party funding priorities are similar for races in elections between 1986 and 1990, and we can assume that a comparable pattern prevailed throughout the 1990s.

One reason the pattern of party funding for legislative candidates is important is that it contrasts with the campaign funding strategy of most PACs; that strategy gives priority to incumbents, particularly those who are very likely to be reelected and those who hold important positions like committee chairs (Cassie and Thompson 1998). PACs do not want to waste contributions on candidates who might very well lose, in part because a contribution might alienate the winners in such races. In other words the effect of most PAC contributions is to increase the funding advantage incumbents have over challengers, while party funding often makes challengers more competitive, at least in close races.

We have emphasized the importance of party funding for state legislative candidates, but we do not want to exaggerate its impact. In the elections of 1986–1992 party contributions in some years represented 10–20 percent of total funding received by candidates in a few larger states such as California, New Jersey, Pennsylvania, and Wisconsin, in North Carolina (Republicans only), and even in some small states—Maine and Idaho. But in a larger number of states the party contributions were considerably smaller, in the 5–10 percent range. Average funding can be misleading because the parties have concentrated on the most closely contested races, sometimes putting most of their funding into ten or fifteen races.

An example of highly concentrated funding can be found in Wisconsin in 1994, when there were three special elections to fill vacancies in the Senate. The Republican Party contributed $246,000 in one race and $131,000 in another (nearly 95 percent of all the spending for those two races), winning both and thereby gaining control of the Senate (Malbin and Gais 1998, 115–116). In a 1984 election in New York the Senate Republican Party spent two-thirds of its funds ($219,000), and the Senate Democrats spent 60 percent ($442,000) on two of the closest Senate contests.

Legislative leaders have strong incentives to raise as much money as possible. If there is a close two-party balance in the chamber, their fund-raising efforts may be crucial in determining whether a leader in the majority can hold onto power or a minority leader can gain majority status. It is not unusual for a leader to be ousted by members of the party caucus because they believe he or she has not worked hard enough or been effective enough in raising campaign money; examples can be found in states as diverse as California, Ohio, and Florida.

The growing role of legislative parties and their leadership in raising and distributing funding to legislative candidates is obviously very important for the candidates who receive such assistance, but it has broader implications as well. It has enhanced and in some ways changed the role of legislative party leaders. The campaign funding operation is usually run by a legislative party campaign committee, but the responsibility for raising money and the power to distribute it to candidates rest with leaders—the presiding officers of the two chambers and the majority and minority leaders. One House Speaker bluntly explained to us that because he alone was able to raise large sums of money he could personally determine how it was distributed.

Legislative leaders have expressed mixed opinions as to whether they have greater influence in dealing with their colleagues because they have raised funds for them. A former Speaker in Iowa told us that he believed this was true particularly for freshmen. "You develop a level of trust and friendship with them that carries over into the session, and if they need help you go down and help them in the district." A former Speaker from Wisconsin, on the other hand, did not think that fund raising increased his influence. "You are expected to maintain the majority, finance the election, raise the money. It does not enhance your power; you can only fail at this."

Alan Rosenthal has argued that legislative leaders' growing responsibility for fund raising has changed their role as leaders for the worse:

> Nowadays, legislative leaders spend a good deal of their time and energy on the upcoming campaign, with campaigning a never-ending activity within, as well as outside, the legislature. . . .The legislature today is awash in partisan campaign politics, to the detriment of the legislative institution and the legislative process. Legislative leaders are turning into campaign managers and, as a consequence, are neglecting their institutional duties. None of this serves the legislature well. (1996, 176)

Political parties as well as individual candidates raise much of their campaign funding from PACs. Some observers believe that the leaders of legislative parties are in a stronger position to raise money from PACs than are leaders of state party organizations. The reason is simply that the interest groups that operate PACs are very often trying to get specific legislation passed or defeated in the legislature, and legislative party leaders—particularly those in the majority—usually have great influence over the fate of such legislation in the House or Senate. Legislators who have received substantial campaign funding from leaders may be particularly willing to support their position on legislation.

Spending Money and Winning Elections

The most comprehensive study of the impact of spending on legislative elections covered eighteen states for 1992 (or 1991 or 1988 in the case of three of the states) (Cassie and Breaux 1998). The states ranged in size from California, Illinois, and Pennsylvania to Idaho, Maine, Montana, Utah, and Wyoming. The strongest connection between campaign spending and winning elections occurs in the larger states with more professional legislatures. These are the states where the cost of elections is higher. In the smaller states elections cost less, a candidate can run a viable campaign less expensively, and therefore there is less connection between spending and winning.

In most of the states the winner outspends the loser in a substantial majority of the races, at least 70 percent and very often more than 80 percent of the time. It is not surprising to learn that incumbents outspend challengers a high proportion of the time—usually 85 percent of the cases—except in smaller states where this occurs two-thirds to three-fourths of the time. These data suggest that the ability of incumbents to raise more money is a major reason why they usually win, but we also know that incumbents have many advantages other than money. It is worth noting that in two-thirds of the eighteen states the proportion of incumbents defeating challengers was larger than the proportion outspending them (Cassie and Breaux 1998).

In many races in the larger states the gap in spending between incumbent and challenger is huge. In California three-fourths of the challengers spent no more than 25 percent of what the incumbent spent, and in Illinois, New Jersey, and Pennsylvania at least 60 percent of the challengers fell that far behind in spending.

The authors of this study conclude that there is a strong but not always simple connection between campaign funding and winning legislative elections. In the high-population states, elections cost a great deal more than in the smaller states, in part because expensive television advertising is essential in the large states. On the other hand, television advertising is not essential and often is not used in smaller states, where the districts are smaller and door-to-door campaigning is more feasible. Cassie and Breaux estimate that in 1992 the threshold of funding a candidate needed to be competitive in a House race was about $100,000 in California, $15,000 in Illinois and Pennsylvania, $5,000 in Oregon, $3,000 in Missouri, and only $1,000 in some of the smallest states like Maine and Montana. "Having money does not guarantee that a candidate will be competitive and have a chance to win. [But] a lack of money, whether it is in comparison to one's opponent or simply a certain dollar amount, virtually guarantees that a challenger cannot be competitive." The authors conclude that "what money 'buys' is an opportunity to compete and that money only 'buys' elections when one's opponent does not have sufficient funds" (1998, 111).

Public Funding for State Legislative Races

Only two states—Minnesota and Wisconsin—provided public funding for state legislatures in the 1990s, although several of the new public funding programs taking effect in 2000 include campaigns for the state Senate and House. It is difficult to prove conclusively that the availability of public funding in these two states has made the elections more competitive. One way of estimating this is to see whether public funding evens up the playing field by reducing the funding advantage normally enjoyed by incumbents.

In four elections from 1986 through 1992 the average spending by challengers was calculated as a percentage of the average spending by incumbents for eighteen states. In larger and medium-sized states spending for challengers was much lower than for incumbents, but the gap was smaller in Minnesota and Wisconsin. In Minnesota the average spending for challengers was half as much as for incumbents, a higher proportion than for most states of comparable size. In Wisconsin the average spending for challengers was 65 percent of that for incumbents, which is considerably higher than any other state except the smaller ones (Moncrief 1998, 54).

In the 1992 Assembly election in Wisconsin, challengers in contested races outspent the incumbents they were opposing 21 percent of the time. Although that percentage may seem small, it is much higher than in most medium- and large-sized states for which data are available. In the Minnesota House election that year, however, only 5 percent of challengers outspent the incumbent. But in these two states only 7–9 percent of challengers actually beat incumbents.

These data suggest that public funding for legislative races has accomplished more in Wisconsin than in Minnesota. One reason for the differences between the two states is that the states use different formulae in allocating funds, and the Minnesota formula tends to favor the majority party in a district. In Wisconsin in 1992, for example, challengers averaged twice as much as incumbents in public funds received, while in Minnesota incumbents averaged more than challengers (Cassie and Breaux 1998, 103).

One reason that public funding does not appear to have had a huge impact on spending levels and outcomes in Wisconsin and Minnesota is that the grants of public funds were modest in size. In Minnesota races from 1988 through 1994 the average amount of public funds for House races received by those accepting such funding ranged from $4,500 to $8,600; on the average this represented 28 percent of all campaign funds received by such candidates. In the Wisconsin Assembly, averaging figures for the 1990 and 1994 elections shows that the average candidate getting public funding received $6,000, representing 30 percent of all the candidate's funding (Malbin and Gais 1998, 71).

By some criteria, however, Minnesota appears to have a more successful public funding program for legislative races than Wisconsin does. There is stronger bipartisan support for public funding in Minnesota, where more than 90 percent of legislative candidates usually accept public funding. In Wisconsin about 90 percent of Democratic candidates but less than half as many Republican candidates do so (Malbin and Gais 1998, 65, 71). Also there are often more uncontested legislative races in Wisconsin than in Minnesota.

NATIONAL TRENDS AND LEGISLATIVE ELECTIONS

National political trends have some impact on state legislative races, just as they affect congressional races. In a presidential election year the party of the winning presidential candidate may gain some legislative seats, and in the following midterm election the presidential party usually loses some legislative seats. These gains and losses may be large or small depending on how strongly the political winds are blowing in favor of one or the other political party.

If the political winds are strong enough, and the party balance in a legislative chamber is close enough, these national trends can help to explain changes in party control of the state senate or house. The direction and magnitude of such changes are illustrated in Figure 7-1. The bars show the net partisan gains and losses in control of chambers for the elections from 1972 through 1998, with Democratic gains above the horizontal line and Republican gains below for all states except nonpartisan Nebraska. (National political trends should be strongest in the forty-five states with legislative elections in even-numbered years because that is when presidential and congressional elections are held. But the four states electing in odd-numbered years are included in the calculations because they should not be completely immune to national trends.)

Figure 7-1 shows that the party winning the presidential election made a net

Figure 7-1 Democratic and Republican Gains and Losses in Legislative Chambers, 1972–1998

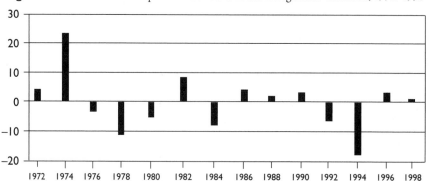

gain of chambers in three elections and lost in four elections, but these gains and losses were relatively small. In midterm elections, however, the party controlling the White House suffered a net loss of state legislative races in six of seven cases, sometimes by large margins. A party making significant legislative gains in a presidential election may be more likely to suffer midterm losses. The Republicans gained a net of fourteen chambers in the two Ronald Reagan election years and lost a net of thirteen in the two elections held in the middle of his two terms.

Landslide elections at the national level, particularly in midterm, are likely to have the greatest effect on state legislative races. The party out of power made very large congressional gains in 1974 and 1994. In 1974, in the so-called Watergate election, the Republicans lost 23 legislative chambers and more than 600 legislative seats. The 1994 election in the middle of President Clinton's first term was a huge victory for the Republican Party, which captured 18 chambers, including 3 southern chambers for the first time in modern history, and gained more than 500 seats, one-fourth of them in the South.

Legislative contests are more likely to be affected by national trends in some states than in others (Campbell 1986). National elections are more likely to affect legislative races in states where there is close two-party competition and most seats are contested. In the past, when Democrats held large majorities in most southern legislatures, a national Republican landslide was not enough to shift partisan control of southern legislatures. A state party that runs a particularly strong candidate for governor or other statewide offices is likely to pick up some legislative seats. Even state legislatures with a close two-party balance may be somewhat isolated from national trends if a large proportion of the districts are safely Democratic or Republican.

PARTISAN IMPLICATIONS OF LEGISLATIVE DISTRICTING

The partisan balance in a state legislature depends not only on the election results but on the way district lines are drawn. It is far from certain, for example, that a party winning 55 percent of the total vote cast for legislative candidates will win approximately 55 percent of the seats in the legislature. Most state legislatures draw the district boundaries (subject to gubernatorial veto and to possible judicial review), and the legislature may have some flexibility in determining what kinds of districts are drawn.

Most states use single-member districts exclusively, but there are four state senates and eleven state houses that consist of only multimember districts or some combination of single- and multimember districts. A multimember district is one in which the residents of a district have a chance to elect several legislators to represent them in the district, rather than just one. From the early 1970s through the

1990s there was a steady decline in the use of multimember districts in state legislatures, in part because courts in some states ruled that multimember districts discriminated against racial and ethnic minorities. For example, in a county that elected five legislators and in which one-fourth of the population was black, the chances of electing at least one black legislator were greater if there were five single-member districts—one of which might include an area with many black voters—than if all five were elected countywide by a white majority.

The effects of at-large districts on partisan minorities are similar. If one-fourth or one-third of the voters were Democrats and were somewhat concentrated geographically, they would be better able to elect at least one Democratic legislator if one or two districts had at least a large minority of Democrats. The use of multimember districts in some parts of the state does not necessarily handicap one party because the Republicans may have a majority in some multimember districts while the Democrats have a majority in multimember districts elsewhere in the state.

Even when single-member districts are used exclusively, the minority party may win a smaller share of seats than its share of the popular vote. To take an extreme example, if the Democratic Party won every district with exactly 52 percent of the vote in each, it would have 100 percent of the legislative seats. In reality this does not happen because Democrats and Republicans tend to be unevenly distributed across the state, with each being a majority in some districts. Nevertheless a party that wins a large majority of votes across the state is likely to win an even larger majority of seats—even if district lines are drawn impartially.

This is because of what political scientists call "wasted votes." Votes are wasted in a sense when they are cast for a losing candidate. If, for example, each party wins its districts with an average of 65 percent of the vote, and the Democrats get a majority in 60 out of 100 districts, the Republicans will have wasted votes in those 60 districts and the Democrats will have wasted votes in only 40 districts. Therefore, mathematically, the Democrats could win 60 districts with only 53 percent of the vote. With the same conditions the Democrats could win 70 districts out of 100 with 56 percent of the vote.

If one party has a majority in both chambers of the legislature and also controls the governorship, it can draw district lines in such a way that the minority party wastes even more of its votes and gets even fewer seats from its share of the vote. This method of drawing district lines is usually called gerrymandering. What tactics the majority party uses depends on the way Democratic and Republican voters are distributed in a particular area.

Assume that the Republicans control the legislature and governorship and they are drawing districts within a county, city, or metropolitan area that has 250,000 persons and is entitled to five seats in the legislature:

1. If there are 50,000 Democrats and 200,000 Republicans in the area, the Democrats should be entitled to one seat. But the Republicans could draw five districts that average 40,000 Republicans and 10,000 Democrats, making it unlikely that even one Democrat is elected.

2. If, however, 100,000 of the 250,000 residents are Democrats, it will be difficult for the Republicans to deny them a seat. Yet they might limit the Democrats to one instead of the two they deserve by creating one district that is overwhelmingly Democratic (40,000–10,000) and four districts with smaller Republican margins (35,000–15,000).

3. The Republicans might even be able to win three of the five seats, even though they were in a 150,000–100,000 minority, by following the same tactic. They could create two districts with a 42,000–8,000 Democratic margin and three districts with a 28,000–22,000 Republican margin.

Sometimes, if Democratic and Republican voters are not neatly concentrated in different locations, the majority party must create strange-looking, noncompact districts to accomplish its partisan goals. Such gerrymandering has been going on for almost two centuries. In 1811 Massachusetts governor Elbridge Gerry signed a districting bill that favored the Democrats over the Federalists. Upon seeing a map of the districts, someone described one of them as a "salamander"; his companion suggested calling it a "Gerrymander." The courts have not seriously challenged the practice of partisan gerrymandering. In 1986 the U.S. Supreme Court stated for the first time that the courts might declare partisan gerrymandering unconstitutional. But the standards the Supreme Court set were so high or perhaps so vague that to date the courts have not declared any partisan gerrymander unconstitutional.

As we pointed out in Chapter 1 the courts have cracked down on racial gerrymandering that they believe dilutes the voting rights of African Americans. But during the 1990s the courts also struck down some districting plans that appeared designed to maximize the representation of African American voters, arguing that race should not be the primary factor in drawing district lines.

GROWING TWO-PARTY COMPETITION FOR CONTROL AND DIVIDED GOVERNMENT

There is a trend in the American states toward more frequent cases of divided government: the control of one or both chambers of the legislature by the party that does not control the governorship. This is important because the governor is the leader of his or her party and usually draws the bulk of legislative support for programs from members of this party. If members of the other party control one or both chambers of the legislature, the governor must change strategy, try to build bipartisan support for his or her programs, and probably compromise more often. We will return to the governor's party leadership role in the legislature in the next chapter.

Between 1965 and 2000 every state except Georgia and Hawaii experienced divided government at least once. (Nebraska with its nonpartisan legislature is not counted.) From ten to fifteen of the states had divided government from the mid-1940s to the mid-1950s, and the number varied from twenty to twenty-five from the mid-1960s through the 1970s. Table 7-2 shows that the proportion of states that had divided government was half or slightly more than half consistently in the 1980s and 1990s. (Note that the occasional state with an independent or third-party governor was by definition divided.)

It is obvious from the table that throughout most of the period there were more—often many more—united Democratic than united Republican governments. The greatest contrast was from 1975 through 1978 (the period after Watergate), when twenty-seven states had united Democratic governments and one or two had united Republican governments. It was only in the last three time periods (1995–2000) that there were more united Republican governments.

Table 7-2 Unified and Divided Government by Two-Year Time Periods, 1965–2000 (number of states)

Two-year Term	Unified Democratic	Divided Democratic Governor	Unified Republican	Divided Republican Governor	Independent Governor	Total Divided
1965–1966	25	6	3	14		20
1967–1968	16	9	9	14		23
1969–1970	13	6	14	15		21
1971–1972	16	11	10	11		22
1973–1974	16	13	8	11		24
1975–1976	27	7	1	12	1	20
1977–1978	27	9	2	10	1	20
1979–1980	20	12	4	13		25
1981–1982	17	10	5	17		27
1983–1984	24	9	4	12		21
1985–1986	17	16	4	12		28
1987–1988	13	13	6	17		30
1989–1990	14	13	5	17		30
1991–1992	18	9	3	17	2	28
1993–1994	16	13	3	15	2	30
1995–1996	8	10	15	15	1	26
1997–1998	6	10	12	20	1	31
1999–2000	10	8	14	15	2	25

Source: Data compiled from authors' research.

The table 7–2 shows that, with occasional exceptions, during the 1965–2000 period divided government more often meant a Democratic or split legislature and a Republican governor than a Republican or split legislature and a Democratic governor. Fiorina (1994) has argued that as legislatures grow more professional they are more attractive to Democratic candidates; therefore the more professional legislatures are more likely to have Democratic majorities, even if the state elects a Republican governor. Divided government occurs most frequently in states where traditionally one party has been strongest and has usually controlled the legislature, but the other party sometimes is able to win the governorship.

To better understand the changing pattern of divided government in the more recent period (1981–2000) we need to look more closely at trends among the states (Table 7-3). Before the mid-1960s the southern states consistently had Democratic governors and legislatures. By the mid-1980s they still had Democratic legislatures, but most of them had elected a Republican governor at least once, and thus divided government had begun to appear in the South.

Only three states consistently had a Democratic governor and legislature during the 1981–2000 period: Georgia, Maryland, and Hawaii. Ten more states, most of them southern or border states, consistently had Democratic legislatures but had Republican governors with some frequency.

At the Republican end of the scale no state consistently had unified Republican government during this twenty-year period; South Dakota came closest but once had a split legislature. Five states in the Plains and Rocky Mountain area (Kansas, Idaho, Wyoming, Colorado, and Utah) consistently had Republican legislatures (or a split legislature in one case) and sometimes Democratic governors.

New York and Delaware always had divided government because the two chambers of the legislature were almost always under different partisan control. In New York the Democratic majority in the Assembly and the Republican majority in the Senate have carried out a redistricting every ten years (without interference from the other chamber) to ensure another decade of control. Alaska always had divided government, often because of a split legislature.

We know that in recent years voters have become more independent in their voting patterns and more likely to split their tickets. In any state that traditionally has been under control of one party, like those in the South, it is much easier for the minority party to find a strong, experienced candidate who may be able to win the governorship than to find 50–100 viable candidates to run for legislative seats across the states. There are other reasons for divided government becoming more frequent. Voters seem to be more willing to cross party lines to vote for a candidate running for a visible office like governor than for a legislative seat. Moreover, as legislatures have become more professional and legislators often serve longer terms, they become more entrenched in office and more difficult to defeat.

Therefore it is particularly important that by the mid-1990s the Republican

Table 7-3 Unified and Divided Government by State, 1965–2000 (number of years)

State	Unified Democratic	Divided Democratic Governor	Unified Republican	Divided Republican Governor	Independent Governor	Total Divided
Georgia	36	0	0	0		0
Hawaii	36	0	0	0		0
Kentucky	31	1	0	4		5
Maryland	32	0	0	4		4
Mississippi	29	0	0	7		7
Louisiana	28	0	0	8		8
Arkansas	26	0	0	10		10
Alabama	24	0	0	12		12
Texas	22	0	0	14		14
Florida	20	6	2	8		14
North Carolina	20	4	0	12		16
Connecticut	20	2	2	8	4	14
New Mexico	20	2	0	14		16
West Virginia	20	0	0	16		16
Oklahoma	20	0	0	16		16
Rhode Island	20	0	0	16		16
Missouri	20	0	0	16		16
South Carolina	18	2	0	16		18
Tennessee	18	0	0	18		18
Virginia	18	0	1	17		18
Massachusetts	16	0	0	20		20
Nevada	12	14	0	10		24
Washington	12	8	0	16		24
New Jersey	12	6	8	10		16
California	12	0	0	24		24
Pennsylvania	8	8	8	12		20
Wisconsin	8	4	6	18		22
Minnesota	8	2	0	12	2	16
Alaska	6	14	2	10	4	28
Oregon	6	12	0	18		30
Montana	4	16	6	10		26
Delaware	4	12	4	16		28
Maine	4	12	0	10	10	32
Michigan	2	6	4	24		30
Illinois	2	6	4	24		30
New York	0	20	6	10		30
North Dakota	0	24	8	4		28
Colorado	0	22	10	4		26
Vermont	4	18	10	4		22
Ohio	2	10	10	14		24

Table 7-3 (*continued*)

State	Unified Democratic	Divided Democratic Governor	Unified Republican	Divided Republican Governor	Independent Governor	Total Divided
Idaho	0	24	12	0		24
Iowa	4	2	12	18		20
Kansas	0	20	14	2		22
Wyoming	0	20	14	2		22
Utah	4	16	16	0		16
Indiana	2	14	16	4		18
Arizona	4	10	20	2		12
New Hampshire	0	12	20	4		16
South Dakota	0	8	26	2		10

Source: Data compiled from authors' research.

Party had succeeded in ending the Democratic control of southern legislatures in five states, with more sure to follow. This end of one-party control created the possibility of an occasional unified Republican government in southern states, as occurred in Florida after the 1998 election.

In the 1994 elections the Republicans made major gains in both branches of state governments. They made net gains of eleven governorships and eighteen legislative chambers, and they increased the number of legislatures where they controlled both chambers from nine to nineteen. In twenty-seven states control of the legislature or the governorship or both changed—always in a Republican direction (except for changes in two states involving independent governors). But in the 1994 election no state shifted from a united Democratic government to a united Republican one. Eleven states shifted from a divided government to a united Republican one; seven shifted from a united Democratic to a divided government; nine remained divided but with some Republican gain, such as capturing one legislative chamber. This suggests that even in a Republican landslide many voters were splitting their tickets. As long as such a voting pattern continues, half or more of the states are likely to have divided governments in the years to come.

CONFLICTING TRENDS IN LEGISLATIVE ELECTIONS

The story of state legislative elections is one of contrasting trends. On the one hand, incumbents have become more difficult to defeat because they are more professional, experienced politicians who are often able to raise much more campaign funding than challengers. On the other hand, in those states where term limits have been imposed on legislators (about one-third of them), a smaller proportion of elections include incumbents, and those running for reelection have had less time to become entrenched in office.

On the one hand, there has been a decline in the number of contested elections, particularly when incumbents are running. Incumbents are often so strong that they discourage anyone from running against them—or at least discourage candidates who are capable of being competitive. On the other hand, political parties are making increasing efforts to recruit viable candidates and to support them with campaign services and financial assistance. This does not guarantee that every race will be contested or competitive, but it increases the chances that both parties will contest districts that have the potential to be competitive.

The most dramatic changes are occurring in the South, where the Republican Party has been contesting more districts, winning more seats, and in some legislative chambers winning a majority of seats. In recent years this has not led to a higher proportion of contested races because there has been a decline in the number of seats that Democrats contest, particularly in those districts that have become safely Republican. As the balance between Democratic and Republican members grows closer in more southern legislatures, both parties will intensify their efforts to recruit stronger candidates and provide them with more support, but they will continue to target those races that are likely to be close.

Because legislative contests are relatively low visibility races, and because many districts appear to be safe for one party, voters who consider themselves Republicans or Democrats are probably more likely to vote for a candidate of their party, if a viable candidate is running, than they would be in more visible statewide or congressional races. But voters will continue to cross party lines often to vote for incumbents or for nonincumbents who campaign well enough to attract public attention. In a large district a nonincumbent must have enough resources for television and radio advertising, the costs of which keep rising. In smaller districts a strong campaign is not necessarily expensive.

8 Political Parties in State Legislatures

Political parties have a pervasive influence on the way most state legislatures operate. Almost all legislatures are organized along party lines, from the leadership of the chambers to the committee system. The members of each party are organized in a caucus, which selects the party leadership. The power of these leaders depends very much on their political skills and their style of leadership. For the party that also controls the governorship, the legislative party's agenda is developed in large part by the governor. In legislatures where the parties are well organized and skillfully led, and where each party represents quite different interests in the state, partisanship plays a large role in the decision-making process and the outcome of roll call votes.

PATTERNS OF LEGISLATIVE ORGANIZATION

In every state except Nebraska legislators are elected on partisan tickets. Most state legislatures are organized along party lines: each party chooses its own leaders, the majority party selects the presiding officer, and committee seats are allocated between the two parties. There are variations on this pattern, and a few southern state legislatures are not yet organized completely along partisan lines.

Some minimum representation of the two major parties is essential if the legislature is to be organized along party lines or to show any traces of partisanship in its voting on issues. Where the minority party holds only a handful of seats, partisanship cannot flourish. For many years the Democratic Party dominated legislatures in the Deep South. The Republican share of legislative seats did not reach one-fifth of the membership until the latter part of the 1980s or 1990s in Arkansas, Mississippi, Louisiana, Alabama, South Carolina, and Georgia.

Partisan Organization

Most state legislatures are organized strictly along party lines. (The nonpartisan Nebraska legislature is an obvious exception.) There is usually strict party discipline in the vote to elect the Speaker of the house or the presiding officer of the senate. The majority party chooses its candidate and unites behind that candidate. Buchanan (1963, 141) has described the vote on the presiding officer as "the indispensable glue for holding a legislative party together."

Most legislative parties have an organization structure that includes a floor leader, assistant leaders or whips, and other officers. The rules of the legislative chamber usually recognize members of the majority and minority leadership in a variety of ways, such as priority of recognition on the floor to make motions. The majority party usually controls the organization of committees, with membership allocated to the two parties roughly according to the size of their membership in the chamber and the chairmanship of committees going to a member of the majority party.

There are a handful of legislatures, particularly in the Deep South, where the Democrats still have a large majority, and these may not have a partisan structure. In several of these states the minority party has no leadership or organized structure, and it may be less likely to be adequately represented on the more important legislative committees.

Bipartisan Coalitions

Until the mid-1990s the leadership in several southern states was chosen by a bipartisan coalition, usually consisting of the more conservative Democrats and the modest number of Republicans. Texas was the best example of this system. The House Speaker would put together a conservative bipartisan coalition and select committee chairs who were loyal to him. Republicans worked within this system instead of organizing as a minority party during the 1980s, despite an increase in the number of Republican representatives and the election of a Republican governor. A real two-party system did not develop in the Texas House until the early 1990s.

A different form of bipartisan coalition can develop in state legislatures that have two fully organized political parties. Usually this occurs when there is a deep division in the majority party caucus over choosing the party's nominee for presiding officer in the house or senate and supporters of the candidate who loses in the caucus refuse to support the winner. The candidate who is behind, or sometimes the one who is ahead, tries to form a coalition with members of the minority party.

The split in the majority party may have one or more sources. Sometimes there are ideological differences, as occurred in New Mexico, particularly during the 1970s and 1980s, when conservative Democrats formed a majority coalition with Republicans, leaving liberal and moderate Democrats in the minority. Sometimes there are simply clashes of personality and personal ambition, as occurred in the Kentucky Senate in 1997. Sometimes members of both parties are rebelling against a house Speaker or senate president whom they perceive to be arbitrary or unfair in making decisions and allocating committee assignments, or who has held power too long. These factors led to bipartisan coalitions in North Carolina, Oklahoma, and Connecticut in 1989.

What can the minority party gain by joining such a coalition? If that party believes that its members have been treated unfairly by the presiding officer, it may bargain for a change in formal rules or informal procedures. The minority party may get committee chairmanships or better committee assignments for some of its members.

How stable is such a bipartisan coalition? It may be more stable if the members are in basic agreement on ideology and major issues or if the new presiding officer has a popular style of leadership. Several factors can cause instability. The North Carolina House coalition formed in 1989 gradually lost its cohesion because of policy and partisan differences (Jewell and Whicker 1994, 78). Personal rivalries led to a split in the Democratic Party in the California Assembly in 1980; the next year Willie Brown was elected Speaker by a bipartisan coalition. However, during his first term partisan issues divided the coalition and Brown reunited the Democratic Party, going on to serve twelve years as a powerful and partisan Speaker. Sometimes the life of a coalition is very brief. In 1989 a bipartisan coalition ousted the Connecticut House Speaker, Irving Stolberg, who was perceived by some as being too strong and holding power too long. His replacement, Richard Balducci, offered the minority Republicans nothing, but he restored unity in the Democratic Party within less than a day and served two successful terms as Speaker (Jewell and Whicker 1994, 77–80).

PARTY LEADERSHIP

The fact that legislatures are organized along party lines does not guarantee that partisanship will have a major effect on decision making. To a great extent, the leaders of the parties make them into more or less effective vehicles for negotiating compromises, making decisions, and passing legislation. Fundamentally the leaders have two sources of power and influence: those that are institutional and those that are personal. We look first at the rules and procedures of the legislature and the legislative parties that make it possible for leaders to determine the membership of committees, set priorities for the legislative agenda, and influence what happens on the floor of the House and Senate. But a major reason why some party leaders are much more successful than others is that some have greater skill and experience in working with their colleagues, arranging for compromises, and mobilizing votes. Some leaders are particularly adept in recognizing what their colleagues need and what incentives will persuade them to go along with the leader on a bill.

Institutional Sources of Power

In the large majority of legislatures that are organized along party lines the structure of organization is similar. The presiding officer of the house, known as the Speaker, performs a dual role—both institutional and partisan. The Speaker presides over the house, interprets its rules, usually has considerable power over assignments of bills to committee and shaping the house agenda, and ultimately is responsible to the house. But the Speaker is also the leader and most powerful member of the majority party in the house and carries much of the responsibility for passing the majority party's legislative program. The Speaker derives power from both these positions and is in a position to provide many types of assistance to members of the majority, and even to members of the minority, whose assistance may sometimes be needed to pass bills.

Both the majority and minority parties have floor leaders who carry on much of the day-to-day work of the legislature. The majority leader is in reality second in command to the Speaker within the majority party. The minority leader is in command of the other party, but being in the minority, he or she usually has less power to get things accomplished.

There are two different organizational patterns in the senate. In twenty-six of the state senates the lieutenant governor, elected by the voters, presides over the senate and usually has the title of senate president. But in most senates the rules do not give the lieutenant governor much power beyond the formal authority of presiding; in practice there are differences among the states about how frequently the lieutenant governor exercises that power. How much additional power he or she has (such as membership on leadership committees) may depend on whether the lieutenant governor belongs to the same political party as the senate majority. In senates where the lieutenant governor presides, the senators choose their own leader from the majority party, who has the title of president pro tem.

Eight states do not have a lieutenant governor, and in sixteen others the lieutenant governor does not preside over the senate. In these twenty-four states the senate picks the presiding officer, who has the title of president of the senate; it usually also picks a senator with the title of president pro tem who must preside when the senate president does not. There has been a gradual trend among the states to eliminate the lieutenant governor from the senate entirely.

In the senate as in the house, majority and minority leaders—also referred to as floor leaders—are chosen by the two parties. As in the house, the minority leader is clearly in charge of the minority party. There are some variations, however, in the role and the power of the senate majority leader. Generally speaking, where the lieutenant governor is president of the senate, the senator chosen as president pro tem is less powerful than senators in states where the members choose the president of the senate. Where the top elected senator has less power, the majority leader usually has more. Leadership power includes control over committee assignments, assignment of bills to committees, and the agenda of bills coming to the floor. The distribution of power may depend on personality, political skills, and experience and not just formal power. In Minnesota, for example, for most of the 1980s and 1990s the long-term majority leader, Roger Moe, exercised more power than did the elected president. In several states the elected president of the senate appoints the majority leader, which obviously enhances the president's power. Finally, in Illinois and Ohio the same person serves both as president of the Senate and majority leader, and the same person is president pro tem of the Senate and majority leader in New York (Jewell and Whicker 1994, 59–60).

One of the major sources of power for most legislative leaders is the ability to make appointments of members and chairs to legislative committees. Unlike congressional leaders, who are somewhat handicapped by the seniority system, legislative leaders in all but a few states can make committee appointments with little regard to seniority. They usually select committee chairs who have some seniority in order to get experienced persons in those jobs, but they are not bound by rigid seniority rules. In states where rigid term limits have been adopted, it may actually be difficult to find enough senior members to fill chairmanships as well as memberships on most important committees.

When there is a contest for a major party leadership, the contestants sometimes offer such key committee positions to those who will support them. Once in office, leaders often select members and chairs for committees who share the party's and the leader's views on the major issues that those committees will address. A chair can refuse to reappoint a legislator as chair or member of a committee who has failed to reflect the party's position on such issues adequately.

The rules of the legislature normally give the majority party roughly the same proportion of seats on committees that it has in the chamber, but the majority party sometimes claims a larger share on a few major committees. In legislatures where one party is numerically weak, it may get very little representation, at least on the most important committees. The chairs of committees are filled by members of the majority party; in the rare cases where there are exceptions to this rule, a very unimportant committee is usually involved.

The majority leadership selects the chairs and majority party members of committees. We might assume that the minority party leadership selects the minority party committee members, but the actual practice varies from state to state, depending on rules and sometimes on informal understandings that may change over a period of years. In some states the minority party leaders have absolute control over appointing their party's members to committees, including both chambers in Iowa and Colorado and the Senate in Ohio and Washington. In other states, including the House in Oregon and Maryland and both chambers in Texas, the majority party leaders appoint minority as well as majority members to committees without consulting the minority leadership. A third pattern of appointments that falls between the first two is one in which the majority leadership has authority to appoint minority members on its own but in practice consults the minority leadership and usually accepts its recommendations. This is by far the most common practice, followed by legislatures in such states as Indiana, Wisconsin, Minnesota, Maine, and New Hampshire (Jewell and Whicker 1994, 91–95).

One would expect that in legislatures with two strong, rather closely balanced parties, the majority party leaders would give the minority party leaders total control over appointing their own members to ensure that same power if they became minority leaders, but this is not always the case. Connecticut, Minnesota, Ohio, and Indiana are examples of states with strong parties where minority leadership control over such appointments is not absolute but is dependent on understandings with the majority leadership.

Oregon offers an example of the risks involved when majority leadership claims too much power. In 1985 the new Democratic Speaker of the Oregon House, Vera Katz, put a stop to the practice of letting the minority party choose its own committee members, although she agreed to let the minority leader discuss the list she had drawn up. Because there was a close two-party balance in the House and on committees, she was trying to keep some important committees from becoming too conservative. But, given the close party balance, it was not surprising that in 1991 the Republicans recaptured the House, chose a Speaker, and happily retained former Speaker Katz's procedure for choosing committee members.

Why is this an important issue? If the majority leaders almost always accept the candidates for committees proposed by the minority party, what difference does it make if a few names are occasionally turned down? The threat of a rejection may limit the minority leader's choice in proposing a committee appointment. The minority may fail in an attempt to appoint a particularly skilled or outspoken member to a committee. If the liberals are likely to have only a modest majority among Democratic members of a committee, the majority leader may try to prevent the minority party membership from being heavily conservative.

Remember that the ability to appoint committee members is an important source of the leader's power. The most serious threat to the minority leadership may occur if a significant number of minority party legislators owe their committee assignment to the majority leaders and may be subject to pressure from them (rather than from the minority leader) on a key vote. In the late 1980s in the Kentucky House, where the minority Republican Party was weak, Democratic Speaker Don Blandford said that Republican members sometimes offered him support on issues if he would give them better committee assignments than the Republican leader had recommended. He turned them down. In 1991, however, Speaker Blandford, who was engaged in a feud with the minority leader, threatened to stop accepting his committee recommendations. The threat worked, and the Republican Party agreed to select a new minority leader who was acceptable to Blandford.

Another important institutional power that the majority party leadership holds is control over the agenda. Once a committee has reported a bill to the house or senate, the majority leadership largely determines what priority, if any, the bill has in getting to the floor of the chamber for debate and a vote. Particularly when it is late in the session, priorities become very important. A bill that is pushed to the head of the calendar usually has a better chance of being passed than one that is postponed for a couple of days or sent back to committee for a few changes. The majority leaders also work with the committee chairs, whom they have appointed, urging them to move quickly on some bills, to make changes in others, and to let some bills die a quiet death in committee.

Sometimes the majority leader works closely with the presiding officer to make these decisions. Sometimes the work is done by a rules committee, which usually consists of several leaders of the majority party (and occasionally a token member of the minority leadership). The committee not only determines when bills will be placed on the house or senate calendar but whether they will be sent back to the original committee or to another committee for further consideration.

Leadership Skills and Styles

The political effectiveness of legislative leaders does not depend only on their formal power under the rules of the chamber or of the party. It also depends on their personal skills, experience, and leadership style. To be effective, leaders must adjust to the political realities they face. The job of leading a majority party is different from leading a minority party, just as the job of leading the governor's party is different from leading the opposition party.

A successful leader understands the problems legislators face in their districts and knows how to help them deal with these problems. This may be as simple as speaking at a fund-raising dinner for the member in the district or as complicated as getting an appropriation to update and improve buildings in a state park or a community college located in the district. There are many ways in which a leader may facilitate or delay passage of a bill that is of particular concern to a legislator whose support the leader needs on major legislation.

Party leaders have increasingly played an important role in recruiting legislative candidates and raising campaign funds for both incumbent and nonincumbent legislative candidates. Leaders who are hard working and skillful in raising and allocating campaign funds presumably are more powerful, but it must be recognized that legislators often have high expectations for funding and are critical of leaders who do not measure up to these standards.

Legislative leaders follow different styles of leadership depending in part on their personality and experience. Most important, however, leaders must adjust their style of leadership to fit the expectations of the membership. During the 1990s in many legislative bodies those expectations began to change. For many years some of the house Speakers, senate presidents, and majority leaders who appeared to be most successful and in some cases had very long tenures used what is sometimes called a command style of leadership. They typically consulted most of the time with a relatively small circle of leaders and trusted advisers; they tried to maintain tight control over the agenda; they applied heavy pressure on members to vote the right way; and if necessary they were willing to use tough reward-and-punish tactics to whip members into line.

Vern Riffe, Democratic Speaker of the Ohio House for ten terms from 1975 through 1994, is a good example of a command leader. He ran a tight ship, consulting with a small group of leaders, rewarding members who were loyal to him, and punishing those who were not in a variety of ways. Near the end of his term other legislators predicted that future speakers would not be able to duplicate Riffe's style because the members would not accept it. John Martin, who became Speaker of the Maine House also in 1975, followed a similar style, dominating the decision-making process in the House and rewarding and punishing members. Maintaining control of the House in Maine was probably easier than in Ohio because Maine had a "citizen" legislature made up of part-time members, some of whom served for only a few years. Martin reluctantly stepped down as Speaker early in 1994, however, after surviving an attempt to oust him a year earlier. The legislature had decided it was time for a new Speaker and a different style of leadership and asked him to step down.

As the members of most legislatures have grown more professional, they have become more resistant to this style of leadership. Female legislators appear to be particularly uncomfortable with strong leadership. Most female legislative leaders we have interviewed say that their own leadership style is less confrontational and more consensus-building and inclusive. Therefore it is not surprising that most rank-and-file female legislators believe that anyone in leadership should have a leadership style similar to that used by women leaders. In some cases rank-and-file members forced strong, domineering leaders like Martin to step down from their posts earlier than they would have preferred. Whatever the reason for a turnover of leadership, the new leaders usually had little opportunity to act as command leaders.

Many of the leaders who have come into power since the early 1990s have used a coordinating style of leadership. They are vigorous in their efforts to control the agenda and build the coalitions necessary to get legislation passed. They know how to reward members who support them without blatantly punishing those who are less cooperative. They encourage broad participation among as many members as possible and try to be accessible to their colleagues. This is a good description of the leadership style of Democrat Roger Moe, who has been Minnesota's Senate majority leader since 1991. Moe is a strong, skillful leader who follows a strategy he calls "pragmatic inclusion"; he consults widely with his colleagues as he builds coalitions to get bills passed.

We have interviewed women leaders who believed they were elected to leadership positions because their colleagues wanted someone who knew how to negotiate and compromise and perceived these women as having such skills and style. Republican Joann Davidson, who replaced Vern Riffe as Ohio House Speaker, has not tried to adopt his leadership style; she has consulted widely with her colleagues but has also worked vigorously and with considerable success to shape compromises and get legislation passed.

Another style of leadership, which is even more permissive, might be labeled as consensus leadership. These leaders may be less concerned with promoting particular legislative goals than with building the broadest consensus within the party or if necessary within the legislatures as a whole. In filling committee chairmanships and memberships, they may be less interested in putting loyal partisans in the most important jobs than in trying to satisfy as many members of their party as possible in an effort to keep them cooperative. This may be a more common style of leadership in some of the less professional legislatures in smaller states today.

No two leaders are exactly the same, of course, and not every one falls neatly into one of these categories of leadership style, but the trend toward coordinating or consensual leadership is clear. It is sometimes argued that legislative leaders are weaker than they used to be. What is really happening is that the expectations of rank-and-file members about leaders are changing and the job of leadership has become more complex and more challenging than in the past.

Although command leaders often held onto their posts for as long as possible, coordinating and consensus leaders are often more willing to move on after a few terms. The term limits movement that is spreading across many legislatures will force leaders to serve shorter tenures. This will not only make command leaders virtually extinct in these bodies but will also make it much harder for leaders to learn how to perform their complex jobs well in those few short years.

The Party Caucus as a Tool of Leadership

In the large majority of legislatures that are organized along party lines, the members of each party in each chamber meet from time to time in a party caucus. How frequently the caucuses meet and how they operate depend in part on the character of the two-party system in the legislature. Party caucuses have the potential to play an important role in legislative decision making, but this is unlikely to occur if one party has a much larger share of legislative seats than the other or if the legislative parties are traditionally weak. If a legislative party is deeply divided over major issues, the caucus is unlikely to be an arena where greater party unity can be built.

Even in a legislative party that is relatively strong and cohesive, the frequency of caucus meetings and the uses to which they are put depend heavily on the preferences and the strategy of the party leaders. It is the leaders who decide how often the caucuses meet, what bills are discussed, and how much emphasis is placed on mobilizing the membership to support a position on pending legislation.

The leadership can use the caucus to provide members with information about bills that are coming up and amendments that may be offered and to brief members on the tactics that leaders plan to follow. The caucus gives members an opportunity to express their views, sometimes including views dissenting from the position taken by the leadership. These discussions may help the leaders to estimate how much support there is for the leaders' position on issues and to decide whether some changes have to be made to present a more united front when the bill gets to the house or senate floor. Some leaders in the caucus often take a straw vote (an unofficial vote that is not binding on anyone) on proposed legislation. If the straw vote reveals splits within the party, the leadership can delay bringing a bill to the floor while it tries to work out a compromise. If it shows that most members are in agreement on a position, the straw vote may put pressure on the small number of dissenting members to go along with the party majority. In most legislative parties the caucuses are held in private, giving leaders and rank and file a chance to discuss issues frankly without revealing disagreements or tactical plans to members of the other party.

Despite these apparent advantages to a caucus, some leaders would prefer to build a coalition by negotiating privately with individual members. They are afraid that a caucus may be hard to handle and may even get out of control. A vigorous debate in the caucus may lead to an escalation of differences rather than laying the groundwork for compromise. Some leaders may vary their tactics, depending on the amount of intraparty disagreement they anticipate on a bill.

Because leaders differ in their tactics, and because they come and go every few years, there may be significant differences from time to time within a particular legislative party in the ways in which the caucus is used. Therefore it is difficult to classify every legislative party caucus by the functions it performs. But caucuses tend to have more important functions in states with relatively strong legislative party systems.

In every legislature that is organized along definite party lines, each party will hold a meeting of its caucus at the beginning of a new legislature to choose its leaders and its nominee for the presiding officer of the house or senate. In some legislative parties the caucus serves no other function and does not meet again until another legislature has been elected. But in about two-thirds of the parties the caucus is used for other purposes as well.

The most active and significant caucuses are those whose major purpose is to build party cohesion and mobilize the members behind a position on issues. Straw votes are common, and if there is substantial consensus leaders may put pressure on the dissenters to get in line. Caucuses designed to build cohesion and mobilize votes are most likely to be found in legislatures with strong parties such as New York, New Jersey, Connecticut, Pennsylvania, Ohio, Indiana, Michigan, and Minnesota. Strong caucuses are somewhat more likely to be found in the majority than in the minority party. A former Speaker of the House in Massachusetts said about the caucus, "I use it as much as possible to make collective decisions about what our party's policy should be on issues" (Jewell and Whicker 1994, 103). The Senate president in Indiana described the Republican caucus there as "reasonably democratic and consensus building" but made it clear that he considered the caucus to be a significant source of power for his leadership (p. 103).

In a few of the caucuses that operate this way, the leaders may ask for a binding vote on a few issues—particularly on appropriations bills. A binding vote means that all members of the caucus are supposed to go along with the majority of members on the issue. Leaders are usually cautious about seeking binding votes. A former Speaker of the Connecticut House told us, "On the budget, we did not try to ram things down their throats. Instead we had lots of discussion about alternatives, before reaching a decision on a party position" (Jewell and Whicker 1994, 101).

A second category of party caucuses are those in which policies and legislative proposals are frequently discussed fully enough that the leadership can assess the opinion of the members. The leadership does not use the caucus in an effort to mobilize votes, though that may be done in private. This type of caucus is found in states that do not traditionally have strong parties, including a number of western states and an increasing number of border and southern states. Kentucky is a good example of a state where the majority Democratic Party in both chambers uses the caucus in large part to assess the position of members on issues and often delays bringing a bill to the floor if party members are seriously divided on it. Other examples of state parties that often use the caucus in this fashion, particularly in the majority party, are Washington, Utah, Idaho, New Mexico, Tennessee, Texas, and North Carolina.

In the final category, caucuses are used simply to provide members with information about pending legislation. The information may come from party leaders or from members of the committee reporting the bill. This type of caucus is used more in western states and southern states, and it is particularly likely to be found in minority parties because there is often less need for them to take a position on bills. A few years ago the Vermont Senate minority leader said, "Republican senators don't like to debate in caucus and then have a position taken on the floor. We have never tried to do that. We spend time in caucus listening to committee chairs and discussing issues" (Jewell and Whicker 1994, 106). Examples of such caucuses are found in the minority parties in Utah, South Dakota, Kentucky, Missouri, Tennessee, and South Carolina.

THE GOVERNOR AS PARTY LEADER

The governor is at the same time the head of the party and the head of the government. His or her success as party leader is vital to success in electoral coalition building as well as legislative coalition building (Morehouse 1998, chap. 7). Governors of strong party states such as New York are endorsed in a convention, and legislative party cohesion is traditionally strong. The California Democrats experimented with endorsing for governor in 1990, but they gave up the practice. And so in 1998 Gray Davis was sent out to primary against multimillionaires without formal party backing. The California Democratic legislative party has offered moderate support for its governor in the past, and therefore much depended on Governor Davis's leadership. Texas traditionally has been a weak party state with divisive primaries and factional coalitions. In those states where the party is weak or divided, governors face legislatures in which sit remnants of the factions that opposed them in the primary contest. Thus the ability of the governor to get legislative approval for his or her program presented in the state-of-the-state address depends on party leadership developed over time by coalition building (Ehrenhalt 1998, 5–6).

Surprisingly, few political scientists have studied the relationship between the political efforts of party leaders and gubernatorial candidates to capture the nomination and their success when in office in passing the party program. Several works have dealt descriptively with the legislative leadership of governors (Sabato 1983; Jewell and Olson 1988, 244–249; Muchmore and Beyle 1980). In *Governors and Legislatures: Contending Powers,* Rosenthal (1990) describes executive-legislative jockeying as well as legislative independence from or dominance over the governor. He assumes institutional conflict, as the title suggests, and does not focus on legislative voting on gubernatorial initiatives.

Working with Legislative Leaders

The governor works closely with the legislative leaders in his or her party as well as with the leaders of the opposition party in the legislature when they are in the majority. When the governor has a majority in a chamber, this party leadership includes the Speaker of the house or the presiding officer of the senate, majority leaders, and chairs of committees. This majority gives the governor a control over legislation that is absent when the governor has a minority. The governor's leaders support the governor's program and see that bills within it are guided through the legislature.

The governor may influence votes with resources such as appointments, public works projects, and the like. The leaders also have possession of resources such as patronage, power of recognition, flow of legislation, appointments, campaign money, and access to the governor. Governors head the ticket on which legislators campaign for election, and legislators hope the governor's coattails will help them win. Many of those who attend the party nominating convention are state legislators as well as local party leaders who benefit from the governor's power and have a stake in the governor's success. Legislators are positively oriented toward their governor because they share the same policy affiliation.

Governors and Divided Government

Governors in half of the states have minority parties in the legislature, and their strategies in these situations are different. Little attention has been paid to the consequences of divided government at the state level (Morehouse and Jewell 1992). In a divided government the governor lacks many of the advantages that accrue to a governor who is backed by a majority. The leaders are members of the opposition party and are in a position to control the legislative timetable and agenda. The ability of the governor to get his or her program passed under conditions of divided government depends upon the strength of the statewide party as well as the cohesion of the legislative party.

If the opposition has only a modest majority, the governor will mobilize support within the minority governing party and seek to expand this coalition by offering personal or constituency benefits to some members of the opposition. Opposition leaders will recognize a greater need to compromise if the governor is politically strong and has widespread public support. In 1997 legislative sessions in both Oregon and Washington, Republican legislative leaders realized the need to hold their party together as well as to do business with the Democratic governor's minority. From the leadership's point of view there was little point in sending the Democratic governor bills that he could successfully veto. Washington governor Gary Locke vetoed a bill containing a series of tax cuts that went further than he was willing to allow. After that, GOP leaders concluded that if the legislature was to get anything done on the budget, it could only be in cooperation with the governor (Gurwitt 1997).

On the other hand, a governor whose statewide party is weak or divided, and who faces a strong opposition legislature, will need to accommodate some of the priorities of the opposition party to get legislation passed. Members of the governor's party may object to these compromises and vote against the program.

When the governor's statewide party is weak, the legislative party is usually weak as well, and divided government may not have an impact. In weak party states divided government often occurs when partisan control of the governorship has rotated, but the legislature traditionally remains in the hands of one party. With less cohesive parties the governor expects less success in winning unanimous support from members of his or her own party but greater success in wooing some members of the opposition party. A governor who is elected from the traditional minority party, such as Tennessee Republicans, would be able to unite the small legislative party contingent but would need to obtain a significant number of votes from the rival majority.

Occasionally governors are elected as independents or third-party candidates. Recent examples are Angus King of Maine, elected in 1994 and 1998; Jesse Ventura of Minnesota, elected in 1998; and Lowell Weicker of Connecticut and Walter Hickel of Alaska, both elected in 1990. They must try to get legislation enacted without having any base of political party support in the legislature. Some are more successful than others.

Angus King, who was elected as an independent in Maine after years of deadlock between a Republican governor and a Democratic legislature, proved adept at compromise and at building bipartisan coalitions to support many of his legislative proposals. He was also very experienced and effective in using the media, particularly television, to win broad public support for his program, and he won a landslide victory when he sought reelection. Jesse Ventura won election in Minnesota as a Reform Party candidate by defeating well-known Democratic and Republican candidates. Despite having limited political experience, he developed a centrist position on some issues and had initial success in getting some of his proposals passed by a legislature in which partisan control was divided between the two chambers.

Lowell Weicker, an experienced Republican politician who had been defeated when he ran for reelection as a U.S. senator, was elected governor of Connecticut in 1990 on a third-party ticket. The state was facing a severe revenue shortage as a result of an economic slowdown, and Weicker proposed the adoption of an income tax, accompanied by a cut in the sales and corporate taxes. With great difficulty, Weicker won enough votes from legislators in both parties to pass his tax program. But he chose not to run for reelection, a race he might well have lost. Walter Hickel had been elected governor of Alaska as a Republican and also had served in President Richard Nixon's cabinet, but he had lost three more elections for governor before running on a third-party ticket and winning in 1990. He was a controversial governor, proposing some projects that angered environmentalists, and he decided not to run again at the end of his term.

The Governor's Program

Speaking for the party, the governor has the responsibility of defining the issues and making the commitments that form the basis of his or her legislative program. How do the issues proceed from a gleam in the governor's eye to a set of administration bills introduced by party leaders in the legislature? How does the governor determine which issues are most important to address? This question has been asked, and the answers are reassuring. Studies of public desires and policy over time in the states show that policy has responded to public ideology, resulting in a high level of correspondence between the two (Erikson, Wright, and McIver 1993).

The governors of all states go into office with a platform that is the work of the candidate and the party (or factions of it). This platform reflects enough of the governor's major policy priorities so that it can be used as a basis for his or her legislative program. Each year the governor presents a state-of-the-state address to a joint gathering of both legislative houses. In this address the governor outlines the substance of the program he or she wants passed for the session. Shifts in the liberalism or conservatism of measures proposed to address policies occur over time, but there appear to be some policies that are perennial, some that are cyclical, and some that are transitory.

Perennial issues include delivery of traditional state services such as education, highways, corrections, health care, law enforcement, and welfare. These policy areas account for nearly 75 percent of average state expenditures, and much of the state's economic well-being and quality of life is tied to the adequate and efficient delivery of these services. Cyclical policies are those in which interest grows, peaks, and declines. Taxes, environment, economic development, consumer protection, and government reorganization are examples. Finally governors may confront issues that are transitory and emotionally charged such as the death penalty, the drinking age, drug testing, and AIDS research and treatment (Herzik 1991).

The issues identified by governors in their state-of-the-state speeches are translated into governor's program bills that are introduced in most states by the governor's party leaders in the house or senate or by legislators whom the governor may specify. The governor's budget message follows shortly afterward, and other special messages on high-priority programs are given throughout the legislative session. Through the power of initiation alone, the governor's influence over the legislature is substantial. The governor sets the agenda for public decision making and largely determines what the business of the legislature will be in any one session. Few major state undertakings get off the ground without the governor's initiation (Crew and Hill 1995). The governor frames the issues, determines their content, and decides their timing.

Resources at the Governor's Disposal

The success of the governor in getting the program passed will depend on his or her ability as a party leader. All governors have resources at their disposal, but their skill in using them marks the difference between a successful and an unsuccessful governor. A governor who has built up a good-sized coalition within his or her party can expect to have a nucleus of support in the group that has worked together and shared the fruits of winning. Friendships, loyalty, psychological rewards—all have a part to play in the legislative coalition that must be fashioned to pass the governor's program. Half of all governors have had legislative experience, which helps them garner support for their programs. Breakfast sessions with the governor at the mansion help along the way. Here are some additional resources at the governor's disposal:

1. Patronage. The amount of patronage at the governor's disposal differs from state to state. Jobs, contracts, and other favors are not put at the governor's disposal the way they used to be, but governors can still use skill in doling out their store of treasures at times of maximum advantage to themselves. Most governors have at least 100 or so appointments to make to boards and commissions (Bernick and Wiggins 1991, 80). Although some of these are more ceremonial than substantive, legislators covet them to prove their ability to reward friends. The promise of a future appointment to the bench may keep a legislator loyal.

2. Media. The governor has guaranteed access to newspapers, radio, and television that the legislator cannot command. The governor has repeated opportunities to speak, to capture the headlines, and to appeal to public sentiment as a way of bringing attention to his or her legislative program. If the governor's press relations office times them strategically, this news is on the evening TV news programs and in the morning papers. In addition to these means of direct access to the citizens are the daily press conferences held by most governors. No single legislator or group of legislators can hope to command the audience held by the governor largely and simply because of his or her position.

3. Promise of campaign support or threat of opposition. The support of the governor in an election campaign can be a powerful stimulus to a legislator, particularly one from a constituency where his or her election is in doubt. Hence the legislator in the governor's party has a personal stake in

the governor's success. In states like Connecticut and Minnesota where parties are strong, party leaders at the state or local level may recruit candidates for the nomination. In those two states as well as in Ohio, Indiana, Pennsylvania, and Colorado local parties endorse and work for candidates in legislative primaries.

4. Calling of special sessions. All governors have the capacity to call the legislature into special session. Special sessions became a political tool for governors to call attention to important aspects of their legislative program. Governors also called special sessions to get the people of the state to become aware of the immediacy of a financial crisis and their program to cope with it. The legislators are then in the position of going along with the proposals of the governor or taking the consequences, which can be serious if the electorate is really alarmed. Gov. John Rowland called the Connecticut legislature into special session in December 1998 to approve a $374 million downtown Hartford football stadium for the NFL's New England Patriots, which he saw as key to the redevelopment of the crumbling city. Momentum for relocation of the Patriots and the downtown development of Hartford proved too much for the opposition. The governor got what he wanted, until the Patriots withdrew from the deal.

Most of these resources depend on the governor's skill at using them. A governor at odds with the legislative leaders will find that many of these resources will fade. A governor faced with a strong rival sitting in the legislature may discover that his or her influence cannot go far because the rival may be building a personal power base using the very resources the governor has.

PARTISAN DECISION MAKING IN THE LEGISLATURE

In some state legislatures many of the most important legislative decisions are made along partisan lines; in others partisanship has little or no influence on policymaking. How do we explain the differences?

We must look at the level of two-party competition in the state and the balance of parties in the legislature. We must examine the constituency base of the two legislative parties and see how much they differ. We have just discussed the governor's role as a party leader in the legislature, and variations in the governor's role obviously affect the level of partisanship in legislative decision making. Legislative leadership is organized along party lines. We have discussed the skill and style of legislative leaders, and we recognize that some take a more partisan approach than others and some are more successful than others in mobilizing partisan support. We have said that leaders differ in their use of the caucus as a tool for mobilizing partisan support.

Makeup of the Legislative Parties

Partisanship is most likely to be important when there is a close balance between the two parties in the legislature. In these conditions the majority party must stick together to get legislation passed, and the minority party has some realistic chance of winning if it can remain cohesive. In legislatures where one party has held the majority for a long time, a growing minority party is more likely to become cohesive if it has elected a governor and is trying to help him or her adopt a legislative program.

Some of the states where legislative decision making is most strongly partisan are among the more heavily urbanized states in the Northeast and Midwest. In such states each of the legislative parties usually represents certain distinctive interests. The Democrats represent the central cities, which are likely to have many working-class voters and racial and ethnic minorities. The Republicans represent higher-income suburbs, small towns, and sometimes rural areas. Each of the political parties is aligned with particular interest groups associated with its party loyalists, such as the link between the Democratic Party and labor unions. Good examples of such states are New York, Pennsylvania, Ohio, and Illinois.

It is in the states where the parties represent distinctive interests that party caucuses are most important. When legislators represent constituencies with similar interests, they are more willing to go along with the decisions made in the caucus. In those cases the leaders can use the caucus more effectively as a vehicle for assessing the viewpoints of members and mobilizing them to support measures that the majority of the caucus supports.

Partisanship is less likely to be important in states where neither of the legislative parties represents a cohesive group of interests. For example, in many of the southern states the majority Democratic Party has represented the most conservative rural constituencies along with urban working-class districts and at least a few districts with a majority of black voters. The minority Republican Party may have been more cohesive because it represented upper-income suburbs. In border states such as Kentucky and Tennessee the Democrats have represented a diverse majority of urban and rural districts, while the Republicans have represented an even more diverse minority: the wealthiest suburban districts and the poorest rural districts in Appalachia, a traditionally Republican area.

During the 1990s the balance of power shifted in many of the southern states. Increasing proportions of conservative voters abandoned the Democratic Party and began voting for Republicans, including those running for legislative seats. The Republican legislative parties built conservative coalitions including suburban and rural areas. Democratic Parties built more liberal coalitions that included some African American and Latino voters, including central cities and some other districts with middle-income voters. As a result the two parties not only were more evenly balanced in some southern legislatures but also represented different interests and viewpoints, laying the groundwork for more partisanship in decision making.

The development of more evenly balanced parties representing distinctly different interests in any legislature does not guarantee that partisanship will have a major impact on a large proportion of important legislative decisions. But it does give those governors and legislative leaders who are skillful enough a greater opportunity to mobilize the support of legislators in their own party.

It is important to recognize that, even in heavily partisan legislatures, partisan alignments do not develop on every issue that comes to a vote. Legislative parties are more likely to take opposing stands on major economic and social issues such as education, health, and welfare services; the control of the economy; the regulation of business and labor; environmental protection; tax policy; and the rights of women and various minority groups. These are issues on which the state parties have made commitments to their allies among the interest groups and the issues that have usually dominated gubernatorial campaigns, in other words the issues on which the parties represent different interests and viewpoints. There is also more likely to be party voting on those issues that are part of the governor's legislative program or on which he or she has taken a strong stand.

Some issues do not produce partisan voting because they cut across the normal partisan and interest group alignments. One example is bills regulating the sale of alcoholic beverages. Another is abortion, which deeply divides both Democrats and Republicans, even though the Democratic Party tends to be pro-choice and the Republicans pro-life. More generally, the political parties often avoid taking stands on issues that involve standards of morality and personal conduct because these issues frequently divide their supporters and arouse strong feelings among voters. Some issues are too localized or specialized to become partisan, such as bills regulating barber shops, providing some funding for a football stadium to attract a professional team, or raising the speed limit on highways.

Voting in Committee and on the Floor

Legislative decision making begins in the committees, where the majority party almost always has the chairmanship and a majority of members; but this does not guarantee that most committee decisions will follow partisan lines. In legislatures with weak parties, votes in committee may be unanimous or cut across party lines. Where parties are strong, committee votes may follow party lines. Sometimes party leaders or the caucus will put pressure on their committee members to support the party position. In some committees the majority party members may meet separately to agree on the stand to take on a bill and pending amendments. The level of partisanship may vary from one committee to another, being strong on committees that often deal with issues on which the parties have taken a stand (such as taxation, education, or health care) rather than with issues such as highways, agriculture, or local government.

The level of partisanship in committee decision making can have an impact on the votes taken on the floor of the house and senate because legislators often take their voting cues from members of the committee who are handling the bill. If there is a straight party vote in committee on a particular bill, votes taken on the house or senate floor are also likely to follow party lines. If there is bipartisan support for a bill in committee, there is more likely to be bipartisan support on the floor.

The clearest measure of partisanship in the legislature is the roll call votes taken in the house and the senate. We know where to look for heavily partisan roll call votes: in legislatures with close two-party balance and particularly those where the two parties represent districts with distinctly different interests. We know that voting can be affected by the skill of leadership and the activity of the caucus. And we know that not all bills are likely to produce party-line votes.

In the last analysis, of course, there will not be a strongly partisan vote on a bill unless most legislators are willing to support the party's position on the bill. What would lead members to vote the "party line"? There are a number of reasons. Many legislators strongly believe in the principles represented by the party; that is why they are active in politics. Moreover, the person who is elected in a district usually wins, at least in part because he or she shares the viewpoints of a majority of persons in the district. A Colorado legislator said, "I am very much a part of the district. I am very much in line with what they think—I reflect fairly well the composition of the district" (Jewell 1982, 98). On some issues there may be a consensus in the district. On issues where voters are divided, the legislator often finds that most of those who voted for him or her agree with the viewpoint of the legislator and the legislator's party. A Kentucky legislator said, "I told the voters in advance how I stood on the issues. I believe in majority rule—the majority puts me in—and I have to follow the majority whose positions I have committed myself to" (Jewell 1982, 121).

Sometimes legislators succeed in getting elected even though they are quite a bit more liberal or conservative than a majority of their constituents. Such legislators may find it more difficult to support the party on a high proportion of roll calls. A Republican elected in a working-class district, for example, has to weigh his or her views and the party leader's demands against the pressure from groups in the district.

The Record of Roll Call Voting

We have said that Senate and House roll call votes provide the clearest, most direct measure of partisanship in legislative decision making. Unfortunately there is no comprehensive collection of roll call votes for all state legislatures in recent years. The situation is even worse: relatively recent data and analysis of roll call voting are available for only a few states. But with a limited number of examples we will try to show how and why partisanship in roll calls varies among the states.

There are various ways of measuring the degree of partisanship that occurs on roll call votes. We cannot learn much about partisanship on roll calls taken on noncontroversial bills, when all, or almost all, legislators vote for (or against) the bill. Therefore most studies include only roll calls on which at least 10 or perhaps 15 percent of the legislators vote in the minority.

The simplest way to measure partisanship is to calculate the roll calls on which a majority of Democrats oppose a majority of Republicans; these are often called party votes. The best, most specific way of comparing the voting pattern of the two parties is an index of difference, which can range from 100 (completely different) to 0 (completely alike). If, for example, 90 percent of Democrats and only 15 percent of Republicans voted for the bill, the index would be 75; if 90 percent of Democrats and 85 percent of Republicans voted for the bill, the index would be only 5.

Because one party may be more united than the other, it is often useful to measure the party cohesion of each party separately. On a cohesion scale, a score of 100 means that all members of a party voted together, 50 means a 75–25 split in party ranks, and 0 means that the party members were split 50–50. Party cohesion scores are often used just for party votes.

If you were examining the party loyalty of all legislators, you could calculate the percentage of times the member voted on nonunanimous bills with a majority of his or her party members; this might apply only to party votes. If you averaged the party loyalty scores of all Republicans, for example, you could calculate a party loyalty score for the Republican Party. A similar approach would be to create a governor's support score by calculating the percentage of times a legislator voted for the governor's program; this percentage could then be averaged for all Democratic and all Republican legislators.

It might seem as if there were more indexes than necessary, but each one measures a somewhat different aspect of partisanship. Some measure partisanship in the legislature as a whole, and others measure cohesion within one party. We will find different measures used in the examples that follow, but we will compare state legislatures by using the governor's support score in Table 8-1 and the index of difference in Table 8-2.

There were a significant number of roll call studies on individual state legislatures or groups of legislatures from the mid-1950s through the mid-1970s. During that period the parties were more likely to take opposite sides on bills, and each party was relatively more cohesive on legislative roll call votes in northeastern and midwestern states than in western and southern states. In a number of the northeastern and midwestern states the two parties took opposing stands on 50–75 percent of roll calls, the average index of difference was between 50 and 65, and the average cohesion index for each party (when parties took opposing sides) was often 65–85 percent (Jewell and Patterson 1977, 384–385).

More impressionistic analysis by political scientists suggests that this general pattern still prevails. Party voting is relatively high in legislatures of states like Connecticut, Massachusetts, New York, New Jersey, Pennsylvania, Illinois, Indiana, Ohio, Michigan, Minnesota, and Wisconsin and in a few western states including California, Washington, and Colorado. But party voting is relatively low in most western states like North Dakota, Idaho, Montana, Oregon, Alaska, Nevada, and New Mexico. (See state chapters in Appleton and Ward 1997.) Party voting has been very low in most southern states, though we will see that it is beginning to develop.

One of the very few comparative studies of roll call voting in the 1980s was undertaken by Sarah Morehouse (1998, chap. 7), who examined votes on bills that were part of the legislative program proposed by the governor. We have said that bills that were part of a governor's program were likely to produce higher levels of partisanship voting in roll calls than most other bills. Examining the 1983 legislative session in ten states, Morehouse calculated the average gubernatorial support scores for Democratic and for Republican legislators and then calculated the differences between support for the governor by Democrats and Republicans. She found that the sharpest partisan differences on the governor's bills occurred in Connecticut and Minnesota (a difference in gubernatorial support scores of 84 and 64, respectively, in these two states). A more modest partisan split occurred in New York, Illinois, California, and Tennessee (with differences ranging from 46 in New York to about 20 in the other three states). Partisanship had even less impact in Colorado, Kansas, and Oregon (from 11 to 15) and no impact in Texas (see Table 8-1). The pattern of differences among the states on these bills is comparable to the more impressionistic differences we reported earlier.

Connecticut, Minnesota, New York, Illinois, and more recently California have a tradition of strong legislative parties. Kansas and Oregon have had relatively weak legislative parties, and the Texas legislature was not even organized along party lines in 1983. Although the Tennessee legislature traditionally was under strong Democratic control, in 1983 a Republican governor received strong support from his legislative party and was often opposed by the Democrats. There are scattered reports of roll call voting in a few state legislatures during the 1980s

Table 8-1 Differences between Democratic and Republican Legislators in Levels of Support for Governors' Bills in 1983

State	Differences in Partisan Support
Connecticut	84
Minnesota	64
New York	46
Illinois	19
Colorado	15
Tennessee	21
California	19
Oregon	16
Kansas	11
Texas	0

Source: Sarah McCally Morehouse, *The Governor as Party Leader* (Ann Arbor: University of Michigan Press, 1998).

and 1990s. In Connecticut, for example, almost two-thirds of the roll calls in the 1981–1982 session were party votes; the average cohesion index averaged about 70 (an 85–15 split) for each party (Swanson 1984, 36).

A study of voting patterns on the most important bills in the Illinois legislature found that the proportion of party votes dropped from about 55 percent in the 1995 session to about 13 percent in the 1997 session, perhaps because in the latter session the very close partisan balance in the legislature discouraged leaders from bringing bills to the floor that might lead to partisan conflict. On those party votes that did occur, both Democratic and Republican Parties had very high indexes of cohesion—about 92 in the 1995 session and 83 in the 1997 session (Pernaciarro and Van Der Slik 1996, 1998).

In the California Assembly, where Democratic Speaker Willie Brown was very powerful for many years, the average proportion of legislators voting for Brown's position on a number of bills on major issues from 1983 through 1988 was 80 percent for Democratic members and only 40 percent for Republicans, for an index of difference of 40 (Clucas 1995, 150).

Iowa is an example of a state that used to be heavily rural and dominated by the Republican Party. As a result, there was a low level of partisanship in legislative role call voting. During the 1960s the state became more urbanized, the legislature became more evenly balanced between parties, and the legislative parties came to represent more different constituencies. The result was a growth in partisan voting; the proportion of party votes rose from about 30 percent in the late 1940s and early 1950s to about 50 percent in the late 1950s and 1960s (Wiggins 1972; Euchner 1990). By the 1980s Iowa was a strong party state.

As we would expect, partisanship is usually higher on those issues on which one or both parties have well-established positions. This can be seen in the 1980s in Iowa, where the Democrats controlled the House and a Republican held the governorship. During the years 1983, 1985, and 1989, the Democratic house party caucus established priorities for a number of important legislative initiatives. On roll calls related to these bills Democratic unity was very high; the index of Democratic cohesion was 91 in 1983, 79 in 1985, and 89 in 1989. In 1983, in fact, Democratic cohesion was 100 percent on more than half of the roll calls on these bills. Not surprisingly, Republican cohesion was lower on roll calls for this Democratic agenda: 72, 65, and 70, respectively, in the three sessions. Both parties had somewhat less cohesion on bills that were not Democratic priorities (Euchner and Jewell 1990).

We have said that the weakest levels of partisanship in roll call votes have been found in southern and border states, where the Democrats controlled most of the southern legislatures by lopsided margins until the 1990s. Even when the two-party balance became closer, the two legislative parties in most southern states did not quickly come to represent constituencies with distinctly different interests.

A good example of weak legislative partisanship occurred in Kentucky, where the Democrats held comfortable majorities in the legislature, especially the House, during the 1980s and early 1990s, and where the parties did not really represent different interests. On a series of roll calls on important issues from 1982 through 1986, there were party votes on less than one-third of Senate roll calls and somewhat more than half of those in the House. The average index of difference on these key roll calls was only about 31 in each chamber (Jewell and Miller 1988, 210–211).

In the 1980s the Republican share of House seats grew from 5 percent to 15 percent in Mississippi and from 14 percent to 28 percent in South Carolina—not enough to play a major role in legislative decision making. Therefore it is not surprising to find that during the 1980s the average index of difference dropped slightly in Mississippi, from 40 to 30, and in South Carolina, from 31 to 24 (Anderson 1998; Graham and Whitby 1989).

In those southern state legislatures where the two-party balance is getting closer, and the parties now represent more distinctively different constituencies, there is some evidence of increasing partisanship on roll call votes as measured by the index of difference. During the 1980s in the Florida House the index increased from 42 to 67, in Virginia from 47 to 62, and in Texas from 38 to 58 (Anderson 1998). The Republican share of House seats had grown to 35–40 percent in all three states by the end of the 1980s.

Table 8-2 summarizes data on the index of party difference in nine states in the 1980s; three of the states also appear in Morehouse's study of gubernatorial support. The states are ranked from the highest to the lowest index of difference.

Table 8-2   Index of Party Differences on a Sample of Roll Calls on Bills

State	Index of Difference	Years
Florida	67	1988
Virginia	62	1988
Texas	58	1987
Tennessee	52	1988
Nevada	49	1987
California	40	1983–1988
Kentucky	31	1982–1986
Mississippi	30	1988
South Carolina	24	1984–1987

Sources: Data for Ky. from Malcolm E. Jewell and Penny M. Miller, *The Kentucky Legislature* (Lexington: University Press of Kentucky, 1988). Data for Calif. from Richard A. Clucas, *The Speaker's Electoral Connection: Willie Brown and the California Assembly* (Berkeley: Institute of Governmental Studies Press of the University of California, 1995). Data for S.C. from Cole Blease Graham Jr. and Kenny J. Whitby, "Party-Based Voting in a Southern State Legislature," *American Politics Quarterly* 17:181–193. Data for Fla., Va., Texas, Tenn., Miss., Nev. from Bruce Anderson, "Party Voting in State Legislatures," Paper presented at the annual meeting of the Southern Political Science Association, Atlanta, 1998.

In most of the states a sample of roll calls was picked; in a few cases roll calls are on bills covering key issues where partisanship should be somewhat above average.

The highest indexes of party difference are found in Florida, Virginia, Texas, and Tennessee. The lowest scores are in South Carolina, Mississippi, and Kentucky. It is remarkable that the voting on roll calls is so partisan in states like Texas, Florida, and Virginia, where the Democratic Party used to have very large majorities but where Republicans gained seats rapidly in the 1990s. Less surprising are the low scores in South Carolina, Mississippi, and Kentucky, where parties have been relatively weak.

As more recent data become available on roll call voting in southern states, we are likely to find evidence that partisan voting increased during the middle to late 1990s and will continue in the future. In both Texas and Florida, for example, the bipartisan coalitions that often appeared in the 1980s were replaced by very close two-party competition in the 1990s; in the late 1990s the Republicans held a narrow lead in the South Carolina House. As southern Republican Parties continue to gain legislative majorities from time to time in more southern and border states, partisan voting is likely to increase.

THE FUTURE ROLE OF POLITICAL PARTIES IN LEGISLATURES

There are some trends that may weaken partisan voting and the importance of partisanship in decision making in state legislatures, in both North and South. As legislators have grown more professional, they have become better able to resist pressure, and party discipline has probably declined. The job of legislative leadership has grown more difficult and requires more skill than it did a few years ago. In states that have adopted strict limitations on legislative terms, leaders have less time to learn their job and develop experience, and their short terms in office may reduce their power.

On the other hand, the Democratic and Republican legislative parties represent different constituencies and stand for different policies in more of the states. In the increasing number of states where there is a close balance between the number of Democratic and Republican members, each party has a greater incentive to stick together because a shift of a few votes either way can determine the outcome of a roll call on a bill. There are additional tools available to legislative party leaders, if they have the skills to use them. They have more staff, and they are making increasing use of party caucuses. Perhaps the greatest change is the increasing role that party leaders are playing in recruiting legislative candidates and providing them with campaign funding and services. All of these developments have the potential for increasing partisanship in legislative decision making.

The level of partisanship is likely to vary from time to time in a state, depending on closeness of the two-party balance and the strategy and skill of the leaders. Some leaders prefer to follow a partisan strategy, relying almost entirely on their party to provide the votes needed to pass bills. The success of a bipartisan strategy may depend on how well leaders of the two parties work together.

The level of partisanship will continue to vary from state to state and is likely to be higher in northeastern and midwestern states with long traditions of legislative partisanship than in southern states where legislative partisanship is a more recent development. In those southern states where partisan competition in the legislature is just beginning to become close, it will be interesting to see when and how the decision making process becomes more partisan.

9   State Parties and National Politics

From the beginning of this book we have disputed the assertion that state political parties are declining or that they are becoming mere pawns of the national parties. In fact, both the national and state political party organizations are growing in many respects. They have become more professionalized, with larger staffs and bigger budgets. They devote a great deal of effort to raising money and use some of these funds to provide services to candidates. The congressional parties and the state legislative parties have organizations separate from the national and state party headquarters that raise and distribute funds to candidates.

The relationships between the national and state parties are changing and growing more complex. Much of the complexity is related to the raising and distribution of campaign funds. For this reason we will spend a considerable amount of time discussing the roles and interrelationship of national and state parties in campaign funding later in this chapter.

STATE PARTIES AND THE PRESIDENTIAL NOMINATING PROCESS

It is also true that state party leaders and organizations now play a less direct and less important role in some aspects of national politics than used to be the case. The most significant changes have occurred in the presidential nominating system. At one time governors, mayors, and other powerful party leaders played major roles in the selection of presidential nominees, largely through their influence over the selection of delegates to national conventions. There were two reasons that role was diminished during the 1960s and 1970s. One reason was the decline in the role of traditional state and local party organizations. The second was the growing importance of presidential primaries, over which state and local leaders had limited influence, and the changing role of the national convention, which was reduced simply to ratifying the winner of the presidential primaries as the party's nominee.

In Chapter 3 we described why the traditional state and local party organizations, which depended heavily on the patronage system, lost much of their power. Without a strong patronage system it was difficult to maintain discipline over party workers. A new breed of party activists, interested in issues and committed to particular candidates, could not be disciplined because they had little interest in patronage. State and local party leaders no longer were able to hand-pick delegates to the national convention and tell them which presidential candidate to support.

Presidential nominations are now decided almost entirely by primaries held in the states. From the 1940s through the 1960s about one-third of the states had primaries in both parties (or occasionally in just one). In the 1996 and 2000 elections four-fifths of the state parties were using primaries rather than caucuses. Although a small minority of state parties still use the caucus system, the outcomes of primary elections attract much more media attention and have a much bigger impact on nominating processes because primaries directly measure the presidential preferences of voters.

Governors and other key political leaders do not have much opportunity to influence the outcome of presidential primaries. It is true that presidential candidates may seek the endorsement of a governor, particularly early in a campaign, and such an endorsement may help to mobilize some party activists and influence some voters. The active support of most Republican governors, for example, was a major reason why Gov. George W. Bush got a head start in the 2000 presidential nominating race. But there is no reason to believe that such endorsements are of major importance in helping a candidate to carry a state. Winning a state requires campaigning as extensively as possible in the state, particularly in small states that have early primaries, like New Hampshire. And above all it requires running television and radio commercials to reach a significant portion of the voters. In other words, for the most part, candidates seeking the presidential nomination are trying to reach the voters directly rather than indirectly through political leaders like governors.

By the time the primaries are over, and sometimes much earlier, one candidate has usually won enough delegates to clinch the nomination, and the national convention simply rubber-stamps this choice. The governors and other state leaders who attend the convention have no alternative but to join the other delegates in voting for the presidential candidate chosen by primary voters.

The states have one very important role to play in the presidential nominating process. They determine whether the state will use a primary or a caucus, what form the primary or caucus will take, and, very important, when it will occur. This is done by a state law adopted by the legislature and signed by the governor (and not directly by the state parties). But the legislature and governor are usually responsive to the wishes of the state parties, and the state law often permits each of the parties to use different procedures for its primary or caucus.

The national political parties, particularly the Democratic Party, have established some guidelines that must be followed. The Democrats prohibit winner-take-all primaries and have rules designed to produce diversity in the delegates to the national convention. The parties discourage the use of open primaries for the choice of delegates. They also establish time frames intended to prevent the primary-caucus season from beginning too early in the presidential election year.

Within the time frame set by national parties the states are free to schedule their primary or caucus whenever they wish. During the 1990s and continuing in 2000 more and more states decided that they should hold their presidential primaries earlier so that both the political leaders and the rank-and-file voters in their state would have more influence over the choice of a nominee. Because the early primaries are becoming more crucial in the choice of a nominee, states with late primaries are often effectively left out of the selection process. In 1980, 20 percent of the Republican delegates had been chosen after four weeks of primaries and 35 percent after six weeks; in 1996, 35 percent had been picked after four weeks and 77 percent after six weeks. The figures for Democratic delegates were comparable (Mayer 1997). In 2000 the crucial primary date was March 7, when eleven states, including California and New York, held their primaries. This was just five weeks after the first primary in New Hampshire and three months before the final primaries.

The scheduling of state primaries can have an important impact on the nomination. The trend toward front-loading has made it almost impossible for a candidate who is not one of the front-runners to come from behind and take the lead in the early weeks of the primary season when a large proportion of delegates are being chosen. This has made it more important for candidates to get a head start as George W. Bush did in 1999 for the 2000 nomination.

The front-loading phenomenon had one other impact on state parties. In presidential election years some states have held their state primaries at the same time as the presidential primary to increase voter turnout in both primaries and to save money. Relatively few states nominate a governor in presidential years, but they do nominate other candidates. If only one party has a serious contest for the presidential nomination (with no incumbent running, for example), this linkage may increase turnout more in that party's state primary than in the other, with unpredictable results. The front-loading trend, however, has pushed many of the presidential primaries to an earlier date than is ideal for state primaries, and a few states that have held their state primaries later in the year have separated the two types of primaries.

There is one other linkage between presidential nominations and state politics that deserves mention. It is possible that party leaders and activists in a state may be so deeply divided over the choice of a presidential nominee that state party unity is undermined, at least for a few years. Even though today state party leaders play much smaller roles in the nominating process, it is possible that a presidential election will attract to a state party new groups of political activists who are committed to a particular candidate for the presidential nomination. The newcomers may have an ideological position that is different from or at least stronger than that of veteran party activists. This phenomenon occurred during Ronald Reagan's campaigns from 1976 through 1984 and made many state Republican parties more conservative.

The clearest examples of these divisions in the Republican Party during the 1990s came from activists who are strongly committed to the religious right. Perhaps they worked in presidential races for Pat Robertson in the 1988 race or in more recent years for other presidential candidates who appealed to the religious right. In state races many of them have supported candidates who emphasized issues promoted by the religious right. Some of these activists will remain active in the party, perhaps trying to win leadership positions in the state and local parties.

ELECTING MEMBERS OF CONGRESS

The state parties have a larger role to play in the nomination and election of U.S senators and representatives than do national parties. Elections to the U.S. House and Senate are at the intersection of state and national politics. The state and local parties are very interested in electing their candidates for congressional offices, and from their perspective the U.S. Senate race is second in importance only to the gubernatorial contest. The Senate race takes on added importance to the party when an incumbent or recent governor of that party runs for the Senate, as frequently happens. Candidates for these congressional races usually run their own campaigns but are likely to get various kinds of help from the state and local party organizations, such as registering voters and getting out the vote. State and local parties, and occasionally the national party, are often active in recruiting the best possible candidate to challenge a congressional incumbent or to run when no incumbent is running. Both the national congressional campaign committees and the state parties help to raise money for congressional candidates, a topic we will return to later in this chapter.

Members of the U.S. Senate and the House are very often among the most important leaders in the state party organization. If the party does not control the governorship, they may assume even more influence. U.S. representatives assume greater importance in states with only a few congressional districts. Both senators and representatives usually have some influence over the selection of a party chair and have a voice in the state party's budgetary priorities. Individuals who regularly work in their campaigns are valuable members of the party's pool of activists.

In discussing gubernatorial elections, we have pointed out that incumbents in the Senate usually have a somewhat better chance of getting elected (about 87 percent) than do governors (about 80 percent). Governors and senators both run statewide, which means that their constituencies include a wide variety of different and sometimes conflicting interests. The increasing two-party competition at the state level means that relatively few states now consistently elect either Democrats or Republicans in statewide races. We know that one reason senators are somewhat more likely than governors to get reelected is that voters usually do not hold them personally responsible when Congress raises taxes or cuts back spending for popular programs. In fact, voters seldom know much about what positions senators take and how they vote on most issues, unlike governors, whose positions generally are more widely known.

Members of the U.S. House have a slightly better chance of being reelected (about 93 percent) than do U.S. senators. Of course, in the long run they are handicapped by having to face the voters three times as often as senators do. Representatives enjoy the same advantage as senators. Their positions and voting record on issues are not well known, and they are seldom held responsible by their constituents for something Congress has done or failed to do.

But representatives have a number of advantages that senators lack, most of which result from the fact that they come from individual districts that are much smaller than a senator's constituency, particularly in a state with five to ten million people or more. The average House district has about 600,000 residents. A single district should be easier to represent because it is more homogeneous, with a smaller number of possibly conflicting interests. It may be entirely located in a central city, several suburbs, or a small town–rural area. A single district is much more likely to be safely Democratic or Republican than most states are. A representative in one of the more populous states is better able than a senator to know a district well and to become well acquainted with its leading citizens. A representative has more time and much more opportunity to provide services to individuals who have problems in dealing with the government and to help communities or businesses receive assistance from the government. Finally a single district has a much smaller pool of potential challengers who are experienced and politically skillful.

Members of the U.S. House often maintain a close working relationship with state legislators located in their districts. Some members of Congress served in the state legislature and have maintained personal friendships with former colleagues. Members of Congress, particularly representatives, work closely with state legislators in trying to obtain federal projects and programs for communities in their districts. They may even cooperate in providing services to individual constituents. U.S. representatives and state legislators of the same party sometimes hold joint town meetings or campaign together in their district.

U.S. representatives have another reason for maintaining good working relationships with members of the state legislature, particularly those in their party. Every ten years many state legislatures have to redraw both congressional and legislative districts. Even if the state neither gains nor loses any congressional seats, boundaries at both levels must be redrawn to meet the judicial requirement that they be approximately equal in population.

Each state party naturally would prefer to gain seats in both the congressional delegation and the state legislature. Every U.S. representative has slightly different priorities: making a few changes in district boundaries to produce a district that is a little safer in partisan terms while avoiding major boundary changes because they have been working hard to cultivate their present constituents. If the state is losing one or more House seats as a result of the census, the stakes are particularly high. Those members of the U.S. House who are popular and have established good contacts in the legislature have an advantage over other members.

The state and national parties work most closely together during election campaigns. Cooperative action becomes particularly important in states where close races are anticipated for seats in the Senate or the House. The national party organizations are efficient in targeting races that are likely to be close, but they may fail to identify some of the races that will be close. The national party and congressional party organizations can send resources in the form of money or services, a topic covered later in this chapter. They may succeed in running coordinated campaigns in some parts of the state. Staff members from the national party may arrive to give advice to congressional candidates; such advice is sometimes resented if the candidates don't believe that the experts from Washington know anything about politics in their state. National leaders such as the president often visit states to raise money and campaign for congressional candidates.

The national party sometimes will provide similar forms of assistance to a gubernatorial candidate who is in a close race. The national party has several reasons for wanting to win as many gubernatorial races as possible, particularly in heavily populated states. Usually the party that controls the governorship is healthier and stronger than the one that does not. A strong party, of course, can help elect candidates for Congress and the presidency. Someone who is elected or reelected governor with substantial help from the national party leadership has reason to be supportive of those leaders in a variety of ways.

STATE PARTIES: CAPTIVES OR PARTNERS?

State parties need money to hold their own in today's technological campaigns. The national committees have vastly greater fund-raising potential than the states, and they are widely perceived as dominating their weaker partners in exchange for the money to function as effective organizations. It is possible to examine this money relationship because much of it is reported to the Federal Election Commission (FEC) and the rest to state campaign finance agencies. This section is concerned with the money relationship between the state parties and their national partners. Are strong state parties better able to maintain their independence, and do the national committees bestow their largess on weaker parties hoping to increase their capability? What do the national committees consider when they target state parties for funding?

Fifty years ago a landmark report, "Toward a More Responsible Two-Party System," noted that the two parties operated "as two loose associations of state and local organizations, with very little national machinery and very little national cohesion" (APSA 1950, v). It further stated that there was no central figure or organ that could claim authority to take up party problems, policies, and strategy. The report called for a change in state organization, methods, and objectives in the interest of creating a higher degree of party responsibility. "Consideration should be given to the development of additional means of dealing with rebellious and disloyal state organizations"(p. 6).

Most of the party reforms since that report have dealt with the relationship between the state and national parties, particularly with respect to national control over the membership of national committees and conventions. In the past two decades national-scale fund-raising capabilities have further altered that relationship. To understand this connection between the national committees and their state parties, party executive directors in thirty political parties in fifteen states were sent a questionnaire. The questions asked about the impact of hard and soft money coming from the national parties on their party's activities and autonomy, their relationship with their legislative campaign committees, and their views on campaign finance reform. These questionnaires and the follow-up interviews are an extremely valuable source of information about the condition of state parties today, and we will quote the directors frequently. Their names and the year of the interview are listed in parentheses after each quotation.

The fifteen states (including nine of the largest) and therefore thirty state parties were also examined for contributions and spending for both state and national candidates. The FEC reports for two-year election cycles for presidential and congressional elections—the year preceding the election and the election year. The election cycle of 1995–1996 was studied extensively, and the following election cycle of 1997–1998 was reported in time for a brief comparison. Therefore state money raising in a presidential election year could be compared with money raising in a gubernatorial election year (thirty-six states elected governors in 1998). Campaign finance reports filed with the state election agencies as well as the FEC were collected and examined.

In the presidential election of 1996 the national parties raised vast sums of soft money for issue advocacy. Hence this inquiry tests the monetary relationship between the state party and national party during an election cycle when the national party would be expected to dominate.

The Rules: Federal Money, Nonfederal Money, and State Money

Laws and regulations that apply to congressional and presidential candidates are not the same as those in effect in state legislative and gubernatorial elections. Laws that apply to what parties on the state level may receive and spend are very different from those that apply to what the national parties may receive and spend. The constitutional mandate of federalism applies to the financing of politics at the different levels of government, but as we shall see this mandate is extremely difficult to understand.

Federal money. To begin with, there are limits on how much money may be given to national and state parties to support federal candidates. Corporations and labor unions may not contribute to or spend money directly for candidates or parties in connection with a federal election. PACs may give up to $15,000 a year, and individuals up to $20,000, to a national party for expenditures to affect a federal election. (Both individuals and PACs may give $5,000 to state parties to use for federal candidates.) This money—which may be given to parties for federal elections, plus the money that may be given to federal candidates by individuals, PACs, or parties—is called federal money, or hard money, and is regulated by federal law.

State and national parties are allowed to spend federally regulated money on behalf of individual congressional candidates if it is spent in direct coordination with the candidate. The Federal Elections Campaign Act strictly limits the amount a party committee may spend in coordination with a federal candidate ($35,000 for a House candidate in 2000). State party committees are allowed to spend the same coordinated amounts in House and Senate races as the national party organizations. But a state party may assign its spending authority to a national party committee, in effect doubling the amount the national committee can spend ($70,000 for a House candidate). These assignments, known as agency agreements, effectively allow a national committee to spend the total amount allowed the national and state party committees in a House or Senate race. Because these expenditures are coordinated expenditures, both the party and the candidate share control over them, thereby giving the party some influence over how these monies are spent. This fact is considered by the state committees before they enter into agency agreements with the national party committees. They want to be sure a congressional or senatorial campaign committee will do justice to their candidate.

Most of the executive directors who answered the questionnaire were satisfied with the agency agreements, claiming that their candidates could usually run their own campaigns. And most executive directors said that the hard money coming from the national committees had little impact on the autonomy of their parties. However, the Illinois Republican director said the national party once wanted to run an issue ad in a southern Illinois district of which the state party did not approve, so they did not enter into a cooperative arrangement for that district (Christine Dudley 1998). The Connecticut Republicans prefer to raise money within the state and the candidates' districts but recognize that coordinated spending "increases competitiveness" (George Gallo 1998). Generally speaking, the national and state party committees work together to determine how best to allocate their resources to provide the greatest benefit to their candidates in targeted races (usually challengers and open-seat candidates) (Corrado 1997). These coordinated expenditures are made only with federally regulated monies.

Federal court rulings could alter these limits on coordinated expenditures for congressional candidates. In 1999 a U.S. district judge removed all limits on how much the parties can spend for their federal candidates. The ruling, in a long-running case from Colorado, threw out spending limits as an unconstitutional infringement on the parties' freedom of speech. The FEC voted to appeal the case (Glasser 1999), and the appellate court upheld the decision in May 2000. Note that we are talking about federal money here, money that is raised and spent for federal candidates according to federal law.

In an earlier round of the Colorado case, the Supreme Court ruled in 1996 that the parties could spend in excess of the federal limits as long as they operated independently of their candidates. The National Republican Senatorial Committee set up spending units to operate independently in the final few months of the 1996 campaign; Democrats later followed suit. Both parties claim it is cumbersome to set up separate entities that are prohibited from coordinating their activities with the candidates they are supporting. The 1999 Colorado ruling, which election lawyers expect will end up back at the Supreme Court, removes the requirement that the parties operate independently of their own candidates if they spend beyond set limits. As the presidential cycle of 1999–2000 began, political parties were planning to raise as much hard (federal) money as possible in anticipation of either coordinated or independent spending.

Nonfederal money. In general, nonfederal money—or soft money as it is commonly called—refers to unlimited contributions that are funneled through the nonfederal accounts of the national parties and state party committees and that are prohibited from being used in connection with federal elections. Soft money may be used for party overhead expenses as well as shared activities that benefit all candidates. Soft money is raised in excess of the federal contribution limits or from federally prohibited sources. Soft money is subject only to the laws of the state where it is spent. Thus if a state allows unlimited corporate and union contributions to state parties, the nonfederal portion of any "generic" party activity in that state can be paid for with unlimited corporate or union funds. On the other hand, if a state imposed contribution limits on parties that were at least as strict as the federal law, there would be no soft money "loophole" in that state. Twenty-four states place limits on contributions to state parties, but some of them allow very generous contributions.

In the states these soft money funds are used to enhance the whole national, state, and local tickets by supporting volunteer and grassroots party-building activities such as voter registration and identification, certain types of campaign material (slate cards), voter turnout programs, and issue advertising without violating the limits imposed on party contributions and expenditures made in connection with a federal election.

Federal court rulings handed down in the late 1980s required the FEC to allocate the costs of state party administrative expenses and the cost of generic (grassroots) activities mentioned above that indirectly affect all candidates in ways that reflected the proportion of federal and nonfederal candidates on the ballot. State parties pay for these general overhead expenses from two funds: federal money for the federal portion and nonfederal money for the state portion. In 1996, a presidential election year, Minnesota parties paid out 60 percent in federal money and 40 percent in nonfederal money for expenses incurred for administrative and grassroots efforts. In 1998, a gubernatorial election year, the allocation formula was 17 percent federal and 83 percent nonfederal.

In 1996 both national parties also spent a significant amount of soft money for the first time on issue advocacy ads designed to promote party issue positions. These ads did not expressly advocate the election or defeat of particular federal candidates and were used to publicize the parties' positions on the administration's health care proposal, the 1995 federal budget debate, President Clinton's first-term record, and issues related to the 1996 congressional races. Increasingly these ads have been run in states and congressional districts with the obvious purpose of helping a particular congressional candidate without explicitly urging people to vote for or against any candidate.

These ads must be paid for with a combination of hard and soft money according to the FEC formula. As we explained, the soft money is raised in the states according to state laws, which may or may not be stricter than the federal limits. For example, in 1996 the Democratic national party committees transferred $1 million in soft money to the Connecticut state party. Much of the money was spent on television ads promoting the record of President Clinton and the Democratic Party. The funds also were used to help pay the salaries of a fifteen-member campaign staff that worked on behalf of both federal and state Democratic candidates. Some of the soft money was contributed directly to state candidates. One candidate for the state Senate received $45,000 from the party soft money account (Common Cause 1998, 6). Although this may sound sensational, this "soft" money came from the national party's individual account because Connecticut law bans money raised from corporations and unions. So the soft money that was transferred to Connecticut was from an account that was raised from individuals by the Democratic National Committee. Naturally the Connecticut Democrats welcomed receipt of the $1 million, but it was not raised in unlimited amounts from corporations and unions. Generally, both the state and the national parties raise soft money to pay for these issue ads.

State money. Many state party executive directors speak of money that is raised and spent according to state laws as state money rather than as nonfederal (soft) money. There are twenty-four states where contributions by individuals and PACs to political parties are limited, and twelve of these states have stricter limits than the federal ones (that is, no soft money loophole). Table 3-2, in Chapter 3, shows what these contribution limits are. In these states the parties have to raise the money to pay for the nonfederal share of administrative and generic activities according to state law. Furthermore, they may not accept soft money from the national party unless it has been raised according to state law.

In twenty-four states (including thirteen of the above) the parties are limited in what they may contribute to statewide candidates. Eleven of the states without contribution limits to parties have limits on party spending for candidates. Their inability to spend much money on their candidates offers an unusual opportunity for the national parties to send soft money funds to these states to be used, for example, for issue advocacy.

One night the Democratic National Committee (DNC) wired $150,000 to the Minnesota Democratic Party account with the instructions that the money be transferred the next morning to a New York advertising agency. This appears to make the Minnesota Democrats into a conduit for the DNC's purposes, but it must be remembered that the issue ads had to be paid for according to the FEC formula for Minnesota (40 percent soft money and 60 percent federal money).

Obviously the regulatory environment in a state structures the way parties try to help their candidates. Malbin and Gais (1998) report that Minnesota's rules for political parties did not accomplish their goal, which was to limit the power of interest groups and increase the importance of parties. Minnesota parties may receive unlimited contributions from individuals and PACs, but they may not contribute more than $20,000 to the governor's campaign. Both these goals would be better served if contributions to the parties were limited and contributions by the parties to candidates were not. We anticipate that state parties faced with spending limits may spend independently to help their state candidates, in line with the Supreme Court's 1996 decision in *Colorado Republican Federal Campaign Committee v. Federal Election Commission,* which held that unlimited independent spending by a political party has the same First Amendment protection as unlimited spending by an individual or group (Malbin and Gais 1998, 123–130). The Colorado ruling applied to federal money, but it may become the entering wedge in a universal application. In fact, in 1999 a federal district court judge in Minnesota ruled that state party independent spending could not be limited.

Thirty-five states have some limitations on contributions to or spending by state parties or both. These parties may not accept or spend national party soft money unless it is in conformity with state law. For instance, New York parties can receive soft money from the national committees if it is raised in $69,900 or smaller increments from individuals and PACs. Seven states limit the total amount of money coming to the state party from the national party. New Jersey has passed a law that limits the amount of soft money from the national committees to a total of $59,000 per year; Hawaii limits soft money to $50,000, and Kansas limits soft money to $25,000 per year. Other states that place much stricter limits of under $5,000 are California, Colorado, Vermont, and West Virginia. Some states (Massachusetts, South Carolina, and Washington) specify that soft money can be unlimited if it goes to administrative and housekeeping accounts (which is not much of a limitation).

Connecticut passed a law in 1998 that bans the receipt of soft money from the national committees. The Connecticut bill passed the state Senate unanimously and the House by a 146–3 vote. The Republican executive director said, "We would prefer not to have soft money exist as an option. We have been forced to beg national officials for some funds simply to compete with the opposition. Our position is that soft money takes the power away from our local base" (George Gallo 1998). The governor said proudly that Connecticut was the first state in the nation to explicitly ban soft money from state politics.

It is important to recognize that the national parties are able to raise unlimited nonfederal (soft money) funds from sources that are not permitted under the federal contribution limits. In 1995–1996 the DNC raised $124 million and the RNC raised $138 million in soft money (about a third of what they raised in total hard and soft funds). These funds, which are placed in nonfederal accounts, are used to support national overhead and fund-raising expenses as well as to support state parties. National committees can raise this money in the states, but they often do so as a joint fund raiser with the state parties, who have insisted that they are entitled to a negotiated share of the "take." According to the Texas Democrats, they are financing a lot of the DNC budget. Texas donors contribute to a huge fund raiser, and the Texas party asks for its share with the threat that its donors may not be as generous the next time if the share is not forthcoming (Jorge Ramirez 1998). The New York Democratic Party asked for 25 percent of all the profits from DNC fund raisers in 1998 but received 7.5 percent. Chair Judith Hope said, "We raised over $1.2 million in 1997. Let me tell you what the DNC contributed to the state party in 1997: $6,600" (Nagourney 1998, B1). No wonder the New York parties want their share: More soft money is raised by the national parties in New York than any other state.

This discussion was intended to emphasize the fact that the rules under which each state party operates are sovereign with respect to what the party may raise and spend for state candidates. The national committees may not give money to a state party unless the contribution conforms to rules in that state. On the other hand, federal rules with respect to congressional candidates are sovereign. State parties may not support their congressional candidates with state money (unless, of course, it is raised according to federal standards). Areas of overlap are the administrative and generic expenses to benefit the whole ticket; these are paid from both federal and nonfederal (or state) money accounts according to a formula set by the FEC for each election cycle.

National Parties and State Parties: Financial Partners

Table 9-1 reports the total picture of state party finances for the fifteen selected states, including funds raised for state election accounts as well as the state-raised percentage of funds in the federal and nonfederal accounts for 1995–1996. The data were gleaned in part from each state party's campaign finance reports filed with the state elections division. These reports contained the party's contributions and expenditures for state election activity for state candidates. Also collected were each state party's campaign finance reports filed with the FEC, which contained contributions and expenditures for combined state and national party activity (allocated between federal and nonfederal money according to ballot composition).

The states are arranged by population in Table 9-1. The first column represents all money raised from all sources. Included here are funds raised by the state committees as well as legislative campaign committees (LCCs), plus what was raised by the state and national committees for the "allocable" activity (activity allocated between federal and nonfederal funding). The second column lists funds raised by the state parties as a percentage of the entire state funding from all sources. The third and fourth columns give the total funds raised for the federal account and the amount raised by the state toward this account. The fifth and sixth columns give the funds raised in the nonfederal, soft money account and the percentage of state funds raised for that account.

The 1950 American Political Science Association Committee on Political Parties would gaze with amazement and approval at the financial division of responsibility between the state and national parties displayed in Table 9-1. This was a presidential election–year cycle; none of the fifteen states had gubernatorial elections during the period that might have demanded a greater share of state

Table 9-1 State Party Percentage of Various Categories of Funds, 1995–1996
(thousands)

State Party	Funds Raised from All Sources[a]		Funds Raised for Federal Account[b]		Funds Raised for Nonfederal Account[b]	
	Total	% from State Party	Total	% from State Party	Total	% from State Party
California						
Democratic	$32,877	39	$8,110	88	$11,889	36
Republican	24,147	38	7,900	68	7,002	0
Texas						
Democratic	14,441	32	4,617	65	5,141	55
Republican	9,698	11	5,093	90	3,496	40
New York						
Democratic	15,573	78	1,912	86	1,534	96
Republican	27,641	76	2,328	98	4,256	80
Florida						
Democratic	23,238	62	3,306	37	5,459	29
Republican	31,951	62	5,756	85	6,471	78
Pennsylvania						
Democratic	15,840	54	2,459	36	4,776	0
Republican	14,839	65	2,570	69	2,630	8
Illinois						
Democratic	16,464	60	2,854	56	3,662	32
Republican	17,222	70	3,265	68	1,882	6
Ohio						
Democratic	17,311	50	3,259	51	5,399	25
Republican	24,406	56	6,357	77	4,448	27
New Jersey						
Democratic	10,101	62	1,969	78	1,855	90
Republican	21,743	65	3,313	87	4,348	96
Georgia						
Democratic	12,905	51	3,174	83	3,125	54
Republican	31,358	83	2,497	73	2,900	16
Tennessee						
Democratic	5,072	42	1,443	22	1,478	0
Republican	7,892	45	2,944	75	1,376	0
Minnesota						
Democratic	12,435	39	4,512	70	2,968	47
Republican	11,585	59	3,069	95	1,664	71
Colorado						
Democratic	8,525	36	2,496	55	3,080	38
Republican	8,432	34	2,256	73	1,362	14
Connecticut						
Democratic	3,758	35	1,360	75	1,059	7
Republican	3,142	46	1,134	75	557	100

Table 9-1 (*continued*)

State Party	Funds Raised from All Sources[a]		Funds Raised for Federal Account[b]		Funds Raised for Nonfederal Account[b]	
	Total	% from State Party	Total	% from State Party	Total	% from State Party
Oregon						
Democratic	4,499	5	2,480	65	1,785	4
Republican	2,171	7	1,694	72	335	25
Kansas						
Democratic	3,089	21	1,542	64	886	87
Republican	1,189	36	684	68	79	70

Sources: Campaign finance reports filed with the secretaries of state, elections divisions, in the fifteen states as well as state reports filed with the FEC.

[a]This includes funds raised for state election accounts as well as funds raised for federal and nonfederal accounts.

[b]This includes total funds raised by state committees, national committees, and senatorial and congressional campaign committees for the state.

funding. The major effort on the state level was elections for the state legislature. Thus it is impressive that the thirty state parties contributed an average of 50 percent of the total fund raising in a presidential election year, and some states contributed a great deal more than that. Except for the Oregon parties, which are dependent on their national parties for sustenance, the parties maintained their autonomy while substantially helping their national parties.

"State party organizations must raise at least enough funds under federal rules to pay the federal portion of their general overhead expenses" (Biersack 1996, 111). Apparently this is not a great problem for the state parties since the average state share contributed toward the federal account in 1996 was 73 percent. In the 1997–1998 cycle the state parties contributed an average of 79 percent toward the federal account. The state Democratic Parties raised 70 percent of their hard money, and the state Republicans 85 percent of the hard money total. In other words, state parties contribute a very large share of the money raised according to federal law to be used by their party for overhead expenses.

The national parties have been raising nonfederal money in huge amounts since 1995, and they are running short of the federal funds needed to pay, for instance, for congressional races. Meanwhile the state parties raise money in smaller contributions to conform to state law or simply because their citizens are not large donors and money raised this way conforms to federal law as hard money. Some state parties, such as the Connecticut and Ohio Democrats, "sell" federal money for nonfederal money to their national partners and make a profit by doing so—a 10–15 percent commission according to Common Cause (1998).

Most state party executive directors claim that they are not dependent on soft money even in a presidential election year. According to the executive director of the Georgia Republicans, "We are not addicted, but we take what we can get" (Joe King 1998). Other executive directors claimed soft money was somewhat useful but that they could get by without it if it were cut off for some reason. The executive director of the Pennsylvania Republicans said it was valuable for voter contacting but that they were not very dependent upon soft money (Hank Hollowell 1998). State parties do not raise nonfederal money as avidly as they raise federal money, and the average percentage contributed by the state party to the soft money account is about 40 percent. There is a great diversity among the states with regard to this form of funding, which leads to speculation about which states are most likely to receive this federal largess. These are the funds that pay for a large portion of the administrative and generic activities and issue advertising.

According to the Illinois Republican executive director, national parties use several criteria in deciding how to bestow nonfederal money upon a state party in a presidential year (Christine Dudley 1998):

1. Targeted state party: closeness of the race for president, senator, and members of Congress.
2. Ability to present a case for needed funds.
3. Strength of state party organization.
4. State laws regulating campaign finance.

The first criterion is the closeness of the race for president in the state. If close, then soft money is usually forthcoming in large amounts. In 1996 California was a targeted state because of the closeness of the race (13 percent margin of victory for President Clinton). New York, with a 28 percent margin for the president, was not targeted and had to raise most of the modest amount of nonfederal money itself. A second standard is the ability to present a good case to the national party for the use of the funds. Christine Dudley made a case for slate cards and absentee ballots and voter identification programs (1998), and Table 9-1 shows that the national Republicans funded 94 percent of the nearly $2 million contributed to the Illinois Republicans. The strength of the state party organization and its leadership is another of the criteria. The strictness of the state laws regarding the raising and contributing of money may have an impact since the national parties must abide by these rules when sending soft money; however, this factor did not appear to affect the amount of nonfederal money bestowed upon a state.

A statistical examination of the reasons why national parties contribute nonfederal (soft) money to their state parties showed that the closeness of the presidential race explained a sizable portion (27 percent). This is a start toward explaining the causes of national party assistance to state parties in a presidential election year.

In the midterm elections, when the national parties focus on races for the

Senate and the House, the closeness of those races may determine the amount of nonfederal money allocated to the state parties. In addition, thirty-six states have gubernatorial races in those years, and a friendly occupant in the governor's mansion is an asset two years hence. Soft money raising increased continuously from 1992 until the 1995–1996 presidential cycle (when it reached a high of $124 million for Democrats and $138 million for Republicans). Understandably the midterm election cycle of 1997–1998 showed a decrease of 14 percent over the presidential election cycle. In spite of this the amount of soft money more than doubled since the midterm election of 1994: Republican soft money accounts raised $131.6 million, a 151 percent increase over 1993–1994, and Democrats collected $92.8 million, an 89 percent increase.

In 1998 the Republican Party sent $47 million and the Democratic Party sent $54 million in hard and soft money to their respective state parties. These figures did not include soft money contributions to state candidates directly (RNC— $11,108, DNC—$3,764). They do not appear generous when we consider that the national Republican Party (including the Senate and House affiliates) raised $362 million and the national Democratic committees raised $218 million.

Perhaps a table comparing the presidential election year money relationships with the gubernatorial election year money relationships would help. Table 9-2 gives that comparison. In 1996, the presidential election year, the national parties sent more money to their state partners than they did in 1998. This was the beginning of the use of issue advertising, which is paid for with both hard and soft money. The national parties wanted to win the presidency, so they sent generous amounts of soft money to their state affiliates. Table 9-2 gives the percentages of federal (hard) and nonfederal (soft) money that were dispersed to the state parties. Surprisingly the percentage of hard (federal) and soft (nonfederal) money in the total outlay for each state party in each year did not change very much. What changed, of course, was the total amount between a presidential and a midterm year. The Democrats, who raised $124 million in soft money in 1996, gave more than half of it to their state parties. The Republicans, the superior money raisers, raised $138 million in soft money and gave 36 percent of it to their state parties. We noted that one major reason for giving generously to a particular state party was the closeness of the race for president.

The midterm election year of 1998 was not as robust for the national committees. The amounts and the percentages dropped. This is particularly noticeable in the nonfederal transfers to the states. The Democrats, whose soft money fund raising dropped from $124 million to $93 million, dropped its national committee transfers from $54 million to $12 million. The Republicans, whose national soft money account dropped from $138 million to $132 million, went from $48 million to $21 million in state transfers. The hard money transfers from the national committees also dropped from 1996 to 1998, as Table 9-2 shows.

Table 9-2 National Party Committees' Transfer of Funds to State Parties (thousands)

Party Organization Federal or Nonfederal Funds	Democrats		Republicans	
	1996	1998	1996	1998
National committee				
Federal	$20,155	$3,300	$18,078	$7,003
Nonfederal	54,194	12,280	48,219	20,701
Senate committee				
Federal	4,656	12,151	396	2,957
Nonfederal	5,860	15,597	1,642	11,631
Congressional committee				
Federal	4,229	3,486	—	2,638
Nonfederal	4,545	6,888	385	1,989
Total for all committees				
Federal	29,040	18,940	18,474	12,598
Nonfederal	64,599	34,765	50,246	34,321
Total funds	93,639	53,705	68,720	46,919
Percentage of federal and nonfederal money going to states				
Federal	31%	35%	27%	27%
Nonfederal	69%	65%	73%	73%

Source: Federal Election Commission.

Lest you think the national committees abandoned their state partners, have a look at the Senate and congressional committees. Recall that this is a congressional election year and the national parties want congressional majorities. The Democrats wanted to hold or increase their numbers, as is evident by their giving to the state parties. The Democratic Senatorial Campaign Committee increased its federal and nonfederal transfers from $10.5 million to $28.5 million in the effort. The Republicans increased their money on behalf of their senators from $2 million to $15 million. The Republican congressional committees also increased their totals. Clearly it was a year to pay attention to Congress. We suspect that certain states received money depending upon the closeness of their Senate or House races. This suspicion has yet to be proved. As long as soft money can be raised, it will be distributed to state parties and the criteria for its distribution remain a fertile question.

A final observation, which puts some of this money discussion into perspective, is the comparison between the amounts of money transfers from the national committees to their state partners and the magnitude of gubernatorial spending for 1998. A sobering observation is the amount spent by the gubernatorial candidates for all thirty-six gubernatorial races in 1998, which was $471 million! (Beyle 1999). The total amount of money given by the national parties to all states in 1998 was $100 million (Table 9-2). The cost of the California gubernatorial race alone was $125 million, and the national committees gave their California partners about $11 million that year. Even if we subtract the extravagant primary, the gubernatorial general election cost $53 million, and the national parties obviously did not fund much of it. Lest we think the national committees are capturing their state partners by overpowering them with money, we should have a look at some of our larger states.

A PARTNERSHIP OF STRENGTH

Many state political party organizations are becoming stronger, not weaker. The old-style patronage-driven, labor-intensive party operation has disappeared. For those who bemoan its demise, the executive director of the Minnesota DFL said, "Even my church uses caterers for funerals" (Kathy Czar 1998). Parties have adapted themselves to the new technology and provide valuable services to state and national candidates. They began this process of adaptation well before the infusion of money from their national committees. In fact, party development within state parties paralleled the resurgence of national party organizations. As the national parties became stronger and richer, they needed to build up their state partners because of the increasing competition in every state. This remedy was suggested fifty years ago by the APSA report titled "Toward a More Responsible Two-Party System."

The relationship between the national parties and their state parties has never been closer than it is today. Ironically, in view of the APSA report, it was also predicted that the state parties would become "nationalized" and would lose their independence as they became financially bound to their wealthy national partners. Since the late 1970s the national parties have built up their state parties, providing cash grants, professional staff, data processing and consulting services, and expertise in fund raising, campaigning, media, and redistricting. State parties now are proficient in voter list development and get-out-the-vote efforts. Far from the predicted party decline, however, they have become "parties in service" (Aldrich 1995). They have developed mutually beneficial relationships with candidate-centered campaigns and legislative campaign committees. And they contribute on average half of all party money spent within their borders in a presidential election year.

In view of this evidence, it is clear that state parties are not decomposing, as academics and journalists have been predicting, but they have been adapting to the media-driven society in which they find themselves. They provide needed technical information and financial resources to candidates. They have maintained their autonomy as they became more professionalized and durable.

10 Conclusions

Throughout this book we have developed the main themes articulated in the introduction:

- State political parties are alive and well, and they are constantly changing.
- The political party system in each of the states is different because of variations in traditional political culture and current political realities.
- The role of money in state party and electoral systems is changing and becoming more complex.
- The relationships between national and state parties are changing and becoming more important.

We expect these trends to continue in the twenty-first century, but our crystal ball is much too cloudy for any predictions about exactly what changes will occur in the years ahead. Our society is changing in many ways that are obvious to all of us, and few of these changes were clearly foreseen a decade ago. Nearly all institutions—corporations, universities, voluntary groups, and even churches—must continually change in order to survive or at least to be effective in a changing world. There is no reason why state and national political parties should be an exception to this rule.

We have described some of the ways in which state and local parties are changing. Parties must win the support of voters for their candidates instead of simply mobilizing party loyalists and getting them to the polls. To attract new activists and workers to the ranks, political parties must give them a chance to influence policy instead of relying primarily on patronage. As state elections become more competitive at the statewide level, and two-party balance in many legislatures becomes closer, it is more important than ever for political parties to target races and recruit party candidates. Because many of a party's candidates can run their campaigns independently, the party must be able to offer them various kinds of services, from money raising and issue development to getting potential voters to the polls. It goes without saying that state parties must make good use of computer technology and the Internet for record keeping, research, and communication with other party organizations and individuals. To carry out these functions and provide these services effectively, the state parties must raise more money than ever and make skillful choices about priorities for spending it.

EVALUATING THE PARTIES

How effectively are state parties adapting to the changes that have been occurring? As some party functions assume greater importance, are they getting higher priority from the parties? Some parties are adapting better than others, of course, and some functions are getting more attention than others. Most state parties realize that providing funding and services to their candidates has become a major part of their responsibilities, but in practice some aspects of the job are done better than others.

The Nominating Process

We believe that as statewide elections become more competitive, the political parties need to give greater attention to nominating the strongest possible candidate. As we have seen (in Chapter 4), the state parties that make endorsements in statewide races sometimes fail to get their endorsee nominated. This may happen because the party convention has not endorsed the strongest candidate available or has failed to unite behind the candidate who is endorsed. In some parties the state and local party organizations have failed to provide enough support, financial and otherwise, to get even a strong endorsed candidate nominated. This suggests that some state parties need stronger leadership and need to take the whole endorsement process more seriously.

We are surprised that the endorsement system has not spread to more state organizations. One would think that some of the state parties that have been losing elections because they have had weak nominees would at least explore the possibility of experimenting with the endorsement process, which works—however imperfectly—in a number of states.

Almost fifty years ago V. O. Key, Jr. (1956, chap. 6) concluded that the growth of the direct primary had contributed to the "atrophy of party organization" by minimizing the role of state and local parties in the nominating process. Preprimary endorsements, however, can help the parties emerge. We discovered that many of the state convention delegates who reported that they favored continuation of the endorsement system gave as one of their major reasons the fact that it enhanced the role of party activists (see Chapter 4). These findings suggest that the adoption of a well-organized endorsement system might not only improve the quality of candidates nominated but also strengthen the party organization at the state and local levels.

Open primaries weaken the parties' influence over the nominating process because they permit voters who are not registered or otherwise identified with a party to vote in the party's primary. There has been a trend toward more states using open primaries and, in closed primary states, toward permitting unaffiliated voters to enter a party's primary without prior party registration. The most dramatic example occurred in California, where, in 1996, the voters initiated a shift from a closed primary to a blanket primary—the most extreme form of open primary—but in June, 2000, the U.S. Supreme Court declared the blanket primary to be unconstitutional.

Recruiting and Supporting Candidates

State parties are making a greater effort to recruit and support candidates for office than they have in the past—at the statewide, congressional, and legislative levels. A major change has been the development of legislative party campaign committees—in which leaders play a key role—to recruit candidates, raise campaign funds, and provide legislative candidates with funding and campaign assistance. The responsibilities are shared in varying degrees with the state party organizations. Despite these efforts, we know that in many states many legislative seats go uncontested in every election.

There are several reasons why the parties leave many seats uncontested. Because parties usually have limited influence over nominations, they cannot guarantee that a potential recruit will be unopposed in the primary, and this reality hurts their recruiting efforts. The seats that go uncontested are, almost by definition, in areas where the party has a weak local base and it is hard to find candidates who will run when the prospects of winning are poor. The parties have developed sophisticated methods of targeting legislative districts based on past voting records. The advantage is that the party can more accurately identify districts that can be competitive if a good candidate can be found. If the party has limited resources, as it always does, it makes sense to use these resources for races that could be won, not for those that are hopeless.

The disadvantage of targeting is that this technique can also identify districts that are probably hopeless for the minority party, however strong the candidate. It may serve the party's interest, at least in the short run, not to try to recruit candidates in such districts or to provide much support to candidates who run on their own initiative. As a matter of strategy, one party—the Republicans, for example—may avoid running candidates in hopeless districts because doing so might cause the opposing party—in this case the Democrats—to turn out more voters in such districts. These voters would also cast votes in close statewide races that could tip the balance in favor of Democratic candidates.

On the other hand, two arguments can be advanced for recruiting candidates in apparently hopeless districts. It is a way to try out untested candidates and give them campaign experience. If a candidate does better than expected, he or she might be recruited for some other local office that could be winnable. Or conditions could change in a few years that would make the district less hopeless for an experienced candidate. The second argument for contesting hopeless seats is that some voters in such districts will respond to a choice if offered one. We know from examining gubernatorial primaries and general elections that candidates regarded by the experts as having no chance (as measured by their inability to raise much money) often get at least 20 or 30 percent of the vote. Members of the minority party in a district, city, or county who repeatedly find that their party is running no candidate for several offices may eventually shift their party allegiance or simply stop voting in most elections.

We have some doubt about whether political parties are doing a good enough job in identifying and grooming strong candidates for major statewide office, such as governor or senator. Often when a governor or senator steps down after several terms in office, there are several candidates eager to replace the incumbent, but they are not necessarily strong candidates. Even in states with relatively strong parties, a party that loses control of the governorship after several terms in power sometimes does a remarkably poor job of providing strong candidates to challenge the incumbent in subsequent elections.

An example of this occurred in New York, traditionally a strong party state. Republican Nelson Rockefeller was elected governor four times in the 1958–1970 period. The Democrats won the governorship in the next five elections, 1974–1990 (the last four times with Mario Cuomo). The last two times the Republicans ran hopelessly weak candidates who won less than one-third of the vote; obviously in those races the Republican endorsement process was ineffective. A similar situation took place in Ohio, which through the years has been one of the most competitive states in the country, with two strong parties. But in 1998, when Republican governor George Voinovich completed his second term and ran for the Senate, the Democrats ran a relatively unknown candidate whom Voinovich beat comfortably. As the 2000 election approached with the other Republican Senate seat on the ballot, Democrats were so desperate that for a while some of them promoted Jerry Springer. Springer was best known as the host of a national television talk show that was notorious because of the fistfights and wrestling matches that often broke out among the show's guests. The Democrats clearly needed to spend more time finding and grooming a suitable candidate.

How Effective Are State Parties?

We believe that state parties play a much more vital role in the political system than appeared to be the case in the 1950s and 1960s. But we have tried to avoid exaggerating the strength of state parties and have described some of their shortcomings.

These include the frequent inability to select nominees even in endorsing states; the gaps that occur in recruiting and supporting candidates, particularly for the legislature; and the ideological splits—particularly among party activists—that seriously divide some parties.

A number of political scientists have argued that political parties, especially at the state level, suffer from a variety of other weaknesses. This argument is made particularly well by Coleman (1994). It is always difficult to measure how much and in what ways party organizations actually affect the outcome of elections. Some surveys of legislative candidates (Frendreis and Gitelson 1999) have indicated that local party leaders may exaggerate the effectiveness of their organization's campaign activities. Election campaigns, particularly at the statewide and congressional levels, remain candidate-centered; the services provided by state parties to candidates give them influence but not usually control of the campaigns. Many party activists working in campaigns are strongly committed to particular issues and may help to nominate candidates who are not moderate enough to win election. In some states, such as Minnesota, that use preprimary party endorsements, there is concern about declining participation of party activists in local caucuses that select convention delegates, in part because it may enable relatively small numbers of zealous activists to control the caucuses.

The more serious questions about the effectiveness of state as well as national parties concern the attitude of voters toward the political system in general and the parties in particular. Public opinion surveys repeatedly show that many voters are disillusioned and cynical about politicians, campaigning, and political parties. There seems to be increasing criticism of negative advertising, which can be blamed on party organizations as well as candidates.

It is absolutely clear that over a number of years there has been a serious drop in voter turnout for elections at the federal, state, and local levels. Between 1960 and 1996 the percentage of the voting-age population voting in presidential elections fell from 65 percent to just above 50 percent; and between 1962 and 1998 the turnout for U.S. House races in nonpresidential years fell from 47 percent to 36 percent (Stanley and Niemi 2000, 12–13). It is not obvious to what extent a decline in turnout is caused by growing cynicism about the political system. Political parties can be blamed because their efforts to get out the vote are not more effective. A less obvious point is that when parties fail to nominate a full slate of candidates, voters have less incentive to vote. In 1998 there were forty-two U.S. House districts (almost 10 percent of the total) with only one candidate running.

It is often said that it is unrealistic to think that state and national parties can be growing more vigorous while the party loyalty of voters has been declining. But this is an outdated argument. As we have seen (Bartels 2000), the proportion of persons who are identified strongly with a party has been increasing steadily, and the proportion who are pure independents (not leaning toward either party) has been decreasing since 1972. The proportion of those identifying with a party who vote for that party's candidates for president has been going up steadily since 1972, and in congressional races a similar though less dramatic increase in party voting has been occurring since 1978 (Bartels 2000). We know the proportion of partisans voting for their party's candidate for governor, Congress, and president has generally ranged from 75 percent to 85 percent, with defections occurring largely when voters cast their ballot for an incumbent of the other party.

It is almost certainly true that fewer voters automatically cast a straight party vote when they go to the polls and that more split their ticket, particularly to vote for incumbents. But this is not a new phenomenon. From 1956 through 1996 the proportion of congressional districts carried by one party for president and another for the House seat averaged almost one-third, without any obvious trends over that forty-year period (Stanley and Niemi 2000, 44). Party loyalty among these voters in recent years has been growing stronger, not weaker, in a period when the parties show many signs of greater vitality.

DIFFERENCES AMONG THE STATE PARTIES

It is difficult in a book like this on comparative state politics to describe and explain the political differences among the states and the variations among 100 state parties. We can present tables that show how each state ranks on such factors as voter turnout, competitive primaries, and the frequency of divided government. And we can provide examples from individual states to illustrate points we are making. But there is not enough space to describe the political environment, the parties, and elections in each of the states, even if we knew each of the states well enough to provide such information. We hope students who discover that their state or state party ranks high or low on some scale will try to figure out the reason why and will gain some perspective on politics and parties in their state by learning what patterns are most common in the states.

Some of the differences among the state parties result from the impact of important past or present political leaders in the state. Political practitioners often think that political scientists do not pay enough attention to the human dimension, which is hard to quantify. For example, it is hard to understand the New York Republican Party without knowing something about former governor Nelson Rockefeller. Huey Long died in 1935, but his legacy still has some effect on the political culture of Louisiana. Republican politics in California has been shaped in part by former governors Earl Warren and Ronald Reagan. Illinois politics has been shaped in part by two of Chicago's mayors—Richard Daley and his son of the same name—who have served a total of more than thirty years. And, of course, the Kennedys have dominated Massachusetts Democratic politics since 1960.

There are several ways to measure the strength of state party organizations.

We think this is best accomplished by examining how well parties perform their important functions, including selecting and uniting behind party nominees, recruiting candidates and providing them with tangible support, attracting and organizing a pool of party activists, raising money, and, in the legislature, developing capable leaders and relatively cohesive parties.

Political scientists and their students can often learn more about state party systems, not only by compiling comparative data but also by observing and talking to politicians and party activists, preferably in more than a single state. When we visit state endorsing conventions and listen to the speeches and discussions on the floor, we can sense that the participants have a stronger commitment to the political party in some states than in others. There is a very strong commitment, for example, in both parties in Connecticut and in Minnesota. In New York conventions we sense that the long tradition of strong parties is being eroded in a variety of ways. There is no such tradition in California, where some ambivalence exists about the party's role in nominations. In New Mexico, with its tradition of weak parties, we think the delegates sometimes are not sure what endorsements are all about.

Through the years we have talked with leaders and members of many state legislatures about such things as leadership, representation, and party cohesion. It is clear that partisanship plays a larger role in the legislative process in some states than others. One explanation for the differences is the two-party balance in the legislature, and another is the degree to which each legislative party represents a set of constituents with different needs and interests. But another important factor is the strength of partisan norms, the extent of commitment the members feel to their party. Legislators with such a commitment usually feel comfortable supporting party positions on important issues. Leaders often told us that party discipline is a thing of the past, but party loyalty is as strong as ever.

Many years ago a political scientist in the New York legislature explained how the political norms of the state conditioned newly elected legislators to have strong partisan loyalties:

> It is brought about by the fact that legislators bring certain political values with them from their local party organizations to the legislature. . . . The legislator has been born within the party atmosphere of the local political arena and bred on basic political values, such as strong leadership, intraparty bargaining and compromise, all of them enveloped with the strongest and highest value, that of partisanship. As he enters the arena of lawmaking, he discovers that essentially the same values prevail there as well. . . . It is no hardship for him at all to accept strong legislative leadership for he had dealt with, and profited from, strong local party leadership. . . . He arrives in Albany as a trained party regular and almost automatically joins his colleagues who consider conformity as the highest party value. (Hevesi 1975, 171)

The political party system is also affected by the laws under which the parties operate and the elections are conducted. Of course, laws are passed by the legislature and signed by the governor. In states where the parties are strong, one would expect that the laws would help parties to remain strong. In states that have been governed most of the time by one party, we might expect that the law would support the political interests of that party, but this is not always so.

Take the case of endorsements. It is true that in several states where party endorsements are provided for by law, strong state parties that nominated by convention for many years were able to insist on a preprimary endorsement system as the price for agreeing to direct primaries; examples are Connecticut, Rhode Island, New York, and Colorado. But in Minnesota, another strong party state where the parties have long made endorsements under party rules, the legislature has never passed an endorsement law. Several states that have used informal endorsement procedures for years, such as Illinois and Ohio, have never enacted them into law.

The issue of open versus closed primaries in the state is a more puzzling one. Many voters prefer open or blanket primaries because they have maximum freedom to vote in the primary of any party. But party leaders recognize that closed primaries, open only to voters registered with the party holding the primary, are more likely to result in the nomination of a candidate who is in the party mainstream and will prevent "raiding" by voters in the other party. We would expect that a party that is strong by most criteria would get closed-primary laws enacted.

It is true that many strong party states have closed primaries, including New York and Pennsylvania as well as Connecticut and Ohio (both of which have some exceptions). But other strong party states, such as Illinois, Indiana, Michigan, and Minnesota, do not. Illinois had closed primaries for many years until 1972, when the U.S. Supreme Court ruled that the lead time required for a voter to change party registration was much too long. Oddly enough, instead of shortening the required lead time, Illinois adopted an open primary. The Supreme Court decision applied to two other strong party states with long lead times, New Jersey and Rhode Island, but these states kept their closed primary, shortened the lead time, and now permit unaffiliated voters to register with a party on election day.

It is interesting to note that every southern state except Florida and North Carolina has open primaries. As Republican Parties in the South grew stronger and began to have contested primaries, an increasing number of conservative Democrats began voting in Republican primaries without having to change registration. One might have thought that southern legislatures, which were still under Democratic control, would have adopted closed primaries to make it a little more difficult for conservatives to participate in Republican primaries, but they made no serious effort to do so. Republican leaders in Florida and North Carolina have discovered there are advantages to closed primaries; once a voter shifts registration to Republican, he or she is likely to stay registered in that party and party registration makes it easy for campaign workers to identify Republicans.

It is surprising that state political systems differ in so many ways at a time when there are so many nationalizing forces in our society. This seems especially strange when we are talking about differences that are heavily based on the state's political culture, history, and norms. Millions of people live and vote in states where they did not grow up. Why should anyone who moves from Wisconsin to Louisiana know or care about the legacy of Huey Long? Would a businessperson who moves from Oregon to New York and gets elected to the legislature ten years later share any of the partisan norms of his colleagues? Does a person who spent her twenties and thirties in an open primary state and voted regularly in primaries become frustrated when she moves to a closed primary state and has to register as a Democrat or a Republican?

There are more fundamental reasons for wondering how long the differences in state political systems will persist. All of us get our information about the world of politics and public issues from the same television networks and newspapers carrying similar news. Our impressions of politicians, parties, and governmental institutions are shaped by the media. We have begun the new millennium with an enormous amount of information literally at our fingertips via the Internet.

Others may be tempted to say that the differences among state political systems will fade away in the first few years of the millennium. We are not convinced, partly because the nationalizing trends in this country have been developing for many years without seeming to erase many of the differences among the states.

MONEY AND POLITICS

Schoolteachers and professors sometimes use true-or-false questions when they give quizzes; unfortunately in political science things are seldom that simple. For example, we could begin this section by asking very simply, "Does money buy elections?" Neither "yes" nor "no" is a correct answer. "It depends" comes closer to the truth. What we really want to know, and what we have tried to explain in several chapters of this book, is under what conditions does campaign funding assume critical importance in the outcome of elections.

We know that campaign funding has a different impact in races with incumbents and those without. We know that it has a different effect in primaries and in general elections. For that reason we have discussed campaign funding in primaries and in general elections in separate chapters, and in each case we have separated elections with incumbents from those without.

Unless an incumbent is politically very weak, most experts expect that he or she will win. Therefore the incumbent usually finds it easy to raise money and often spends much more campaign money than is probably necessary to win comfortably. Moreover, because most governors are regarded as tough opponents and because they can raise a lot of money and raise it early, they are usually able to discourage some of the strongest potential opponents from running at all. These political realities explain why it is difficult to separate cause and effect completely. Does the governor win because he or she can raise and spend so much money, or can the governor raise and spend so much money because most experts realize he or she is likely to be reelected? We must also remember that the governor, unlike most challengers, does not need to spend a lot of campaign funds to become well known to the voters and to develop as positive an image as possible.

For these reasons elections without incumbents running probably provide a clearer test of the influence of money on the outcome. These elections are not always different because in some races there are nonincumbent candidates who are much better known than others and are perceived as more likely winners, and there are some who are candidates of a party that usually dominates state politics. Such candidates can usually raise money much more easily and perhaps get a head start to discourage a potentially strong opponent from running. Generally speaking, we have seen that if one candidate for whatever reason raises and spends a lot more money than his or her opponent that candidate usually wins; a candidate who is unable to raise much money usually loses. But if both candidates can raise enough to carry out a normal campaign by the standards of that state, relatively small differences in spending, such as a 55–45 percent contrast, are unlikely to be decisive.

In general election campaigns a candidate who lags somewhat behind in spending may win because there are more voters in the state who are loyal to his or her party. Primary campaigns are different because, by definition, partisanship plays no role in the race. Therefore money assumes greater importance, particularly in races without an incumbent. We have found that if one candidate has a very large funding advantage, that candidate is usually the winner—unless another candidate is much better known (such as Gray Davis in California) and therefore has a head start. Often several candidates can spend at least enough money to run a viable campaign in the state, and modest differences in spending are usually not decisive. But if some candidates cannot meet these minimum requirements, they are usually left far behind in the race.

The only prediction that can be made about the role of money in state elections is that it will keep changing. In recent years more states have been adopting bold new programs of public campaign funding linked to strict limits on spending and contributions. This trend may continue, but there have also been a series of court decisions overruling very low limits on contributions.

The Federal Election Commission keeps changing the rules governing the role of national parties in financing elections, rules that sometimes have an impact on state parties. Every time new rules are adopted, the parties' lawyers start looking for loopholes and often find new ways in which the parties can spend campaign money. Moreover, the federal courts (including the Supreme Court) continue to debate the proper role of parties in funding campaigns, a debate that may give parties much greater flexibility in spending money on campaigns. Meanwhile Congress continues to debate a variety of proposals to reform federal campaign finance laws, with particular emphasis on banning or limiting soft money. Passage of such reforms would force the party lawyers to start looking again for loopholes.

THE EVOLVING PARTNERSHIP OF STATE AND NATIONAL PARTIES

The relationships between the national and state parties have been changing at an increasing rate and will continue to change. Some of the most important changes concern the financial relationships between the national and state parties, and we have just finished explaining why these relationships continue to be in flux. If the FEC and the courts give the national parties more flexibility in campaign funding, this will surely lead to closer financial linkages between national and state parties.

In its regulation of campaign financing the FEC has tried very hard to separate federal elections, which it can regulate, from state elections, which it cannot, but these distinctions are unrealistic. In reality, state and local parties are heavily involved in the effort to elect presidential and congressional candidates, as they should be. Local party activists participate in phone banks, campaign door to door, and organize rallies in support of federal candidates. They do most of the work in getting voters registered and getting them to the polls, efforts that simultaneously benefit the party's federal, state, and local candidates (as even the FEC has recognized). The national parties have an interest in getting governors elected, and they sometimes even provide direct assistance to state legislative candidates, particularly if they are in states where there is a close two-party balance in the legislature. They are more active in the election preceding the legislative session when the legislature will redistrict congressional and legislative seats.

In our analysis of changing patterns of state party competition (Chapter 2), we emphasized that the revitalization of a state party that has long been in the minority, and its increasing ability to elect statewide and legislative candidates, almost always are consequences of successful efforts by the party's presidential candidates to win the state. Individuals in a state who first became active in politics in order to work for presidential candidates often remain active in state politics and begin working for state and legislative candidates as well. This pattern of party growth has been most obvious in southern states in the second half of the twentieth century. State parties and their candidates do better if the party's national candidates can do well in the state; national candidates have better prospects for success where state parties are strong and are winning elections.

The relations between national and state parties are not always smooth. They often have different priorities, and this may lead to differences of opinion over how to spend scarce resources. A presidential candidate, particularly an incumbent, will insist on hoarding financial resources in an effort to win by a larger landslide, while state parties are pleading for more financial help to elect senators, governors, and other candidates who are in danger of being beaten. Sometimes ideological or other divisions in a state result in a situation where the leadership of the state party is out of step with the leaders of the national party. Sometimes state-national party linkages break down simply because of personality conflicts.

STATE PARTIES: NEW RESPONSIBILITIES AND CAPABILITIES

Many state political parties are becoming stronger, not weaker. They have adapted to the new technology, and they provide valuable services to state and national candidates. In fact, their adaptation to the technological age paralleled the resurgence of national party organizations. As the national parties became stronger and richer, they needed to build up their state partners because of increasing competition in every state. Far from the predicted decline, state parties have become "parties in service" (Aldrich 1995). They provide services such as polling, campaign seminars, advertising, and fund raising. The more effective and extensive these services, the more important they are to ambitious candidates as they seek election and reelection. State parties maintained their autonomy as they became more professionalized and more durable. And they contribute on average half of all party money spent within their borders in a presidential election year.

At any given time the working relationship between the national party and a particular state party will depend on the ability of the two sets of leaders to overcome the differences that arise because the two parties have somewhat different priorities and needs and because some disagreements over financing are inevitable. In the long run the relations between national and state parties seem certain to become closer, and national and state election campaigns will become more intertwined.

References

Abramowitz, Alan I., John McGlennon, and Ronald B. Rapoport. 1986. "An Analysis of State Party Activists." In *The Life of the Parties*, ed. Ronald B. Rapoport, Alan I. Abramowitz, and John McGlennon. Lexington: University Press of Kentucky.

Aistrup, Joseph A., and Mark Bannister. 1997. "Kansas." In *State Party Profiles*, ed. Andrew M. Appleton and Daniel S. Ward. Washington, D.C.: Congressional Quarterly.

Aistrup, Joseph A., and Ronald Keith Gaddie. 1999. "Candidate Emergence in the New Southern Party System." Paper presented at the annual meeting of the Southern Political Science Association, Savannah.

Aldrich, John H. 1995. *Why Parties?* Chicago: University of Chicago Press.

———— 2000. "Southern Parties in State and Nation." *Journal of Politics* 62.

American Political Science Association Committee on Political Parties. 1950. "Toward a More Responsible Two-Party System." *American Political Science Review* 44: supplement.

Anderson, Bruce. 1998. "Party Voting in State Legislatures." Paper presented at the annual meeting of the Southern Political Science Association, Atlanta.

Appleton, Andrew M., and Anneka Depoorter. 1997. "Washington." In *State Party Profiles*, ed. Andrew M. Appleton and Daniel S. Ward. Washington, D.C.: Congressional Quarterly.

Appleton, Andrew M., and Daniel S. Ward, eds. 1997. *State Party Profiles: A Fifty-State Guide to Development, Organization, and Resources.* Washington, D.C.: Congressional Quarterly.

Atkeson, Lonna Rae, and Randall W. Partin. 1995. "Economic and Referendum Voting: A Comparison of Gubernatorial and Senatorial Elections." *American Political Science Review* 89: 99–107.

Barone, Michael, William Lilly III, and Laurence J. DeFranco. 1998. *State Legislative Elections: Voting Patterns and Demographics.* Washington, D.C.: Congressional Quarterly.

Barone, Michael, and Grant Ujifusa. 1995. *The Almanac of American Politics, 1996.* Washington, D.C.: National Journal.

———— 1979–1999. *The Almanac of American Politics,* 1980–2000. Washington, D.C.: National Journal.

Barrilleaux, Charles J. 1986. "A Dynamic Model of Partisan Competition in the American States." *American Journal of Political Science* 30: 822–840.

Bartels, Larry M. 2000. "Partisanship and Voting Behavior, 1952–1996." *American Journal of Political Science* 44: 35–50.

Beck, Paul A. 1996. *Party Politics in America.* 8th ed. New York: Longman.

Bernick, E. Lee, and Charles W. Wiggins. 1991. "Executive-Legislative Relations: The Governor's Role as Chief Legislator." In *Gubernatorial Leadership and State Policy,* ed. Eric. B. Herzik and Bren W. Brown. New York: Greenwood Press.

Berry, Frances Stokes, and William D. Berry. 1992. "Tax Innovation in the States." *American Journal of Political Science* 36: 715–742.

Berry, William D., and Bradley C. Canon. 1993. "Explaining the Competitiveness of Gubernatorial Primaries." *Journal of Politics* 55: 454–471.

Beyle, Thad L. 1996a. "The Cost of Winning." *State Government News* 39 (April): 10–14.

———— 1996b. "Governors: The Middlemen and Women in Our Political System." In *Politics in the American States,* 6th ed., ed. Virginia Gray and Herbert Jacob. Washington, D.C.: CQ Press.

———— 1999. "The Governors." In *Politics in the American States,* 7th ed., ed. Virginia Gray, Russell L. Hanson, and Herbert Jacob. Washington, D.C.: CQ Press.

———— 2000. "The Cost of Winning." *State Government News* 43 (February): 20–23.

Bibby, John F. 1992. *Politics, Parties, and Elections in America.* 2d ed. Chicago: Nelson-Hall.

———— 1998. "State Party Organizations: Coping and Adapting to Candidate-Centered Politics and Nationalization." In *The Parties Respond,* 3d ed., ed. L. Sandy Maisel. Boulder: Westview Press.

———— 1999. "Party Networks: National-State Integration, Allied Groups, and Issue Activists." In *The State of the Parties,* 3d ed., ed. John C. Green and Daniel M. Shea. Lanham, Md.: Rowman and Littlefield.

Biersack, Robert. 1996. "The Nationalization of Party Finance, 1992–1994." In *The State of the Parties,* ed. John C. Green and Daniel M. Shea. Lanham, Md.: Rowman and Littlefield.

Brace, Paul. 1993. *State Government and Economic Performance.* Baltimore: Johns Hopkins University Press.

Breaux, David A., and Anthony Gierzynski. 1998. "Candidate Revenues and Expenditures in State Legislative Primaries." In *Campaign Finance in State Legislative Elections,* ed. Joel A. Thompson and Gary F. Moncrief. Washington, D.C.: Congressional Quarterly.

Bryan, Frank M. 1974. *Yankee Politics in Rural Vermont.* Hanover, N.H.: University Press of New England.

Buchanan, William. 1963. *Legislative Partisanship: The Deviant Case of California.* Berkeley: University of California Press.

Bullock, Charles S. III, and David J. Shafer. 1997. "Party Targeting and Electoral Success." *Legislative Studies Quarterly* 22: 573–584.

Campbell, James E. 1986. "Presidential Coattails and Midterm Losses in State Legislative Elections." *American Political Science Review* 80: 45–83.

Carey, John M., Richard G. Niemi, and Linda W. Powell. 1997. "Incumbency and the Probability of Reelection in State Legislative Elections." Paper presented at the annual meeting of the American Political Science Association, Washington.

Carlson, James M. 1989. "Primary Divisiveness and General Election Outcomes in State Legislative Races." *Southeastern Political Review* 17: 149–157.

Carsey, Thomas M. 1996. "The Influence of Campaign Themes on Voting Behavior in Gubernatorial Elections, 1982–1994." Paper presented at the annual meeting of the Midwest Political Science Association, Chicago.

Cassie, William E., and David A. Breaux. 1998. "Expenditures and Election Results." In *Campaign Finance in State Legislative Elections,* ed. Joel A. Thompson and Gary F. Moncrief. Washington, D.C.: Congressional Quarterly.

Cassie, William E., and Joel A. Thompson. 1998. "Patterns of PAC Contributions to State Legislative Candidates." In *Campaign Finance in State Legislative Elections,* ed. Joel A. Thompson and Gary F. Moncrief. Washington, D.C.: Congressional Quarterly.

Chen, Edwin. 1997. "Devolution, Disgust Lure Members to Statehouse Bids." *Los Angeles Times,* December 16.

Chubb, John E. 1988. "Institutions, the Economy, and the Dynamics of State Elections." *American Political Science Review* 82: 133–154.

Clark, Peter B., and James Q. Wilson. 1961. "Incentive Systems: A Theory of Organization." *Administrative Science Quarterly* 6: 129–166.

Clucas, Richard A. 1995. *The Speaker's Electoral Connection: Willie Brown and the California Assembly.* Berkeley: Institute of Governmental Studies Press of the University of California.

Cohen, Jonathan, and John Sides. 1998. "The Incidence and Importance of Crossover Voting in a Blanket Primary: Washington State Senate Elections 1986–1996." Berkeley: Institute of Governmental Studies, University of California, Working Paper.

Coleman, John J. 1994. "The Resurgence of Party Organization: A Dissent from the New Orthodoxy." In *The State of the Parties,* ed. Daniel M. Shea and John C. Green. Lanham, Md.: Rowman and Littlefield.

——— 1996. "Party Organizational Strength and Public Support for Parties." *American Journal of Political Science* 40: 805–824.

Common Cause. 1998. *Party Soft Money.* Washington, D.C.: Common Cause.

Congressional Quarterly's Guide to U.S. Elections. 1994. 3d ed. Washington, D.C.: Congressional Quarterly.

Cook, Elizabeth, Ted Jelen, and Clyde Wilcox. 1994. "Issue Voting in Gubernatorial Elections: Abortion and Post-Webster Politics." *Journal of Politics* 56:187–199.

Corrado, Anthony. 1997. "Statement of Anthony Corrado." Waterville, Maine: Colby College. Unpublished manuscript.

Cotter, Cornelius, James L. Gibson, John F. Bibby, and Robert J. Huckshorn. 1984. *Party Organizations in American Politics.* New York: Praeger.

Crew, Robert E., Jr., and Marjorie Renee Hill. 1995. "Gubernatorial Influence in State Government Policymaking." *Spectrum* 68: 29–39.

Ehrenhalt, Alan. 1998. "It Pays to Know Where the Bodies Are Buried." *Governing* 11 (9): 5–6.

Elazar, Daniel. 1972. *American Federalism: A View from the States,* 2d ed. New York: Crowell.

——— 1984. *American Federalism: A View from the States,* 3d ed. New York: Harper and Row.

Epstein, Leon.1986. *Political Parties in the American Mold.* Madison: University of Wisconsin Press.

Erikson, Robert S., Gerald C. Wright, and John P. McIver. 1993. *Statehouse Democracy: Public Opinion and Policy in the American States.* New York: Cambridge University Press.

Euchner, Jonathan P. 1990. "Partisanship in the Iowa Legislature." Paper presented at the annual meeting of the Midwest Political Science Association, Chicago.

Euchner, Jonathan P., and Malcolm E. Jewell. 1990. "Party Caucus Influence in the Iowa Legislature." Paper presented at the annual meeting of the American Political Science Association, San Francisco.

Finkel, Steven E., and Howard A. Scarrow. 1985. "Party Identification and Party Enrollment: The Difference and the Consequences." *Journal of Politics* 47: 620–642.

Fiorina, Morris P. 1994. "Divided Government in the United States: A Byproduct of Legislative Professionalism?" *American Political Science Review* 88: 304–316.

Frendreis, John, and Alan R. Gitelson. 1999. "Local Parties in the 1990s: Spokes in a Candidate-Centered Wheel." In *The State of the Parties,* 3d ed., ed. John C. Green and Daniel M. Shea. Lanham, Md.: Rowman and Littlefield.

Gibson, James L., John P. Frendreis, and Laura Vertz. 1989. "Party Dynamics in the 1980s: Change in County Party Organizational Strength, 1980–1984." *American Journal of Political Science* 33: 67–90.

Gierzynski, Anthony. 1992. *Legislative Party Campaign Committees in the American States.* Lexington: University Press of Kentucky.

Gierzynski, Anthony, and David A. Breaux. 1998. "The Financing Role of Parties." In *Campaign Finance in State Legislative Elections,* ed. Joel A. Thompson and Gary F. Moncrief. Washington, D.C.: Congressional Quarterly.

Gimpel, James. 1996. *National Elections and the Autonomy of American State Party Systems.* Pittsburgh: University of Pittsburgh Press.

——— 1999. "Contemplating Congruence in State Electoral Systems." *American Politics Quarterly* 27: 133–140.

Glasser, Susan B. 1999. "The Lid Lifts on Party Spending." *Washington Post,* national weekly edition, April 5.

Goodhart, Noah J. 1999. "The New Party Machine: Information Technology in State Political Parties." In *The State of the Parties,* 3d ed., ed. John C. Green and Daniel M. Shea. Lanham, Md.: Rowman and Littlefield.

Graham, Cole Blease, Jr., and Kenny J. Whitby. 1989. "Party-Based Voting in a Southern State Legislature." *American Politics Quarterly* 17: 181–193.

Green, John C., John S. Jackson, and Nancy L. Clayton. 1999. "Issue Networks and Party Elites in 1996." In *The State of the Parties,* 3d ed., ed. John C. Green and Daniel M. Shea. Lanham, Md.: Rowman and Littlefield.

Green, Paul M. 1997. "Illinois." In *State Party Profiles,* ed. Andrew M. Appleton and Daniel S. Ward. Washington, D.C.: Congressional Quarterly.

Grofman, Bernard, Michael Migalski, and Nicholas Noviello. 1986. "Effects of Multi-member Districts on Black Representation in State Legislatures." *Review of Black Political Economy* 14: 55–78.

Gross, Donald A., Robert K. Goidel, and Todd G. Shields. 1998. "Money, Turnout, and Electoral Outcomes in Gubernatorial Elections." Paper presented at the annual meeting of the American Political Science Association, Boston.

Gurwitt, Rob. 1997. "The Unrevolution." *Governing* 11 (2): 20–26.

Hansen, Susan B. 1983. *The Politics of Taxation.* New York: Praeger.

——————— 1999. " `Life Is Not Fair': Governors' Job Performance Ratings and State Economies." *Political Research Quarterly* 52: 167–188.

Herzik, Eric B. 1991. "Policy Agendas and Gubernatorial Leadership." In *Gubernatorial Leadership and State Policy,* ed. Eric B. Herzik and Brent W. Brown. New York: Greenwood Press.

Hevesi, Alan G. 1975. *Legislative Politics in New York State.* New York: Praeger.

Hogan, Robert E. 1999. "The Effects of Primary Divisiveness on General Election Outcomes in State Legislative Elections." Paper presented at the annual meeting of the Southern Political Science Association, Savannah.

Jackson, Robert A. 1997. "The Mobilization of U.S. State Electorates in the 1998 and 1990 Elections." *Journal of Politics* 59: 520–537.

Jacobson, Gary. forthcoming. *The Politics of Congressional Elections,* 5th ed. New York: Longman.

Jewell, Malcolm E. 1982. *Representation in State Legislatures.* Lexington: University Press of Kentucky.

——————— 1984. *Parties and Primaries: Nominating State Governors.* New York: Praeger.

——————— 1994. "State Legislative Elections: What We Know and Don't Know." *American Politics Quarterly* 22: 483–509.

——————— 1995. "Explaining Republican Gains in Southern State Legislatures." Paper presented at the annual meeting of the Southern Political Science Association, Tampa.

Jewell, Malcolm E., and David A. Breaux. 1988. "The Effect of Incumbency on State Legislative Elections." *Legislative Studies Quarterly* 13: 495–514.

——————— 1991. "Southern Primary and Electoral Competition and Incumbent Success." *Legislative Studies Quarterly* 16:129–144.

Jewell, Malcolm E., and Penny M. Miller. 1988. *The Kentucky Legislature.* Lexington: University Press of Kentucky.

Jewell, Malcolm E., and David M. Olson. 1988. *Political Parties and Elections in the American States,* 3d ed. Chicago: Dorsey.

Jewell, Malcolm E., and Samuel C. Patterson. 1977. *The Legislative Process in the United States,* 3d ed. New York: Random House.

Jewell. Malcolm E., and Marcia Lynn Whicker. 1994. *Legislative Leadership in the American States.* Ann Arbor: University of Michigan Press.

Johnson, Donald B., and James R. Gibson. 1974. "The Divisive Primary Revisited: Party Activists in Iowa." *American Political Science Review* 68: 67–77.

Jones, Ruth S. 1984. "Financing State Elections." In *Money and Politics in the United States,* ed. Michael J. Malbin. Washington, D.C.: American Enterprise Institute for Public Policy Research.

Karp, Jeffrey A., and Susan A. Banducci. 1997. "Oregon." In *State Party Profiles,* ed. Andrew M. Appleton and Daniel S. Ward. Washington, D.C.: Congressional Quarterly.

Kelley, Anne E. 1997. "Florida." In *State Party Profiles,* ed. Andrew M. Appleton and Daniel S. Ward. Washington, D.C.: Congressional Quarterly.

Kenny, Patrick J. 1988. "Sorting Out the Effects of Primary Divisiveness in Congressional and Senatorial Elections." *Western Political Quarterly* 41: 756–777.

Kenny, Patrick J., and Tom W. Rice. 1984. "The Effects of Primary Divisiveness in Gubernatorial and Senatorial Elections." *Journal of Politics* 46: 904–915.

————— 1987. "The Relationship between Divisive Primaries and General Election Outcomes." *American Journal of Political Science* 31: 31–44.

Key, V. O., Jr. 1956. *American State Politics: An Introduction.* New York: Knopf.

————— 1958. *Politics, Parties, and Pressure Groups,* 4th ed. New York: Crowell.

————— 1964. *Politics, Parties, and Pressure Groups,* 5th ed. New York: Crowell.

Kone, Susan L., and Richard F. Winters. 1993. "Taxes and Voting: Electoral Retribution in the American States." *Journal of Politics* 55: 22–40.

Kousser, J. Morgan. 1974. *The Shaping of Southern Politics: Suffrage Restrictions and the Establishment of the One-Party South, 1880–1910.* New Haven: Yale University Press.

Kousser, Thad. 1999. "Hedgers, Raiders, and Sincere Voters in Blanket Primaries: Theory and Evidence." Paper presented at the annual meeting of the Western Political Science Association, Seattle.

Levy, Clifford J. 1998. "Led by Pataki, Fund Raising in Governor's Race Outstrips the Past." *New York Times,* February 15.

Leyden, Kevin, and Steve Borrelli. 1995. "The Effect of State Economic Conditions on Gubernatorial Elections: Does Unified Government Make a Difference?" *Political Research Quarterly* 48: 275–290.

Lieberman, Joseph I. 1966. *The Power Broker.* Boston: Houghton Mifflin.

Lockard, Duane. 1959. *New England State Politics.* Princeton: Princeton University Press.

Lubenow, Gerald C., ed. 1995. *California Votes: The 1994 Governor's Race.* Berkeley: Institute of Governmental Studies Press, University of California, Berkeley.

Lublin, David, and D. Stephen Voss. 1999. "Racial Redistricting and Realignment in Southern State Legislatures." Paper presented at the annual meeting of the Southern Political Science Association, Savannah.

Magleby, David, and Marianne Holt. 1999. "Outside Money: Soft Money and Issue Ads in Competitive 1998 Congressional Elections." Unpublished paper.

Maisel, L. Sandy. 1994. "Political Parties at the Century's End." In *The Parties Respond,* 2d ed., ed. L. Sandy Maisel. Boulder: Westview Press.

Maisel, L. Sandy, Linda L. Fowler, Ruth S. Jones, and Walter J. Stone. 1994. "Nomination Politics: The Roles of Institutional, Contextual, and Personal Variables." In *The Parties Respond,* 2d ed., ed. L. Sandy Maisel. Boulder: Westview Press.

Malbin, Michael J., and Thomas L. Gais. 1998. *The Day after Reform: Sobering Campaign Finance Lessons from the American States.* New York: Rockefeller Institute Press.

Martorano, Nancy, B. Bruce Anderson, and Keith E. Hamm. 1999. "State Legislative Seat Contestation in the South." Paper presented at the annual meeting of the Southern Political Science Association, Savannah.

Mayer, William G. 1997. "The Presidential Nominations." In *The Election of 1996,* ed. Gerald M. Pomper. Chatham, N.J.: Chatham House.

McGlennon, John. 1997. "Virginia." In *State Party Profiles,* ed. Andrew M. Appleton and Daniel S. Ward. Washington, D.C.: Congressional Quarterly.

Mileur, Jerome M. 1997. "Massachusetts." In *State Party Profiles,* ed. Andrew M. Appleton and Daniel S. Ward. Washington, D.C.: Congressional Quarterly.

Miller, Penny M., and Malcolm E. Jewell. 1990. *Political Parties and Primaries in Kentucky.* Lexington: University Press of Kentucky.

——————— 1997. "Kentucky." In *State Party Profiles,* ed. Andrew M. Appleton and Daniel S. Ward. Washington, D.C.: Congressional Quarterly.

Miller, Penny M., Malcolm E. Jewell, and Lee Sigelman. 1988. "Divisive Primaries and Party Activists: Kentucky, 1979 and 1983." *Journal of Politics* 50: 459–470.

Miller, Warren E., 1988. *Without Consent: Mass-Elite Linkages in Presidential Politics.* Lexington: University Press of Kentucky.

Miller, Warren E., and M. Kent Jennings. 1986. *Parties in Transition.* New York: Russell Sage.

Miller, Warren E., and J. Merrill Shanks. 1996. *The New American Voter.* Cambridge, Mass.: Harvard University Press.

Monardi, Fred M. 1999. "Campaign Techniques in State Legislative Elections." Paper presented at the annual meeting of the Southern Political Science Association, Savannah.

Moncrief, Gary. 1998. "Candidate Spending in State Legislative Races." In *Campaign Finance in State Legislative Elections,* ed. Joel A. Thompson and Gary F. Moncrief. Washington, D.C.: Congressional Quarterly.

Montjoy, Robert, William Shaffer, and Ronald Weber. 1980. "Policy Preferences in Elites and Masses: Conflict or Consensus?" *American Politics Quarterly* 8: 319–344.

Morehouse, Sarah McCally. 1981. *State Politics, Parties and Policy.* New York: Holt, Rinehart, and Winston.

——————— 1998. *The Governor as Party Leader.* Ann Arbor: University of Michigan Press.

Morehouse, Sarah M., and Malcolm E. Jewell. 1992. "Divided Government and Legislative Support for the Governor's Program." Paper presented at the annual meeting of the Southern Political Science Association, Atlanta.

Muchmore, Lynn, and Thad L. Beyle. 1980. "The Governor as Party Leader." *State Government* 53: 121–124.

Nagourney, Adam. 1998. "Fight Widens over Keeping Party Funds: New York's Democrats Demand a 25 Percent Share." *New York Times,* January 17.

National Conference of State Legislatures. 1994. "Incumbent Reelection Rates in 1994 State Legislative Elections." Unpublished paper.

New York Times. 1996. "Portrait of the Electorate." November 10.

Niemi, Richard G., Harold W. Stanley, and Ronald J. Vogel. 1995. "State Economies and State Taxes: Do Voters Hold Governors Accountable?" *American Journal of Political Science* 39: 936–957.

Norrander, Barbara. 1992. *Super Tuesday.* Lexington: University Press of Kentucky.

Parent, T. Wayne. 1997. "Louisiana." In *State Party Profiles,* ed. Andrew M. Appleton and Daniel S. Ward. Washington, D.C.: Congressional Quarterly.

Partin, Randall W. 1995. "Economic Conditions and Gubernatorial Elections." *American Politics Quarterly* 23: 81–95.

——— 1999a. Unpublished data provided to authors.

——— 1999b. "Revisiting Campaign Spending in Governor's Races." Paper presented at the annual meeting of the Midwest Political Science Association, Chicago.

Patterson, Samuel C. 1968. "The Political Culture of the American States." *Journal of Politics* 30: 187–209.

——— 1982. "Campaign Spending in Contests for Governor." *Western Political Quarterly* 35: 457–477.

Patterson, Samuel C., and Gregory A. Caldeira. 1983. "Getting Out the Vote: Participation in Gubernatorial Elections." *American Political Science Review* 77: 675–689.

——— 1984. "The Etiology of Partisan Competition." *American Political Science Review* 78: 691–707.

Peirce, Neal R. 1972. *The Megastates of America.* New York: Norton.

Pernaciarro, Samuel J., and Jack R. Van Der Slik. 1996. "Roll Call Voting in the 89th General Assembly." In *Almanac of Illinois Politics—1996,* ed. Craig A. Roberts and Paul Kleppner. Springfield: Institute of Public Affairs, University of Illinois at Springfield.

——— 1998. "Roll Call Voting in the 90th General Assembly. In *Almanac of Illinois Politics—1998,* ed. David A. Joens and Paul Kleppner. Springfield: Institute of Public Affairs, University of Illinois at Springfield.

Price, David E. 1992. *The Congressional Experience.* Boulder: Westview Press.

Purdum, Todd S. 1998. "California Governor's Race: A New Height in Spending." *New York Times,* February 13.

Rakove, Milton. 1975. *Don't Make No Waves, Don't Back No Losers.* Bloomington: Indiana University Press.

Ranney, Austin. 1976. "Parties in State Politics." In *Politics in the American States: A Comparative Analysis,* 3d ed., ed. Herbert Jacob and Kenneth Vines. Boston: Little, Brown.

Rosenthal, Alan. 1990. *Governors and Legislatures: Contending Powers.* Washington, D.C.: CQ Press.

——— 1996. *Drawing the Line: Legislative Ethics in the States.* Lincoln: University of Nebraska Press.

——— 1998. *The Decline of Representative Democracy: Process, Participation, and Power in State Legislatures.* Washington, D.C.: CQ Press.

Rosenthal, Cindy Simon. 1995. "New Party or Campaign Bank Account: Explaining the Rise of State Legislative Campaign Committees." *Legislative Studies Quarterly* 20: 249–268.

Sabato, Larry. 1983. *Goodbye to Goodtime Charlie: The American Government Transformed,* 2d ed. Washington, D.C.: CQ Press.

Salmore, Stephen, and Barbara Salmore. 1997. "New Jersey." In *State Party Profiles,* ed. Andrew M. Appleton and Daniel S. Ward. Washington, D.C.: Congressional Quarterly.

Scheele, Raymond H. 1972. "Voting in Primary Elections." Ph.D. dissertation, University of Missouri.

Schlesinger, Joseph A. 1966. *Ambition and Politics: Political Careers in the United States.* Chicago: Rand McNally.

Schneider, Paige. 1997. "Factionalism in the Southern Republican Party: The Impact of the Christian Right." Paper presented at the annual meeting of the Southern Political Science Association, Norfolk.

Scott, Steve. 1998. "Governor." *California Journal* 29 (7): 11–13.

Simon, Dennis M. 1989. "Presidents, Governors, and Electoral Accountability." *Journal of Politics* 51: 286–304.

Simon, Dennis M., Charles W. Ostrom, Jr., and Robin F. Marra. 1991. "The President, Referendum Voting, and Subnational Elections in the United States." *American Political Science Review* 85: 1177–1192.

Sorauf, Frank J., and Paul A. Beck. 1988. *Party Politics in America,* 6th ed. Glenview, Ill.: Scott, Foresman.

Squire, Peverill. 1992. "Challenger Profile and Gubernatorial Elections." *Western Political Quarterly* 45: 125–142.

————1998. *"Uncontested Seats in State Legislative Elections."* Unpublished manuscript.

Squire, Peverill, and Christina Fastnow. 1994. "Comparing Gubernatorial and Senatorial Elections." *Political Research Quarterly* 47: 705–720.

Stanley, Harold W., and Richard G. Niemi. 2000. *Vital Statistics on American Politics, 1999–2000.* Washington, D.C.: CQ Press.

Stein, Robert. 1990. "Economic Voting for Governor and U.S. Senator: Electoral Consequences of Federalism." *Journal of Politics* 52: 29–53.

Stone, Walter J., and Ronald B. Rapoport. 1998. "A Candidate-Centered Perspective on Party Responsiveness." In *The Parties Respond,* 3d ed, ed. L. Sandy Maisel. Boulder: Westview Press.

Sundquist, James L. 1973. *Dynamics of the Party System.* Washington, D.C.: Brookings Institution.

Svoboda, Craig J. 1995. "Retrospective Voting in Gubernatorial Elections." *Political Research Quarterly* 48: 135–150.

Swanson, Wayne R. 1984. *Lawmaking in Connecticut: The General Assembly.*

Tompkins, Mark E. 1988. "Have Gubernatorial Elections Become More Distinctive Contests?" *Journal of Politics* 50: 192–205.

Trish, Barbara. 1997. "Iowa." In *State Party Profiles,* ed. Andrew M. Appleton and Daniel S. Ward. Washington, D.C.: Congressional Quarterly.

Van Dunk, Emily. 1997. "Challenger Quality in State Legislative Elections." *Political Research Quarterly* 50: 793–808.

Van Dunk, Emily, and Ronald Weber. 1997. "Constituency-Level Competition in the United States, 1968–1988: A Pooled Analysis." *Legislative Studies Quarterly* 22: 141–160.

Verba, Sydney. 1965. "Comparative Political Culture." In *Political Culture and Political*

Development, ed. Lucian W. Pye and Sydney Verba. Princeton: Princeton University Press.

Walker, Jack L. 1969. "Diffusion of Innovation among the American States." *American Political Science Review* 63: 880–899.

Weber, Ronald E., and Kevin B. Smith. 1991. "Voter Turnout in U.S. Gubernatorial Elections: A Pooled Analysis." Paper presented at the annual meeting of the Midwest Political Science Association, Chicago.

Weissert, Carol S. 1997. "Michigan." In *State Party Profiles,* ed. Andrew M. Appleton and Daniel S. Ward. Washington, D.C.: Congressional Quarterly.

Wielhouwer, Peter W. 1995. "Strategic Canvassing by Political Parties, 1952–1990." *American Review of Politics* 16: 213–238.

———— 1999. "The Mobilization of Campaign Activists by the Party Canvass." *American Politics Quarterly* 27: 177–200.

Wielhouwer, Peter W., and Brad Lockerbie. 1994. "Party Contacting and Political Participation, 1952–1990." *American Journal of Political Science* 38: 211–229.

Wiggins, Charles W. 1972. *The Legislative Process in Iowa.* Ames: Iowa State University Press.

Winters, Richard F. 1996. "Reconsidering the Tax-Economy-Vote Link by Integrating Diverse Approaches in the Study of American State Politics." Paper presented at the annual meeting of the American Political Science Association, San Francisco.

———— 1998. "Fate Choice and Fate Control in Reelecting American Governors, 1978–1996." Paper presented at the annual meeting of the Midwest Political Science Association, Chicago.

Wright, Gerald C., Jr. 1974. *Electoral Choice in America.* Chapel Hill: Institute for Research in Social Science, University of North Carolina, Chapel Hill.

———— 1998. Unpublished data set.

Wright, Gerald C., Robert S. Erikson, and John P. McIver. 1985. "Measuring State Partisanship and Ideology with Survey Data." *Journal of Politics* 47: 469–489.

INTERNET SOURCES

A complete listing of Web sites maintained by state political parties, as well as links to many other Web sites on political topics, can be found at *www.campaignline.com/bandwagon.* This Web site is operated by *Campaigns and Elections* magazine.

SUPREME COURT CASES

Baker v. Carr (1962)

Buckley v. Valeo (1976)

Colorado Republican Federal Campaign Committee v. Federal Election Commission (1996)

Colorado Republican Party v. Federal Election Commission (1999)

Elrod v. Burns (1976)

Eu, Secretary of State of California v. San Francisco County Democratic Central Committee (1989)

Hunt v. Cromartie (1999)

March Fong Wu, Secretary of State of California, et al. v. San Francisco County Democratic Committee, et al. (1989)

McMillan v. Escambia County of Florida (1981)

Miller v. Johnson (1995)

Nixon v. Shrink Missouri Government PAC (2000)

Rutan v. Republican Party (1990)

Shaw v. Reno (1993)

Index

A

Abortion, 83, 90–91, 112, 129, 131, 188, 189–190, 245
Abramowtiz, Alan I., 86, 88
Academic standards, 188
Activists, 82, 88–92, 108
Add-on system of public financing, 69–70
Advertising
  attack ads, 155
  interest groups and, 152–153
  issue advocacy ads, 152, 262, 269
  television advertising, 148, 155
African American interest groups, 154
African American voters, 221
Agency agreements, 260–261
Aggregate voting data, 176
Aistrup, Joseph A., 37, 73
Aldrich, John H., 47–49, 50–51, 53, 57–58, 72, 88–89, 94–95, 98, 271, 283
Allen, George, 91
Almanac of American Politics, The, 186
American Federation of State, County, and Municipal Employees, 62
American State Politics: An Introduction (Key), 22
Anderson, B. Bruce, 37
Anderson, Bruce, 250
Appleton, Andrew M., 76, 77, 91, 248
Appointments, 242
Atkeson, Lonna Rae, 177, 182, 191
Attack ads, 155
Autonomous state party systems, 177–180

B

Bailey, John, 74, 85
Baker v. Carr (1962), 16
Balducci, Richard, 229
Banducci, Susan A., 77

Bannister, Mark, 73
Barone, Michael, 163, 186
Barrilleaux, Charles J., 94
Bartels, Larry M., 38, 46, 276, 277
Beasley, David, 125, 131, 134, 163
Beck, Paul A., 84, 126
Benson, Joanne, 113
Bernick, E. Lee, 242
Berry, Frances Stokes, 194
Berry, William D., 120, 194
Beyle, Thad L., 142, 145, 164, 165, 238, 271
Bibby, John F., 48–49, 62, 73, 75, 90, 93, 95
Biersack, Robert, 267
Bipartisan coalitions, 228–229
Blanchard, James, 195
Blandford, Don, 233
Blanket primaries, 128, 274, 279. *See also* Open primaries
Blount, Winton, 131
Borrelli, Steve, 193
"Bought" nominations, 131–136
Brace, Paul, 191
Branstad, Terry, 91, 159–160
Breaux, David A., 201, 204, 212, 213, 216, 217
Breaux, John, 81
Brickley, James, 130
Brown, Jerry, 161
Brown, Kathleen, 147, 161–162
Brown, Willie, 212, 229, 249
Bryan, Frank M., 159
Bryan, William Jennings, 24
Buchanan, William, 228
Buckley v. Valeo (1976), 174
Bullock, Charles S. III, 56
Bush, George, 192
Bush, George W., 134, 144, 163, 165, 169, 254, 255

Bush, Jeb, 144
Businesspeople, as gubernatorial
    candidates, 144

C

Caldeira, Gregory A., 94, 199
Campaign finance, 280–282
    federal money, 6, 68, 260–261
    general elections, 163–175
    gubernatorial candidates, 163–175
    hard money, 6, 68, 260–265
    impact of spending on legislative
        elections, 216
    legislative elections, 211–218
    nonfederal money, 261–263
    primaries, 281
    regulation of, 65–69, 260–265, 282
    relationship between state parties and
        national partners, 258–271
    role in state politics, 5
    soft money, 6, 68–69, 259
    state elections, 280–282
    state money, 65, 263–265
    state party organization and, 61–70
Campaigns, 147–158
    campaign strategy and tactics, 154–156
    candidate-centered, 2–3, 48, 179
    interest groups and, 152–154
    for legislative elections, 208–210
    media and, 156–158
    organizing campaigns, 148–150
    role of state parties, 150–152
Campbell, James E., 219
Candidate-centered campaigns, 2–3, 48, 179
Candidates. *See also* Incumbency
    candidate-centered campaigns, 2–3, 48,
        179
    for Congress, 143–144, 261
    deciding to run, 144–145
    endorsements, 106–118
    in general elections, 142–147
    for governor, 142–144, 172–175
    for legislative elections, 201–202
    party assistance for, 57–61, 283
    recruiting and supporting, 52–57, 274–275
    searching for, 137–138
    strong candidates, 112–113
Canon, Bradley C., 120

Carey, John M., 203
Carlson, Arne, 112
Carlson, James M., 138
Carsey, Thomas M., 161
Carter, Jimmy, 16, 181, 189
Cassie, William E., 214, 216, 217
Cellucci, Paul, 112, 133–134
Checchi, Al, 64, 135, 164, 165
Check-off system of public financing, 69–70
Chen, Edwin, 144
Chiles, Lawton, 73
Christian Coalition, 74, 131
Christian right, 73, 83, 91–92, 112, 131,
    137, 154, 256
Chubb, John E., 177
Clayton, Nancy L., 89
Clean election laws, 173
Clements, William, 125, 159
Cleveland, Grover, 23
Clinton, Bill, 16, 35, 125, 183, 189, 219,
    262, 268
Clinton, Hillary Rodham, 189
Closed primaries, 103–104, 279
Clucas, Richard A., 249
Coalitions, bipartisan, 228–229
Cohen, Jonathan, 128
Cohesion index, 248
Coleman, John J., 94, 276
Coleman, Norm, 113, 185
*Colorado Republican Party v. Federal Election
    Commission* (1999), 67
Committee for Responsible Government, 62
Committee on Political Parties of the Amer-
    ican Political Science Association, 265
Committee votes, 245–246
Common Cause, 262, 267
Competition
    changing patterns of, 282–283
    divided government and, 221–225
    growth in, 37–46
    historical patterns of national party
        competition, 22–24
    incumbency and, in legislative elections,
        202–208
    levels of, in primaries, 118–120
    measuring partisanship and two-party
        competition, 28–33
    measuring party strength and, 92–94

national trends and state party
competition, 25–28
New Deal realignment and post-war
period, 24
party registration and, 43–45
patterns of, 10
Republican growth in the South and,
33–37
sectional politics and, 22–24
trends in two-party competition, 28–37
two-party, 21–46
Congress
candidates for, 143–144, 261
electing members of, 256–258
involvement with state party organization,
80–81
limits on coordinated expenditures for
congressional candidates, 261
members as candidates for governor,
143–144
Congruent voting patterns, 179–180
Consensus leadership, 235
Constitutions, state, 7–10
Consultants, 48–49
Conventions, 107–109
Cook, Elizabeth, 189
Cook County Democratic Party, 84
Cooper, Bill, 75, 113
Corrado, Anthony, 261
Cotter, Cornelius, 49, 93, 95
County parties, organizational strength of, 94
Crew, Robert E., Jr., 242
Cuomo, Mario, 81, 113, 115–116, 144,
170, 188, 275
Curry, Bill, 115
Curtis, Steve, 92
Czar, Kathy, 271

D

Daley, Richard J., 84, 277
Daley, Richard M., 161, 277
D'Amato, Alfonse, 81, 113
Davidson, Joann, 235
Davis, Dean, 159
Davis, Gray, 64, 135, 147–148, 150, 155,
162, 165, 238, 281
Dayton, Mark, 135
Debates, 157–158

Delegates, 108
Democratic National Committee, 263, 264,
269
Democratic Senatorial Campaign
Committee, 270
Depoorter, Anneka, 91
DiPrete, Edward, 169–170, 188
Districting, and partisanship, 219–221
Divided government
competition and, 221–225
governors and, 239–241
legislative elections and, 221–225
Divisive primaries, 138–139
Dudley, Christine, 261, 268
Dukakis, Michael, 16, 27, 74, 129, 182, 186

E

Earl, Anthony, 162
Economic impact on voting behavior,
190–193
Economic voting hypothesis, 177
Edgar, Jim, 161
Edwards, Edwin, 74, 81, 188
Edwards, James, 125
Ehrenhalt, Alan, 238
Eisenhower, Dwight, 26, 27, 33, 35
Elazar, Daniel, 11, 13
Elrod v. Burns (1976), 87
Emerging parties, 3–5
Endorsements
candidate nominations and, 106–118
evaluating, 273
funding and other tangible resources,
114–116
future of, 116–118
impact on nominations, 109–110
party commitment to, 110–111
party strength and, 96, 98
process of, 107–109
regulation of, 29
of strong candidates, 112–113
success of, 110–116
types of, 106–107
unity and, 113–114
Engler, John, 73, 93, 130, 134, 169
Epstein, Leon, 76
Erikson, Robert S., 39, 89, 90, 108, 181,
182, 185, 186, 241

Eu v. San Francisco County Democratic Central Committee (1989), 8, 76–77
Euchner, Jonathan P., 250
Evaluation of parties, 273–277
  effectiveness of state parties, 275–277
  nominating process, 273–274
  recruiting and supporting candidates, 274–275

F

Factionalism, 91
Fastnow, Christina, 182
Federal Election Commission (FEC), 6, 68, 258, 261, 262, 281–282
Federal Election Commission v. Colorado State Republican Party (1996), 261, 263–264
Federal Elections Campaign Act, 260
Federal money, 6, 68, 260–261
Federalism, 260
Fieger, Geoffrey, 130
Finkel, Steven E., 127
Finney, Joan, 73
Fiorina, Morris P., 223
First Amendment, 263
Floor votes, 245–246
Florida Lawyers Action Group, 64
Florio, Jim, 160, 187
Folsom, James, Jr., 169, 188
Fordice, Kirk, 125, 169
Foster, Mike, 74
Fowler, Linda L., 52
Francis, Mike, 74
Freeman, Mike, 113, 115, 135
Frendreis, John, 48, 60, 78, 276
Frendreis, John P., 94

G

Gaddie, Ronald Keith, 37
Gais, Thomas L., 64, 70, 174, 214, 217, 218, 263–264
Gallen, Hugh, 187
Gallo, George, 261, 264
Gambling, 163
General elections, 141–142, 175. *See also* Governors; Legislative elections
  campaigning for office, 147–158
  candidates, 142–147

  impact of primaries on, 136–140
  issues in the campaign, 158–163
  role of money, 163–175
Gerry, Elbridge, 221
Gerrymandering, 17, 221
Gibson, James L., 49, 78, 93, 94, 95
Gibson, James R., 138
Gierzynski, Anthony, 201, 204, 212, 213
Gimpel, James, 25, 179–180
Gitelson, Alan R., 48, 60, 78, 276
Glasser, Susan B., 261
Glendening, Parris, 169
Goidel, Robert K., 199
Goldwater, Barry, 26, 33, 91
Goodhart, Noah J., 51
Governors
  campaign finance, 163–175
  campaign support from, 242–243
  candidates for, 142–144, 172–175
  costs of campaigns, 163–166
  divided government and, 239–241
  election outcomes, 166–172
  elections for, 175
  incumbency, 145–147, 166–172, 182–185
  independent or third-party, 240–241
  legislative program of, 241–242
  media as resource for, 242
  nominations for, and party system strength, 96–97
  as party leaders, 238–243
  patronage as resource for, 242
  public funding for, 172–175
  resources for, 242–243
  special sessions called by, 243
  support score, 247
Governors and Legislatures: Contending Power (Rosenthal), 238
Graham, Cole Blease, Jr., 250
Graves, Bill, 73
Green, John C., 89
Green, Paul M., 84
Grofman, Bernard, 18
Gross, Donald A., 199
Ground wars, 148
Gubernatorial elections. *See* Governors
Gun control, 83, 131, 153
Gurwitt, Rob, 239

H

Hague Machine, 84
Hamm, Keith E., 37
Hansen, Susan B., 191, 194
Hard money, 6, 68, 260–265
Harman, Jane, 135
Harper, John, 170–171
Hayden, Mike, 169
Headlee, Richard, 130
Herzik, Eric B., 241
Hevesi, Alan G., 278
Hickel, Walter, 240–241
Hill, Marjorie Renee, 242
Hodges, Jim, 163
Hogan, Robert E., 139
Hollowell, Hank, 268
Holt, Marianne, 60
Hooker, John Jay, 130, 169
Hope, Judith, 264–265
House of Representatives. *See* Congress
Huckshorn, Robert J., 49, 93, 95
Humphrey, Hubert, 27
Humphrey, Hubert III, 113, 115, 135, 185
Hunt v. Cromartie (1999), 17

I

Ideology
    ideological splits, 131
    impact of activists on parties, 88–92
    impact on voting behavior, 185–195
Incentives, for party workers, 85–88
    material incentives, 86–87
    purposive incentives, 86, 88
    solidary incentives, 86, 87–88
    types of, 86
Income tax, 194
Incongruent voting patterns, 179–180
Incumbency, 280–281
    assets and liabilities of, 129–130, 202–204
    competition and, 202–208
    in gubernatorial elections, 145–147,
        166–172, 182–185
    in legislative elections, 202–208
    nominating process and, 129–130
    outcomes of primaries and, 129–130
    running on the record, 158–160
    voting behavior and, 182–185

Independents, 240–241, 276–277
Index of party difference, 247–248
Initiatives, 8
Institutional sources of power, 230–233
Interest groups, 64, 82–83
    advertising and, 152–153
    in campaigns, 152–154
Issue-advocacy ads, 152, 262, 269
Issues, 158–163
    impact on voting behavior, 185–195
    incumbency and, 158–160
    nominating process and, 130–131
    nonincumbents and, 160–163

J

Jackson, Andrew, 15, 101
Jackson, John, 89
Jackson, John S., 89
Jackson, Robert A., 198, 199
Jacobson, Gary, 181
James, Fob, 131, 134, 135, 163
Jelen, Ted, 189
Jennings, M. Kent, 108
Jewell, Malcolm E., 18, 75, 81, 86, 88, 126,
        128, 132, 138, 181, 201–202, 207,
        212, 229, 231–232, 237–239, 246,
        248, 250
Johnson, Donald B., 138
Johnson, Lyndon, 19, 46
Jones, Ruth S., 52, 62
Junkins, Lowell, 159–160

K

Karp, Jeffrey A., 77
Katz, Vera, 232
Kelley, Anne E., 73
Kempthorne, Dirk, 144
Kennedy, John, 26, 27, 84, 277
Kennedy, Robert, 26, 277
Kenney, Patrick J., 138
Kevorkian, Jack, 130
Key, V. O., Jr., 22, 25, 89, 92–93, 100–101,
        139, 273
Kezer, Pauline, 111
King, Angus S., Jr., 183, 240
King, Bruce, 188
King, Edward, 74, 129, 132

King, Joe, 268
King, Martin Luther, Jr., 13
Koch, Edward, 115
Kone, Susan L., 193, 194
Kousser, J. Morgan, 101, 128

L

Labor unions, 82–83, 154, 260
Landslide elections, 219
Larson, John, 115
Latino interest groups, 154
Law enforcement, and gubernatorial
    candidates, 144
Leadership
    consensus leadership, 235
    governors as party leaders, 238–243
    legislative leaders, 238–239
    party caucus as tool of, 235–238
    party leadership in legislatures, 229–238
    skills and styles of, 233–235
    state party leadership, 72–76
Legislative elections, 201–226
    campaigning, 208–210
    candidates for, 201–202
    conflicting trends in, 225–226
    contested and competitive races, 204–208
    divided government and, 221–225
    electoral competition and incumbency,
        202–208
    financial role of political parties in, 211–215
    financing, 211–218
    impact of spending on, 216
    incumbency and, 202–204
    national trends in, 218–219
    nominating process for, 201–202
    partisan implications of legislative
        districting, 219–221
    public funding for, 217–218
    as route to governorship, 143
Legislative organization, 227–229
    bipartisan coalitions, 228–229
    partisan organization, 227–228
Legislatures, political parties in, 227–252
    future role of, 252
    governors and legislative leaders, 238–239
    governors as party leaders, 238–243
    institutional sources of power, 230–233
    leadership skills and styles, 233–235
    legislative program of governors, 241–242
    makeup of legislative parties, 244–245
    partisan decision making in legislatures,
        243–251
    party caucus as tool of leadership,
        235–238
    party leadership, 229–238
    patterns of legislative organization, 227–229
    roll call voting record, 247–251
    special sessions, 243
    state party organization and, 81–82
    voting in committee and on the floor,
        245–246
Lehrman, Lewis, 115–116, 144
Levy, Clifford J., 64, 68
Lewinsky, Monica, 183
Leyden, Kevin, 193
Lieberman, Joseph I., 85
Lindauer, John, 135–136
Local primaries, 126–127
Local-level party organization, 77–79
Lockard, Duane, 85
Locke, Gary, 239
Lockerbie, Brad, 58
London, George, 113
Long, Earl, 13
Long, Huey, 13, 277
Lotteries, 163
Lubenow, Gerald C., 162
Lublin, David, 17, 37
Lungren, Dan, 147–148, 150, 162

M

Magleby, David, 60
Maisel, L. Sandy, 47, 52
Malbin, Michael J., 64, 70, 174, 214, 217,
    218, 263–264
Malone, Joseph, 112
Marra, Robin F., 178
Martin, John, 234
Martinez, Bob, 188
Martorano, Nancy, 37
Material incentives, 86–87
Maubus, Ray, 169
Mayer, William G., 255
McCarthy, Eugene, 26
McGlennon, John, 86, 88, 91
McGovern, George, 27

McIver, John P., 39, 89, 90, 108, 181, 182, 185, 186, 241
McKinley, William, 24
McMillan v. Escambia County of Florida (1981), 17
Media
 as governor's resource, 242
 role in campaigns, 156–158
Migalski, Michael, 18
Mileur, Jerome M., 74
Miller, Penny M., 75, 81, 86, 88, 138, 250
Miller, Warren E., 38, 108
Miller v. Johnson (1995), 17
Milliken, William, 130
Moe, Roger, 231, 235
Monardi, Fred M., 210
Moncrief, Gary, 211, 217
Mondale, Walter, 27
Money. *See* Campaign finance
Montjoy, Robert, 89
Moore, Arch, 170, 188
Morehouse, Sarah McCally, 64, 93, 238, 239, 248, 251
Muchmore, Lynn, 238
Muskie, Edmund, 27

N
Nagourney, Adam, 265
National Conference of State Legislatures, 203, 208
National Federation of Independent Businesses, 83
National politics. *See* State parties, and national politics
National referendum theory, 177
National Republican Senatorial Committee, 261
National Rifle Association, 83, 153
Netsch, Dawn Clark, 161
New Deal, 24
New England Patriots, 243
Niemi, Richard G., 146, 192, 193, 203, 276, 277
Nixon, Richard, 26, 27, 33, 35, 46, 240
Nixon v. Shrink Missouri Government PAC (2000), 174
Nominating process, 100–102. *See also* Endorsements

"bought" nominations, 131–136
 campaign skills and, 130–131
 endorsements and, 106–118
 evaluating, 273–274
 as function of state party organization, 52–57
 for governors, and party system strength, 96–97
 impact of endorsements on, 109–110
 impact of primaries on general elections, 136–140
 incumbency and, 129–130
 issues and, 130–131
 for legislative elections, 201–202
 levels of competition in primaries, 118–120
 presidential nominations, and state parties, 253–256
 primary election outcomes 128–136
 searching for candidates, 137–138
 voter participation in primaries, 121–128
 voting requirements for primaries, 102–106
Nonfederal money, 6, 68–69, 259
Nonincumbency, and issues, 160–163
Normal division of the vote, 186
Norms, political, 278–279
Nottingham, Edward W., 67
Noviello, Nicholas, 18

O
Olson, Allen, 189
Olson, David M., 181, 238
Open primaries, 104–105, 279
Ostrom, Charles W., Jr., 178
Outcomes
 campaign skills and, 130–131
 of gubernatorial elections, 166–172
 incumbency and outcomes of primaries, 129–130
 issues and, 130–131
 nominating process and outcomes of primaries, 128–136
 of primary elections, 128–136
Owens, Bill, 92

P
PACs (political action committees), 62–63, 65–67, 153, 213–215, 260, 263–264
Parent, T. Wayne, 74, 81

Parties. *See* Legislatures, political parties in;
State parties, and national politics;
State political parties
Partin, Randall W., 166, 177, 181, 182,
191, 192
Partisan gerrymandering, 221
Partisanship. *See also* Competition
bipartisan coalitions, 228–229
competition and, measuring, 28–33
districting and, 219–221
partisan decision making in legislatures,
243–251
partisan organization in legislatures,
227–228
party loyalty and, 181–182
roll call votes and, 247–251
trends, in state politics, 18–19
Party activists, 82, 88–92, 108
Party caucus, as tool of leadership, 235–238
Party cohesion
cohesion index, 248
roll call votes and, 247–248
Party committees, 260
Party headquarters, organization of, 51–52
Party identification, 276–277
competition and, 38–43
Party leadership, 72–76, 229–238
Party loyalty, 277, 278
partisanship and, 181–182
roll call votes and, 247
voting behavior and, 180–182
Party machines, 83–85
Party organization. *See* State party
organization
Party registration, and competition, 43–45
Party strength
competition and, measuring, 92–94
endorsements and, 96, 98
gubernatorial nominations and, 96–97
measuring, 92–98, 277–278
organizational strength of county parties,
94
state parties and national politics, 271
strong parties, 3–4
Party Transformation Study, 93–94
Party voting, 248, 277
Party workers, 83–92

Party-related groups, 79–83
Pataki, George, 64, 67–68, 81, 113, 114,
164, 170
Patronage, 86–87
as governor's resource, 242
party machines and, 83–85
Patterson, Samuel C., 11, 94, 166, 199, 248
Peirce, Neale, 84
Pendergast Machine, 84
Pernaciarro, Samuel J., 249
Perot, Ross, 188
Perpich, Rudy, 188
Political action committees (PACs), 62–63,
65–67, 153, 213–215, 260, 263–264
Political culture, 11–14, 19–20
Political history of states, 10–11
Political norms, 278–279
Political parties. *See* Legislatures, political
parties in; State parties, and national
politics
Political systems. *See* State political systems
Politics. *See* State parties, and national
politics; State politics
Politics, Parties, and Pressure Groups (Key), 22
Polling, 149–150
Poshard, Glenn, 131, 160–161
Powell, Linda W., 203
Power, institutional sources of, 230–233
Prayer in schools, 131
Precincts, 78–79
Presidential primaries, 253–256
Press, Bill, 111
Price, David, 151–152
Primaries. *See also* Nominating process
blanket primaries, 128, 274, 279
campaign spending and, 281
closed primaries, 103–104, 279
divisive primaries, 138–139
impact on general elections, 136–140
incumbency and, 129–130
individual participation in, 125–127
levels of competition in, 118–120
local primaries, 126–127
open primaries, 104–105, 279
outcomes, 128–136
presidential primaries, 253–256
the problematic primary, 139–140

searching for a winning candidate, 137–138
voter participation in, 121–128
voting requirements for, 102–106
Public financing, 69–70, 172–175, 217–218
Purdum, Todd S., 64
Purposive incentives, 86, 88

Q

Quist, Allen, 112, 113, 115

R

Racial gerrymandering, 17, 221
Rakove, Milton, 84
Ramirez, Jorge, 264
Ranney, Austin, 28
Ranney index, 28, 93, 94
Rapoport, Ronald B., 48, 86, 88
Reagan, Ronald, 16, 19, 26, 46, 256, 277
Recruiting candidates, 52–57, 274–275
Referenda, 8, 177
Regulation
    of campaign finance, 65–69, 260–265, 282
    of endorsements, 279
    of party structure, 76–77, 279
Religious right, 73, 83, 91–92, 112, 131, 137, 154, 256
Republican National Committee, 264, 269
Republican Party, growth in the South, 33–37
Republican Women's Club, 80
Rice, Tom W., 138
Richards, Ann, 163, 165, 171
Ridge, Tom, 169
Riffe, Vern, 212, 234, 235
Robertson, Pat, 256
Rockefeller, John D. IV, 188
Rockefeller, Nelson, 275, 277
Rockefeller, Winthrop, 35
Roll call votes, 246
    committee votes, 245–246
    degree of partisanship on, 247–251
    floor votes, 245–246
    partisanship and, 247–251
    party cohesion and, 247–248
    party loyalty and, 247

record of, 247–251
Roosevelt, Franklin, 24
Rosenthal, Alan, 213, 215, 238
Rosenthal, Cindy Simon, 212–213
Rowland, John, 111, 115, 243
Rutan v. Republican Party (1990), 87
Ryan, George, 161

S

Sales tax, 194
Salmore, Barbara, 77
Salmore, Stephen, 77
Sauerbrey, Ellen, 169
Scandals, 183, 188
Scarrow, Howard A., 127
Scheele, Raymond H., 126, 127
Schlesinger, Joseph, 47
Schneider, Paige, 137
School prayer, 131
Scott, Steve, 64, 150, 162
Sectional politics, 22–24
Senate. *See* Congress
Shafer, David J., 56
Shaffer, William, 89
Shanks, J. Merrill, 38
Shaw v. Reno (1993), 17
Shields, Todd G., 199
Sides, John, 128
Siegelman, Don, 163
Sigelman, Lee, 138
Simon, Dennis M., 177, 178
Smith, Al, 22
Smith, Kevin B., 195, 198, 199
Soft money, 6, 68–69, 259
Solidary incentives, 86, 87–88
Sorauf, Frank J., 84
South, Republican Party growth in, 33–37
Southern Politics (Key), 22
Special sessions, 243
Spellman, John, 187
Split-ticket voting, 178, 277
Springer, Jerry, 275
Squire, Peverill, 143, 182, 204
Stanley, Harold W., 146, 192, 193, 276, 277
State autonomy, 177–180
State constitutions, 7–10
State economic voting hypothesis, 177

State legislative elections. *See* Legislative elections
State legislatures. *See* Legislative elections; Legislative organization; Legislatures, political parties in
State money, 65, 263–265
State parties, and national politics, 253–271
  congressional elections, 256–258
  federal money, 260–261
  financial relationships, 258–271, 282–283
  nonfederal money, 261–263
  partnership of state and national parties, 282–283
  presidential nominations and, 253–256
  regulations of campaign finance, 260–265
  state money, 263–265
  strength of, 271
State party committees, 260
State party organization, 47, 98–99
  campaign finance, 61–70
  campaign regulations, 65–69
  functions of, 49–61
  ideology and, 88–92
  incentives to work for the party, 85–88
  legal regulation of party structure, 76–77, 279
  legislatures and, 81–82
  at local level, 77–79
  measuring party strength, 92–98, 277–278
  nominating function, 52–57
  organizational linkages to party-related groups, 79–83
  organizing party headquarters, 51–52
  party machines and patronage, 83–85
  party workers, 83–92
  public financing of elections, 69–70
  recruiting function, 52–57
  registering and mobilizing voters, 57–58
  services to candidates, 57–61, 283
  state party leadership, 72–76
  structure of, 70–83
  targeting function, 52–57
  theories of, 47–49
State political parties
  changes in, 1–3
  differences among, 3–5, 277–280

effectiveness of, 275–277
emerging parties, 3–5
evaluation of, 273–277
linkages with national parties, 5–6
new responsibilities and capabilities, 283
role in campaigns, 150–152
State political systems
  constitutional and legal factors, 7–10, 279
  differences in, 7–14
  geographic, economic, social, and historical factors, 10–11
  patterns of political competition, 10
  political culture, 11–14
State politics
  constitutional, statutory, and judicial factors, 15–18
  national factors in, 14–20
  national political culture, 19–20
  partisan trends, 18–19
Statehouse Democracy, 181
Stein, Robert, 178
Stolberg, Irving, 229
Stone, Walter J., 48, 52
Strong candidates, 112–113
Strong parties, 3–4
Sundlun, Bruce, 170
Sundquist, Don, 130, 169, 171
Sundquist, James L., 24
Survey data, 176
Svoboda, Craig J., 182, 192
Swanson, Wayne R., 249

T
Tammany Hall, 84
Targeting, 52–57, 274
Taxes
  income tax, 194
  increases in, 159–160, 186–187, 193–195
  sales tax, 194
  voting behavior and, 193–195
Television advertising, 148, 155
Third-party and independent candidates, 240–241, 276–277
Thompson, Joel A., 214
Thompson, Tommy, 162, 169
Thone, Charles, 186–187
"Time for a change," 188

Tompkins, Mark E., 191
Toward a More Responsible Two-Party System, 259, 271
Trends
   in legislative elections, 218–219, 225–226
   in state party competition, 25–28
   in state politics and partisanship, 18–19
   in two-party competition, 28–37
Trish, Barbara, 91
Truman, Harry, 26
Two-party competition, 21–46

U

Ujifusa, Grant, 163, 186
Uncontested elections, 274
Underwood, Cecil, 135
Unions, 82–83, 154, 260
United Auto Workers, 130
Unruh, Jess, 212

V

Vallone, Peter, 114
Van Der Slik, Jack R., 249
Van Dunk, Emily, 204, 207, 208
Ventura, Jesse, 14, 113, 171, 185, 198, 240
Verba, Sydney, 11
Vertz, Laura, 78, 94
Vogel, Ronald J., 146, 192, 193
Voss, D. Stephen, 17, 37
Voter participation, in primaries, 121–128
Voter registration and mobilization, 57–58
Voter turnout, 195–200, 276
Voting behavior, 176, 200
   differences between state and national elections, 178–179
   economic conditions and, 190–193
   impact of ideology and issues, 185–195
   incumbency and, 182–185
   influence of national forces on state elections, 177–178
   party loyalty and, 180–182
   state and national party systems, 179–180
   state autonomy and, 177–180
   taxes and, 193–195

voter turnout, 195–200, 276
Voting patterns, congruency of, 179–180
Voting requirements, for primaries, 102–106
   regional variations in types of primaries, 105
   types of closed primaries, 103–104
   types of open primaries, 104–105
Voting rights, 221
Voting Rights Act in 1965, 9

W

Walker, Jack, 13
Wallace, George, 35
Ward, Daniel S., 76, 77, 248
Warren, Earl, 277
Washington Conservative Voters, 62
Washington Education Association, 62
Washington Labor Council, 62
Wasted votes, 220
Weak parties, 3–4
Weber, Ronald E., 89, 195, 198, 199, 204, 207
Weicker, Lowell, 240
Weissert, Carol S., 73
Weld, William, 74, 112
Whicker, Marcia Lynn, 212, 229, 231, 232, 237, 238
Whitby, Kenny J., 250
White, Frank, 35, 125
White, Mark, 159, 188
Whitman, Christine Todd, 62, 160, 187
Wielhouwer, Peter W., 58, 85
Wiggins, Charles W., 242, 250
Wilcox, Clyde, 189
Wilkinson, Wallace, 170–171
Williams, Clayton, 125, 171
Williams, G. Mennen, 27
Wilson, Pete, 111, 134, 144, 147, 161–162
Winters, Richard F., 145, 162, 193, 194
Wright, Gerald C., 39, 89–90, 108, 146–147, 181–182, 185–186, 241

Y

Young Democrats Club, 80